# Novel Judgements

*Novel Judgements* is a book about nineteenth-century Anglo-American law-and-literature. But by redefining law as legal theory, *Novel Judgements* departs from socio-legal studies of law-and-literature, which are often dated in their focus on past lawyering and court processes. This text's 'theoretical turn' renders the period's law-and-literature relevant to today's readers because the nineteenth-century novel, when read 'jurisprudentially', abounds in representations of law's controlling concepts, many of which are still with us today. Rights, justice, morality, each are encoded novelistically in stock devices such as the country house, friendship, love, courtship and marriage. In so rendering the public (law) as private (domesticity), the nineteenth-century novel exposes, for legal and literary scholars alike, the ways in which law comes to mediate all relationships – individual and collective, personal and political – during a period as much under the Rule of Law as the reign of Capital. So the novel passes judgement – a *novel judgement* – on the extent to which the nineteenth-century's idea of law is collusive with that era's Capital, thereby opening up the possibility of a new legal theoretical position: that of a critique of the law and a law of critique.

**William P. MacNeil** is the Dean of the Griffith Law School, Queensland, Australia. Trained in both law and literature, MacNeil has published widely in the field of cultural legal studies and is the author of *Lex Populi: The Jurisprudence of Popular Culture* (Stanford University Press, 2007).

*Discourses of Law*

Series editors: Peter Goodrich, Michel Rosenfeld and Arthur Jacobson
*Benjamin N. Cardozo School of Law*

This successful and exciting series seeks to publish the most innovative scholarship at the intersection of law, philosophy and social theory. The books published in the series are distinctive by virtue of exploring the boundaries of legal thought. The work that this series seeks to promote is marked most strongly by the drive to open up new perspectives on the relation between law and other disciplines. The series has also been unique in its commitment to international and comparative perspectives upon an increasingly global legal order. Of particular interest in a contemporary context, the series has concentrated upon the introduction and translation of continental traditions of theory and law.

The original impetus for the series came from the paradoxical merger and confrontation of East and West. Globalization and the internationalization of the rule of law has had many dramatic and often unforeseen and ironic consequences. An understanding of differing legal cultures, particularly different patterns of legal thought, can contribute, often strongly and starkly, to an appreciation if not always a resolution of international legal disputes. The rule of law is tied to social and philosophical underpinnings that the series has sought to excoriate and illuminate.

Titles in the series:

*Nietzsche and Legal Theory: Half-Written Laws*
Edited by Peter Goodrich and Mariana Valverde

*Law, Orientalism, and Postcolonialism: The Jurisdiction of the Lotus Eaters.*
Piyel Haldar

*Endowed: Regulating the Male Sexed Body*
Michael Thomson

*The Identity of the Constitutional Subject: Selfhood, Citizenship, Culture, and Community*
Michel Rosenfeld

*The Land is the Source of the Law: A Dialogic Encounter with Indigenous Jurisprudence*
C.F. Black

*Shakespearean Genealogies of Power: A Whispering of Nothing in Hamlet, Richard II, Julius Caesar, Macbeth, The Merchant of Venice, and The Winter's Tale*
Anselm Haverkamp

Forthcoming:

*Novel Judgements: Legal Theory as Fiction*
William MacNeil

*Crime Scenes: Forensics and Aesthetics*
Rebecca Scott Bray

*Sex, Culpability and the Defence of Provocation*
Danielle Tyson

*The Rule of Reason in European Constitutionalism and Citizenship*
Yuri Borgmann-Prebil

*Visualizing Law in the Age of the Digital Baroque: Arabesques and Entanglements*
Richard K. Sherwin

The publisher gratefully acknowledges the support of the Jacob Burns Institute for Advanced Legal Studies of the Benjamin N. Cardozo School of Law to the series *Discourses of Law*.

# Novel Judgements

*Legal Theory as Fiction*

William P. MacNeil

LONDON AND NEW YORK

First published 2012
by Routledge
2 Park Square, Milton Park, Abingdon, Oxon OX14 4RN

Simultaneously published in the USA and Canada
by Routledge
711 Third Avenue, New York, NY 10017 (8th Floor)

*Routledge is an imprint of the Taylor & Francis Group, an informa business*

© 2012 William P. MacNeil

The right of William P. MacNeil to be identified as author of this work has been asserted by him/her in accordance with sections 77 and 78 of the Copyright, Designs and Patents Act 1988.

All rights reserved. No part of this book may be reprinted or reproduced or utilised in any form or by any electronic, mechanical, or other means, now known or hereafter invented, including photocopying and recording, or in any information storage or retrieval system, without permission in writing from the publishers.

*Trademark notice*: Product or corporate names may be trademarks or registered trademarks, and are used only for identification and explanation without intent to infringe.

*British Library Cataloguing in Publication Data*
A catalogue record for this book is available from the British Library

*Library of Congress Cataloging in Publication Data*
MacNeil, William P.
 Novel judgements : legal theory as fiction / William P. MacNeil.
  p. cm.
  ISBN 978–0–415–45914–3 (hbk)—ISBN 978–0–415–45915–0 (pbk)—ISBN 978–0–203–93086–1 (ebk)
 1. English fiction—19th century—History and criticism.  2. Law in literature.  3. American fiction—19th century—History and criticism.  4. Law and literature—History—19th century.  5. Culture and law.  6. Sociological jurisprudence.  I. Title.  II. Title: Legal theory as fiction.
 PR868.L39M33 2011
 823'.8093554—dc22

2011001731

ISBN: 978–0–415–45914–3 (hbk)
ISBN: 978–0–415–45915–0 (pbk)
ISBN: 978–0–203–93086–1 (ebk)

Typeset in Minion
by RefineCatch Limited, Bungay, Suffolk

To Lady P
With love and affection

# Contents

|   | | |
|---|---|---|
| | *Acknowledgements* | xi |
| | *List of Abbreviations* | xvii |
| 1 | Pro*lex*omenon: Towards *a* Novel Legal Theory of the Novel *as* Legal Theory | 1 |
| 2 | John Austin or Jane Austen? *The Province of Jurisprudence Determined* in *Pride and Prejudice* | 21 |
| 3 | Jousting with Bentham: Utility, Morality and Ethics in *Ivanhoe*'s Tournament of Law | 47 |
| 4 | The Monstrous Body of the Law: Wollstonecraft vs. Shelley | 75 |
| 5 | Hawthorne's Haunted House of Law: The Romance of American Legal Realism in *The House of the Seven Gables* | 99 |
| 6 | In Boz We Trust! *Bleak House*'s Reimagination of Trusteeship | 131 |
| 7 | Two on a Guillotine? Courts and 'Crits' in *A Tale of Two Cities* | 157 |
| 8 | Beyond Governmentality: The Question of Justice in *Great Expectations* | 181 |

## A Jurisprudential Postscript: Century's Close and the End of the Meta-Narrative of Law?   205

Bibliography   209
Index   227

# Acknowledgements

*Novel Judgements* is a tale of not two, not even three, but four cities; it was conceived in Hong Kong, articulated in Brisbane, written in Ann Arbor and, finally, published in London. Along that highly peripatetic route, and over the more than ten-year period of its protracted composition (interrupted, largely, by *another* book), *Novel Judgements* accrued, for want of a better word, any number of 'debts' – intellectual, emotional, financial. I want to take this opportunity, if not exactly to clear these debts, then at least to acknowledge the invaluable contributions – scholarly and otherwise – of its *creditors*. I italicise 'creditors' because it is hard to *credit* (and debit) what really amount to *gifts* so generously given; which is why what follows is not so much a settling of creditors' accounts as it is an expression of gratitude offered up to this book's many gift-givers. First and foremost, *Novel Judgements* would not have appeared in print without the timely intervention and enthusiastic encouragement of Cardozo Law School's Prof. Peter Goodrich, *il miglior fabbro*, everyone's favourite, with all due respect to Sting, 'Englishman in New York'. To him, I am truly grateful, and honoured to appear in the 'Discourses of Law' series. Next, I would like to thank Dr Colin Perrin, Ms Holly Davis, Ms Rhona Carroll, Mr Martin Barr and the rest of the editorial staff at Routledge in London (including their readers, anonymous and otherwise) for, initially, their unwavering support of my proposal and, later, their untiring efforts, not to mention incredible patience in seeing my manuscript through to publication.

xii • Acknowledgements

Singled out here is that 'sublime *subject* of (legal) ideology', Prof. Renata Salecl of the University of Ljubljana and the London School of Economics for particular praise and appreciation.

I am grateful, as well, to the ever unique and always stimulating intellectual environment – critical, interdisciplinary, theoretical – of the Griffith Law School (GLS); and I want to thank, particularly, its former dean, my predecessor (and fellow Lacanian), Prof. Paula Baron, as well as its former and current heads of school, Prof. Sandra Berns and Dr Afshin Akhtarkhavari, for securing the leave of absence and providing the material and emotional support so necessary for this book's writing. A collective – but nonetheless heartfelt – thank you to the current and former directors of Griffith's Socio-Legal Research Centre (SLRC): to Prof. Brad Sherman, colleague, fellow theorist and friend forever, for assuming – at a critical point in time – the Acting Deanship, allowing me to finish this book; to Mr Kieran Tranter, jurisprude *extraordinaire* and, like myself, *BSG* 'space cadet' wannabe ('Frak!'), for stepping up to the Acting Directorship when I became Dean; and to Prof. Richard Johnstone, for his invaluable feedback about, in particular, this book's 'Pro-*lex*-omenon' and for assisting me, over many conversations, to clarify this book's vexed question of methodology, and what it is, precisely, I *do* when I *do* law-and-literature. The Legal Theory Reading Group listened to, and provided brilliant advice as to how to improve several of these chapters, and I want to express my appreciation to, *inter alia*, the following attendees: Dr Alan Ardill, Ms Merran Lawler, Dr Bede Roshan de Silva-Wijeyeratne, Ms Bronwyn Statham, Assoc. Prof. Charles Lawson, Dr John Touchie and Dr Chris Butler. Also, thanks to my colleagues – both local and global, past and present – for their many lively discussions about, and over law and literature, especially the following GLS, SLRC and GU 'usual suspects': Dr Christine F. Black, Dr Ron Levy, Dr Ian Duncanson, Ms Judy Grbich, Dr Chris Butler, Assoc. Prof. Rob McQueen (now of Monash University), Dr Elena Marchetti, Dr Rebecca Loudon, Dr Fiona Kumari Campbell, Ms Kate Van Doore, Ms Karen Schultz, Ms Nicole Graham, Prof. Mary Keyes, Dr David Ellison, Dr Jeffrey Minson and last, but certainly not least, the irreplaceable Mr Shaun McVeigh (now of the University of Melbourne).

Students, as well, provided invaluable feedback, and I want to thank collectively the members of the Legal Fictions seminar at both Griffith and Hong Kong Universities, each of whom heard many of this book's chapters first as lectures. I single out, in particular: in Hong Kong – Mr Charles Mo, Ms Helena Chan, Mr Mark Chan, Ms Margot Rosato-Stevens, Ms Janine Cheung, Ms Patricia Nadwani, Ms Michelle Ng, Ms Laveena Mahtani; in Australia – Mr Tim Peters, Mr Stephen Burton, Ms Elena Schak, Ms Anna

Farmer, Ms Mietta Olsen, Mr Tarik Kochi, Ms Julie Lovell, Ms Rhiannon Moreton-Robinson, Ms Angela Hayward, Mr Michael Bromley; in India – Ms Manojna Yeluri. Of particular significance and note – as student, later research assistant, now law school colleague – is the incomparable Mr Etueni 'Eddie' Ngaluafe without whose tireless energy, eye for detail, insight and good humour *Novel Judgements* would never have been completed. I want to express my deep appreciation to Mr Ngaluafe, as well as his 'team' of researchers, for stepping in, and seeing this manuscript through to editorial and formatting completion while I was otherwise engaged, including his partner (and GLS colleague), Ms Madonna Adcock-Ngaluafe and GLS students, Ms Catherine Heuser, Ms Jessica Shannon and Ms Sarah Matheson.

Several of this book's chapters have appeared previously in journals or book series, and I would like to acknowledge and thank those publications: first, *Law Text & Culture (LTC)* which published Chapter 1;[1] second, *Australian Feminist Law Journal (AFLJ)* where Chapters 3[2] and 6[3] came out; third and finally, *Studies in Law, Politics and Society (SLPS)*, which printed a version of, now substantially revised, Chapter 5.[4] Thanks, as well, to the editorial teams involved: at *LTC*, Prof. Desmond Manderson and Dr Rick Mohr; at *AFLJ*, Prof. Alison Young, Dr Nina Puren-Philadelphoff and Ms Judy Grbich; at *SLPS*, Prof. Austin Sarat and Prof. Patricia Ewick. As well, various institutions invited me to present parts of this book either as a seminar or lecture, and I am obliged to the following: the School of Law, Birkbeck London; the Department of Law, University of Leicester; the Socio-Legal Research Centre, Griffith University; the Women's Research Network, the Faculty of Law, the Departments of English and Comparative Literature, all of the University of Hong Kong; the Department of English, LaTrobe University; the Department of Criminology, University of Melbourne; the Faculty of Law, Macquarie University; and the Department of Law, Jurisprudence and Social Theory, Amherst College.

Many thanks to the following organisers: Dr Piyel Haldar, Prof. Panu Minkkinen, Ms Clare Inwood, Ms Joanne Pascoe, Ms Mariella Hassell,

---

1 W. MacNeil, 'John Austin or Jane Austen? The Province of Jurisprudence Determined in *Pride and Prejudice*', *Law, Text, Culture* 4(2), 1998, 1–35.
2 W. MacNeil, 'The Monstrous Body of the Law: Wollstonecraft vs. Shelley', *Australian Feminist Law Journal* 12, 1999, 21–41.
3 W. MacNeil, 'Beyond Governmentality: Retributive, Distributive and Deconstructive Justice in *Great Expectations*', *Australian Feminist Law Journal* 13, 1999, 98–117.
4 W. MacNeil, 'A Tale of Two Trials: Revolutionary Enjoyment, Liberal Legalism and the Sacrifice of Critique in Dickens's *A Tale of Two Cities*', in A. Sarat and P. Ewick (eds), *Studies in Law, Politics and Society*, Oxford: Elsevier Science Ltd, 2000, pp. 77–102.

Prof. John Dewar, Prof. Brad Sherman, Dr Irene Tong, Dean Johannes Chan, Ms Vivian Wong, Prof. Elaine Ho, Prof. Akbar Abbas, Dr Linda Johnson, Dr Kirsty Duncanson, Dr Gloria Lappin, Ms Kate Lappin, Prof. Alison Young, Assoc. Prof. Peter Rush and Prof. Austin Sarat. Invaluable feedback was provided by the attendees at these talks; and I would like to thank all of them collectively, but single out some of these friends and colleagues by name: Prof. Les Moran (Birkbeck), Dr Marty Slaughter (Kent), Dr Aileen Kavanagh (Oxford); Dr Marco Wan (Hong Kong); Prof. Michele Goodwin (Minnesota), Prof. David Saunders (Griffith/Paris), Prof. Nasser Hussain (Amherst), Prof. Orit Kamir (Michigan/Hebrew University) and Prof. Martha Umphrey (Amherst). Conferences also afforded me a number of opportunities to air portions of this book. Of particular note here is the 13th Annual Conference of the Association for the Study of Law, Culture and the Humanities (2010), sponsored by the Department of English, Brown University and the Faculty of Law, University of Connecticut, at which I was fortunate enough to present Chapter 6, 'In Boz We Trust! *Bleak House*'s Reimagination of Trusteeship', as the keynote address. In addition to this, I acknowledge, gratefully: the Conference of the Law and Literature Association of Australia (1997 – GLS; 1999 – Beechworth, Victoria; 2000 – Sydney) and the British/European Critical Legal Conference (1997 – Dublin; 1999 – London; 2000 – Helsinki). Many thanks, as well, to the following organisers: Prof. Susan Schmeiser, Asst. Prof. Ravit Reichman, Assoc. Prof. Graeme Orr, Mr Shaun McVeigh, Ms Judy Grbich, Assoc. Prof. Peter Hutchings, Mr James Bergeron, Prof. Penny Pether, Mr Angus McDonald, Dr Ari Hirvonnen, Ms Maria Aristodemou, Dr Adam Gearey, Prof. Patricia Tuitt and Prof. Costas Douzinas.

I want to offer a very belated thank you (and a long overdue apology for its belatedness) to my former LSE law lecturer, Prof. William R. 'Bill' Cornish – Cambridge don, intellectual property lawyer and legal historian *nonpareil*. For me, he opened up, and brought to life the world of eighteenth- and nineteenth-century British legal history; and, in so doing, he enabled me to historicise both law and literature, and undertake the interdisciplinary study of each in this book.[5] 'Across the pond', and almost as long ago in terms of their tuition are my Columbia Law School JSD supervisors, and I want to thank Prof. Patricia Williams, Prof. Mark Barenberg and, especially, Prof. Kendall Thomas, fellow theorist, friend and stalwart.

---

5 See especially his magisterial legal history, the best of its kind and (still) the standard text in the field: W. R. Cornish and G. de N. Clark, *Law and Society in England, 1750–1950*, London: Sweet & Maxwell, 1989.

For their ongoing interest in my work, as much as their early tuition of me, thanks go to Prof. Jane Millgate, my former Victorian literature lecturer at (appropriately enough) Victoria College, University of Toronto – now emeritus, but still the reigning doyenne of Scott scholarship; and to Prof. William Twining, also emeritus, though of the Faculty of Laws, University College London, but, nonetheless, a jurisprudential force to be reckoned with on both sides of the Atlantic, and the person who taught me (and many others) how to read legal theory 'otherwise'. To all of these outstanding scholar-teachers, I am deeply indebted.

Other persons, less pedagogic in their mentorship perhaps, but literally *inspiring* in their interactions with me must be mentioned here. To my former Hong Kong University colleagues, Assoc. Prof. Peter Hutchings (now the Australian Learning and Teaching Council, Sydney) and Prof. Jeremy Tambling (now the University of Manchester), many thanks for their scholarly interventions on, respectively, Shelley and Dickens. To my longstanding friends: fellow globe-trotter and former Dalhousie Law School classmate, Ms Penelope Tham (Hong Kong); and 'the Nancy Mitford of e-mail', Mrs Philip (Jeannette) Strathy (Toronto, Ontario) – huzzah to both for their insights on, respectively, Scott and Dickens. I am grateful, as well, to many family members, and want to thank the following in turn: for her tireless publicising efforts, kudos to my sister-in-law, Mrs John D. (Diana) MacNeil (Dubai, UAE and Lake Tamagami, Ontario); for our ongoing banter about *A Tale of Two Cities*, Dickens and 'the routine', 'snaps' for my sister – 'Monica' to my 'Ross' – Mrs Blair Edwin F. (Mary Patricia) Harding ('Harding Hollow', Brighton, Michigan); for our many discussions about *Pride and Prejudice*, 'hats off' to my mother-in-law and fellow 'Jane-ite', Mrs Muriel Adams ('Blyth House', Southwold, England); for their generous hospitality and support in providing me with the perfect writer's retreat in 'Braigh Mohr Farm' – a kind of Midwestern Walden Pond outside of Ann Arbor, Michigan – my thanks to my parents, Mr and Mrs John Angus (Viberta Marie) MacNeil. Last but, of course, certainly not least, I want to thank from the bottom of my heart and with a deep sense of gratitude and appreciation, my *cara sposa* Ms Pamela Kathryn Adams, aka 'Lady P'; an *Austenian* figure of grace and elegance, but (being the good Glaswegian she is) with a strength and resolve that is more than a match for any would-be *Austinian* sovereign. To her I dedicate this book with much love and affection.

# List of Abbreviations

| | |
|---|---|
| ATTC | *A Tale of Two Cities* |
| BH | *Bleak House* |
| CLS | Critical Legal Studies |
| F | *Frankenstein: or The Modern Prometheus* |
| GE | *Great Expectations* |
| HSG | *The House of Seven Gables* |
| I | *Ivanhoe* |
| IPML | *An Introduction to the Principles of Morals and Legislation* |
| MPL | *My Philosophy of Law* |
| OJQ | *On the Jewish Question* |
| P&P | *Pride and Prejudice* |
| PL | 'The Path of Law' |
| SR | *Scotch Reform* |
| TE | *Three Essays* |
| VRW | *A Vindication of the Rights of Woman* |

CHAPTER 1

# Pro*lex*omenon: Towards *a* Novel Legal Theory of the Novel *as* Legal Theory

**By Way of Introduction: What's Law Got to Do with It? Got to Do with It?**

To (mis)quote the ever fabulous Tina Turner, 'what's law got to do with it, got to do with it?' Only, here, in my riff – and with all due respect to *Private Dancer*[1] – the 'it' means *literature* and its significance for *law*. For the overarching question standing behind and informing this book is as follows: does literature have something significant 'to do with' or, better yet, say about law? Of course, literature, itself, has been quick to provide an answer, not only speaking to, but deriving some, indeed *much* of its dramatic, thematic, even structural core from law. It does so by liberally borrowing from law not only a cohort of characters (barristers, magistrates, bobbies) and range of plot devices (missing heirs, contested legacies, strict settlements), but, above all, a *mise-en-scène* tailor-made for novelistic *agon*: the courtroom. No wonder issues of legal *process* loom so large in law-and-literature scholarship, with the trial and all of its forensic 'tricks' – witnessing, cross-examination, confession – taking pride of place. In a similar vein, and following closely upon the courtroom as a favoured scholarly resource, is substantive *doctrine*; namely, those eminently *litigious* areas of legal rules and principles, largely criminal (e.g. murder, theft, even

---

1 Tina Turner, 'What's Love Got to Do with It?', *Private Dancer*, Capitol Records, 1984.

crimes against humanity), but also civil (e.g. tort, property, trusts), both of which, in gifting fiction with innumerable storylines, have underwritten and informed countless law-and-literature studies. Undertaking these sorts of studies, be they process-oriented or doctrine-inflected – in short, 'socio-legal' research into law-and-literature – are outstanding scholars such as those that decorate the following list, and which I propose to review forthwith, giving a 'snapshot' of the discipline.

Starting from the most recent and working backwards, they include the following: Edward Morgan, on international law's literary aesthetics;[2] Stephen Best, on literature's representation of race and 'the poetics of possession';[3] A. G. Harmon, on the language of contract in the Shakespearean canon;[4] Sandra MacPherson, on inheritance laws in the fiction of Jane Austen;[5] Meredith McGill, on copyright and literary nation-building;[6] Margaret Russett, on the legal 'identity' of the literary work;[7] Lisa Rodensky, on criminal responsibility in Victorian law-and-literature;[8] Jonathan Grossman, on the 'art of the alibi' in literature;[9] Ian Ward, on the law in, and of the Shakespearean literary canon;[10] Nan Goodman, on tortious 'accidents' and literature;[11] Harriet Murav, on the 'legal fictions' of Russian literature;[12] Laura Hanft Korobkin on law, adultery and the novel;[13] Thomas

---

[2] E. Morgan, *The Aesthetics of International Law*, Buffalo: University of Toronto Press, 2007.

[3] S. Best, *The Fugitive's Properties: Law and the Poetics of Possession*, Chicago: University of Chicago Press, 2004.

[4] A. G. Harmon, *Eternal Bonds and True Contracts: Law and Nature in Shakespeare's Problem Plays*, Albany: State University of New York Press, 2004.

[5] S. MacPherson, 'Rent to Own; or What's Entailed in *Pride and Prejudice*', *Representations* 82(1), 2003, 1–23.

[6] M. McGill, *American Literature and the Culture of Reprinting 1834–1853*, Philadelphia: University of Pennsylvania Press, 2003.

[7] M. Russett, 'Meter, Identity, Voice: Untranslating "Christabel"', *Studies in English Literature, 1500–1900* 43(4), 2003, 773–797.

[8] L. Rodensky, *The Crime in Mind: Criminal Responsibility and the Victorian Novel*, New York: Oxford University Press, 2003.

[9] J. Grossman, *The Art of the Alibi: English Law Courts and the Novel*, Baltimore: Johns Hopkins University Press, 2002.

[10] I. Ward, *Shakespeare and the Legal Imagination*, London: Butterworths, 1999. See also, I. Ward, 'A Love of Justice: The Legal and Political Thought of William Godwin', *Journal of Legal History* 25(1), 2004, 1–30.

[11] N. Goodman, *Shifting the Blame: Literature, Law and the Theory of Accidents in Nineteenth Century America*, Princeton: Princeton University Press, 1998.

[12] H. Murav, *Russia's Legal Fictions*, Ann Arbor: University of Michigan Press, 1998.

[13] L. H. Korobkin, *Criminal Conversations: Sentimentality and Nineteenth-Century Legal Sources of Adultery*, New York: Columbia University Press, 1998.

Pro*lex*omenon • 3

C. Grey, on Wallace Stevens's mutually implicated professions of law and poetry;[14] Brook Thomas, on the trial-like 'cross-examinations' between law-and-literature;[15] Alexander Welsh, on copyright and literary biography;[16] Robert Ferguson, on America's 'republic of (legal) letters';[17] Alistair Duckworth, on property law and 'the improvement of the estate' in, once again, Jane Austen;[18] Phillip Collins, on crime and criminality in Dickens;[19] further back to Sir William Holdsworth, on Dickens as 'legal historian';[20] and, going as far back as these *ur*-figures of the (inter-)discipline, to Benjamin Cardozo,[21] John Henry Wigmore,[22] and James Fitzjames Stephen,[23] on, respectively, the 'improving' or 'distorting' aspects of literature upon law, lawyers and legal practice. As different in time and place, issue and focus, as each of these excellent law-and-literature scholars are, *all make this same point*. That is, in responding to the question – does literature have anything to do with or say about law? – they answer resoundingly in the affirmative. Law-as-a-process (of advocates and adversaries, courts and

---

14 T. C. Grey, *The Wallace Stevens Case: Law and the Practice of Poetry*, Cambridge, MA: Harvard University Press, 1991.
15 B. Thomas, *Cross-Examinations of Law and Literature: Cooper, Hawthorne, Stowe and Melville*, New York: Cambridge University Press, 1987. See also, B. Thomas, *Civic Myths: A Law and Literature Approach to Citizenship*, Chapel Hill: University of North Carolina, 2007; B. Thomas, *American Literary Realism and the Failed Promise of Contract*, Berkeley: University of California Press, 1997.
16 A. Welsh, *Strong Representations: Narrative and Circumstantial Evidence in England*, Baltimore: Johns Hopkins University Press, 1992. See also: A. Welsh, *From Copyright to Copperfield: The Identity of Dickens*, Cambridge, MA: Harvard University Press, 1987.
17 R. A. Ferguson, *Law and Letters in American Culture*, Cambridge, MA: Harvard University Press, 1984. See also, R. A. Ferguson, *The Trial in American Life*, Chicago: University of Chicago Press, 2007; R. A. Ferguson, *Reading the Early Republic*, Cambridge, Cambridge, MA: Harvard University Press, 2004; R. A. Ferguson, *The American Enlightenment 1750–1820*, Cambridge, MA: Harvard University Press, 1997.
18 A. Duckworth, *The Improvement of the Estate: A Study of Jane Austen's Novels*, Baltimore: Johns Hopkins University Press, 1971.
19 P. Collins, *Dickens and Crime*, London: Macmillan, 1994.
20 Sir William Holdsworth, *Charles Dickens as a Legal Historian*, New Haven, CT: Yale University Press 1929.
21 B. N. Cardozo, *Law and Literature and Other Essays and Addresses*, New York: Harcourt, Brace & Co, 1931.
22 J. H. Wigmore, 'A List of Legal Novels', *Illinois Law Review* 2, 1907–1908, 574. Reprinted and expanded as J. H. Wigmore, 'A List of 100 Legal Novels', *Illinois Law Review* 17, 1922–1923, 26. See also, R. Weisberg, 'Wigmore's Legal Novels: New Resources for the Expansive Lawyer', *Northwestern Law Review* 71, 1976, 17.
23 J. F. Stephen, 'The Licence of Modern Novelists', in S. Wall (ed.), *Charles Dickens: A Critical Anthology*, Harmondsworth, England: Penguin, 1970, pp. 106–108.

tribunals) speaks and is spoken to by literature-as-a-structure (character, plot, setting). Both participate, as the above cited scholarship clearly demonstrates, in a dialogic relationship; and it is *this* amply evidenced dialogue which explains why *this book aims to do something else* – though, clearly, it is indebted to, and builds upon the innovative and path-breaking scholarship, cited previously. But *Novel Judgements* poses *another* question, one that is more *legal philosophical,* more *jurisprudential* than these socio-legal studies (albeit with large add-ons of history, aesthetics, narratology, and so on). By 'legal philosophical' or 'jurisprudential', this book means, simply, the theory, or, rather, theories of law; that is, law's foundational ideas, its organising notions – like theories of justice, rights, law's morality and the Rule of Law, to give but a few examples. All of which find their fullest expression in what might be called 'the jurisprudential classics' – or the canonical texts of legal theory; for example, those written by Jeremy Bentham, John Austin, Mary Wollstonecraft, John Stuart Mill, Fitzjames Stephen, A. V. Dicey, Oliver Wendell Holmes Jr., and so forth. Can literature tell us anything about these legal theorists and their legal theories? That is, does literature have something to say about law *philosophically* and/or *jurisprudentially,* going *beyond* the socio-legal niceties of legal process's literary representation – of courtroom trials, of good and bad lawyering, of lost or challenged wills, of the police 'in different voices', of murder most foul? If so, what is it?

I want to explore in this book the ways in which literature comments upon, and/or critiques *theories* deemed central to legal philosophy, to jurisprudence. How are these 'concept(s) of law', to echo English jurist Herbert Hart, reflected in, but also refracted by literary texts? That is my central question here; and one which sets this book off from less conceptual, more socio-legal issues about not only literature's representation of legal process (e.g., about the accuracy of equity pleadings in *Bleak House*),[24] but legal doctrine (e.g., the nature of the entail in *Pride and Prejudice*)[25] and/or legal history (e.g., Scott's stance on punishment and, in particular, capital sentences).[26] While many of these issues are important ones, relevant not

---

24 See, for example, J. M. Guest, *The Lawyer in Literature*, Boston: Boston Book Company, 1913. See also, Holdsworth, *Charles Dickens as a Legal Historian*.
25 G. H. Treitel, 'Jane Austen and the Law', *Law Quarterly Review* 100, 1984, 549–586. For a quite different take on law in Austen, see MacPherson, 'Rent to Own'. This article propounds an extremely sophisticated and nuanced reading of *Pride and Prejudice* in light of the history of property law: fee simple, fee tails, entails, strict settlements, leaseholds, and so on, as indices of character, and conveyors of theme.
26 B. Beiderwell, *Power and Punishment in Scott's Novels*, Athens, GA: University of Georgia Press, 1992.

only for a richer understanding of these texts' past import but present significance, there is a danger here; specifically, of (re)producing an 'Old Historicism' in the guise of the New,[27] one marked by an a-theoretical antiquarianism that misses these texts' profound jurisprudential subtexts. Not that law-and-literature scholarship *is* a-theoretical; far from this being true, much of it is profoundly theoretical.

For example, many previously cited 'socio-legal' scholars of law-and-literature – Morgan, Best, Harmon, McGill, Russett, Rodensky, Goodman, Murav, Grossman, to name just a few of the most significant – have re-theorised 'process' itself, reconceptualising legal notions such as war crimes, contract, copyright, possession, *mens rea*, negligence, the trial and evidence through an astonishing array of aesthetic, identic and hermeneutic traditions. Other, like-minded, and, possibly, even more ideologically driven scholars of law-and-literature have extended this theoretical ambit to include the following: feminism (Alison Young, on rape in *The Waste Land*;[28] Larissa Behrendt on Australian colonial captivity narratives and Indigeneity;[29] Michele Goodwin, on *Jane Eyre*'s racialised 'mad woman in the attic';[30] Hilary Schor and Nomi Stolzenberg, on law-and-literature's female 'bastards');[31] deconstruction (Sue Chaplin, on *Antigone*'s 'fictions of origin';[32] Patrick Glen, on Kafka's legal *œuvre*;[33] Terry Threadgold,

---

27 One very successful New Historicist/Feminist collection that avoids this pitfall is the excellent, N. E. Wright, M. W. Ferguson and A. R. Buck (eds), *Women, Property, and the Letters of the Law in Early Modern England*, Toronto: University of Toronto Press, 2004.
28 A. Young, 'The Waste Land of the Law: The Wordless Song of the Rape Victim', *Melbourne University Law Review* 22, 1998, 442–465.
29 L. Behrendt and E. Fraser, 'A Colonial and Legal Narrative', in I. McCalum and A. McGrath (eds), *Proof and Truth: The Humanist as Expert*, Canberra: Australian Academy of the Sciences, 2003.
30 M. Goodwin, 'The Black Woman in the Attic: Law, Metaphor and Madness in *Jane Eyre*', *Rutgers Law Journal* 30, 1999, 597–682.
31 H. Schor and N. Stolzenberg, 'Bastard Daughters and Illegitimate Mothers: Burning Down the Courthouse in *Bastard Out of Carolina* and *Bleak House*', *Yearbook of Research in English and American Literature: REAL* 18, 2002, 109–130. See also, on the topic of women and property, Schor's superb book on Dickens and women: *Dickens and the Daughter of the House*, Cambridge: Cambridge University Press, 1999.
32 S. Chaplin, 'Fictions of Origin: Law, Abjection, Difference', *Law and Critique* 16(2), 2005, 161–180. See her excellent, and more sustained study: *The Gothic and the Rule of Law, 1764–1820*, New York: Palgrave Macmillan, 2007.
33 P. Glen, 'The Deconstruction and Reification of Law in Franz Kafka's *Before the Law* and *The Trial*', *Southern California Interdisciplinary Law Journal* 17, 2007, 23–66.

on Derridean justice in law-and-literature);[34] Foucauldian archaeology (David Miller, on the disciplinary regime of the police in *Bleak House*;[35] Peter Hutchings, on photography as a forensic discipline and Poe's 'Man in the Crowd');[36] or post-Freudian psychoanalysis (Peter Brooks, on confessions and confessionalism in law-and-literature;[37] Susan Stewart and the 'crimes of writing' in, variously, Hawthorne, graffiti and the Meese Report on Pornography).[38]

This heady mix yields rich readings of law/literature in terms of sexual difference, grammatology, power, the unconscious – and, of course, the legal process itself. Which, in its intellectual diversity, is all to the good; and one that *Novel Judgements* mimes in its references to, and functionalisation of Agamben, Althusser, Badiou, Brint, Brooks, Derrida, Foucault, Lacan, Levinas, Luhmann, Salecl, Saunders, Žižek, and so on. But these scholarly developments – though excellent in and of themselves – still beg the question: where are theories that are specifically *legal philosophical* or *jurisprudential*? Here there is a much more glaring deficit; though, even then, some of the legal philosophical/jurisprudential notions mentioned above – e.g., theories of justice – have been addressed in the path-breaking work of the following: Kieran Dolin, on Victorian and Modernist British literature;[39] Ravit Reichmann, on inter-war and post-war fiction;[40] Costas Douzinas, on Greek tragedy;[41] Paul Raffield, on early

---

34 T. Threadgold, 'Deconstruction and the Possibility of Justice: Critical and Cultural Difference', *Law, Text, Culture* 1, 1994, 140–148.
35 D. A. Miller, 'Discipline in Different Voices: Bureaucracy, Police, Family and *Bleak House*', *Representations* 1, 1983, 59–89. For a more sustained version, see his (justly) celebrated book on policing: *The Novel and the Police*, Berkeley: University of California Press, 1988.
36 P. Hutchings, 'Modern Forensics: Photography and Other Suspects', *Cardozo Studies in Law and Literature* 9(2), 1997, 229–244. See also, his excellent book on the novel and criminality: *The Criminal Spectre in Law, Literature and Aesthetics: Incriminating Subjects*, London: Routledge, 2001.
37 P. Brooks, *Troubling Confessions: Speaking Guilt in Law and Literature*, Chicago: University of Chicago Press, 2000.
38 S. Stewart, *Crimes of Writing: Problems in the Containment of Representation*, New York: Oxford University Press, 1994.
39 K. Dolin, *Fiction and the Law: Legal Discourse in Victorian and Modernist Literature*, Cambridge: Cambridge University Press, 1999. See also: K. Dolin, *A Critical Introduction to Law and Literature*, Cambridge: Cambridge University Press, 2007.
40 R. Reichman. *The Affective Life of Law: Legal Modernism and the Literary Imagination*, Stanford: Stanford University Press, 2009. See also: R. Reichman, 'Mourning, Owning, Owing', *American Imago* 64(3), 2007, 433–449.
41 C. Douzinas, *Justice Miscarried: Ethics and Aesthetics in Law*, London: Harvester Wheatsheaf, 1994.

modern English law-and-literature;[42] Maria Aristodemou, on the classic and contemporary novel;[43] Wai-chee Dimock[44] and Gregg Crane,[45] on canonical American literature; Susan Sage Heinzelman[46] and Melanie Williams,[47] on feminist literary jurisprudence. Recently, rights discourse, and the subjectivity it interpellates (the rights-bearer), has provided new ways of reading the *Bildungsroman* in the work of Joseph Slaughter.[48]

*Novel Judgements*, however, *extends* this theoretical ambit taking as its brief a wider range of key legal philosophical/jurisprudential issues in canonical nineteenth century – as well as contemporary 'high' theory – pairing each one with a particular literary analogue: the theme of sovereignty in John Austin and Jane Austen; the vexed matter of law's morality in Sir Walter Scott and Jeremy Bentham; the contentious issue of rights in Mary Wollstonecraft and Mary Shelley; the critique of law's letter in Hawthorn and Holmes; and the heated debates over legal ethics, the Rule of Law and justice in Charles Dickens and, variously, A. V. Dicey, James Fitzjames Stephen and John Stuart Mill. Interwoven throughout these cross-stitched pairings is a third strand – of contemporary theorists, and their contributions, legal and otherwise: Derrida on justice, Lacan on the 'Law of the Father's Name', Levinas on 'the face of the Other', Steven Brint on trust, Žižek on enjoyment, Foucault on governmentality, and so on. In taking jurisprudence not only 'seriously' but with such a broad sweep, *Novel Judgements* has strong affinities with the work of both feminist jurisprude Melanie Williams[49] and Australian Indigenous (Kombumerri–

---

42 P. Raffield, *Shakespeare's Imaginary Constitution: Late Elizabethan Politics and the Theatre of the Law*, Oxford: Hart Publishing, 2011; and P. Raffield, *Images and Cultures of Law in Early Modern England: Justice and Political Power, 1558–1660*, Cambridge: Cambridge University Press, 2004.
43 M. Aristodemou, *Law and Literature: Journeys from Her to Eternity*, Oxford: Oxford University Press, 2000.
44 W. C. Dimock, *Residues of Justice: Literature, Law, Philosophy*, Berkeley: University of California Press, 1996.
45 G. Crane, *Race, Citizenship and Law in American Literature*, Cambridge: Cambridge University Press, 2002.
46 S. S. Heinzelman and Z. Wiseman, *Representing Women: Law, Literature and Feminism*, Durham, NC: Duke University Press, 1994.
47 M. Williams, *Empty Justice: One Hundred Years of Law, Literature and Philosophy: Existential, Feminist and Normative Perspectives in Literary Jurisprudence*, London: Routledge-Cavendish, 2002. See also: M. Williams, *Secrets and Laws: Collected Essays in Law, Lives and Literature*, London: Routledge-Cavendish, 2005.
48 J. Slaughter, *Human Rights, Inc.: The World Novel, Narrative Form and International Law*, New York: Fordham University Press, 2007.
49 For Williams, see above n. 47.

Munaljahlai) scholar Christine Black,[50] and the capacious *theoretical* range of each's law-and-literature *œuvre*. The former develops her notion of a 'literary jurisprudence' across texts as diverse as *Tess of the D'Urbervilles*, the drama of John van Druten and the magic realism of John Fowles; while the latter recuperates notions of an Indigenous legal philosophy from the poetry of Senior Law Man Bill Neidje, as well as the novels of New Zealand Maori Witi Ihimaera and Australian Indigenous writer, Alexis Wright.

Unlike, however, either Williams's or Black's work, *Novel Judgements* is a book that is confined to a specific period (the nineteenth century), and has a particular generic focus (the novel). These sorts of period and generic limits, when coupled with the book's clear jurisdictional restriction to Anglo-American common law culture, set *Novel Judgements* apart not only from Williams's and Black's work, but also, rhetorician James Boyd White,[51] post-structuralist Penny Pether,[52] aesthetics scholar Adam Gearey[53] and ethicist Richard Weisberg,[54] all of whom mix and match the classical with the contemporary, Hardy with W. H. Auden, Shakespeare with Tess of the d'Urbervilles, Shelley's Ozymandias and Faulkner's Yoknapawtapha, the US Constitution with the Australian Outback's 'bush lawyer'. Not that I have any objection to this sort of syncretic scholarship, and I applaud each of these researchers, and acknowledge my debt to all of them. But *Novel*

---

50 C. F. Black, *The Land is the Source of the Law: A Dialogic Encounter with Indigenous Jurisprudence*. London: Routledge, 2010.
51 J. B. White, *When Words Lose Their Meaning: Constitutions and Reconstitutions of Language, Character and Community*, Chicago: University of Chicago Press, 1984; J. B. White, *Heracles' Bow: Essays on the Rhetoric and Poetics of Law*, Madison, Wisconsin: University of Wisconsin Press, 1985; J. B. White, *Justice as Translation: An Essay in Cultural and Legal Criticism*, Chicago: University of Chicago Press, 1990; J. B. White, *Acts of Hope: Creating Authority in Literature, Law and Politics*, Chicago: University of Chicago Press, 1994.
52 P. Pether, 'Regarding the Miller Girls: Daisy, Judith and the Seeming Paradox of *In Re: Grand Jury Subpoena, Judith Miller*', *Law and Literature* 19(2), 2007, 187–207; P. Pether, 'Is There Anything Outside the Class – Law, Literature and Pedagogy *Symposium: The Failure of the Word*', *Cardozo LR* 26, 2005, 2415–2424; P. Pether, 'Measured Judgements? Histories, Pedagogies and the Possibility of Equity', *Law and Literature* 14(3), 2002, 489–543; P. Pether, 'Sex, Lies and Defamation: The Bush Lawyer of Wessex', *Cardozo Studies in Law and Literature* 6, 1994, 171–201; P. Pether, 'Fiduciary Duties, Congreve's *The Way of the World*', *Australian Journal of Law and Society* 7, 1991, 71.
53 A. Geary, *Law and Aesthetics*, Oxford: Hart Publishing, 2001.
54 R. Weisberg, *Poethics and Other Strategies of Law and Literature*. London: Butterworths, 1992. See also his earlier works: *The Failure of the Word: The Protagonist as Lawyer in Modern Fiction*, New Haven, CT: Yale University Press, 1984; *When Lawyers Write*, New York: Little Brown, 1987.

*Judgements* is doing something else; specifically, it is exploring, through a genre-, period-, and jurisdiction-specific study of literature, the literary contribution to the historical construction of the nineteenth-century's legal mindset – what might be called, with a nod to Lacan,[55] its 'juridical imaginary'. 'Imaginary', because this term suggests an imagination underpinning law's symbolic processes and doctrines, institutions and ideas; that is, a realm of limitless legal fantasy, of free-flowing nomological desire, fixed around, and fixated upon controlling images that condense its central juridical concepts – think of how the blindfolded figure of Iustitia concentrates and conveys the Rule of Law's claims to objectivity, impartiality, and neutrality.

It is towards the historical construction of this juridical imaginary that *Novel Judgements* turns its attention, an investigation predicated not just on the 'pastness' of this imaginary's past but its continued *presence*. For a study of the nineteenth-century's juridical imaginary is relevant to the here-and-now because that imaginary still informs, organises and structures contemporary Anglo-American law, including notions such as rights, law's morality, justice, as well as the Rule of Law. So *Novel Judgements* will explore the origins of this juridical imaginary using another vehicle of the imagination, the novel. As the privileged *and popular* medium of its era (like cinema and/or television of our own), the novel is coincident with the emergence of this juridical imaginary, bearing not-so-silent witness to its development. Biographer, feminist legal theorist, and criminal lawyer, Nicola Lacey, has made a similar point in her excellent, *Women, Crime and Character: From Moll Flanders to Tess of the D'Urbervilles*[56] – but she confines her remit to *crime* and its imaginary of intention, responsibility, and punishment.

I want to extend this remit here because, to my way of thinking, the novel is a particularly choice vehicle for exploring the *jurisprudential* imaginary in all its (near-) infinite variety, including but also extending well beyond the criminogenic. After all, it is in this period – the Age of Industrial

---

55 For Lacan's first treatment of the Imaginary, and its false lures of identic wholeness, see: J. Lacan, 'The Mirror Stage as Formative of the Function of the I as revealed in Psychoanalytic Experience', in A. Sheridan (trans.) *Ecrits: A Selection*, New York: Norton, 1997, pp. 1–7. The Imaginary has been picked up, developed and politicised by a range of cultural and critical theorists – Althusser, Castoriadis, Žižek, to name some of the most prominent – all of whom equate it with the realm of ideology, and the images and symbols, identifications and misidentifications that circulate there.

56 N. Lacey, *Women, Crime, and Character: From Moll Flanders to Tess of the D'Urbervilles*, Oxford: Oxford University Press, 2008.

Capital, with its strong contractual and property imperatives – that the law begins to touch upon, and 'reify' (or 'thing'-ify) all aspects of life, including the most private, like the realm of domesticity. The novel, with its focus on this domestic realm – of marriage and manners, hearth and home – provides a unique record of the private sphere's encroaching 'juridification' (or legalisation). To give just one example, think how contractual – rather than sacramental – a wedding has become for the Bennet sisters in *Pride and Prejudice*.[57] Other novels here register similar sorts of legal changes; they do so, however, elliptically and subtly, encoding or allegorising this process of juridification in settings, characters, plots, and themes that are not necessarily recognisable as overtly legal: as historical romances (*Ivanhoe, A Tale of Two Cities, The House of the Seven Gables*), mysteries (*Bleak House, Great Expectations*) and Gothic horrors (*Frankenstein*) – as well as country house comedies (*Pride and Prejudice*). None of these texts – but one: *Bleak House*, and even there the detective story overwhelms the court case – announce themselves, however, as legal dramas.

Of course, the law never goes missing entirely from these narratives. Think of lawyers such as Jaggers (criminal attorney), 'Conversation' Kenge (solicitor), Jaffrey Pyncheon (judge), and Tulkinghorn (civil attorney); the trials of Charles Darnay (for sedition in England, then counter-revolutionary crime in France), Matthew Maule (witchcraft) and generations of Jarndyces – not to mention Clares, Carstones, and Barbarys (over a will 'in Chancery'); criminals such as Compeyson (fraud), Frankenstein's monster (murder), Col Pyncheon (conspiracy), and the Brothers St. Evremonde (rape); offences such as usury (Isaac of York), false witness (Barsad), murder (Clifford Pyncheon); even legal documents, an equity bill (in Nemo's 'law hand'), the deed to Waldo County (secreted behind Col. Pyncheon's portrait) and a long-hidden affidavit (Dr Manette's testimonial). But this abundance of legal detail – of character and *contretemps* – remains just that in much of the critical literature: mere *detail*, on the margins of these texts, peripheral to their meaning. And even if it is addressed, usually such detail is explained away as of purely 'historical' interest, adding little to the actual *explication de texte*. Counterposing this sort of dismissive reductionism, I want to stake a central *theoretical* claim here, one that shifts attention away from the historicity of these texts'

---

57 For an alternative viewpoint of Georgian and Regency marriage *a la mode*, this time rehabilitating Anglicanism, see: L. O'Connell, 'Proper ceremony: the political origins of the marriage plot', unpublished manuscript, forthcoming.

surface (legal) detail, and plumbs, instead, the depths of their (legal–theoretical) deep structure. For what these deep structural depths reveal, once plumbed, is a different scene of explication, an alternative site of understanding; namely, a subtext of jurisprudential and legal philosophical import that releases rather than fixes meaning.

And what a rich, meaning-*ful(l)* subtext it turns out to be, especially given the range of legal theories available for literary representation in the period. This is so because the nineteenth-century common law world witnessed an explosion of legal theories, consequent upon legal positivism's break with natural law at the beginning of the century. That break proclaims law's autonomy from morality, a move often thought of as negative because it insulates the law from politics, economy, and society as well as religion. True. But, equally, this positivistic break can be conceived more *positively*; that is, as liberating the law from faith, and thereby freeing it to rethink its origins, aims, and scope, shorn of theological strictures. In so doing, this break unleashes a host of competing jurisprudential/legal philosophical schools and movements, all of which this book argues the novel taps into and takes on board; for example, the command theory of law, utilitarianism, formalism, retributivism, feminism, Marxism, legal realism, rights theory and liberal legalism, to name a few. These schools and/or movements contest as much as confirm the judicial imaginary's core ideas (Rule of Law, rights, justice, etc.); and it is precisely their *contestatory* potential that emboldens the novelist and his/her novel to 'ask the law question' – as jurisprude Margaret Davies might put it[58] – of the juridical imaginary. So this book is concerned, not only with how the novel represents the juridical imaginary's legal theories (both at the level of idea or school/movement), but how this novelistic rendering of legal theories complicates, challenges, and calls the juridical imaginary to account. Thus, *Novel Judgements* propounds a thesis which resonates with, and echoes that of others – but raises it a notch; principally, about the *subversive* power of literature vis-à-vis not only law[59] but *legal theory*. It is this thesis that I will test here by and through a series of close readings of paired legal and literary texts, their interaction giving rise to what might be called a 'cultural legal intertext'.

---

58 M. Davies, *Asking the Law Question*, Sydney: Law Book Company, 2008.
59 Literature's subversive potential with respect to *law* generally has been argued by a range of writers: Dolin, Goodrich, Pether, Hutchings, Aristodemou, Williams, *et al*. My thesis differs here in its focus; that is, on *legal theory* specifically, and *its* potential subversion by literature.

### Rendering (Novel) Judgements and the Question of Method: Reading Jurisprudentially

It is this cultural legal intertext – meaning the textual space, *between* and generated *by* two overlapping discourses, two interpenetrating disciplines: law-and-literature – in which the novel puts jurisprudence/legal philosophy on trial, judges and finds it . . . *wanting*? What then is the nature of this *novel judgement*? Certainly, the content of the novels here gives us a rogues' gallery of legal theory, not only judged and found wanting, but condemned, as it were, by the court of history: from *Pride and Prejudice*'s Lady Catherine de Bourgh, the obdurate spokeswoman for an oppressive class society 'blessed' by divine natural law, to *A Tale of Two Cites*' Mme. Defarge, the implacable agent of a psychotic revolutionary justice; from *Bleak House*'s attorney, Tulkinghorn, who kills his clients for their own good, to *Great Expectations*' Miss Havisham, whose notion of justice is one of the most retributively vengeful in Victorian fiction. Further, how does this judgement come about; that is, through what techniques of literary/legal form is the tale told, and the case proved? Omniscient narrators, first-person narratives, unreliable focalisers/witnesses, epistolary devices, analepsis (flashback) and prolepsis (foreshadowing), doubled or false endings; all the tricks of narratology – or the science of storytelling – will be investigated here as forms of evidence, of proof. Finally, there is a larger question implied here, subsuming and superseding questions of form and content; namely, the question of legal fiction's efficacy upon legal fact. Specifically, can literature change anything about the law, challenging its organising concepts, its foundational ideals? If so, what sort of space of critique does it open up – gendered? racialised? 'class'-ified?

*Novel Judgements* will argue that nineteenth-century prose fiction gives its readers a host of critics of the law: Elizabeth Bennet, Rebecca of York, Frankenstein's monster, Esther Summerson, Joe Gargery, Sydney Carton, and Holgrave. These 'crits' and their critiques of law can certainly *combust*, and anticipate, with an uncanny prescience, today's feminists, race theorists, ethicists, Marxists, and postmodernists. But can they construct something else? That question is asked, often in bad faith, of legal critique and with an ulterior motive; principally, to shut it down, foreclosing its analysis of law's class, gender and race 'politics' because, purportedly, it offers nothing in its place. This is most certainly *not* the agenda of *Novel Judgements* because driving this text is the sense that these characters' 'novel judgements' can, and do envisage another *nomos*, even call forth a reimagined socio-Symbolic. What does this socio-Symbolic look like? And what kind of *nomoi* – simply, laws – regulate it? How do they operate? When are exceptions made? What of sanctions and penalties? Who applies them?

How are they enforced? These are some of the questions this book will raise and, *en passant*, explore.

As noted earlier, this line of inquiry differs from that of socio-legal perspectives. Instead, my approach opts for a more 'theoretical' perspective; accordingly, it has more of an affinity with avowedly feminist (Aristodemou, Williams, Sage Heinzelman, Schor) or Foucauldian (Hutchings) scholars of law-and-literature, all of whom are theoretically driven (be it by Irigaray, Lacan, Foucault, and so forth). But my perspective diverges from these feminist/Foucauldian approaches, as I have argued previously, because my theoretical paradigm comes, not from cultural or gender studies, but from the law itself; that is, from *jurisprudence*, from *legal philosophy* in all its varieties, be it legal positivism, rights, theories of justice, utilitarianism, realism and all forms of legal critique (class, gender, and race). I reiterate this point at some length here because it goes to the heart of my scholarly agenda. Specifically, I want to restore jurisprudence to its rightful place in the canon of contemporary hermeneutics as a discourse with its *own* unique mode of interpretation, its *own* particular method of analysis. And not just as a discourse capable of interpreting or analysing of legal texts, but, potentially, *all* texts – political, social, economic or, as here, cultural. In short, I want to demonstrate how jurisprudence functions as a *reading* practice of textuality *writ* large which is, as Catherine MacKinnon might put it, 'unmodified',[60] distinctly separate from, and a viable alternative to, for example, deconstruction, psychoanalysis, New Historicism, gender and/or queer theory. For far too long jurisprudence has been content to plunder those fields for paradigms and procedures, *topoi* and treatments – the dissemination of *différance*, the capillaries of power and the 'Law of the Father's Name', to name a few.

*Novel Judgements* puts paid to this one-way traffic and aims to reverse this flow, returning to the overlooked and under-utilised intellectual resources of jurisprudence itself (often perceived, like 'historicism' or 'theory', as languishing in a state of conceptual 'poverty'), engaging its rich and abiding themes of justice, rights, the Rule of Law and law's morality as the subject and source of a new way to read the (cultural) text. So here I will develop and extend an argument adumbrated in an earlier book,[61] all the while modelling what it means to '*read jurisprudentially*'. This reading

---

60 C. MacKinnon, *Feminism Unmodified: Discourse on Law and Life*, Cambridge, MA: Harvard University Press, 1987.
61 W. P. MacNeil, *Lex Populi: The Jurisprudence of Popular Culture*, Stanford, CA: Stanford University Press, 2007.

practice involves, by necessity, an investigation of *method*, the question of which is often skirted in debates over the value, relevance and worth of law-and-literature scholarship. This methodological silence leads to problems on both sides of the law-and-literature divide – particularly for budding scholars or students of the field. Lawyers, on one hand, are often (not always) 'blind' before the literary work, unable to functionalise their extensive and intimate knowledge of law, legal process and (sometimes) legal philosophy beyond the belletristic, failing to translate these rich resources into a sustained analysis of the text-*qua*-text.

Literary critics, on the other hand, come to the text with an impressive arsenal of *recherché* interpretive stratagems, running the gamut from A (Agamben) to Z (Žižek), and are more than able, from their training, to put these stratagems to work in the service of a subtle and sophisticated hermeneutics. But when it comes to questions of *law*, an intellectual diffidence descends and these very same critics retreat, in many (not all) cases, into technicist explanations (cribbed from dictionaries, hornbooks, antiquarian studies), often as out-of-date as they are under-theorised, and relied upon as if there was *no* legal theory already in place with which to conceptualise these questions. *Novel Judgements* proposes a corrective to and for *both*, modelling for lawyers how to *analyse* literature ('reading') in terms of law, and for literary critics, how to *think* about law ('jurisprudentially') in terms of literature. To that end, and without intending to be reductionist – but, nevertheless, seeing the *necessity* for a structured approach in law-and-literature, the systematicity of which opens up rather shuts down debate (think of Barthes's *S/Z*, my personal favourite as a 'how-to' of *practical criticism*), I would like to lay out the following programme for 'reading jurisprudentially', one that follows three stages of analysis.

First, 'reading jurisprudentially' identifies patterns of what might be called subtextual similitude between the literary and legal text: a turn of phrase, a recurrent image or motif, a particular narrative design or shape. For example, Chapter 4 ('The Monstrous Body of the Law: Wollstonecraft vs. Shelley') was inspired by the image of monstrosity found not only in Shelley's but Wollstonecraft's writings; specifically, in *A Vindication of the Rights of Women* where women, when deprived of rights, are characterised as 'monstrous' – a telling phrase for a woman whose daughter will write the most famous monster story of all time. Second, these subtextual analogies are *nominated* expressly, by this mode of reading, as a legal school or theory, rendering the novelistic in terms of the jurisprudential and vice-versa; for instance, designating a setting as a site of natural law, a character as an embodiment of positivism, and so forth. Consider the example offered by Chapter 7 ('Two on a Guillotine? Courts and "Crits" in *A Tale of Two*

*Cities*') where *A Tale of Two Cities*' Sydney Carton, the dissolute and cynical barrister, is identified with the nihilistic drift of critical legal studies and its contempt for law's claims to fairness, neutrality, and justice. Third and finally, a jurisprudential reading converts the analogical into the analytical; that is to say, by exploring the extent to which these novels' subtextual analogies reinterpret, indeed resignify jurisprudence, generating a new *intertext* of the legal and the literary that, potentially, *re*imagines the juridical imaginary. Take the example of Chapter 8 ('Beyond Governmentality: The Question of Justice in *Great Expectations*'): there, in *Great Expectations*, it is Pip's kindly uncle-by-marriage, Joe Gargery, who offers the reader a very different version of justice from the retributive and distributive fantasies of Magwitch and Miss Havisham, one that the late (and much lamented) French philosopher, Jacques Derrida, might identify as turning on the 'ethics of friendship'.

I call these novels' analogies 'subtextual' because their juridical resonances are anything but obvious. More often than not, they are encoded as a-legal persons (damsels in distress, penniless suitors, well-meaning benefactors, unscrupulous and thwarting relations) and places (stately homes, castellated redoubts, haunted houses); and are figured in a range of plot devices, all turning on desire: happy marriages, *mésalliances*, unrequited love, wanton dalliances. Law, if present at all here in any substantive way, is often figured, subtly, even elliptically – in a range of *things*: a lost deed, a long hidden testimonial, an unusual 'law-hand'. This book will take up the interpretive challenge afforded by these *objets trouvés*, using them, as well as the devices of plot, place, *mise-en-scène*, theme and characterisation, to tease out the jurisprudential/legal philosophical subtexts. In so doing, I will develop not only a literary interpretation of the legal theory in question but a legal theoretical interpretation of the respective literary text. Seven close readings of literary texts will be essayed here, and they are as follows. To begin at the beginning: Chapter 2 ('John Austin or Jane Austen? *The Province of Jurisprudence Determined* in *Pride and Prejudice*') and Chapter 3 ('Jousting with Bentham: Utility, Morality and Ethics in *Ivanhoe*'s Tournament of Law') will examine, respectively, two schools of nineteenth-century legal positivism and the two principal exponents of those schools: John Austin and Jeremy Bentham. The jurisprudential theories of both legal theorists will be read in light of what I take to be their novelistic equivalents: Jane Austen's *Pride and Prejudice*[62] and Sir Walter Scott's *Ivanhoe*.[63]

---

62 J. Austen, *Pride and Prejudice*, D. Gray (ed.), New York: Norton, 1993.
63 Sir W. Scott, *Ivanhoe*, G. Tulloch (ed.), London: Penguin, 2000.

I want to suggest here that these novels raise and represent two issues, consequent upon legal positivism's rise to jurisprudential hegemony. First, what is the status of critique (what Bentham calls 'censorial jurisprudence') once the positivist order of 'expository' jurisprudence (John Austin's 'command of the sovereign') is entrenched? Second, what happens to ethics once positivism has banished morality from the closed system of the law? As to the former question, *Pride and Prejudice*'s Mr Darcy will be read as a stand-in for the Austinian sovereign, the embodiment of commanding, expository law; and Elizabeth, as the Benthamic 'censorial' critic, silenced by their marriage – much as Austin's legal positivism silences Benthamite critique and reform. While, as to the second question, *Ivanhoe*'s Jewish usurer, Isaac of York, will be analysed as an instantiation of the Benthamic debates over the abolition of the usury laws, and the need to remove 'the moral' (i.e. anti-usurious feeling) from the law, figured not only the expulsion of the Grand Master of the Templars but, equally, in Isaac's departure for Spain at the close of the novel. That latter leave-taking, however, is highly problematic because, in so doing, Isaac is accompanied into exile by none other than his daughter, Rebecca – who, in turn, personifies a more subtle kind of law's morality; namely, law's relationship with ethics, and especially, its 'ethics of the Other'. Indeed, this chapter will argue Rebecca is the very 'face of the Other' – as the celebrated philosopher of ethics, Emmanuel Levinas might put it – radiating a kindness and care that not only the law but society so desperately needs. Which is why, at the end of *Ivanhoe*, Rebecca's expulsion from England with her father, when read as an allegory of the consequences of legal positivism, is such a disaster for law because, here, the positivists throw the ethical baby out with the legal morality of the bathwater.

Chapter 4 ('The Monstrous Body of the Law: Wollstonecraft vs. Shelley') turns to rights discourse and examines the way in which two proto-feminists of the period debate this discourse. One of these proto-feminists is juridico-political and a radical; the other, literary and, at times, a reactionary – but the two share a commonality not the least of which is bloodline. For they are English literature's most celebrated mother–daughter duo, Mary Wollstonecraft and Mary Shelley, and their respective texts under consideration here are *A Vindication of the Rights of Women*[64] and *Frankenstein*.[65] In the former, Wollstonecraft claims, famously, that

---

64 M. Wollstonecraft, *A Vindication of the Rights of Woman*, C. H. Poston (ed.), New York: Norton, 1988.
65 M. Shelley, *Frankenstein: or The Modern Prometheus*, M. Hindle (ed.), London: Penguin Books, 2003.

persons without rights (i.e. women) are rendered 'monstrous'. I want to raise this question: is Mary Shelley's *Frankenstein* a riposte to that claim? By way of response, I want to explore the possibility that rights are, in and of themselves, monstrous – or, potentially, monster-making. The twist in the tale is vital here because in its story of a creature turning on its creator – and thereby becoming monstrous – *Frankenstein* may provide an allegory of rights themselves; that is, by vividly dramatising how what was, initially, an emancipatory discourse enabling us to own, contract, and so on, ultimately comes to own and reify *us*, turning all rights-bearers into 'the monstrous body of the law'. Is, then, there an alternative to this double bind of 'monstrifying' rights, of which we cannot live with, and cannot live without? This section will suggest that Wollstonecraft and Shelley, positioned as 'scribbling women' in a heavily patriarchal period – at once, inside and outside the law – point the reader to a specifically feminist solution to this juridical dilemma.

Chapter 5 ('Hawthorne's Haunted House of Law: The Romance of American Legal Realism in *The House of the Seven Gables*') turns from the Old World of English (and Scottish) novel judgements to the New World, America and its potential for a new literature, a new law. A potential, as yet unrealised; or so Holgrave, the artist-daguerreotypist, carps in Hawthorne's *The House of the Seven Gables*: 'What slaves we are to bygones times',[66] he protests to love interest, Phoebe, continuing more juristically, 'A dead man sits on all our judgement seats; and living judges do his business'.[67] No wonder the villain of the piece here is the figure of the judge – as dead *and* alive, being doubled in the characters of the magisterial Col. Pyncheon, the colonial builder of the House of the Seven Gables, Hawthorne's 'haunted house of law', and his grasping descendant, Judge Jaffrey Pyncheon, contemporary Whig appointee and politico. In these two depictions of judicial malfeasance, Hawthorne anticipates a kind of anti-legalism that will become typical of American jurisprudence, especially in its marked hostility to the expository, to the posited; specifically, to the judge-made rules of 'black letter' law, seen here as the dead hand of the past warping the present. 'It is revolting to have no better reason for a rule than that it was laid down in the time of Henry IV'[68] – a statement that could just as easily

---

66 N. Hawthorne, *The House of the Seven Gables*, New York: Modern Library, 2001, p. 157.
67 Ibid. p. 158.
68 O. Wendell Holmes, 'The Path of the Law', in R. A. Posner (ed.), *The Essential Holmes: Selections from the Letters, Speeches, Judicial Opinions and Other Writings of Oliver Wendell Holmes Jr.*, Chicago: University of Chicago Press, 1992, p. 170.

have been made by Holgrave, as it was by Oliver Wendell Holmes, Jr. Indeed, this chapter will argue that Holgrave is a prefiguration of Holmes and his jurisprudential successors (Llewellyn, Frank, *et al.*), a kind of proto-legal realist, committed to a programme of juridical reform that re-functionalises the old English common law for its new American context, hovering, as it is, on the brink of industrial take-off. This, of course, means making critique, legal and otherwise, safe for Capital – ironically by neutralising that very agent of change, Holgrave and his (potentially) revolutionary call for, *inter alia*, a new law. No wonder the novel ends with Holgrave (the prophet of the 'new order') marrying Phoebe (the descendant of the old regime) because, in merging the old and the new, critique and convention, Hawthorne's *The House of the Seven Gables* enacts, so this chapter will argue, 'the romance of American legal realism': a love affair that unites, and marries precedent and policy, form and function.

Chapter 6 ('In Boz We Trust! *Bleak House*'s Reimagination of Trusteeship'), Chapter 7 ('Two on a Guillotine: Courts and "Crits" in *A Tale of Two Cities*') and Chapter 8 ('Beyond Governmentality: The Question of Justice in *Great Expectations*') form a kind of closing triptych within this book, advancing a revisionist thesis about one of the greatest of law-and-*littérateurs*, Charles Dickens. Long deemed by law-and-literature studies as the greatest critic *of* the law, I want to ask this startling question: For all his fulminations about and against Chancery's evils, was Dickens in fact an apologist *for* the law? This is an astonishing about-face in Dickens law-and-literature scholarship, and it begins here with a rereading of no less a (putatively) anti-legalist text than *Bleak House*. Chapter 6 will suggest that, while *Bleak House* is, explicitly, a searing critique of equity and its principal device, the trust – the disputed nub of the case of Jarndyce and Jarndyce – it, implicitly, calls for a renewed *trust* in the law. How? That call comes through the tale's *form* rather than content; namely, in a narrative voice that functions as a kind of lawyerly 'social trustee', denouncing injustices as if before the bar of the *socius* itself ('Dead, your Majesty. Dead my lords and gentlemen ... Dead ... And dying thus around us, everyday')[69] and demanding a new social order in which a reformed and reforming law will play a key role.

This rehabilitation of the law in general continues and extends to, more specifically, the common law in Chapter 7's reading of *A Tale of Two Cities*. There, the common law courts are depicted as, ultimately, the guarantor of our safety and security through, paradoxically, their very failure. What is

---

69 C. Dickens, *Bleak House*, New York: Modern Library, 2002, p. 636.

the nature of this failure? This section will suggest that it is the common law's *inability*, unlike the revolutionary tribunals, to get at 'the truth' which enables it to *acquit* rather than convict Charles Darnay of treason. Of course, the collateral damage contingent upon not only Darnay's acquittal but survival is the decline, then demise of Carton – the sacrifice of whom, I argue here, metaphorises the common law's abandonment of critique. That critical loss, however, enables the common law to *live* on: as personified in Charles and Lucie's son – Carton's namesake and, himself, a judge. This endorsement of the common law sets the stage for Chapter 8's examination of Dickens's full-scale search for a theory of justice in *Great Expectations*. Where is that theory to be found? Certainly not in the retributive and distributive fantasies of Magwitch and Miss Havisham, both of whom provide very 'unjust' notions of justice (against the status quo of class or gender). This chapter will suggest that a new template for justice lies with one of the more modest, less front-and-centre characters in the novel: in Joe Gargery and his ethics of friendship ('Ever the best of friends, ain't us Pip?').[70]

In the concluding postscript, I will return to, and summarise my argument, all the while drawing out its inferences for what might be called 'the shape of legal theory to come'. For *Novel Judgements* is not solely a period study. Or, if it is, it is a period study which *prognosticates*; that is, looks beyond its limits, it cadastres, peering into the future. This forward-looking gaze – that takes, as it were, *Novel Judgements* 'back to the future' – is an effect as much as a cause of 'reading jurisprudentially'. For when these textual materials – nineteenth-century legal philosophy, nineteenth-century literature – are laid out, in the manner of a Derridean 'double session', side by side and read jurisprudentially, they produce a new *mediation*: a legal theory of, and from the novel. And what this new mediation – a legal theory of, and from the novel – opens up, articulates and develops is nothing less than a juridical position that will become the nomological signature of our own era, and a riposte to the Rule of Law ideology of the previous age; that is, legal *critique* in all of its *differences* of legal realism, critical legal studies, critical legal feminism, critical race theory, postmodern jurisprudence, and so on. Diverse as these jurisprudential movements may be, they are united in their critique of law's claims to consistency, impartiality, and open access. It will be these postures of legal censure that will come to dominate our era, and which are, I argue, figured in *and* prefigured by characters like Elizabeth Bennet, Rebecca of York,

---

70 C. Dickens, *Great Expectations*, New York: Bantam Books, 1982, p. 436.

Frankenstein's monster, Holgrave, and so on. For each of these characters will assume, at one point or another in their respective narrative proceedings, a judicial role, reviewing, deliberating upon and condemning a dominant and/or hegemonic conception of law (e.g., the Rule of Law, the 'command of the sovereign', natural rights, equity, etc.). But legal critique is not the endgame of these characters' 'judgements'; instead, when read as a whole, they propound a counter-law as much as a critique of law, hailing a new legal dispensation as it discards the old, one that is well and truly 'novel'. So what these acts of 'novel judgement' call forth, and indeed perform is, I will conclude, nothing less than *a novel legal theory* of the *novel as legal theory.*

CHAPTER 2

# John Austin or Jane Austen?
## *The Province of Jurisprudence Determined* in *Pride and Prejudice*

**Recontextualising Jane Austen: Law's Empire and the Jurisprudence of *Pride and Prejudice***

It used to be a truth universally acknowledged that the novels of Jane Austen were narratives in want of context. The Napoleonic Wars, industrialisation and the French Revolution; in fact, all the great and heroic events of the period are conspicuous by their absence in the 'little bit (two Inches wide) of ivory' upon which dear Jane worked with 'so Fine a brush'.[1] Postcolonial critics, however, have sensitised readers to the traces of context on the margins of Austen's *œuvre*, and how, despite this marginality – or perhaps, as the postmodernists of yesteryear would say, precisely because of it – they perform an absolutely central function in terms of the novel's plotting, characterology and thematics. For example, the imperial context of *Mansfield Park* is the principal focus of Edward Saïd's celebrated reading of that text in *Culture and Imperialism*.[2] There, Saïd's reading turns on an often overlooked narrative detail of the novel; namely, the significance of Sir Thomas Bertram's Jamaican estate which, while a literal absence in the

---

1 J. Austen, 'Letter to J. Edward Austen, 16 December 1816', in J. Austen, *Pride and Prejudice*, D. Gray (ed.), New York: Norton, 1993, p. 270. Hereafter referred to as *P&P*.
2 E. Saïd, *Culture and Imperialism*. London: Vintage Press, 1994, pp. 95–116.

text (no scene is actually set there, though some characters – Sir Thomas notably – go missing occasionally from the storyline because of visits there), is, nonetheless, a pervasive imaginative presence (as the site and source of the Bertram family fortune). This chapter's argument addresses a different text, *Pride and Prejudice*, but shadows that of Saïd and repeats many of his critical moves; however, the contextual argument that I propose to advance is not about *the* Empire but what might be called, with a nod to Ronald Dworkin, 'Law's Empire'. For it is my thesis here that some of *Pride and Prejudice*'s principal concerns are legal, and, more precisely jurisprudential, thereby linking Jane Austen, by more than just homophony, with the pioneering jurisprudential thinker of her day, her near contemporary, the utilitarian and positivist jurist, John Austin, the first professor of English law at University College London and the author of the then leading standard text on common law jurisprudence, *The Province of Jurisprudence Determined*.[3]

Indeed, it will be my central thesis that Jane Austen's *Pride and Prejudice* is John Austin's *The Province of Jurisprudence Determined*, and *vice versa*, a process of identification that generates a new cultural legal intertext. Before, however, advancing this intertextual thesis in any detail this chapter will address in the next (and second) section the 'site' of law in *Pride and Prejudice*, attempting to map its 'lawscape'; that is, determining where, in *Pride and Prejudice*, the law is to be 'sighted', especially when none of its principal characters are themselves lawyers – or, for that matter, litigants. This absence of lawyering or courts, however, is not fatal to the cultural legal reading essayed here; in fact, it reanimates such a reading, blowing new theoretical life into it, thereby shifting the reader's understanding of 'the legal' away from issues of persons (barristers, solicitors, etc.) or processes (the entail, etc.) and towards the conceptual, the jurisprudential: specifically, the jurisprudence of legal positivism and its forerunner, Benthamic utility. So the third section of this chapter will identify a range of settings (Meryton, Netherfield Hall) and characters (Charlotte Lucas, Caroline Bingley) that instantiate utility's most celebrated Benthamic formula; namely, the calculus of felicity – rendered here as the *marital* felicity of 'the good match' with all of its strategic connotations of suitable backgrounds and steady incomes.

Counterposed against these largely arithmetical calculations, however, is another form of 'good match', one based much more on bloodline rather

---

3 J. Austin, *The Province of Jurisprudence Determined and The Uses of the Study of Jurisprudence*, London: Weidenfeld & Nicolson, 1954.

than bank balance, on quarterings rather than quarterly statements; and whose spokesperson, this chapter will argue in its fourth section, is as much a foe of modernity's (and utility's) regime of 'contract' as she is of the Darcy–Elizabeth alliance: that figure of *ancien régime* 'status', Lady Catherine de Bourgh. As it turns out, though, Lady Catherine is a *faux* foe because, like the class she stands for – the landed aristocracy – she is a receding figure of power on the (social) text's 'lawscape'. For her claims to governance, to sovereignty, as section five and six maintain, have been displaced, by her nephew, Darcy, and re-situated on an entirely new basis: Austinian command. Which prompts this chapter to ask in its concluding (and seventh) section exactly who wrote *Pride and Prejudice*: John Austin or Jane Austen? This question of *authorship* is directly related to the issue of *authority* – legal and otherwise – sketched above, and solicits a judgement, a *novel* judgement about this novel's uncertain 'politics of the law' as raised, particularly, in its highly ambiguous ending. For that ending is, at once, intensely satisfying in its manufacture of consensus (imaged in the Darcy–Elizabeth marriage) but, equally, deeply disturbing in its censoring of dissensus (with Elizabeth's 'different voice' forever silenced), and points the cultural legal reader towards a legal theory that may go beyond exposition and (reforming) censure, beyond command and its (neutralised) critique: in short, to a jurisprudence of open revolt.

## Austen's 'Lawscape': Siting/Sighting the Law in *Pride and Prejudice*

Where is the law in *Pride and Prejudice*? The question is a necessary one, and must be addressed and resolved as a threshold issue before any cultural legal, let alone jurisprudential reading of the text can be put forward. This is because the law is almost nowhere to be *seen* in the text. After all, only one character, and a minor one at that – Mrs Bennet's brother-in-law, Mr Philips – is a lawyer; and he is not even a 'good' lawyer in the sense of belonging to the socially desirable branch of the profession, the bar. Rather he is a mere pettifogger, an 'attorney' whose portrait would hang, as Caroline Bingley comments ironically, so well next to Darcy's ancestor, the eminent judge (*P&P*, p. 36). This absence of law, however, becomes even more marked when moving from the legal profession to the legal process itself. Oddly, no one seems to 'go to law' in Jane Austen's novel; yet it is set, in large part, among that class of society most likely to litigate: the propertied classes of land and commerce. Sales of goods as much as leases of land seem to be unproblematic in this novelistic world – a distortion, if there ever was one, of the historical record. Even when a public wrong is committed, let alone a private dispute, no one seems to turn to the legal authorities. For example, the law is never invoked – no magistrate notified, no justice of the peace alerted – when the wicked Mr Wickham (who, incidentally and very tellingly, once professed his intention of studying law, *P&P*, p. 131) makes off, for a second time, with another underage female; in this instance, with the fickle Lydia Bennet – a *déclassée* follow-up to the posh Georgiana Darcy – as his willing victim, and against whom he commits, in all likelihood, what would qualify today as a statutory rape.[4]

Though absent from the text in terms of either process or *dramatis personae*, the law is – much like the Empire in *Mansfield Park* – an all pervasive *thematic* presence in *Pride and Prejudice*, informing many of its characters' motivation and, indeed, constituting the key plot mechanism driving its narrative action. What is this law? Further, where is it to be 'sited', as much as 'sighted' in the text? The law I speak of is, specifically, the law of inheritance, and it can be espied in the legal device of 'the entail', much commented upon or alluded to in the text (*P&P*, pp. 19–20) and by a range of characters: Mrs Bennet (*P&P*, pp. 42, 44), Elizabeth (*P&P*, p. 42), Jane (*P&P*, p. 42), Mr Collins (*P&P*, p. 44), Lady Catherine (*P&P*, pp. 107–108). This legal 'sighting', furthermore, has a particular 'site'; that is, at Longbourn, the modest country seat of the Bennet family, and over which the entail obtains. Briefly, an entail settles property on a prescribed line of succession, fixing it so that it cannot be altered by any of those individuals in whom the entailed property vests.[5] The entail on Longbourn is in the male line and is settled upon Mr Bennet's nearest male next-of-kin, his cousin, cleric, and comic relief, Mr Collins. The effect of this settlement is to disinherit and, ultimately, dispossess the Bennet sisters upon the death of their father: an event repeatedly adverted to by Mrs Bennet, and a source of much of the novel's 'gallows humour'.

This instantiation of what a certain strand of psychoanalysis – specifically, Lacanian – would call the 'Law of the Father's Name' activates, as no other device does, the plot of the novel, shifting its setting from the rather static country house comedy of manners – which the opening chapters, with their focus on the *badinage* of Mr and Mrs Bennet, would suggest – to a more dynamic line of action which moves, briskly, from

---

4 Though, in this period, absolutely legal – if morally reprehensible, the age of consent being twelve at common law and awaiting the passage The Criminal Law Amendment Act to raise it to sixteen in 1885. See *The Criminal Law Amendment Act* 1885, 48 & 49 Vict. c. 69.

5 Entail, in: D. M. Walker, *The Oxford Companion to Law*, Oxford: Clarendon Press, 1980.

Longbourn to Meryton, and then onto Netherfield, Hunsford, Rosings, Gracechurch St, and Pemberley. This shift is more than just scenic; it is thematic, particularly in the initial displacement from Longbourn to Meryton. Though the physical distance between the two is slight, the psychic distance is great, as Meryton seems to be *outside* the law as much as Longbourn is clearly *within* it. For all is fixity at Longbourn; its past is a matter of record, its future predetermined, both temporalities having been secured by the legal device of the entail. Nothing, however, is fixed in Meryton, its condition being one of flux, and functioning as a kind of no man's land, belonging to no one in particular but through which everyone in general passes. These displaced persons include those disrupted by war, like Col. Foster's regiment of Capt. Carter, Denny and Wickham; or those orphaned inheritors of property such as Miss King, Wickham's obscure object of desire; or those who belong nowhere and everywhere like the rootless 'new rich', the Bingleys, whose leased manor-house, Netherfield, could act as a metaphor for all of Meryton and its environs. Indeed, every*thing* is 'To Let' in Meryton, not just Netherfield but, so it seems from Mrs Bennet, 'Hay-Park... the great house at Stoke... Ashworth and Purvis Lodge' (*P&P*, p. 198). Further, every*one* is price-tagged: 10,000 outright for Miss King (*P&P*, p. 99); 5,000 *per annum* for Bingley (*P&P*, p. 4); much less for the regimentals, so much so that even Mrs Gardiner warns Elizabeth against an 'imprudent' (*P&P*, p. 95) match with the penniless Wickham. Clearly, exchange values prevail here; and, because everyone and everything has its price and is up for sale, Meryton is a feverish scene of speculation, as all and sundry vie to renegotiate their futures (like Mr Collins and his three offers of marriage) as much as rewrite their pasts (like Mr Wickham and his reinvention of himself as victim rather than 'villain of the piece').

All of which suggests that perhaps Meryton is not so much *outside* the law as previously suggested, and may function as yet another site of law in what might be called *Pride and Prejudice*'s 'lawscape'. Indeed, the constant round of offer, counter-offer, rejection and acceptance that constitutes much of Meryton's social tie suggests a regime which, while very different from that of Longbourn's entailment and its status certainties, is, nonetheless, very much a *juridical* regime: that of contract. Of course, the contract most often negotiated in Meryton is the marriage contract, itself a bargain for a new sort of status. But note the absence of great arranged alliances of the classic status society. Only one such example is proffered in the novel; notably, that of Miss Ann de Bourgh to Darcy, an engagement which even Lady Catherine describes as of a 'peculiar kind' (*P&P*, p. 228) and which never comes to fruition. Thus, even aristocratic marriage in the novel has come under the sway of contract's exchange values. For those actually in

Meryton and subject directly to its regime of contract – like the dispossessed Bennet sisters – the change is even more dramatic. For they enact what the eminent, nineteenth-century legal anthropologist and comparativist, Sir Henry Maine said was the classic move of 'modernity', a move which is also jurisprudential: the movement from status to contract.[6]

The citation of this well-worn formula – the move from status to contract – should not be read, however, as some Whiggish celebration of the shift from Longbourn (the society of status) to Meryton (the society of contract) as allegorising the movement from the realm of necessity to that of freedom. On the contrary, there is no mistaking Meryton as a realm of freedom released from the constraints of necessity. For, here, options, choices, even autonomy itself are constrained by the material conditions within which each of its inhabitants is situated; this, in turn, skews the putatively level playing field of freedom of contract, and, indeed, the entire network of capitalist relations of which it is a symbol. To give just one example, consider Jane Bennet's explanation to the appalled Elizabeth why her close friend and confidante, Charlotte Lucas would entertain, let alone accept a man of Mr Collins's severe limitations: 'Remember that she is one of a large family; that as to fortune, it is a most eligible match' (*P&P*, p. 88). Examples such as these – pointing to material conditions which constrain and distort the freedom of contract and Capital – proliferate throughout the novel, so much so that the representation which emerges of Meryton, and its regime of contract is anything but an 'Eden of the innate rights of man'. Or, if it is a paradisal realm of the Rousseaueque social contract, then it is only so in the highly ironic way Marx – the author of the above cited sobriquet – intended it in *Capital*; that is, as a place where 'alone rule Freedom, Equality, Property and Bentham', so that freedom produces wage slavery, equality leads to substantive inequity, property reinforces rather than challenges *bourgeois* privilege and Bentham masks and mitigates the master–slave relationship between, as he puts it in *Capital*, 'the capitalist; (and) the possessor of labour-power (who) follows as his labourer. The one with an air of importance, smirking, intent on business; the other, timid and holding back, like one who is bringing his own hide to market and has nothing to expect but – a hiding'.[7]

---

6 H. S. Maine, *Ancient Law*, Sir F. Pollock (ed.), Boston: Beacon Press, 1963, p. 165.

7 K. Marx, *Capital: A Critique of Political Economy, Volume I, The Process of Production Capital*, S. Moore and E. Aveling (trans.), F. Engels (ed.), Moscow: Progress Publishers, 1954, p. 416.

## Was that Mr Bennet or Mr Bentham? *Pride and Prejudice*'s Calculus of Felicity

The reference to Bentham here is very apropos *Pride and Prejudice*, particularly the scenes set in Meryton. For if there is any jurist who underwrites Meryton's regime of contract, then surely it is that apostle of utility, Jeremy Bentham, whose *Introduction to the Principles of Morals and Legislation*[8] supplies not just the community's doctrinal core but its very vocabulary. Consider, for example, the language of the two women most anxious to maximise their pleasure and minimise their pain in making a good match: Caroline Bingley and Charlotte Lucas. In one of her poison pen letters to Jane, Caroline Bingley uses a very telling phrase to describe the hoped-for match between her brother, Charles, and Georgiana Darcy. This alliance of 'brass and class' is described as producing 'the happiness of so many' (*P&P*, p. 79), a phrasing which evokes the first principle of utility itself, the 'greatest happiness for the greatest number'.[9] Charlotte Lucas goes even further in her language, so much so that I wonder if she is, indeed, the author of the *IPML*, because from the first scenes in which she is introduced – the visit to Lucas Lodge, following the assembly, and then at the reception at the Lodge – she speaks not only of 'happiness' but 'felicity' (*P&P*, p. 16), that other great Benthamite buzzword with all of its associations of the 'calculus of felicity'.[10] Certainly, 'calculate' is what Charlotte does best; notably, by urging Jane to display, rather than conceal her affection for Bingley after weighing all the advantages and disadvantages of one or the other mode of conduct (*P&P*, p. 15); accepting Mr Collins's offer of marriage out of the 'pure and disinterested desire of an establishment' (*P&P*, p. 82); even pairing off Elizabeth, when staying at Hunsford, with

---

8   J. Bentham, *An Introduction to the Principles of Morals and Legislation*, J. H. Burns and H. L. A. Hart (eds), Oxford: Clarendon Press, 1996. Hereafter, referred to as *IPML*.
9   Bentham writes in a footnote in the *IPML*, at 11a: 'To this denomination has of late been added or substituted the *greatest happiness* or *greatest felicity* principle: this for shortness, instead of saying *that principle* which states the greater happiness of all those whose interest is in question, as being the right and proper, and only right and proper and universally desirable, end of human action'.
10  Indeed, the opening paragraph of the *IPML*, explicitly links utility with this term, arguing that the purpose of this principle is 'to rear the fabric of felicity by the hands of reason and of law' (11). Such 'felicity', moreover, is subject to precise calculations as Bentham clearly demonstrates in the fourth chapter, entitled 'Value of a Lot of Pleasure or Pain, How to be Measured': 'Sum up all the values of all the *pleasures* on the one side, and those of all the *pains* on the other. The balance, if it be on the side of pleasure will give the *good* tendency of the act upon the whole, with respect to the interests of that *individual* person; if on the side of pain, the *bad* tendency of it upon the whole' (40).

Darcy rather than Col. Fitzwilliam because of the former's access to Anglican Church patronage (P&P, p. 118). Indeed, Charlotte is the Benthamite utilitarian *par excellence* – though pushed to its most vulgar Posnerian extreme, anticipating those contemporary Gradgrinds, the law-and-economics movement. Like them, reason is her faculty, and happiness, in its most material sense – of wealth maximisation – is her goal. 'I am not romantic', she says to Elizabeth, in a statement of the obvious if there ever was one, 'I ask only a comfortable home; and considering Mr Collins's character, connections and situation in life, I am convinced that my chance of happiness is as fair as most people can boast' (P&P, p. 84).

The problem with this Benthamite logic, of course, is that it can backfire spectacularly, nowhere more so than when it gives you what you want – proving the truth of the old adage that it's often a curse to get what you wished for. For is there a more chilling, nay ghoulish portrayal in nineteenth-century fiction of the lowest circle of matrimonial hell – outside the Dorothea Brooke – Mr Casaubon marriage in *Middlemarch* – than the picture of the Collinses at Hunsford living together, though in splendid isolation – he in his book room, she in her back parlour – keeping social (and, doubtless, other forms of) intercourse to a minimum? These bleak 'scenes from a marriage' call into question the calculus of felicity, and the happiness it produces, which seems too little by far here. But I would like to argue that utility, as a force of desire (after all, what is felicity? what is happiness?) as much as reason (of calculus, of social planning), is marked by a doubleness which releases not only too little but also too much *jouissance* into the regime of contract as well as Capital; that is, an excess of pleasure which overreaches itself, enacting utility's law of desire – the desire for more – at the very moment at which it undermines its desire for law – and its moderation of the desire for more. Lydia Bennet's amorous career is a graphic illustration of the utility principle run amok: 'untamed, unabashed, wild, noisy, and fearless' (P&P, p. 201). In her, the calculus of felicity becomes the 'thoughtless' (P&P, p. 186) pursuit of pleasure of the crassest kind – 'extravagant in wants and heedless of the future' (P&P, p. 248) – driving her from the seaside pavilions of Brighton to London's *demimondaine* and then finally to a shabby genteel existence, 'unsettled in the extreme' (P&P, p. 249) on the fringe of good society in the North.

Only with the figure of Mrs Bennet, however, does utility reach its real apogee of self-defeating excess, so much so that it produces a kind of paralysis. Hers is probably one of the most interesting pathological characters drawn in Austen's text (and *œuvre*?), condensing as she does a variety of symptoms, figured individually in the other utilitarian characters: Lydia's licentiousness (in Mrs Bennet's own self-confessed fixation with officers in youth, 'I confessed . . . I cried for two days together when Colonel Millar's regiment went away', *P&P*, p. 148), Charlotte's opportunism ('A single man of large fortune; four or five thousand a year', *P&P*, p. 1, is, after all, Mrs Bennet's *beau idéal* as much as Charlotte's) and Caroline's social climbing (Mrs Bennet is, as well, a woman of the middle classes – though the Meryton *petit bourgeoisie* rather than the London *haut bourgeoisie* of the Bingleys – pressing her way, and her family's into the gentry and nobility). These symptoms, once condensed, are then converted, rearticulated and literally written on the 'nervous' body of Mrs Bennet, a reinscription which supplies as vivid a metaphor as there ever was for the hysterical excess of Capital, contract and its law of desire, utility: 'I . . . have', says Mrs Bennet, 'such tremblings, such flutterings all over me, such spasms in my side, and pains in my head, and such beatings in my heart' (*P&P*, p. 184).

## The 'Primal Mother' of Rosings Park: Lady Catherine as a Figure of Totem and Taboo

It is precisely to escape this version of what might be called the 'monstrous maternal'[11] – and the hysterical, nay psychotic logic of Meryton's Capital, contract and utility which it figures – that triggers Elizabeth's departure for Hunsford to stay at the invitation of Charlotte Lucas, now Mrs Collins. This second scene shift in the novel is, however, not so much a departure for Elizabeth as it is a return. This is because, in journeying to the Collinses's vicarage, Elizabeth arrives back, at least thematically, in the same world of status with which the novel opened at Longbourn. Indeed, this world is far *more* status-conscious than Longbourn, being figured in the far grander, even ostentatious Rosings Park, the stately home and seat of the de Bourgh family, and furnished with, among other things, Mr Collins's *objet petit a*, the chimneypiece in one of the drawing rooms – itself, alone, costing 'eight hundred pounds' (*P&P*, p. 51). Certainly, the regime of status is intensified here to a degree that would satisfy any Continental court of the *ancien régime*, its letter of the law being followed strictly: 'Do not make yourself uneasy, my dear cousin, about your apparel' says Mr Collins to Elizabeth on the eve of her first visit to Rosings, 'Lady Catherine is far from requiring that degree of elegance of dress in us, which becomes herself and her daughter . . . She likes to have the distinction of rank preserved' (*P&P*,

---

11 I borrow, with some modification, Barbara Creed's phrase: the 'monstrous feminine', a very rich metaphor for Kristevan abjection. See B. Creed, *The Monstrous-Feminine: Film, Feminism, Psychoanalysis*, London: Routledge, 1993.

p. 105). This put-down, so typical of Collins, serves another purpose in that it confirms Lady Catherine's role as the very embodiment of the old, aristocratic order of the eighteenth-century which, with its compulsions about protocol, its obsessions over precedence ('I am excessively attentive', she says, 'to all those things' (*P&P*, p. 137)), evinces a 'psychopathology of everyday life' in marked contrast to the hysteria of Meryton.

In fact, Lady Catherine, and the world she represents, is quite the reverse of Meryton and its values. Unlike Meryton's *faux* gentry – take the example of the Lucases, only recently in trade, but now reinventing themselves as knighted country squires – Lady Catherine is the 'real thing' (even, one might say, the horrifying *das Ding* of Kant and Lacan).[12] No respectably born chatelaine her, Lady Catherine bears, instead, the coronet, quarterings and honorific befitting a belted earl's daughter; and so ranks, by birth, even above the de Bourghs and the Darcys – to whom she refers to, quite pointedly, as families that are 'respectable, ancient, honourable *though untitled*' (italics mine; *P&P*, p. 228). Indeed, in the social world of the novel, she is its very pinnacle. Accordingly, it is this positioning at the very top of the hierarchy – as the spokeswoman for a, previously, unassailable, but now threatened and soon to be displaced aristocratic hegemon in what is, after all, a revolutionary era – that makes her the implacable class enemy of an 'upstart ... of a young woman without family, connections, or fortune' (*P&P*, p. 229), the irredeemably middle-class, Elizabeth Bennet. For Lady Catherine *is* Elizabeth's principal nemesis; and, more than any other character in *Pride and Prejudice*, she is the 'villain of the piece' exceeding George Wickham's selfishness, Caroline Bingley's spitefulness and Mrs Bennet's meanness of spirit. Though, unlike any of these characters, fortune and rank have given Lady Catherine the power to implement her fantasies of control. And with what, to quote Mr Collins, 'affability' and 'condescension' (*P&P*, p. 45) – in short, 'enjoyment' in its grimly Lacanian–Žižekian[13] sense – her ladyship carries out that control: 'improving' the vicarage and Charlotte's housewifery (*P&P*, p. 107); trading in the acceptable wage slavery of the period – the hiring and firing of governesses – by entrusting that 'treasure', Miss Pope to Lady Metcalf (*P&P*, p. 108); and scheming, since their birth, for Darcy and Anne's marriage ('From their infancy, they have been intended for each other. It was the favourite wish of *his* mother; as well as her's. While in their cradles, we planned the union' (*P&P*, p. 228)).

---

12 See, especially, J. Lacan, *The Seminar of Jacques Lacan, Book VII: The Ethics of Psychoanalysis, 1959–1960*, New York: W. W. Norton, 1992, pp. 71–84.
13 S. Žižek, *For They Know Not What They Do: Enjoyment as a Political Factor*, London: Verso, 1991, p. 3, pp. 7–11, pp. 30–31, pp. 231–234, pp. 237–241 and p. 271.

My depiction of Lady Catherine as the 'villain of the piece', however, is not without its problems, particularly when her character is read through feminist lenses. For what, indeed, is so villainous about a woman being 'authoritative'? 'formidable'? even 'self-important'? (P&P, p. 106) – all adjectives used to describe her. Aren't these the very traits of her nephew, Darcy, the putative hero of the novel? Does this suggest, as all patriarchies have tried to, that what is considered a virtue in man – strength – is deemed a weakness in a woman; that is, an unsexing of her, so that Lady Catherine's strength of character is an affront and, indeed, a challenge to patriarchal ideology? This rehabilitation of Lady Catherine as something like a feminist icon – carried out in the critical literature of, for example, Johanna Smith[14] – is supported, in large part, by the nature of the status claims which Lady Catherine makes in her critique of the law. This critique has some affinities with the feminism of her day and today because, like both these feminists, Lady Catherine objects to a law that excludes women, specifically, the entail obtaining over Longbourn: 'I see no occasion for entailing estates from the female line – It was not thought necessary in Sir Lewis de Bourgh's family' (P&P, p. 108). Her argument for inclusiveness, however, differs markedly from the liberal critique of her day as much as the critical legal feminist position of today because Lady Catherine is certainly no Mary Wollstonecraft declaring the 'rights of woman',[15] even less a Mary Jo Frug, proclaiming the 'politics of difference'.[16]

In fact, it is Elizabeth's claims to, at least conversational equality (she answers back on the matter of her sisters all being 'out', P&P, p. 109) and difference (she refuses, at first, to tell her age, P&P, p. 109) which antagonises Lady Catherine. So instead of 'equality' feminism or 'difference' feminism, Lady Catherine's position might best be described as 'essentialist',[17]

---

14 J. M. Smith, 'I am a Gentleman's Daughter: A Marxist–Feminist Reading of *Pride and Prejudice*', in M. M. Folsom (ed.), *Approaches to Teaching Austen's 'Pride and Prejudice'*, New York: MLA, 1993, p. 70. Smith emphasises, quite rightly, the ambiguities of Elizabeth's 'victory over Lady Catherine' which, while 'in some sense a feminist one, the episode also has antifeminist as well as antiaristocracy elements'. Lady Catherine is, after all a 'titled *woman*' and a spokesperson for 'matrilineal desire'.
15 M. Wollstonecraft, *A Vindication of the Rights of Woman*, C. Poston (ed.), New York: Norton, 1988.
16 M. J. Frug, *Postmodern Legal Feminism*, New York: Routledge, 1992. See especially ch. 3, 'Progressive Feminist Legal Scholarship: Can We Claim "A Different Voice?"'.
17 For a critique of this term and position within a feminist legal context, see: D. Cornell, *Beyond Accommodation: Ethical Feminism, Deconstruction and the Law*, London: Routledge, 1991. See particularly ch. 1, 'The Maternal and the Feminine: Social Reality, Fantasy and Ethical Relation'.

what being more essential than birth itself, particularly the bond between mother and child. Hence, her advocacy of what might be called the Natural Law of the 'Mother's Body'; that is, the 'noble line' (*P&P*, p. 228) of her own birth family – the house of Fitzwilliam, the illustrious (maternal) lineage from which both Ann de Bourgh and Fitzwilliam Darcy descend. For Lady Catherine, this shared genealogical background is the deciding point in sealing Ann and Darcy's union; to wit, both of them enjoy, equally, what the Inquisition would call the *limpieza de sangre*, the 'purity of blood',[18] so conspicuously absent in the Bennet, but especially Gardiner strain. Indeed, in rebuke to Elizabeth's claim of the linguistic 'Law of the Father's Name' ('I am a gentleman's daughter' *P&P*, p. 229), her ladyship says point-blank: 'But who was your mother? Who were your uncles and aunts? Do not imagine me ignorant of their condition?' (*P&P*, p. 229). So much for universal sisterhood – the suggestion being here, in this final showdown at Longbourn, that matriarchy can be just as divisive, just as oppressive, just as ham-fisted as patriarchy at its most primitive.

With this endogamous sanction, an anthropological overtone creeps into Lady Catherine's complaint, one which is heightened by her cry that an alliance with a family that includes the Wickhams would 'pollute the shades of Pemberley' (*P&P*, p. 229). Taboo looms large in such a statement, particularly in the way in which Pemberley is characterised as something approximating a sacred site threatened with 'pollution' – physical, spiritual, communal – and against which all forms of ban are mobilised, including the proscriptive hex of the totemic. All of which suggests a function for Lady Catherine that is indebted as much to Freud's *Totem and Taboo* as it is Frazer's *Golden Bough*; that is, of her ladyship as a tribal totemic figure – even more, for Mr Collins, a *fetish* – who bears comparison with the Freudian 'primal father'. And just in case the reader misses it, this identification is doubled over, and made twice by the text. First, like the primal father, Lady Catherine speaks a sexual prohibition, her ukase refusing the exogamous marriage of Darcy to Elizabeth in favour of the more suitably consanguine marriage to Ann: 'Tell me once for all, are you engaged to him?', her ladyship demands, securing, in turn, Elizabeth's admission, 'I am not' (*P&P*, p. 229). Second – and again, like that of the primal father – Lady Catherine's prohibition is ultimately transgressed; it is Elizabeth's flat refusal ('I will make no promise of the kind', *P&P*, p. 229) not 'to enter into such an engagement' (*P&P*, p. 229)

---

18  P. Johnson, *A History of Christianity*, London: Weidenfeld & Nicolson, 1976, p. 307.

that teaches Darcy to 'hope' (*P&P*, p. 245) that a second proposal might not go amiss.

Unlike, however, the 'primal father' who is himself sacrificed by the tribe in *Totem and Taboo*, the 'primal mother', as the epilogue clearly tells us, muddles on here, still insisting, one imagines, that all and sundry sacrifice themselves – their very subjectivities – to her. This is a psychoanalytic reading of Lady Catherine's role that owes more to Lacan than Freud. For, to my way of thinking, there is no grimmer literary representation of the Lacanian 'mirror phase',[19] and the sacrifice of subjectivity in its looking-glass lures, than in the self-abnegation which Mr Collins's undergoes in his 'misrecognition' of Lady Catherine as his ego-ideal. Collins is lucky, though, in that he still lives to flatter her Ladyship with those rehearsed 'elegant compliments' (*P&P*, p. 46) that gave Mr Bennet so much amusement – a damning comment on not only the sycophancy of his character but the Erastian cringe of the period's latitudinarian Anglicanism. At least, however, Collins *survives*. This fate is not so clearly marked out for Ann de Bourgh, who is repeatedly referred to as 'thin and small' (*P&P*, p. 104), 'pale and sickly' (*P&P*, p. 104) and 'sickly and cross' (*P&P*, p. 104), the suggestion being that she may not live to enjoy her splendid inheritance. What or, more to the point, *who* is killing Miss de Bourgh? I would like to suggest that it is not just aristocratic in-breeding but Lady Catherine's 'ill breeding' (*P&P*, p. 113) that is killing Ann, draining her of life and, possibly, even of blood. For Lady Catherine is of that species of the 'monstrous maternal' that exceeds even that of Mrs Bennet's calibre: she devours her young.

## Elizabeth in the Positivist House of Law: Pemberley's 'Province of Jurisprudence Determined'

With Elizabeth's departure from Rosings the narrative, as well as this argument, reaches a crossroads, literalised in the text by the stay at the inn in Book II, Chapter XVI where she is met by Lydia and Kitty. This crossroads is also an impasse. For where is Elizabeth to go? Having been 'foreclosed' from both instantiations of the status society – the Symbolic Order of the linguistic 'Law of the Father's Name' (Longbourn), from which she is barred by virtue of her sex; and the Imaginary Order of the 'Natural Law

---

[19] J. Lacan, 'The Mirror Stage as Formative of the Function of the I as revealed in Psychoanalytic Experience' in A. Sheridan (trans.), *Ecrits: A Selection*, New York: Norton, 1977 at pp. 1–7.

of the Mother's Body' (Rosings), from which she is tabooed because of the impurity of blood of her kinship network – she now has only the Real of the hystericised, even psychotic economy of Meryton's regime of contract to which to return. This is a temptation that she rightly resists. All of which raises the issue as to whether there is somewhere else, an alternative space, 'another country', as it were, subject to a different kind of law – unfettered by status, but more anchored than contract – in which Elizabeth can assume a subjectivity and establish a social tie. I would like to suggest that such a location presents itself while Elizabeth is on her rural rambles with those centres of moral authority, the Gardiners, during their Peak District holidays in Derbyshire. The scene is a famous one, so I quote at some length:

> The park was very large, and contained a great variety of ground. They entered it in one of its lowest points, and drove for some time through a beautiful wood, stretching over a wide extent ... They gradually ascended for half a mile, and then found themselves at the top of a considerable eminence, where the wood ceased, and the eye was instantly caught by ... a large, handsome, stone building, standing well on rising ground, and backed by a ridge of high woody hills – and, in front, a stream of some natural importance was swelled into greater, but without any artificial appearance. Its banks were neither formal, nor falsely adorned. Elizabeth was delighted.
>
> (Austen, *P & P*, p. 156)

This passage, describing Elizabeth's approach to, and arrival at the ancestral seat of the Darcys and her future home, Pemberley, is justly celebrated by narratologists, like Michael Riffaterre[20] – though not, as might be expected in a novel of realist conventions, for its scenic detail. In fact, quite the reverse, since the passage utilises, as Riffaterre argues very persuasively, a language of descriptive markers that tell the reader virtually nothing in terms of setting; specifically, empty adjectives such as 'large', 'beautiful', 'wide' and 'handsome', creating absolutely no picture for the reader. For what is really being envisaged here, according to Riffaterre, is not so much a picture of a place as it is a 'portrait of a lady', particularly – to continue the Jamesian analogy – of her individual consciousness reacting to a place, registering her 'delight'; and, in so doing, indicating a complete shift in

---

20  M. Riffaterre, *Fictional Truth*, Baltimore: Johns Hopkins University Press, 1990.

point of view, a reorientation of affect and a new love interest. Remember that, however tongue-in-cheek, Elizabeth will confide later to Jane that she first fell in love with Mr Darcy when she first saw his 'beautiful grounds at Pemberley' (*P&P*, p. 240) – a comment that echoes and renders explicit her feeling here that 'To be mistress of Pemberley would be something indeed' (*P&P*, p. 156).

As compelling as I find this reading, I would like to suggest *another* one, not so much as an alternative, but as a complement, stressing the *exteriority* of the physical scene as much as the interiority of Elizabeth's consciousness. For what does this scene represent but a house, specifically a country house in the grand style? Now the country house is a significant structural device and potent symbol in nineteenth- and twentieth-century literature, evoking a range of associations, some national, some cultural, some political, but almost always legal. This is because the country house is *the* house of law – whether natural, positivist or otherwise – the overarching question about it being the legal one of who will inherit, for example, Thrushcross?[21] Tipton?[22] Howards End?[23] Robin Hill?[24] Brideshead?[25] This question of inheritance,

---

21 The elegant home of the new-come Linton family in Emily Brontë's *Wuthering Heights*, a sharp contrast to the much more countrified 'Heights' of their near neighbours, the long established Earnshaws; and the place to which, at the end of the novel, Catherine Linton and Hareton Earnshaw plan to repair as their marital home. See E. Brontë, *Wuthering Heights*, in C. Brontë, E. Brontë and A Brontë, *The Brontës: Three Great Novels*, Oxford: Oxford University Press, 1994, p. 365.
22 The manor of the landed Brooke family in George Eliot's *Middlemarch*, presided over by Mr Brooke of Tipton, and the future home of his niece, Dorothea Brooke, and her second husband, Will Ladislaw. See G. Eliot, *Middlemarch*, Oxford: Oxford University Press, 2008.
23 The country retreat of the *haut bourgeois* Wilcoxes in E. M. Forster's novel of the same name, and the future home of the intellectual, 'chattering class' Schlegel sisters, Margaret and Helen who acquire it, respectively, by marriage (Margaret to Henry Wilcox) and inheritance (Henry leaves the house to Helen's illegitimate child by Leonard Bast). See E. M. Forster, *Howards End*, London: Arnold, 1947.
24 The bespoke home of solicitor, Soames Forsyte, 'the man of property' in Galswothy's *roman fleuve*, *The Forsyte Saga*; and, subsequently, bought as a place of retirement by his uncle, prosperous tea merchant, 'Old Jolyon' Forsyte. Later in the series, 'Robin Hill' is the home of his cousin, the artist 'Young Jolyon' Forsyte and his wife (Soames's ex-wife), Irenee Heron Forsyte. See J. Galsworthy, *The Forsyte Saga*, London: Headline Review, 2007.
25 The stately home of the aristocratic Flyte family in Waugh's novel of the same name; left, at the end of the novel, to Lady Julia Mottram (*née* Flyte), her father, Lord Marchmain, having bypassed his sons, 'Bridey' and the glamorous but now hopelessly sodden Sebastian. See E. Waugh, *Brideshead Revisited*, Harlow: Longmans, 1968.

however, can be as much a burden as a benefit, even a curse, as amply demonstrated by the gothicised, and sinister haunted houses of law, found, throughout the period, both in English literature (e.g., in Dickens's *Bleak House*, the source of controversy in the case Jarndyce and Jarndyce, and the subject of Chapter 6 in this book), and in American literature (e.g., in Nathaniel Hawthorne's *House of the Seven Gables*, the subject of Chapter 5 in this book, and the site of several crimes – murder principally – perpetrated by, or against the Pyncheon family of Salem). Nothing could be further, certainly, from the haunted house of law than the representation of Pemberley here; indeed, the solidity of its foundations ('standing well on rising ground'), the dignity of its prospect ('the top of a considerable eminence'), the symmetry of its architecture ('a large, handsome stone building'), the harmony that obtains between it structure and natural setting ('a great variety of ground', 'a beautiful wood', 'a stream of some natural importance ... swelled into greater, but without any artificial appearance'), the timelessness of the style ('neither formal, nor falsely adorned') – all these details suggest, in their very coherence, integrity and abstractedness the ideal of the English common law, as reimagined by not just the utilitarian Bentham, but his positivist disciple, John Austin.

John Austin's *The Province of Jurisprudence Determined and The Uses of the Study of Jurisprudence*, as much as Bentham's much earlier *Limits of Jurisprudence Defined*[26] visualises the law, along virtually architectural lines. Consider Austin's following description of the law in *The Uses of the Study of Jurisprudence*, and his analogisation of it to a holistic 'structure', glimpsed, initially, by the focaliser of the passage ('he', the young jurisprude) from a distance, and which, as this gap narrows, comes into full view, arresting his gaze – much as Pemberley does for the carriage-driven Elizabeth, touring with the Gardiners:

> [I]f ... approached ... with a well-grounded knowledge of the general principles of jurisprudence, and with the map of a body of law distinctly impressed upon his brain, he ['the student ... of the English Law'] might obtain a clear conception of it (as a system or organic whole) with comparative ease and rapidity ... he might perceive the various relations of its various part; the dependence of its minuter rules on its general principles; and the subordination of such of these principles as are less general or extensive, to such

---

26 J. Bentham, *Limits of Jurisprudence Defined*, H. L. A. Hart (ed.) London: Athlone Press, 1970.

of them as are more general, and run through the whole of the structure.

(Austin, *The Uses of the Study of Jurisprudence*, n. 4, p. 379)

When 'approached', if not from a barouche or landau, then at least from the vantage of his 'jurisprudence', Austin's edifice – his house of law – evokes, for the focaliser ('the student'), a sense of order ('a system or organic whole'), almost Palladian in its proportions: 'the dependence of its minuter rules on its general principles; and the subordination of such of these principles as are less general or extensive, to such of them as are more general, and run through the whole of the structure'. Such language mimics, in its architectonic *argot* ('dependence', 'subordination') and building imagery ('whole of the structure'), Pemberley's elegant lines and environs, as well as, in its focaliser's growing wonder, Elizabeth's appreciation of them – especially in clauses such as 'he . . . might obtain a clear conception' or 'he might perceive'. But, here, Austin's *longueur* differs decidedly from Elizabeth's in that Pemberley is already a finished product. This is certainly not the case for the common law, however much Austin desires it 'whole'. For the common law's 'structure' requires massive conceptual repair work before this vision can become a reality. Until then, its 'whole' remains riddled with *holes*; and its foundations, so shaky that only a 'well *grounded*' (italics mine) legal theory will cement them. So Austin's jurisprudential project here is to draft a plan or blueprint ('the map of a body of law') which, if 'impressed on the brain', enables one to see beyond the common law's 'arbitrary and unconnected rules'[27] to the 'organic' method underlying its surface madness – 'the various relations of its various part'.

What measure will release this organicism – the 'dependence' and 'subordination' of part to whole, particular to general? That is, how is this 'map of the body of law' to be executed, and its vision realised? Surely Austin's first step would be to clear the feudal debris of natural law – 'law improperly so called' in *The Province of Jurisprudence Determined*[28] – still littering the juridical grounds of the house of law, obscuring its nomological foundations. This conceptual clean-up, however, only served to set the stage for a more far-reaching remodelling of Austin's: that of his 'expository' agenda,[29] and its imperatives of systematic classification. In order to

---

27 Austin, *The Uses of the Study of Jurisprudence*, above n. 3, p. 379.
28 Austin, *The Uses of the Study of Jurisprudence*, above n. 3.
29 John Austin writes that: 'As principles abstracted from positive systems are the subject of general jurisprudence, so is the exposition of such principles its exclusive or appropriate object' (ibid. p. 366).

carry out this agenda though, Austin needed to re-set the common law on a firmer foundation, one that is 'posited' – *viz.*, man-made – and which discarded natural law's moral baggage or philosophical 'nonsense upon stilts',[30] be it 'trad' (Aquinian scholasticism) or 'rad' (revolutionary rights). So the 'positivist' house of law Austin constructs, and which Austen figures in Pemberley, is very different from, and indeed hostile to the law of status, either in the form of the 'Law of the Father's Name' (the 'rights of *man*', imaged in Longbourn) or the 'Mother's Body' (the divinely ordained hierarchy of birth, represented in Rosings), with all their respective gender and class sanctions (no women need apply at Longbourn; no *bourgeois* at Rosings). Instead of these sanctions, a Rule of Law doctrine would hold sway in the positivist house of law, guaranteeing equal access to all. The same access, in fact, that obtains at Pemberley, as evidenced by Mrs Reynolds's obliging tour of the house (*P&P*, III, I), indicating that this space is not only open to the nobility (Col. Fitzwilliam, Lady Catherine, Miss de Bourgh), the gentry (Darcy, Georgiana) and their class allies, the *haut bourgeoisie* (the Bingleys and Hursts), but the very middle-class Gardiners of Cheapside and Elizabeth herself.

## Austen's Austinian Sovereign: The Command of Mr Darcy and the Censure of Elizabeth-as-Censor

Anchoring this site of open access and free movement, and giving it a centre – in sharp contrast to the flux of Meryton – is Fitzwilliam Darcy himself who, as master of Pemberley, functions also as the utilitarian 'sovereign' of this house of law, weighing pleasures and pains in his calculations of felicity – a connection which Elizabeth makes explicit when she ruminates: 'As a brother, a landlord, a master, she considered how many people's happiness were in his guardianship – How much pleasure or pain it was in his power to bestow. How much good or evil must be done by him' (*P&P*, p. 158). Speculation, however, about the nature of Darcy's 'sovereignty' is almost instantly resolved by the good reports of Mrs Reynolds: the 'best landlord and best master' to his staff and tenants (*P&P*, p. 159); a 'good brother' to his sister, gifting her with 'whatever is to give her pleasure' (*P&P*, p. 159); and a man of the most benevolent 'good-nature' who has never had a 'cross word' for his old housekeeper since he was 4 years old (*P&P*, p. 158). Now given the source, this testimonial may sound like one of those

---

30 J. Bentham, 'Anarchical Fallacies', in J. Waldron (ed.), *Nonsense Upon Stilts: Bentham, Burke and Marx on the Rights of Man*, New York: Methuen, 1987.

sentimentalisations of the feudal order which abound in romance literature, usually ventriloquised by old retainers, nurses or mammies who love their masters, charges or white folk more than themselves. Indeed, it this archconservative caricature – Mrs Reynolds's representation of her master as the benign *grand seigneur* – that is precisely what Darcy's 'civility' (*P&P*, p. 165) and 'stately' manners (*P&P*, p. 164) suggest, initially, to the Gardiners: the deportment of a 'great' man (*P&P*, p. 164), the lord of all he surveys, conferring his favour one day, withdrawing it just as readily another.

I would argue, however, for *another* role for Darcy: not so much the feudal satrap as the utilitarian sovereign in the best Benthamite mode. Rather than the motive of *noblesse oblige*, Darcy seems guided by a sense of the 'greatest happiness for the greatest number' in his dealings with people. Nowhere does this seem more the case than in his handling of the Lydia–Wickham elopement; there, he blames himself and his pride for failing in his public 'duty to step forward, and endeavour to remedy the evil' by making Wickham's 'worthlessness . . . so well known, as to make it impossible for any young woman of character, to love or confide in him' (*P&P*, p. 205). By securing Wickham's marriage to Lydia at the price of clearing his debts, settling monies upon Lydia, purchasing his commission and even standing up as groomsman at the ceremony – doubtless to his extreme mortification – Darcy performs, as Elizabeth, says an 'unexampled kindness' (*P&P*, p. 234) for the little community at Longbourn; namely, an act which, indeed, secures the greatest happiness for the greatest number. Darcy himself, however, complicates this claim that he is the utilitarian sovereign, at least of the reforming Benthamite stripe when he retorts to Elizabeth: 'I thought only of you' (*P&P*, p. 235). Far from being motivated by the principle of utility – and its calculations for the widest distribution of happiness – his objective has been a personal one, focused and specific: Elizabeth herself. Now I want to ask: why? Why does Mr Darcy, master of Pemberley, whom even Lady Catherine treats as *primus inter pares*, coax, cajole and bribe his nemesis Wickham into marriage, restore Mr Bingley to Jane, and even endure the none-too-subtle jibes of Mrs Bennet for a woman whose connections and 'condition in life is so decidedly beneath . . . (his) own' (*P&P*, p. 125). What is the attraction?

Of course, the obvious answer is love. As he says at Hunsford, 'You must allow me to tell you how ardently I admire and love you' (*P&P*, p. 123). But why does Mr Darcy love Elizabeth? What is there that is loveable about her when, in her own words, her 'behaviour to (him) was at least always bordering on the uncivil', never speaking without 'wishing to give . . . (him) pain' (*P&P*, p. 244). A quick review of her behaviour confirms that all she has done to provoke his love is snipe (as at the Meryton, Netherfield and Rosings where all is pointed innuendo), shout (as at Hunsford where innuendo is dropped for direct insult at his condescending proposal) or burst into tears (as at Pemberley when she receives the news of Lydia's catastrophic elopement). In what resides her attraction, aside from, as Elizabeth herself playfully suggests at the close of the novel, her 'impertinence' (*P&P*, p. 244)? Here, a romantic reading of the novel would have Darcy looking through Elizabeth's 'impertinence' and straight into her soul through those windows to which he pointedly, and much to the chagrin of Miss Bingley, refers as her 'fine eyes' (*P&P*, p. 19). But I would like to suggest that it is precisely this 'impertinence' – this resistance to Darcy, be it either passive (as at Meryton, Netherfield, Rosings or Pemberley), or active (as at Hunsford) – which is the source of Elizabeth's appeal and a choice example of the law of desire: of wanting precisely that which you cannot have.

I want to link, however, this psychic condition with earlier claims to Darcy's sovereign status because it is exactly this 'desire for the desire of the Other' that confirms his political and juridical role, though conceived now more in Austinian rather than Benthamite terms. For John Austin departs from, as much as disseminates his old mentor's theories, largely dropping the utilitarian frame of Bentham's philosophy, and its reformist agenda,[31] in favour of a definition of sovereignty which focuses on power[32] – a power which I think is at work in, and underpins the Darcy–Elizabeth match. The source of this power, according to Austin, is the sovereign who is nothing more than the one whose 'commands' are habitually 'obeyed';[33] hence, the popular sobriquet of the 'command theory of law' to describe his jurisprudence.[34] Indeed, if there is an Austinian sovereign in *Pride and Prejudice*, whose commands are, obeyed, it is Darcy. 'He is the kind of man', says the most querulous, least obliging character in the novel, Mr Bennet, 'to whom I should never refuse anything should he condescend to act' (*P&P*, p. 242). And almost everyone else in the world of the novel evinces a similar 'habit

---

31 W. L. Morison, *John Austin*, London: Edward Arnold, 1982, p. 2.
32 Austin writes in *The Province of Jurisprudence Determined*, that law is a species of command and that: 'A command is distinguished . . . by the power and the purpose of the party commanding to inflict an evil or pain' (above n. 3, p. 14).
33 Austin writes: 'The superiority which is styled sovereignty . . . is distinguished from other superiority, and from other society, by the following marks or characters: 1. The *bulk* of the given society are in a *habit* of obedience or submission to a *determinate* and *common* superior' (above n. 3, pp. 193–194).
34 See for example, M. D. A, Freeman, *Lloyd's Introduction to Jurisprudence*, London: Sweet & Maxwell, 1994, pp. 213–214.

of obedience' towards Darcy, either sooner (like Bingley, who needs his 'permission', as Elizabeth puts it, to court Jane, *P&P*, p. 239) or later (like Wickham who is, eventually, induced to marry Lydia). All, of course, excepting one: Elizabeth Bennet. Her refusal to obey Darcy is one of the constants of the novel, ranging from her decline of his offer to dance at Lucas Lodge ('Mr. Darcy with grave propriety requested to be allowed the honour of her hand; but in vain. Elizabeth was determined', *P&P*, p. 18) to her spectacular refusal of his proposal at Hunsford (where he is 'the last man in the world whom I could ever be prevailed upon to marry', *P&P*, p. 126).

Why Elizabeth refuses Darcy is attributable to her defining trait – one that Darcy, himself, says, at the end of the novel, attracts him in the first place: her 'liveliness of mind' (*P&P*, p. 244) that enables her to see through, and critique his 'arrogance', 'conceit' and 'selfish disdain for the feelings of others' (*P&P*, p. 126). Certainly, Elizabeth is *the* critical intelligence of the book, both as a suspicious close reader of texts (think of how well she construes the real import of Caroline Bingley's letters) as well as of character itself, which she reads just as sceptically: the superciliousness of the Bingley sisters ('proud and conceited', *P&P*, p. 11), the thoughtlessness of Mr Bingley (particularly his 'want of attention to other people's feelings', *P&P*, p. 90), the silliness of Collins ('Can he be a sensible man?', is her reaction, even before she meets him, to his letter of introduction, *P&P*, p. 44), the forwardness of her younger sisters ('Vain, ignorant, idle and absolutely uncontrouled', with Lydia a 'determined flirt' and Kitty sure to 'follow' Lydia's lead, *P&P*, p. 149), the glibness of her father (she had 'never been blind to the impropriety of her father's behaviour as a husband', *P&P*, p. 152), the opportunism of Charlotte (upon the announcement of Charlotte's engagement, she feels the 'pang of a friend disgracing herself and sunk in her esteem', *P&P*, p. 84), even the amiability of her confidante and ally Jane ('you are a great deal too apt you know, to like people in general', *P&P*, p. 11).

This repeated emphasis on Elizabeth's capacity to critique – in short, to censure – suggests a jurisprudential analogue to parallel Darcy's sovereignty; that is, as the 'censorial' jurist, who is not merely content to say what the law *is* (the 'expository' project of Austin)[35] but what it *ought* to

---

35 Austin writes in *The Province of Jurisprudence Determined*: 'Having suggested the *purpose* of my attempt to determine the province of jurisprudence: to distinguish positive law, the appropriate matter of jurisprudence, from the various objects to which it is related by resemblance, and to which it is related, nearly or remotely, by a strong or slender analogy' (above n. 3, at p. 13).

be[36] – like some Benthamite reformer alert to the discrepancies, as well as, the iniquities of the juridical but also political status quo. Elizabeth's embodiment, however, of this reformist agenda is as much a limitation as it is an advantage; in fact, by my lights, it is precisely this role as censorial critic that explains why, for all her acuity, she is duped by Wickham. This is because Wickham tells her the story that Elizabeth, as the Benthamite reformer, the censorial jurist – in other words, the critical legal lawyer – wants to hear: that of natural merit overlooked, even wronged by hereditary privilege in Darcy's supposed refusal to bestow the beneficed living of Kympton on him – a narrative even Jane suspects. By allowing Elizabeth to be so 'blind, partial, prejudiced and absurd' (*P&P*, p. 135) in favour of Wickham at the expense of Darcy, Austen ironises critique and shifts the philosophical, political but particularly jurisprudential orientation of the novel away from Bentham, and his advocacy of the 'censorial' agenda, and towards Austin, and his focus on power, propped up by the 'expository' law. For John Austin – as much, if not more than Jane Austen – is motivated by a profoundly conservative vision of the law, and, indeed, politics and society;[37] critique has no place here, or, if it does, it must be brought to heel, co-opted, even silenced. 'Censorial jurisprudence' must, and is, in turn, *censored* in the work of John Austin as well as Jane Austen.

This is why, I would like to suggest, Darcy marries Elizabeth. In so doing, the Austinian sovereign is co-opting his greatest critic – the 'censorial' jurist – who, in her refusal to obey, threatens the delicate equilibrium of the 'expository' order of the positivist house of law. This co-optation of

---

36 Bentham writes in the *IPML*, essentially of his own project: 'To know what is meant by jurisprudence, we must know, for example, what is meant by a book of jurisprudence. A book of jurisprudence can have but one or the other of two objects: 1. to ascertain what the *law* is: 2. to ascertain what it ought to be. In the former case it may be styled a book of *expository* jurisprudence; in the latter, a book of *censorial* jurisprudence; or, in other words, a book on the *art of legislation*' (pp. 293–294).

37 Indeed, Austin's principal modern advocate, Morison, calls his outlook 'reactionary' in ch. 4, 'Austin: Conservative or Reformer' (above n. 31, p. 123). Jane Austen's conservatism, particularly with regard to *Pride and Prejudice*, has been emphasised by the following critics: A. M. Duckworth, *The Improvement of the Estate: A Study of Jane Austen's Novels*, Baltimore: Johns Hopkins University Press, 1971, pp. 116–128, pp. 140–143 and M. Butler, *Jane Austen and the War of Ideas*, Oxford: Clarendon Press, 1975, pp. 197–198, pp. 203–207, pp. 210–213.

critique by a reconstituted status quo is, as Gramsci has taught us,[38] the standard ideological move of 'modernity' because it produces the appearance of a society based on 'consent' when, in fact, it is predicated upon silence. This, in fact, is precisely what Darcy does to Elizabeth in marrying her: he silences her. So much so that from the moment he makes his second proposal at Longbourn, she loses her voice. Consider her response to his proposal which we never actually hear spoken, but which is rendered through the most tortured circumlocution, obscured by a welter of strained subordinate and coordinate clauses:

> Elizabeth feeling all the more common awkwardness and anxiety of his situation, now forced herself to speak; and, immediately, though not very fluently, gave him to understand, that her sentiment had undergone so material a change, since the period he alluded, as to make her receive with gratitude and pleasure, his present assurances.
>
> (Austen, *P & P*, p. 235)

We hear nothing directly here; and nor do we ever really hear directly from Elizabeth again, much to the concern of Jane ('My dear, dear Lizzy, I would – I do congratulate you – but are you certain?', *P&P*, p. 240) and the alarm of Mr Bennet ('What are you doing? Are you out of your senses to be accepting this man?', *P&P*, p. 242). All in fact we do hear is a kind of ventriloquism in which Elizabeth celebrates her sovereign, arguing that he has 'no improper pride' (*P&P*, p. 242). Gone, indeed, is critique. So Elizabeth's fate is sealed; she will be mistress of Pemberley, metonymised in terms of its economy of objects, which her mother gloatingly itemises, 'how rich and great you will be! What pin-money, what jewels, what carriages you will have! . . . a house in town! Ten thousand a year!' (*P&P*, p. 243). These credits, however, are offset by the tremendous debt to be paid; the sacrifice of Elizabeth's very self, her 'different voice' as Carol Gilligan might put it,[39] in order to reign as the silent chatelaine of the house of law.

---

38 A. Gramsci, *An Antonio Gramsci Reader: Selected Writings 1916–1935*, D. Forgacs (ed.), New York: Schocken Books, 1988. Gramsci writes, for example, 'The spontaneous consent given by the great masses of the population to the general direction imposed on social life by the dominant fundamental group; this consent is "historically" caused by the prestige (and consequent confidence) which the dominant group enjoys because of its position and function in the world of production' (p. 307).
39 C. Gilligan, *In a Different Voice: Psychological Theory and Women's Development*, Cambridge, MA: Harvard University Press, 1982.

## Who Wrote *Pride and Prejudice*? The Politics of the Law in Aust*in* and Aust*en*

I stress the word 'reign' in connection with Elizabeth's new role, because it is Darcy who continues to 'rule' at Pemberley, even when this rule is challenged in a minor way by Elizabeth's flippancy; namely, those acts of connubial rebellion which give so much 'astonishment' to Georgiana (*P&P*, p. 249), but which, interestingly, the reader never hears dialogised. Indeed, Darcy's rule is secured by Elizabeth's reign; her occasional dissent attests to an overarching consent that, more than anything else, ensures the persistence of Pemberley and the social, political and *legal* values for which it stands. For what is the last scene of the novel but a rendering of Pemberley as the site of class reconciliation, visited not only by that emblem of status, Lady Catherine (curious to see how Mrs Darcy 'conducted herself', *P&P*, p. 249), but also by the relations from Cheapside, the Gardiners, who gave her ladyship so much offence and of whom, tellingly, the last line of the novel speaks. Why are the Gardiners the last characters to be referred to in *Pride and Prejudice*? On one level – the sentimental one – it is because, as the reader is told, they were the 'means of uniting' Elizabeth and Darcy (*P&P*, p. 250). So they seem to be *the* great romantic allies of Pemberley. But I would also like to suggest, on the basis of a more material reading – that of class analysis – that the Gardiners are also its greatest threat. For who are the Gardiners but the urban, affluent, educated *bourgeoisie*? This is precisely the class leading the calls for reform in England (for example, in coming years, the Reform Bill of 1832), and revolution elsewhere.

Clearly, in any other country, Mr Gardiner would be a Marat *manqué*, inciting the mob not only to burn Pemberley (and Rosings, Netherfield and Longbourn) to the ground, but to send all of its inhabitants to the guillotine. Imagine the 'affability' and 'condescension' of Lady Catherine in the tumbrils, or better yet hanging from the entrails of Mr Collins! I allude to the sanguinary sentiment of the Jacobins – not content to rest until the last aristocrat was hanging from a lamp-post by the last priest's entrails[40] – because it is against this political background that Jane Austen is writing; she, after all, had a cousin married to a French count who perished in the Terror.[41] As well, it is this political future to which, with just as much if not

---

40 From Diderot's '*Dithyrambe sur la fête des Rois*': '*Et des boyaux du dernier prêtre/Serrons le cou du dernier roi*' (trans.: 'And with the bowels of the last priest/let us strangle the last king').
41 For the extremely romantic, indeed 'novelistic' story of Eliza, Comtesse de Feuillide, see the detailed and informative account of the Austen-Leigh family in: G. H. Tucker, *A Goodly Heritage*, Manchester: Carcanet, 1983, pp. 45–50.

more trepidation, John Austin looks forward in anticipating not just the Reform Act but Chartism and the 'making of English working class'. Hence, in light of these political threats, both past and future, it is absolutely critical that the middle-class Gardiners be integrated into the house of law, now positivised as the Austinian 'command of the sovereign' rather than the 'divine right of kings'. Why is that space – of assimilation, of reconciliation – to found other than at Pemberley? Because it is here in one of the most famous architectural flights of Austenian fancy that the Austinian 'province of jurisprudence' finds its 'determination' in mediating a very English compromise through a law which, in marrying 'pride' (Mr Darcy) to 'prejudice' (Elizabeth), preserves the forms of status (the organicism of the old order, imaged in the country house at harmony with nature) all the while embracing the emergent forms of contract (the interests of commercial and industrial capital for which the Gardiners speak).

All of which returns me to the question which entitles not only this section but this chapter: who wrote *Pride and Prejudice*? Was it Jane Austen or John Austin? This question of authorship is closely related to each author's relation to authority, and the troubling issue of Austin's but, particularly, Austen's politics as either transgressive or regressive, either liberal or conservative.[42] I would like to argue, by way of conclusion, that they are both and neither liberal and/or conservative, a doubling which mimics the classic move of legal ideology of facilitating change at the very moment it conserves tradition. For example, Austen's politics, as much as Austin's, are liberal in that they both attack the world of status: he, in his assault on natural law, and the uncoupling of the positive law from morality; she, in her satires of the aristocracy (here in Lady Catherine, but also in Sir Walter Elliot, Miss Elliot and the Viscountess Dalrymple in *Persuasion*) and the Established Church (here in Mr Collins but also in Mr Elton in *Emma*). Both, however, are conservative in the sense that the house of law each constructs becomes a sort of positivist panoptical prison-house in which are consigned Austen's 'censorial' heroines – Elizabeth at Pemberley, but also, Marianne Dashwood at Delaford, even Emma at her old home,

---

42 For the former, classic 'subversive' reading of Austen, particularly *P & P*, see: D. W. Harding, 'Regulated Hatred: An Aspect in the Work of Jane Austen', *Scrutiny* 8, 1940, 346–347, 351–354, 362; and M. Mudrick, *Jane Austen: Irony as Defense and Discovery*, Princeton: Princeton University Press, 1952, pp. 107–113, pp. 116–120, pp. 123–125. The standard, 'reactionary' readings of Austen are Duckworth, *The Improvement of the Estate: A Study of Jane Austen's Novels* and Butler, *Jane Austen and the War of Ideas* (above n. 37). For Austin, the same debate about politics – conservative or liberal?– is staged internally in Morison's text, above n. 31.

Hartfield – and over which an Austinian sovereign commands: Mr Darcy, Col. Brandon and Mr Knightley. But I would like to suggest that Jane Austen goes one step further than John Austin in that she actually supersedes both readings – the liberal and the conservative – at the very moment she authorises each, opening up a space for a third reading: what might be called the critical legal reading. For in rendering, at the close of the novel, both Elizabeth and Darcy as so thoroughly *in situ* at Pemberley, Austen points us to the critical legal insight that, far from being empty – and, hence, belonging to everyone because it belongs to no one – the house of law is *inhabited.*

Who inhabits this house of law? That is *the* question which Critical Legal Studies (CLS) will ask and answer, variously, and depending upon its particular stripe, as the ruling class (CLS in its Marxist form), the patriarch (CLS in its feminist form) and the coloniser (CLS in its race theory form). Austen has been quick to anticipate these answers, entwining these strands into the enraced, engendered and classified body of Mr Darcy. In exposing this white, male ruling class body behind, and indeed controlling the letter of the law, Austen contests, as much as confirms the positive law which Darcy represents, anticipating not only Austin's 'expository' legal positivism but its 'censorial' critique. Indeed, Austen may see even further than this binary of exposition–censure, pointing us, instead, towards a new juridical imaginary with a jurisprudence of, and in open revolt against Austin's very notion of sovereignty. So, in answer to the question, 'Who wrote *Pride and Prejudice?*', clearly Jane Austen; however, in so doing, Austen proleptically writes, critiques and then goes beyond that of Austin's *The Province of Jurisprudence Determined.* For in figuring jurisprudence as a stately home, Jane Austen renders a novel judgement that looks not just to this edifice's 'determinations' – that is, its boundaries – but past them, to the angry and incensed crowds (the critical legal mob?) massing at its gates, rattling its portcullis, ready to breach its barriers, then storm, ransack and put to the torch the positivist house of law.

CHAPTER 3

# Jousting with Bentham: Utility, Morality and Ethics in *Ivanhoe*'s Tournament of Law

## Law's Violence and the Last of England: *Ivanhoe*'s End and the Departures of Rebecca, Isaac and Beaumanoir

Let me begin at the end by repeating Rowena's query at the close of *Ivanhoe*:[1] why must Rebecca leave England and accompany her father, Isaac of York, into self-imposed exile in Moorish Spain? Rebecca, herself, is quite clear on this point, answering Rowena emphatically: she leaves because of *violence*. '[T]he people of England are a fierce race', says Rebecca; consequently, she continues, their country is 'no safe abode for the children of my people' (*I*, p. 399). Rowena's response to Rebecca raises, impliedly, a counter-argument to violence: that of right, rather than might; of legitimacy, rather than usurpation. In short, *law* is her proffered solution, as represented in and by its principal novelistic upholders: her husband, Wilfred, who 'has favour with the King' (*I*, p. 399); and the King himself – Richard I – who is 'just and generous' (*I*, p. 399). With law-*ful(l)* protectors like these, who

---

1 Sir W. Scott, *Ivanhoe*, G. Tulloch (ed.), London: Penguin, 2000. Hereafter referred to as *I*. *Ivanhoe* has attracted some excellent literary historical scholarship, the most significant being, of course, that of Jane Millgate, the doyenne of Scott scholarship. See her superb bibliographical and biographical analysis: 'Making It New: Scott, Constable, Ballantyne and the Publication of *Ivanhoe*', *Studies in English Literature, 1500–1900* 34(4), 1994, 795–811.

48 • Novel Judgements: Legal Theory as Fiction

would threaten '[s]he who nursed the sick-bed of Ivanhoe' (*I*, p. 399)? Rebecca is unconvinced by these promises of protection and is right to remain so. For it is her character – so I hazard – that is threatened most directly by the Lionheart's return and the law he (re)institutes. What is the nature of this law? Certainly it is one that expels as much as compels, the narrative's ending witnessing a flurry of departures: not only the Yorks, but Maurice de Bracy, Waldemar Fitzurse and, most notably for my purposes, the Grand Master of the Templars, Lucas de Beaumanoir. I want to link Beaumanoir's leave-taking with that of Rebecca's and Isaac's exodus because, when read together, this trio of voluntary exiles identifies – so the claim runs here – the precise jurisprudential basis of the Lionheart's restored legal order. That basis is none other than the law (re)conceived as the sovereign's command, one where there is neither space nor scope for appeals to natural rights or divine justice. So the form of legality that obtains at the end of *Ivanhoe* is, jurisprudentially speaking, a version of legal positivism that vacates (seemingly) any sense of a 'higher law'. It is this act of desacralisation that, as I shall argue at the close of this chapter, Scott dramatises in both the egress of Beaumanoir (emblematising Ecclesia's morality of law, 'participated' in the *lex aeterna*, God's law) and the exit of the Yorks, both Isaac (instantiating the immorality of usury, as *contra naturam*) and Rebecca (as the Levinasian 'face of the other', or ethics en-*visaged*).

The curious jurisprude might well wonder at this juncture precisely what type of legal positivism fills the lack left here by these removals. J. R. R. Dinwiddy's[2] acute observation notwithstanding – namely, that the period could find no two figures more dissimilar than Scott and Bentham – I want to advance this thesis; namely, that *Ivanhoe*'s positivist sovereignty, and the legality it commands, is decidedly Benthamic (rather than, say, Austinian) in its origin, operation and ends. This Benthamism not only figures as the diegesis's organising legal regime; it is that diegesis's principal object of critique, *Ivanhoe* rendering judgement on, and over three topoi central to Bentham's jurisprudence in terms that are – strangely enough for such a conservative author as Scott – practically proto-Marxist (especially the Marx of *On the Jewish Question*). This chapter takes up *Ivanhoe*'s engagement, 'marxified' and otherwise, with these Benthamic topoi in the following order. In the second section, I argue how the narrative's ambiguous representation of Isaac – as, at once, sympathetic *and* anti-Semitic –

---

2 Who maintains that Scott and Bentham provide in this period 'antithetical viewpoints', with the former having 'ignored' the latter, as much as the latter 'ignored' the former. See: J. R. R. Dinwiddy, *Radicalism and Reform in Britain, 1780–1850*, London: Continuum, 1992.

accords with, but also undercuts Bentham's *apologia* for Isaac's profession in his *Defence of Usury*. A defence which, ironically, is predicated upon the disappearance of the usurer himself, the loss of whom the novel vividly realises in his dispatch of Isaac: first to Torquilstone's *donjon*; then to Muslim Iberia. In the third section, I hold that *Ivanhoe* gives, in the figure of Beaumanoir, a vivid characterological depiction of 'Judge & Co'., conflating Bentham's common law *bête noire* – the corrupt judge – with the civilian inquisitor-as-fanatic, whose codes – either reactionary (i.e., ecclesiastical) or radical (i.e., Jacobinical) – threaten, even when redesigned *à la* Bentham's pannomion, 'the return of the (judicial) repressed' so decried by utilitarian reform. In the fourth section, I argue that Scott's King Richard not only enacts (distributing goods and favour across a wide spectrum; meting out punishment along Benthamic lines) but also exposes (in his selfish caprice) the problematic nature of utilitarianism's *ur*-principle; specifically, the 'fundamental contradiction', even fatal flaw that lies at the heart of 'the greatest good for the greatest number' in its all too eager sacrifice of empathy (of the one) to the egotism (of the many).

This last assertion – of Ricardian England, hitherto a power vacuum, now recast as a princely state turning on the utility principle – makes ever more paradoxical the leave-taking with which this chapter opened and to which I will return in the chapter's concluding fifth section: Rebecca's tragic choice to depart England. Why then does she go? Especially if Richard's rule is but a magnification of Rebecca's ethics, aggregating her highly personal and private 'care of the Other' into a collective calculus of felicity, maximising group pleasure and minimising group pain? That Rebecca leaves England, her ethics intact, and resisting this analogy of scale – that Richard's reign does on a macro-level what her healing does on a micro-level – goes to her perspicacity as not only a critic of the law, but a censor of Bentham. For Rebecca sees through not only feudalism's rules of chivalry at Torquilstone and Templestowe, but the precarious nature of utility itself, and how its greatest number's good always turns out to be looking out for what's good for number one, suspending the law, rendering the state of exception, the rule. It is this (Schmitt-like) decisionism that Rebecca senses lurking behind the Plantagenets' feudal version of legal positivism, a jurisprudential insight that, I want to argue lastly in this chapter, transforms this most 'romantic' of the Waverley series – all tourneys and turrets, crosiers and crusaders – into a novel judgement[3] of no less

---

3 For a very different sort of reading of Scott's thematic of legalism, see: B. J. Beiderwell, *Power and Punishment in Scott's Novels*, Athens, GA: University of Georgia Press, 1992.

a figure of juridical science than that anti-romantic *non pareil*, Jeremy Bentham who, in his imposition of a utility maximising sovereign of (re-) distributive command, inscribes a violence at the very heart of posited law that makes a fugitive of ethics (Rebecca) at the very moment it banishes morality (Beaumanoir, Isaac).

### Defending Usury, But Dispatching Isaac: Bentham and Scott on Moneylending

Despite the back-to-front reading of utility essayed in the introduction above, Benthamism – and its critique – is as conspicuous at *Ivanhoe*'s beginning as it is at its end. I want to locate this dual thematic's early emergence precisely at the moment of Isaac's appearance in the storyline: as a wayfarer seeking shelter for the night in the Anglo-Saxon manor of Rotherwood (*I*, pp. 46–48). How, though, is Isaac of York, the medieval Jew and man of faith, connected in any way with Jeremy Bentham, the modern secularist and sceptic? Their shared identity, I contend, lies not so much in *who* they are (Jew/Gentile; believer/freethinker),[4] but in *what* they do. Both, in their respective ways, defend usury. For Bentham, that defence was mounted explicitly in a celebrated pamphlet, entitled appropriately enough, *Defence of Usury*;[5] while for Isaac, this defence comes more by implication – in the form of a sympathetic rendering of the usurer that amounts to an apologia for the profession, especially when one compares Scott's character to that of his forerunner, Shakespeare's Shylock.[6] Even so: *sympathetic*? Modern-day readers may look askance, even balk at this assertion, pointing to the anti-Semitic qualifiers Isaac, as a Jewish usurer,

---

4 On the specific issue of Isaac's (and Rebecca's) Jewishness, see: J. Lewin, 'Jewish Heritage and Secular Inheritance in Walter Scott's *Ivanhoe*', *ANQ* 19(1), 2006, 27–33. M. Ragussis, 'Writing Nationalist History: England, the Conversion of the Jews, and Ivanhoe', *ELH* 60(1), 1993, 181–215. A. Cagidemetrio, 'A Plea for Fictional Histories and Old-Time "Jewesses" ', in W. Stollers (ed.), *The Invention of Ethnicity*, New York: Oxford University Press, 1989, pp. 14–43. More general treatments of this issue include: L. G. Zatlin, *The Nineteenth Century Anglo-Jewish Novel*, Boston: Twayne Publishers, 1981, ch. 1. A. A Naman, *The Jew in the Victorian Novel*, New York: AMS Press, 1980. E. Rosenberg, *From Shylock to Svengali: Jewish Stereotypes in English Fiction*, 1960, Stanford, CA: Stanford University Press, ch. 4.
5 J. Bentham, *Defence of Usury*, London: Routledge, 1787. Hereafter referred to as *DU*.
6 See, for example, on this comparison: S. Mergenthal, 'The Shadow of Shylock: Scott's *Ivanhoe* and Edgewoth's *Harrington*', in H. Alexander and D. Hewitt (eds), *Scott in Carnival: Selected Papers of the Fourth International Scott Conference, Edinburgh 1991*, Aberdeen: Association for Scottish Literary Studies, 1993, pp. 320–331.

attracts throughout the text; namely, adjectives such 'mean and unamiable' (I, p. 47), 'trembling' (I, p. 61), 'churlish' (I, p. 96), 'unbending' (I, p. 180). Other, more fully articulated character traits ascribed to him and his profession are no better; Isaac is portrayed as either pushily presumptuous 'jost[ling]' decayed gentry, like the Montdidier descendent, for a place at the tournament, I, p. 69) or gleefully money-grubbing (his hands 'trembled for joy' at Gurth's delivery of Ivanhoe's prize money, I, p. 99). But one thing this 'wretched usurer' (I, p. 313) never does, despite all the imprecations to that effect by Prior Aymer[7] and others,[8] is this: *Isaac never charges interest.*

Of course, Shylock, infamously, demanded his 'pound of flesh'; by way of contrast, Isaac never engages in, let alone insists upon this sort of transaction and its, literally, *sharp* practices. If anything, these practices work the other way, Isaac being the subject – rather than the source – of any number of shakedowns. Prince John, after all, treats him like his own personal (and proto-) ATM machine: 'Here Isaac', commands His Royal Highness, rather loftily for one so chronically short of a bob and about to make 'a touch', 'lend me a handful of byzants' (I, p. 75). This is gentle treatment when compared to Front-de-Bœuf who thinks nothing of torturing Isaac in his dungeon's chamber of horrors – Torquilstone's 'treasure' room (I, p. 184) – in order to extract his fortune: 'Now, choose betwixt such a scorching bed and the payment of a thousand pounds of silver' (I, p. 182). Even relatively benign figures in the text, such as the outlaw Robin of Sherwood and his merry men, have no problem clipping Isaac for a zecchin or a mark, eagerly ransoming him (I, p. 285). But never do we see Isaac conduct himself so throughout the narrative. In fact, the one loan we do see Isaac make turns out to be interest free; namely, that of the horse and equipment offered, *gratis*, to Ivanhoe for the tournament (I, pp. 64–65). In short, Isaac is a usurer *without* usury. This characterological depiction complicates, indeed *shifts* responsibility away from the Jews for the claims, hitherto made by the text, about the ever-rising tide of debt in England as owing to 'usurious interest' (I, p. 66), gnawing like a 'canker' (I, p. 66) at many a noble estate. Instead, such responsibility is placed squarely on the Christian mainstream.

This is precisely Bentham's position in the *Defence of Usury*, a tract that identifies faith – especially, the Christian faith, and its 'self-denying' (*DU*,

---

7 'Foul usuries and extortions' (I, p. 286) is how the pleasure-loving prior describes the basis of Isaac's wealth.
8 Front-de-Bœuf, in a popular smear, calls Isaac a 'usurious blood-sucker' (I, p. 184), while Beaumonoir refers to Isaac as a 'wretched usurer' (I, p. 313).

Letter X, 19) theology of 'sin' (*DU, Letter* XI, 22) – as the jurisprudential source for usury, giving that offence its peculiarly Blackstonian connotation of *contra naturam* criminality. Indeed, Bentham is at his expository *and* censorial best when parsing what Dworkin would call usury's 'semantic sting', de-theologising this very loaded term, freighted as it is with moral wrongdoing, as a sign that denotes nothing more than a loan with interest above a certain rate. As an act of legislative prescription, that rate – 5 per cent since the reign of Queen Anne[9] – constitutes, for Bentham, an all-too-human juridical creation that is as easily combusted as it is constructed; that is, overturned, allowing, instead, an interest rate that is floating rather than fixed, one mutually agreed upon by the parties to a transaction, free from any transgressive taint. Bentham's argument here is not only consonant with the ideological agenda of his nascent legal positivism – expunging morality's remainder from the law, trumpeting its manmade rather than natural or divine origin – but has a practical payoff. For the *Defence of Usury*'s reissue in 1816 responds to, but also reactivated a debate that it kick-started when first published in 1787: one over the abolition of legal limits upon interest on loans. This issue of abolition had become urgent again because money was tight in the post-Waterloo England;[10] and the usury law – on the statute books since the Tudor period[11] – was hotly contested both on the floor of Parliament and closed sessions of its select committees[12] as the contributing, if not principal cause

---

9 Statute of 12 Anne, c. 16.
10 S. Homer, *A History of Interest Rates*, New Brunswick, NJ: Rutgers University Press, 1963, pp. 160 and 205. See also: J. H. Clapham, *An Economic History of Modern Britain: The Early Railway Age, 1820–1850*, Cambridge: Cambridge University Press, 1926, p. 28; P. Matthias, *The First Industrial Nation: An Economic History of Britain, 1700–1914*, London: Hartwell, 1969, p. 147.
11 Statute of 37 Hen. VIII, c. 9, s. 3 where it was enacted that: 'no person or persons ... shall have, receive or accept or take in lucre or gains for the bearing or giving day of payment of one whole year and for his or their money or other things that shall be due for the same wares, merchandises, or other things, above the sum of 10 pounds in the hundred'. This rate of 10 per cent was affirmed, after a brief repeal under the Statute of 5 & 6 Edw. VI, c. 20, by the Statute of 13 Eliz., c. 8 where s. 5 held, 'all usury, loan or forbearing of money ... above the sum of 10 pounds for the loan or forbearing of a hundred pounds for one year ... shall be ... punished' by forfeitures. It is this statute which remained the basis of the usury laws until their repeal in 1856, though with minor amendments. See: Statute of 21 Jac. I, c. 17, amending the Statute of 13 Elizabeth, c. 8. Statute of 12 Carl. II, c. 13, amending the above.
12 The story of the nineteenth-century campaign against the usury laws is a long and involved one, replete with many parliamentary false starts, legislative road blocks and select committee detours. But briefly: on 12 February 1816, Brougham kicked off the

of the post-war depression. In the wake of this sort of governmental deliberation, a veritable 'battle of books' was sparked amongst the 'chattering class'[13] that, in turn, was closely followed and reviewed by journals across the political spectrum: Conservative, Liberal, Radical.[14] No wonder Bentham's pamphlet was taken up once again, embraced by the era's principal reformers – Brougham, Onslow and others. For despite its title as a

campaign in the House of Commons, calling for the (partial) repeal of the usury laws (*Parl. Deb. XXXII, 1 Feb.–6 March 1816*, 393). Subsequently, Brougham passed the baton of leadership to Onslow who, on 22 May 1816, motioned for leave to repeal the usury laws. The motion was opposed and defeated, *Parl. Deb. XXXIV, 26 Apr.–2 July 1816*, 723. Undeterred, Onslow in 1818 raised his motion again, this time requesting a select committee be empanelled, and mandated to draft a set of recommendations on the future of the usury laws. The 1818 Committee – consisting of Onslow, Sugden (later Lord St. Leonards), and others (like pro-usury law MP, Preston) – met, reviewed the usury laws and recommended, on 22 May 1818, their abolition, *Parl. Deb. Vol. 5, 3 Apr.–11 July 1821*, 176. Bills – or motions – to that effect were raised in the House in Feb. 1819, April 1821, Feb. 1824, Feb. 1826; but in each case failed, were withdrawn, or simply went no further and lapsed into abeyance. The campaign petered out towards the end of the 1820s, a change of leadership – from the now retired Onslow to Poulett-Thompson (later Lord Sydenham) doing little to re-energise calls for abolition. Indeed, abolition was a dead letter for most of the 1830s and 1840s – though the ambit of the usury laws was successively restricted (first to three-month – Statute of 3 & 4 Will. IV, c. 98, s. 7, then twelve-month bills – Statute of 1 Vict., c. 80). The usury laws were finally abolished, as if in the backwash over the repeal of the much more contentious Corn Laws, in 1854 by the Statute of 13 & 14 Vict., c. 56.

13 Some of these texts include: J. Grahame, *Defence of the Usury Laws Against the Arguments of Mr Bentham*, Edinburgh: Printed for A. Constable, 1817. J. Bentham, *Reasons Against the Repeal of the Usury Laws*, London: J. Murray, 1825. F. Neale, *Essay on Money-Lending: containing a defence of legal restrictions on the rate of interest, and an answer to the objections of Mr. Bentham*, London: W. Pickering, T. White (printer), 1826.

14 Which, strangely enough, for this partisan period, resulted in something like a consensus with the *Defence of Usury* earning approval ratings from all three major periodicals – and *not* just from Benthamic organ, the radical *Westminster Review*. Rather the tract being favourably received by the liberal-minded Whig *Edinburgh Review* (*Edinburgh Review*, 27 Dec. 1816) and, even more surprisingly, by that strident Tory mouthpiece – and 'killer of Keats' – the *Quarterly Review* (*Quarterly Review*, 33 Dec. 1825) to which, not uncoincidentally, Scott was a leading supporter and key contributor. For more on Scott's involvement in the *Quarterly Review*, see these two excellent sources: K. Wheatley, 'Plotting the Success of the *Quarterly Review*' and S. Ragaz, 'Walter Scott and the *Quarterly Review*', both in J. Cutmore (ed.), *Conservatism and the Quarterly Review*, London: Pickering & Chatto, 2007. Even a cursory review of that invaluable online resource, the *Quarterly Review* Archive confirms the extent of Scott's involvement with the journal, having written reviews on poetry, biography, church history and military logistics, among other topics. See: J. Cutmore (ed.), *Quarterly Review Archive*. Available at: www.rc.umd.edu/reference/qr (accessed 10 October 2010).

'defence', this text is anything but that. In effect, Bentham's *Defence of Usury* is an *attack* on 'usury', the best defence, as ever, being an offence; and one which, as here, is designed to banish usury as a sign from the legal lexicon, as much as obliterate it as a substantive offence from the legislative record, making it not only undoable but unsayable, even unthinkable.

This is exactly what Scott does in *Ivanhoe*, if only impliedly rather than directly; that is, he allegorises the erasure Bentham's *Defence* polemicises, usury's exile from England being metaphorised in and with Isaac the usurer's novelistic departure for the safe haven of 'Boabdil the Saracen('s)' (*I*, p. 336) realm. Here Bentham, doubtless, would object vehemently, countering that this outcome – Isaac's leave-taking – is not the one his tract would dictate. Indeed, the *Defence* might very well suggest the precise opposite; specifically, an ending where Isaac would stay on in England, free of persecution, because his usurious practices have become the norm for commercial transactions rendering all of us – Christian or Jew – potential usurers. Instead, then, of being a 'marginal man' confined to the perimeter of society, Isaac turns out to be absolutely central; that is, something very much like the 'practical Jew' in Marx's *On the Jewish Question*,[15] whose self-interested and utility maximising 'egotism' (*OJQ*, p. 24) is so universalised under the conditions of Capital that it becomes the fulcrum around which the society of exchange turns: 'The Jew has emancipated himself ... because, through him ... money has become a world power and the practical Jewish spirit has become the practical spirit of the Christian nations. The Jews have emancipated themselves insofar as the Christians have become Jews' (*OJQ*, p. 23). Following on from this, one might say – echoing the sloganeering of the *soixante-huitards* as much as the writings of Marx – that in the futurity of the free market, *we are all Jews!* Strangely enough, however, this group identification means that those who are *born* as Jews are no longer necessary, the otiose surplus of which Scott most definitely picks up on in *Ivanhoe* and thematises by dispatching Isaac to his near doom in the *donjon* at Torquilstone, as if presaging the fate of European Jewry in the twentieth-century's genocidal camps.

I want to argue that Isaac can go missing from the narrative without affecting the storyline's arc because his literal absence here is more than offset by his figurative presence in every other character in the novel: the greed of Prince John – whose 'eager desire' (*I*, p. 69) for a 'large loan from the Jews of York' (*I*, p. 69) approximates Isaac's undisguised 'joy' (*I*, p. 99)

---

15 K. Marx, 'On the Jewish Question' in *Works of Karl Marx 1844*, A. Blunden and M. Grant (eds), 1844. Hereafter referred to as *OJQ*.

at Ivanhoe's prize money; the display of Prior Aymer – whose tournament finery of '[f]ur and gold' (*I*, p. 70) find its match in Isaac, 'richly . . . even magnificently dressed' (*I*, p. 69); the cunning of Fitzurse – who is likened to, as is Isaac, a 'spider', the former spinning 'meshes' (*I*, p. 133) of intrigue, the latter 'sucking the blood of his miserable victims' (*I*, p. 70). Not that the reverse holds: though bits and pieces of Isaac's character disseminate throughout the Christian mainstream, they – and especially their Catholicism – are most certainly are not inscribed in him, as Friar Tuck's comical – and failed – efforts at conversion show (*I*, pp. 279–280). Yet the notion that 'we are all Isaac' because 'we are all Jews', even 'we are all usurers', *takes* something from Isaac, robs him of his uniqueness; specifically, his difference *as* a Jew, the theft of which – even if Isaac remains, as here, true to the faith of his fathers – *de-judaifies* him. How? By assimilating Isaac into the social mainstream, Scott renders him all but invisible, effectively a non-being. This is why *Ivanhoe* is such a powerful example of a 'novel judgement', the narrative launching here its first volley in a full-scale critique of the Benthamic project. For with Isaac's increasing distance, even disappearance from the tale, the text teases out the violence – indeed, racist core – that is latent in the *Defence*, its legal positivist agenda of decriminalising usury (thereby fracturing the law–morality nexus) participating in, possibly *exacerbating* the persecution of the Jews in its liquidation of the usurer.

## Was that 'Judge & Co.' or Judge and Code? The Trials and Tribulations of Lucas de Beaumanoir

This paradox at the very centre of Bentham's legal positivism – reproducing, indeed magnifying the problem (anti-Semitism) its law reform was designed to rectify (anti-usury) – is at work, as well, in the way its anti-judicial bias exacerbates rather than erases law's violence. Consider Richard's command at the end of the story ordering the Grand Master of the Templars, Lucas de Beaumanoir, to '[d]issolve thy Chapter, and depart with thy followers' (*I*, p. 393). Here the King's aim is not just *displacement* – that is, the removal of the Templars – but the *replacement* of their culture of violence, exchanging a system of judgement organised around a person (Beaumanoir) for that of a *process* (i.e., the King's 'justice' (*I*, p. 393)). This juridical substitution is all the more urgent because the 'person' in question – the Grand Master – is, for all his professions of piety, even more vicious than any of *Ivanhoe*'s other robber barons. Only consider the word-of-mouth that precedes his appearance in the text, Rabbi Nathan ben Samuel warning Isaac of his 'cruelty' (*I*, p. 302) especially to the 'Children of the Promise' (*I*, p. 302) whose 'murther' (*I*, p. 303) is, for him, 'an offering of . . . sweet savour' (*I*, p. 303). Beaumanoir, himself, confirms his sanguinary reputation by wholeheartedly endorsing, when he first arrives on the narrative scene, the sentence meted out to the learned Miriam of York, 'burned at a stake' (*I*, p. 311), her medical skills misrecognised as witchcraft. What really appals, however, about the Grand Master's blood-lust here is that it is cloaked in, and by the legitimacy of *law*, Miriam having been sent to her fiery end by a trial – *so-called*. 'So called' because here a deeply flawed jurispathology holds sway, presided over by a bitter and twisted emblem of the Rule of Man: the 'hanging judge' of Beaumanoir, himself. Who, in turn, promises a repeat performance of his 'rough justice' when he sits as the adjudicator of Miriam's 'pupil' (*I*, p. 344), Rebecca: 'With . . . [her] we will deal as the Christian law and our own high office best warrant' (*I*, p. 311).

A critique of judgement looms here, one that summons up Bentham's vexed relationship with the common law, especially that of his *bête noire*, 'Judge & Co.',[16] whose malign influence cast a shadow throughout his long lifetime over English courts. At first blush, though, Beaumanoir – the canon lawyer from abroad – bears little resemblance to the English judge, who, by virtue of the local adversarial system, stands, umpire-like, at a remove from the curial fray, a mere arbitrator between competing parties and their conflicting claims. But then this common law conception of the judge was not the principal object of critique in Bentham's anti-judicial broadside, *Scotch Reform*. There, the judges singled out for particular scorn were *civilians* rather than common lawyers, hailing from Scott's native Caledonia,[17] then (and now) a jurisprudential province of Roman law.[18] This connection, of course, brings Beaumanoir back into the picture because it from precisely this legal system that he derives his authority, threatening to 'appeal to Rome' (*I*, p. 393) when the King challenges him. Given this, Beaumanoir may not only be the judge that Bentham had in mind in *Scotch Reform*; he

---

16 J. Bentham, 'Scotch Reform' (1843) in J. Bowring (ed.), *The Works of Jeremy Bentham*, vol. 5, Edinburgh: William Tait. Available at: http://oll.libertyfund.org/title/1996 (accessed 2 January 2009). Hereafter referred to as *SR*.
17 Though, that said, English judges do come in for some of the general drubbing that Bentham administers to the Scottish judiciary: 'In Scotland, as in England, and elsewhere, the system of judicial procedure has been, in the main, the work, not of legislators but of judges: manufactured, chiefly in the form – not of real statutory law – but of jurisprudential law, consisting of general inferences deduced from particular decisions' (*SR*, p. 12).
18 Not that Bentham saw, in terms of the bottom line – the ends of justice – all that much difference between Scotland's 'Rome-bred technicalism' and the 'English-bred technicalism', south of the border (*SR*, p. 73).

could very well be Bentham's *worst nightmare*, the Grand Master's inquisitorial authority rendering him a kind of *uber*-judge, far more powerful in his 'hands on' approach to legal proceedings than any of the common law judiciary. Think of the total control Beaumanoir exerts over the course of the Templestowe trial: calling witnesses;[19] cross-examining testimony;[20] challenging evidence.[21] So the Grand Master's representation amounts to a composite of the judge-as-Benthamite bogeyman, concentrating in one figure all the disagreeable traits of the bench, be it civilian or common law, inquisitorial or adversarial, Scots, Continental or English: traits such as high-handedness, officiousness, bias, and so forth.

Every trait, that is, except one: specifically, 'corruption' (*SR*, p. 14). For all the abuse heaped on Beaumanoir by the text – as superstitious, as overbearing, as fanatical – the venality associated with Judge & Co. is not one of them. 'Fees' (*SR*, p. 13) and the 'fee-gathering system' (*SR*, p. 15) that loom so large for Bentham's judges[22] do not figure in Beaumanoir's scale of values at all, 'despising', as he does, 'treasure' (*I*, p. 303). In point of fact, Beaumanoir is driven neither by the gain of 'gold and silver' (*I*, p. 302) nor the sirens of 'sensuality' (*I*, p. 303) but aims, as his minion Mountfitchet points out, at 'reformation' (*I*, p. 307). This last term would have strong positive connotations for Scott's original and largely Protestant audience, and would have disallowed any easy sectarian reading, rife in a period hotly debating Catholic emancipation, of the Grand Master as a papist 'bigot' (*I*, p. 304). If anything, Beaumanoir exudes more the spirit of John Knox and his *ethos* of Calvinist restraint: that of the Presbyterian 'ascetic' (*I*, p. 304) – a figure of anathema, incidentally, for both Scott (for whom it spelled the demise of dignified worship)[23] *and* Bentham (for whom it meant the end of

---

19 Such as the fawning Albert de Malvoison, the hapless Higg and Torquilstone's all-too-gullible 'men-at-arms': Scott, *Ivanhoe*, p. 327, eagerly attesting to Rebecca's abilities in spell-casting (Scott, *Ivanhoe*, pp. 327–328) and shape-shifting: Scott, *Ivanhoe*, p. 328.
20 Like that of Bois-Guilbert's oblique reference to 'The scroll!' (Scott, *Ivanhoe*, p. 329), deemed a device of Rebecca's 'witcheries' (ibid.).
21 Like the Old Testament Hebrew that decorates Higg's unguent-containing case, thereby converting 'Scripture into blasphemy' (ibid. p. 325).
22 As Bentham puts it: 'By primeval indigence, and inexperience on the part of the sovereign, judges are left without salaries, but left with the power to pay themselves by fees. Hence, as we have seen, a constant opposition between the ends of justice and ends (the original, and then actual ends) of judicature' (*SR*, p. 12).
23 Scott maintained, according to Leslie Stephen, that it was the Scottish Episcopal Church – that branch of the Anglican Communion in North Britain – that offered the 'religion for a gentleman' and was the implacable foe of Presbyterian 'dogmatism' – the Kirk in which he was reared. See: L. Stephen, *Hours in a Library*, vol. 1, London: J. Murray, 1917, p. 151.

utility).[24] This point is important because, in 'ecumenising' Beaumanoir's defects as both Reformed and Roman, both Kirk and chapel, Scott, the Episcopalian convert, makes the same anti-confessional point, paradoxically, as the Establishment-loathing Bentham did in his attacks on what he called 'Church of Englandism'.[25] For, here, both rise above simple anti-clericalism and shift their critiques, as if in tandem, from the narrower issue of the subject (the judge, the clergyman) to the larger one of structure (law, education). In chiming in together as chary of *any* belief-system, and the set of ethico-moral values associated with that system, having purchase on public office – judicial, educational or otherwise – the two of them air the proto-positivist sentiment that the state is separate from faith, the law from morality.

All of which suggests that Beaumanoir, as the emblem and agent of that morality, may present far more of a threat to the law than 'Judge & Co'. Only, ironically, the danger of this threat resides in the former's sincerely held religious convictions rather than the latter's much more biddable corruption. This reversal points to another, even more contemporary judicial referent, one that is evoked by Beaumanoir's self-denying zealotry and which speaks to the passionate neo-puritanism, rife in revolutionary times – like Scott's – that welcomes morality back into the law with open arms, effectively erasing the line between the secular and the sacred. This referent is suggested by the fact that Beaumanoir, as canon lawyer and Catholic cleric, most definitely lives by a code – not necessarily a bad thing for Bentham who spent a lifetime arguing on behalf of[26] and drafting codes.[27] But here the code of Beaumanoir is organised around a distinctly anti-Benthamic principle; namely, a higher law that is neither posited by man, nor recognisable as an 'is', but which consists of a set of 'oughts' that say, 'Thou shalt not!' With such a broad normative sweep and such grand rhetorical gestures, this Mosaic-like code is a far cry from anything envis-

---

24 Citing, famously, in the *Introduction to the Principles and Morals of Legislation*, the principle of asceticism 'as constantly opposed to' the principle of utility. J. Bentham, *An Introduction to the Principles and Morals of Legislation*, J. H. Burns and H. L. A. Hart (eds), Oxford: Clarendon Press, 1996, p. 2000.
25 See, for example: J. Bentham, *Strictures on the Exclusionary System as Pursued in the National Society's Schools*, London: E. Wilson, 1816; also, J. Bentham, *Church of Englandism and Its Catechism Examined*, London: E. Wilson, 1818.
26 J. Bentham, 'Legislator of the World', in P. Schofield and J. Harris (eds), *Writings on Codification, Law and Education*, New York: Oxford University Press, 1998.
27 J. Bentham, *Constitutional Code: Vol. 1*, F. Rosen and J. H. Burns (eds), Oxford: Clarendon Press, 1983.

aged by Bentham's science of legislation, being much closer, in its jurisprudential spirit, to the French Revolution's *Declaration of the Rights of Man*.[28] Even closer in spirit – both politically and legally – is it to Blackstone's much more reactionary efforts to order, organise and clarify the English common law in what amounts to the crypto-code of his celebrated *Commentaries*.[29] Of course, Bentham, famously, loathed both Blackstone and the French Revolution, denouncing the former in his *Comment on the Commentaries*[30] and lambasting the latter in his *Anarchical Fallacies*.[31] According to Bentham, each of these juridical projects grounded their respective 'law' on the chimerical foundations of the Law of Nature: in the case of the French revolutionaries, on the 'nonsense upon stilts'[32] of natural rights, everywhere in theory but nowhere in fact; in that of Blackstone, on the fantasmatic flummery of a higher law, the eternal law of God, informing, ordering and underpinning nature's chain of being.[33]

With Scott's character of Beaumanoir, these two antithetical poles of natural law – the 'divine right' of reaction and the Revolution's 'rights of man' – converge, the former turning into the latter, the latter merging with the former. This claim may strike the reader as odd in that, at least initially, neither kind of *Recht* figure very much in the makeup of Beaumanoir, the *lex natura* having gone on walkabout here. For little or no appeal is made by him to said law's 'higher power', be it secular or, even more strangely, sacred. I say 'strangely' because, for all his presumption to be God's lawyer, carrying out *His* will, only once – upon Bois-Guilbert's death – does the Grand Master actually reference the deity: 'This is indeed the judgement of God ... *Fiat voluntas tua*' (*I*, p. 392). If anything, it is Rebecca who talks repeatedly of the 'Great Father',[34] and best embodies

---

28 'Declaration of the Rights of Man and the Citizen', in *The Human Rights Reader*, W. Lacquer and B. Rubin (eds), New York: New American Library, 1979.
29 W. Blackstone, *Commentaries on the Laws of England*, Chicago: University of Chicago Press, 1979.
30 J. Bentham, *A Comment on the Commentaries and A Fragment on Government*, J. H. Burns and H. L. A. Hart (eds), London: Athlone Press, 1977.
31 J. Bentham, 'Anarchical Fallacies', in J. Waldron (ed.), '*Nonsense upon Stilts: Bentham, Burke and Marx on the Rights of Man*', New York: Methuen, 1987.
32 Ibid. p. 53.
33 Bentham, *A Comment on the Commentaries*, above n 30.
34 While journeying home, back from the tournament, and their two trains meet, Rebecca beseeches Rowena for assistance in these terms: 'Then rising, and throwing back her veil, she implored them her in the great name of God whom they both worshipped, and by that revelation of the Law in which they both believed, that she would have compassion upon them, and suffer them to go forward under their safeguard' (*I*, p. 160). Or in

the natural law tradition of both rights (speaking her mind, asserting her independence) and responsibilities (healing the sick, accompanying her father). By way of contrast, Beaumanoir's faith is of a peculiar kind because it is Christianity without Christ, even without God; instead, it sees enemies everywhere, indeed *the* Enemy, Satan (referred to, repeatedly, as 'the Ancient Enemy' (*I*, p. 306) and 'Sathanas' (*I*, p. 325)). Such paranoia has a political as much as a theological relevance; for it is, after all, the Schmitt-like, proto-totalitarian leader who sees the world in terms of 'enemies' and 'friends' – and *judges* accordingly, embracing the latter, executing the former. All of which may serve to identify Beaumanoir as a *particular* revolutionary leader-*cum*-judge of the period, one whose fastidious fanaticism is in stark contrast to the atheistic Bois-Guilbert's Sadean libertinism, ever 'enjoying' its 'philosophy in the bedroom',[35] and which approximates 'the Incorruptible' himself: that Arras *avocat*, Robespierre, ever demanding 'Off with their heads!'

So Robespierre is Beaumanoir and Beaumanoir is Robespierre, the revolutionary inquisitor segueing into the reactionary one and vice-versa, because both, ultimately, are true *believers*, their sense of a 'higher purpose' – divine or human, political or theological – not only blurring the boundaries between governmentality and God/Reason but obscuring, in their obsession with the state of the soul (be it that of communicant or citizen), *reality* itself. No wonder something as bellicose as trial by combat comes as a relief here, precisely because it operates on the most tangible level of the *real* – the physical blow – and eschews the epistemic violence of natural law's imperative to *know* the *logos* of Reason or the mind of God. Yet trial by combat may be all *too* real in that it substitutes the *threat* of violence, hazarded by Templestowe's inquisitor, with *actual* violence. This exchange, however, turns out to be, paradoxically, far less aggressive in its effects, the latter (actual violence) being far milder, indeed much more salutary than the former (the threat of violence). For trial by combat *saves* Rebecca from the fires of the faggot. Furthermore, it remains open to question whether, in fact, this fierce curial mode, all swinging maces and thrusting lances, actually *kills* Bois-Guilbert. As the text tells the reader, he dies not so much from a blow ('the spear of Ivanhoe did but ... touch ... (his) shield', *I*,

---

Ivanhoe's sick room at Torquilstone, while tending her wary patient, Rebecca assures him that 'a Jew may do good service to a Christian, without other guerdon than the blessing of the Great Father, who made both Jew and Gentile' (ibid. p. 237).

35 D. A. F. de Sade, *Justine, Philosophy in the Bedroom and Other Writings*, New York: Grove Press, 1990.

p. 391), as from what Slavoj Žižek might call 'the Real of his desire',[36] consumed by and 'a victim . . . of his own contending passions' (*I*, p. 392).

That said, there is no getting away from a harsher truth here; namely, that trial by combat *is* brutal, its legal process foregrounding, indeed showcasing the Coverian 'pain and suffering'[37] that still remain – however menacingly – in the backdrop of the Grand Master's inquisitorial proceedings. What's more, this mode of trial is *anything but* a feudal flourish that Scott, donning his cap as legal historian, has revived for the sake of some sort of antiquarian picturesque. Though an anomaly by this time, trial by combat was still a viable adjectival alternative at common law, having been invoked only recently – and for the last time in English legal history – in the appeal from that *cause célèbre* of a murder trial, *Ashford* v. *Thornton*.[38] Of which proceeding, Scott, ever the advocate must have known – as literary critic Gary Dyer argues persuasively.[39] With all due respect, however, to this path-breaking analysis, I would argue that Scott goes further than Dyer claims, *Ivanhoe* invoking, with the allusion to *Ashford* v. *Thornton*, a curial *concept* as much as a case citation. For the jurisprudential point that Scott makes here is that the common law trial, as *adversarial* – meaning dispute driven – is, always/already, a trial by combat; that is, it is a nomological *agon* in which 'damsels in distress' (i.e., Rebecca) stand in for litigants, and lawyers are metaphorised as champions (i.e., Bois-Guilbert, Ivanhoe), nominated by, and duking it out for their clients as armed combatants.

This is exactly why Bentham wanted to do away with the common law altogether because, in its courtroom processes, he saw an anachronistic slug-fest, a curial version of the medieval period's 'extreme sport' of choice, the tournament. For both gave the victor's laurels not to right but might (dependent on physical strength in one case, and the power of cash in the other) and resolved conflict, *ex post facto*. In *Truth versus Ashhurst*, Bentham would call this kind of legality 'dog law',[40] the common law waiting for its breach to occur *before* springing into prosecutorial action. Instead of this delayed reaction, what was needed, according to Bentham, was a law based on prophylaxis: that is, one acting pre-emptively and *ante facto*. How

---

36  S. Žižek, *The Sublime Object of Ideology*, London: Verso, 1989.
37  R. Cover, 'Violence and the Word', *Yale Law Journal* 95(7), 1986, 1601.
38  *Ashford* v. *Thornton* (1818) 1 B & Ald 405.
39  G. Dyer, 'Ivanhoe, Chivalry, and the Murder of Mary Ashford', *Criticism* 39(3), 1997, 383–408.
40  J. Bentham, 'Truth versus Ashhurst; or Law as It Is Contrasted with What It Is Said to Be,' in J. Bowring (ed.), *The Works of Jeremy Bentham*, vol. 5, Bristol, England: Thoemmes Press, 1995, p. 236.

was this law to be realised? Bentham is clear: through nothing less than a *code* – though one based not on the theologico-political delirium of natural law but the legislative science of utility. Such a code Bentham called a *pannomion*[41] because it was not only comprehensive in its textual detail, but all-embracing in its jurisdictional reach, proleptic of each and every *actus reus*. In short: a 'total' law. How this pannomion comes to be crafted in the first place is implicit in Bentham's theory of discourse and, with it, his critique of 'legal fictions'.[42] For Bentham theorised a language that was so *totalising* that, in its codifying aspirations, it aimed at nothing less than the closure of the gap between the legal signifier and the signified, thereby sealing off the space from which fictions seeped into law. In carrying out this sort of linguistic *and* legal lock-down, Bentham's pannomion renders any sort of judicial process these fictions solicit, like the dodgy hermeneutics of 'Judge & Co.', unnecessary, if not irrelevant.

As a Scots-trained advocate, *au fait* with a proto-pannomial civilian system, Scott, surely, would have seen the folly of Bentham's 'total' law, and its claims to be immune to interpretation, free from uncertainty. From the practical task of parsing Scots or Roman codes alone, Scott would know, more than any other law-and-*littérateur*, the extent to which the sign of law is utterly riven with indeterminacy and, as such, is forever *fractured*. Within the fault-lines of this fracture, adversarialism's competing curial arguments take shape because it is here that legal language's fundamentally aporetic structure shows itself. This disclosure fissures from the start Bentham's dream of a closed legal order of signs because law's linguistic core of *un*-meaning threatens a new species of legal fictions which, in turn, calls forth, even *demands* the uncanny return of the interpreting judge. The danger here is that this judicial return would take the form of Beaumanoir who, as something like the Lacanian letter endowed with the executory power of *coupure*, would *cut* through the pannomion's knot of codified confusion, relieving it of polysemy, restoring the moral absolutism of 'one right answer': specifically, *his answer*, and, with it, *his* strange amalgam of bias and inflexibility. All of which confirms the truth of Lacan's law: that you get back in reverse form that which you desire most. So in searching for a law free of the Solomonic whim of 'Judge & Co.', Bentham may set the stage for a judicial monomania far more dangerous, indeed far more violent: that of 'Judge *& Code*'. This vision of (legal) judgement is fully

---

41  J. Bentham, *An Introduction to the Principles of Morals and Legislation*, J. H. Burns and H. L. A. Hart (eds), London: Athlone Press, 1996, p. 305.
42  C. K. Ogden, *Bentham's Theory of Fictions*, Edinburgh: Edinburgh Press, 1932.

realised in Scott's character of Lucas de Beaumanoir, the code-trained civilian, who is ever at war with (in his grimly objective demand for certitude), but always enacting (in his subjective exercise of 'wild' discretion) the profound ambiguity rupturing, at its very crux, law and its judicial processes.

## *Avant la Loi*: Rebecca, Ivanhoe and the Return of the King-as-Benthamite

Two of these judicial (and quasi-judicial) processes – Templestowe's trial by combat and the heavily regulated tournament at Ashby-de-la-Zouche which presages it – book-end the narrative, framing the storyline's centrepiece: that is, the 'awful event' (*I*, p. 243) of the assault on Torquilstone, and with it, its (dis)organising thematic of law's violence. Not that law is very much in evidence there – at least, at first blush. For the attestation rendered here favours *violence* plain and simple, Rebecca's act of witnessing, recording for the benefit of the bedridden Ivanhoe (and the reader) the following: the 'cloud' (*I*, p. 246) of arrows launched into the air; the scaling (and abseiling) of thick 'outer' (*I*, p. 247) walls; the breaching of inner 'barriers' (*I*, p. 246); the parry and thrust of 'hand to hand' (*I*, p. 246) combat. Yet the striking feature of this extremely vivid sequence of events is stylistic, rather than sensational; that is, for all its visceral power, this scene remains very much a *mediated* one, *focalised* and *vocalised* by an intervening narrational agent (Rebecca), whose reportage here (to Ivanhoe) contrasts sharply with the much more direct depictions, indeed grim and grisly realisations of Torquilstone's earlier and later torments – e.g., Isaac's torture (*I*, pp. 179–186), Front-de-Bœuf's immolation (*I*, pp. 252–258), Ulrica's last hurrah on the battlement (*I*, pp. 269–271).

Why is this second-hand account significant? Because it shifts the scene's centre of gravity away from the visual and towards the verbal, thereby foregrounding the dialogic, even hermeneutical significance – rather than representational punch – that attaches here. For what do Rebecca and Ivanhoe actually *do* here but *debate* the nature of the violence confronting them? This conversational exchange brings the law very much back into the picture because, here, Ivanhoe characterises the siege of the castle as a rule-bound act of *legality* and casts chivalry in terms redolent of *the* topos of jurisprudence, the Rule of Law: 'Chivalry! – why maiden, it is the nurse of pure and high affection – the stay of the oppressed, the redresser of grievances, the curb of the power of the tyrant – nobility were but an empty name without her, and liberty finds the best protector in her lance and sword' (*I*, p. 248). Here, chivalry is apostrophised by Ivanhoe in terms that evoke, and are near identical to the Rule of Law; that is, as a 'law of rules' to which *all* are subject ('the curb of the power of the tyrant', *I*, p. 248) and to which *everyone* has access, regardless of rank or status (be they 'the oppressed', or the 'nobility', *I*, p. 248). Sealing that identification is Ivanhoe's observation that, like the Rule of Law, chivalry extends the benefit of its procedures (the 'redresser of grievances', *I*, p. 248) to each of its subjects, including sanctions ('lance and sword', *I*, p. 248) which here *guarantee* – rather than punitively circumscribe – that subject's civil 'liberty' (*I*, p. 248).

This encomiastic flight of Ivanhoe's (juridical) fancy is interrupted, however, by Rebecca, who – like some Benthamite censor[43] – *censures it*, all the while propounding an alternative (novel) judgement: a critique of the 'fantastic chivalry of the Nazarenes' (*I*, p. 250). For, according to Rebecca, this legality is destined to be become a dead letter, unreadable but for a few clerks ('the ignorant monk', *I*, p. 249) and unheeded by those 'drunken churls' (*I*, p. 249) to whom it is recited as an empty precedent (by barristerial 'vagabond minstrels', *I*, p. 249), having become un-interpretable, a meaningless ornament, like 'the rusted mail which hangs as a hatchment over the champion's dim and mouldering tomb' (*I*, p. 249). Yet for all her logical parsing – and puncturing – of Ivanhoe's fancy of chivalry-as-law here, Rebecca is far from inured to its sheer 'blood 'n' guts' impact, her act of witnessing becoming an affidavit of *affect* ('high and pure affection', *I*, p. 248) that attests not only to the 'terror' (*I*, p. 243) this phenomenon arouses, but to a kind of exaltation or ecstasy that it releases. All of which elevates Rebecca's experience of chivalry's laws to a legalist version of that most 'Romantic' of states of being: what this chapter calls jurisprudential 'sublimity' (*I*, p. 243).

The only problem, however, with this 'jurisprudential sublime' is that it can flip over all too easily into a kind of psychotic vertigo, confusing heights and depths. This symptomatic loss of perspective explains why Rebecca is all too willing to plunge off the battlements here. For the space of Torquilstone is one in which the law has gone insane, its rule system divided and fighting each other; and its armed camps of the Black Knight (right)

---

43 Bentham writes on this distinction: 'There are two characters, one or the other of which every man who finds anything to say on the subject of law, may be said to take upon him; that of the Expositor, and that of the censor. To the province of the Expositor, it belongs to explain to us what, as he supposes, the Law is: to that of the Censor, to observe to us what he thinks it ought to be' (J. Bentham, *A Fragment on Government; or, a Comment on the Commentaries*, 2nd edn, London: E. Wilson and W. Pickering, 1823, pp. xii–xiii).

and Front-de-Bœuf (might), being a legalistic equivalent of the Hobbesian *bellum omnium contra omnes*, 'the war of all against all'.[44] What or *who* will put a stop to this *nomomachia* if not the Leviathanic sovereign, the return of whom – the return of the king? – is so longed for, and ultimately realised at the end of *Ivanhoe*? For that is the core juridical problem here: the law is (minimally) functional, yet unanchored in any identifiable or 'posited' source of sovereignty. There is, of course, that *simulation* of sovereignty, Prince John. But he remains just that: a simulacra, a facsimile, a pale imitation of authority. So John displays all trappings of royalty (a 'sort of comeliness', a 'splendour' of dress and equipage, *I*, p. 71) but commands none of its obedient respect; accordingly, his pronouncements – like his ill-conceived caprice to make Rebecca the tournament's queen of 'Love and Beauty' (*I*, p. 76) – chop and change with the prevailing winds blowing through his 'cabal' (*I*, p. 133) of high caste hangers-on, who seem to be the real sovereign here. Consider how quickly the Prince resiles from his tournament mischief-making once it becomes clear that, as far as his underlings are concerned, Rebecca's proposed coronation has neither their support nor their approval, being a step too far for even these taunting louts: 'This passes a jest, my lord', said Bracy; 'no knight here will lay lance in rest is such an insult is attempted' (*I*, p. 76).

John is countermanded so easily here because, as it turns out, he is little more than a puppet figure; yet another 'tool' (*I*, p. 137) deployed to provide the *appearance* of legality to a palace revolt, cloaking the machinations of its principal engineer, that medieval Machiavel (or Dick Cheney?), 'Noble Waldemar Fitzurse' (*I*, p. 137). For Fitzurse aspires to be nothing less than 'the power behind the throne' – that is, the 'future Chancellor' (*I*, p. 136) – who, once having secured the crown for his dupe, will nullify the remnants of the old constitutional order and thereby end the ongoing 'crisis' (*I*, p. 136) of the state by rendering permanent the Johannine regency. In so doing, Fitzurse will transform emergency into the norm, making exception, the rule. For the England of *Ivanhoe* resembles nothing less than an Agamben-*esque* 'state of exception'[45] – though one *in reverse*. Here its legality is indeterminate – *sous rature*, present *and* absent – because England's *sovereignty* has been suspended (rather than the other way around), creating a vacuum of governance, juridical, political and otherwise. Not that a *restoration* will fill, necessarily, the black hole of this

---

44 T. Hobbes, *Leviathan*, M. Missner (ed.), New York: Pearson Longman, 2008, p. 86.
45 G. Agamben, *State of Exception*, K. Attell (trans.), Chicago: University of Chicago Press, 2005.

66 • Novel Judgements: Legal Theory as Fiction

chaotic 'failed state', as is so often the case in cinematic[46] and/or televisual stagings[47] of *Ivanhoe* that 'arthurianise' Richard as 'the once and future king' who has only to show himself undisguised to ensure fealty. The problem with this loyalist reading is that the text flatly contradicts it, Richard having to fight, indeed claw his way back to power – at the tournament, at Torquilstone – his subjects, a motley band of brigands, literally 'out-law' in their remove beyond the jurisdictional reach of the 'king's justice' and its sheriffs. By way of contrast, lawful authority – meaning the claim of royalist legitimacy – is ruthlessly and relentlessly parodied (and thereby undone) in the text's comic portrayal of the clownish Athelstane of Coningsburgh; his 'visionary throne' (*I*, p. 157) functions here as a 'saxonised' version of that of the Stuart pretenders in Scott's earlier *œuvre* – the most notable being *Waverley*'s Bonnie Prince Charlie[48] – with Cedric, a Sassenach stand-in for that diehard Jacobite dreamer, the Baron of Bradwardine.

So legitimacy is certainly *not* the ground for Richard's claim here, however much the reader may want to identify it as such, importing, from other sources – T. H. White?[49] J. R. R. Tolkien?[50] even Erroll Flynn?[51] – the rhetoric of the *right*-ful king. For 'right', or *Recht* – that is, law – seems alien to Richard, who appears first in the text as a figure a-*nomos*; that is, as the wandering Black Knight, *Le Noir Faineant* (*I*, p. 114), who is, literally, anomised, meaning alone, estranged and outside the socio-Symbolic's law. In fact, it is Richard who has put himself in this position – outside the law – in the first place, having suspended his own sovereignty and installing, in its stead, the regency of his brother, John. All of which points to and underlines the nature of Richard's rule, and why he, more than anyone else in the text, is 'the man who *must* be king'. For by this act of abrogation – that is,

---

46  *Ivanhoe*, Directed by D. Canfield. Film. UK/USA: Columbia Pictures, 1952.
47  *Ivanhoe*, Directed by S. Orme, UK/USA: A&E Television Networks, 1997; *Ivanhoe*, Directed by D. Coupland, UK/USA: Columbia Pictures, 1982; *Ivanhoe*, Directed by D. Maloney, UK: BBC, 1970; *Ivanhoe*, Directed by P. Rogers, B. Coote and H. Smith, UK: Screen Gems Television, 1958.
48  W. Scott, *Waverley*, Andrew Hook (ed.), London: Penguin, 1972.
49  There, with Richard a type of Arthur, aka 'Wart'. See T. H. White, *The Once and Future King*, New York: Putnam, 1958.
50  With Richard as a precursor of that other great king-in-disguise (and exile), Aragon, aka 'Strider', aka 'Estel'. See J. R. R. Tolkien, *The Lord of the Rings*, Boston: Houghton Mifflin, 1965.
51  With Richard *as Richard* (and played by South African/British stalwart in Hollywood, Ian Hunter) in, for example in, *The Adventures of Robin Hood*, Directed by M. Curtiz and W. Keighley, USA, Warner Bros. 1938.

the surcease of his own power – he establishes himself, beyond all doubt, not only as a legal positivist avatar of the 'commanding' sovereign, but as a precursor of what Carl Schmitt would come to call the 'decisionist' sovereign.[52] In short, he commands the abeyance of his *own* commands, deciding upon, *as* 'the Law', the end *of* 'the Law'.

This is, of course, a species of imperative that not only contests *and* confirms Richard's role as sovereign but promulgates a new world (dis)order where any and all are displaced, if not dispossessed by and through the law. Think of the other anomic characters in the text, each repeating the ruse of Richard's disguise because they too have been consigned *hors-loi*. For example, even when he drops the assumed identity of a palmer 'just returned from the Holy Land' (*I*, p. 32), Wilfred of Ivanhoe takes to the field at Ashby under yet another alias, that of *Desdichado*, or the 'Disinherited' (*I*, p. 82). This sobriquet flags the deprivation of Wilfred's rightful inheritance not once but twice: first, by his own father for disobedience, having confounded Cedric's schemes for dynastic cross-breeding by falling in love with Rowena, Athelstane's intended (*I*, p. 157); second, by Prince John, his *de facto* liege, for disloyalty – or, rather, for his overarching loyalty to his *de jure* liege – the king – with the consequence that his estate is now forfeit, and to be transferred to a more reliable minion, Front-de-Bœuf (*I*, pp. 117–118). Or take the example of Robin/Locksley, who, like many an 'English yeoman' (*I*, p. 368) of the period, is driven by the 'tyrannical exercise of ... forest rights and other oppressive laws' (*I*, p. 368) to a life of petty thieving, who, with his henchmen – a 'gang' (*I*, p. 102) of similarly evicted Sherwood itinerants – are literally in their masking 'visors' (*I*, p. 103), 'the boys in the 'hood'.

But if disorder prevails *outside* in what might be called *Ivanhoe*'s 'green world'[53] – that is, its liminal space of Sherwood's forested outlawry – then anarchy is the order of the day within the castellated walls of the narrative's overarching image (and crass send-up) of the *civis*; namely, the Norman redoubt, Torquilstone. Why? Because the bedlam that is this bastion issues from, and is predicated upon a *crime*; in fact, *the* originary offence, the slaying of the father. No wonder that the atmosphere which obtains at Torquilstone is so 'anything goes' because prohibition, in the form of the paternal function – that is, the Law of the Father's Name – has been

---

52 C. Schmitt, *Political Theology: Four Chapters on the Concept of Sovereignty*, G. Schwab (trans.), Cambridge, MA: MIT Press, 1985.
53 N. Frye, *The Anatomy of Criticism: Four Essays*, Princeton: Princeton University Press, 1957, pp. 101 and 182–183.

foreclosed all too thoroughly here by 'parricide' (*I*, p. 258). This parricide is confirmed by that strange and tragic figure, Ulrica (aka, Urfried – another example of disguise), the 'madwoman in the turret', who confesses to a horrified Cedric the ignominious role she played – as a 'temptress' (*I*, p. 256) – in fomenting enmity between Front-de-Bœuf *père et fils*. This enmity *exceeds* that of Oedipus; indeed, the depth of rancour evidenced here is more suggestive of a paternity that readers of *Totem and Taboo* would recognise instantly as 'primal'. For *that* father is not one who says 'No!' to incest but who, on the contrary, is a figure of *jouissance* – or 'enjoyment' in its most libidinous sense. Though this figure enjoys *only for himself*, thwarting his son(s)' access to 'the feminine' by monopolising *eros*: an act of sexual hording which will end only with his death. Which is precisely what happens to Front-de-Bœuf senior; his murder, aided and abetted by his treacherous 'paramour' (*I*, p. 217), allows his insatiable son to take to his place as Ulrica's lover, bedding (though never wedding) her.

Not that Front-de-Bœuf senior is the only dead father in *Ivanhoe*. Consider the deceased King Henry and his own highly vexed relationship with Prince John. Described as a 'rebellious son' (*I*, p. 137) by the text, here John's rivalry with his father takes on something of the quality of psychoanalysis's – and jurisprudence's – privileged complex (Oedipus *Lex*?), the struggle of which is not so much 'worked through' as (re)projected onto his sibling rivalry with Richard.[54] This is why Richard's return, unsurprisingly, comes as such a psychic as well as physical relief – because he puts an end to this sexual and sovereign confusion. His storming of Torquilstone, for example, not only re-establishes sovereignty around a king whose commands are obeyed, but restores the sexual status quo by rescuing Rowena from a Ulrica-like fate as yet another Saxon heiress auctioned off and earmarked for the enrichment (and pleasure) of a Norman 'favourite': the *faux*-courtly lover, De Bracy. But more than these feats of – as Wilfred might put it – 'derring do' (*I*, p. 248), Richard, for all his *Recht*-lessness (and recklessness) ends up doing 'the right thing' in doing 'the *rights* thing'; namely, by restoring his vassal's possessory rights to the Ivanhoe estate. In so doing, Richard ensures the feasibility of Wilfred's suit with Rowena and the *material* basis for the success of their marriage. So Richard turns out to be a sovereign driven by what contemporary political theory would recognise as a distributivist logic, divvying up the 'goodies' of this society but with an eye to 'justice as fairness'.

54 Indeed, the history of the Norman dynasty is one for father–son struggles, going back to, as the text details, the bypassing by William the Conqueror, in the line of succession for the English throne, that of his first born, Robert, Duke of Normandy in favour of 'William the Red and Henry, his second and third brothers': *I*, p. 134.

Even *too* fair at times. Think how lightly, for example, he treats Prince John, who gets off scot-free, not even upbraided for his treachery, but is encouraged to take refuge with Queen Eleanor ('thou wert best go to our mother ... and abide with her until men's minds are pacified', *I*, p. 395). Beaumanoir, of course, is invited to share the King's 'hospitality' (*I*, p. 393) – or take his leave, which he does, willingly, if in a huff, his 'dignity' (*I*, p. 393) mortally offended. De Bracy slips off to the 'service of Philip of France' (*I*, p. 396) – but so effortlessly that he may very well have been allowed, with royal connivance, to get away. Not that Richard allows all of John's *frondeurs* such leeway; both Malvoisins – Philip and Albert – are 'executed' (*I*, p. 396), while Fitzurse is subjected to 'banishment' (*I*, p. 396). But there *is* a logic to Richard's sentencing *praxis* here, his 'quality of mercy' extending only to those whose punishment (like John's) may be more trouble than their worth, the pains involved clearly outweighing the pleasures. For measure these pains and pleasures, Richard clearly does, meting out his 'afflicative' (execution) or 'restrictive' (relegation, banishment) penalties in a post-Beccarian style redolent of Bentham's *The Rationale of Punishment*.[55] All of which suggests that if Richard is any particular *kind* of sovereign – the one who not only commands, but whose commands are supported by 'corporal' and 'privative' sanctions – then he is, in philosophical terms, a *utilitarian* one in the best Benthamite mode, ever computing even in his punitive capacity the 'calculus of felicity', and its yield of 'the greatest happiness for the greatness number'.[56]

Utilitarian? Richard? The Lionheart, a ... *Benthamite*?! The cultural legal reader – let alone Scott or Bentham scholar – might very well look askance at this characterisation, especially in light of the fact that the text goes out of its way to render Richard anything *but* Benthamic or utility driven: as 'rash and romantic' (*I*, p. 401), rather than rational; as capricious, rather than calculating; as egotistic, rather than altruistic. This, of course, is precisely the sort of double-edged critique that Marx,[57] as well as numerous other left-wing pundits of law and politics (critical legal studies for example), have lodged against utilitarianism generally[58] and Benthamism

---

55 J. Bentham, *The Rationale for Punishment*, London: R. Heward, 1830.
56 A principle first adumbrated in Bentham, *A Comment*. Later and more fully developed in *IPML*.
57 K. Marx, *Capital: A Critique of Political Economy*, S. Moore and E. Aveling (trans.), F. Engels (ed.), New York: International Publishers, 1967, vol. 1, p. 416.
58 Especially in its modern incarnation, law-and-economics. For the definitive critique of that movement from a Lacanian and feminist perspective, see J. L. Schroeder's brilliant book, *The Triumph of Venus: The Erotics of the Market*, Berkeley: University of California Press, 2004.

specifically. Namely, that its claims to promote 'the greatest good for the greatest number' can all too easily turn into looking out for number one, utility's distributivist remit becoming in the process, its reverse; that is, an allocative heuristic, gauging the margins, testing possible substitutes and otherwise charting the never-ending circuit of goods in a system hardwired for the 'wealth maximisation' of its autonomic 'free agents'. Here, then, is the bottom line of utility; lurking behind its notion of the collective's 'greatest good', is a fundamentally self-interested subject, incapable of thinking beyond anything but his *own* 'felicific calculations', indeed fortuitous *speculations* in commerce, finance and property. A subject, in short, very much like Scott who, despite his play-acting as the 'Laird of Abbotsford', was, first and foremost, Britain's most (and least) successful literary *entrepreneur*, his eye squarely fixed on the main chance, knowing exactly how many pence were in a pound and never letting his aristocratic affectations get in the way of his intensely *bourgeois* love of lucre.[59]

So it is Scott, capitalist of letters *and* Tory nostagist, who not only anticipates but goes well beyond Marx's (and other radicals') critique of Bentham, seeing through the deeply conflicted *nature* of utility as much as utility's equally problematic notion of *nature*. 'Nature has placed mankind', writes Bentham in his celebrated opening of *Introduction to the Principles and Morals of Legislation*, 'under the governance of two masters, *pain* and *pleasure*'.[60] Here nature is neither a gift from God (*lex natura*) nor a trace of the social contract ('natural rights'), but rather a material construct of *nurture*: a 'family romance' of punishment (the Lacanian paternal 'No!') and reward (the Kleinian maternal breast) which attracts, indeed solicits cathexes, be they one's deepest held desires or intensely felt dreams: in short, *fantasy*. In this psychoanalytic sense, is there anything more 'natural' than utility, and its imaginary of pleasure and pain, its fantasmatic law 'written on the body', as much as inscribed in our minds, both conscious and unconscious? This psychical point is important because it explains why utility is so *reversible*, its Kant-like rational calculations – a kind of arith-

---

59 For Scott on money, as well as his extensive printing and publishing endeavours (initially successful but ultimately ruinous), one has only to consult the many excellent biographies on the 'author of Waverley'. See, for example: J. G. Lockhart, *Memoirs of the Life of Sir Walter Scott*, Boston: Mifflin and Co., 1901; R. H. Hutton, *Sir Walter Scott*, London: Macmillan, 1929; H. J. C. Grierson, *Sir Walter Scott*, New York: Clarendon Press, 1979; D. Daiches, *Sir Walter Scott and his World*, London: Thames & Hudson, 1971; C. Orman, *The Wizard of the North: The Life of Sir Walter Scott*, London: Hodder & Stoughton, 1973.
60 J. Bentham, *An Introduction to the Principles of Morals and Legislation*, J. H. Burns and H. L. Hart (eds), London: Athlone Press, 1970, p. 11.

metical 'categorical imperative' – all too easily transmogrifying *à la* Lacan into something like Sade's transgressive *jouissance* in which, under its superegoic injunction 'Enjoy!', pleasure is taken as pain, and pain as pleasure. Here, utility-as-fantasy turns into, as Slavoj Žižek would put it, a *plague*,[61] afflicting all with its psychotic delusions of putative happiness. To that end, is there a more vivid depiction of the *victim* of such a 'plague of fantasies' than *Ivanhoe's* character of Bois-Guilbert, who undergoes a veritable Kant/Sade transformation here, his reason turning into passion; his judgement, into abandon; his law, into crime? A metamorphosis which, for most of the text's other characters remains unseen – all other characters, that is, except one. That character who *sees* is, of course, *Rebecca*.

### Throwing the Baby out with the Bathwater: *Ivanhoe's* Exile of Ethics (Rebecca) and Morality (Beaumanoir)

In fact, Rebecca turns out to be the only character in *Ivanhoe* gifted with *second* sight, envisioning not only what happens in front of her (such as the siege of Torquilstone) but what lies ahead, in futurity. Think of how clearly she apprehends the perilous position that English Jewry occupies, today royal favourites, tomorrow the mob's target: 'Like Damocles at his celebrated banquet, Rebecca perpetually beheld, amid ... gorgeous display, the sword which was suspended over the heads of her people' (*I*, p. 195). Moreover, this perspicacity is never obscured by ameliorations in the Jews' status, however tangible and durable they may seem: 'the pomp and wealth ... which she witnessed in the houses of ... wealthy Hebrews, had not blinded her to the precarious circumstances under which they were enjoyed' (*I*, p. 195). Nor is this insight dimmed by promises of protection which, however sincerely intended, always turn out to be false, like that entreaty which opened this chapter and closes *Ivanhoe*; namely, Rowena's impassioned plea that Rebecca remain in England, renounce her faith ('your unhappy Law', *I*, p. 400) and live as her 'sister' (*I*, p. 401) under the protection of not only Ivanhoe but the king himself, who – as noted at the start of this chapter – is ever 'just and generous' (*I*, p. 399). This blandishment falls, quite rightly, on deaf ears here. For Rebecca knows, more than anyone else, just how easily this 'justice' can become scapegoating, this 'generosity', genocide because of a fundamental flaw, a basic *lack* in utility itself.

What is this lack? It is nothing less than the *ethical* principle itself, and its desire for 'the desire of the Other'. Surely, if this principle is embodied

---

61  S. Žižek, *The Plague of Fantasies*, London: Verso, 1997.

anywhere in the text, then it is in that sublime, indeed Levinasian 'face of the Other': that of Rebecca herself, and her much commented upon physiognomy. With its 'brilliancy of ... eyes' (*I*, p. 72), its 'superb arch of ... eyebrows' (*I*, p. 72) and its 'well formed aquiline nose' (*I*, p. 72), this visage becomes the text's principal site of desire, its Antigone-like ethics taking the form of 'Do not give up on your desire!'.[62] Rebecca, however, does more than en-*visage* desire's ethical principal; she *enacts* it, using her knowledge of medicine to heal the sick, be they rich (Ivanhoe) or poor (like the lame Higg, 'son of Snell', *I*, p. 525), arousing in each *their* desire.[63] So Rebecca's desiring (and desired) ethics operates on the level of the singular – or 'the One' – at variance with, indeed in bold contrast to 'the Many' of utility, whose quantum of the group ('the greatest number') threatens to obliterate the needs of the individual as its 'greatest good'. This is why Rebecca *must* leave England; her departure is prompted as much by the violence of what will soon be that nation's organising principle – *utilitas* – as its people. For utility and its apostles – Lord Brougham, James Mill, Edwin Chadwick – are soon to preside over (in the 1820s, and onwards), and reverse what by the *annus horribilus* of 1818[64] has become the parlous 'condition of England', carrying out a reformist agenda – in politics, education, public welfare, economy *and* law – that will lay the groundwork for the progressive Victorian administrative state-to-come.[65]

The price to be paid for this 'progress', however, is tremendous, teleology (collective wellbeing) ever trumping deontology (individual rights) by sacrificing the interests of the minority to those of the majority – a competition which is over before the contest even begins. For these so-called 'competing' interests are neither coincident with, nor reconcilable under utility, their failure to resolve – other than in the crass victory of majoritarianism – constituting that principle's 'fundamental contradiction', if not fatal flaw. One wonders how the Reformers ever hoped to pull

---

62 J. Lacan, 'The Paradoxes of Ethics or Have You Acted in Conformity with Your Desire?', in J.-A. Miller (ed.) and D. Porter (trans.), *The Seminar of Jacques Lacan: Book VII The Ethics of Psychoanalysis 1959–1960*, New York: W. W. Norton, 1992, p. 314.
63 After all it is Higg, 'resolute in the service of his benefactress' (Scott, *Ivanhoe*, p. 334), who delivers Rebecca's scroll demanding a champion to Isaac at York. And of course it is Ivanhoe who, to the end of his days, indulges his 'recollection of Rebecca's beauty and magnanimity' (ibid. p. 401).
64 J. Chandler, *England in 1819: The Politics of Literary Culture and the Case of Romantic Historicism*, Chicago: University of Chicago Press, 1998.
65 O. MacDonagh, 'The Nineteenth-Century Revolution in Government: A Reappraisal', *History Journal* 1, 1958, 52–67.

off their utilitarian *coup d'état* with such a lopsided scale, the excessive majoritarian weight of the 'greatest happiness' principle forever tipping the social balance in favour of the plural rather than the singular, opening the way for a law that forcibly assimilates the individual into the group, brutally dissolves the One into the Many – which, paradoxically, turns out to be a One of a particular kind, the egotist. Not surprisingly, it is the reactionary Scott who provides a critique of Reform's collective *violence* and the 'tragic choices' its legislative yardstick, utility, necessitates; but in terms – and herein lies the *real* surprise – which eschew conservatism's communitarianism and which *out*-reform the Reformers by suggesting, in Rebecca's departure, the *re*gress utility's *pro*gress may entail for an individual who, quite simply, does good *for others* as her own 'greatest happiness'. That individual does not figure in utility's calculations because, by its profoundly self-regarding measure, no such person exists. Or should exist. Because in the collectivity Reform creates, everyone is a stranger to another, released from the ties of *sittlichkeit*, lacking responsibility, even connection. This is why Rebecca votes with her feet, rejecting the false equivalence that her 'ethics of the good' are to the social part, what the Benthamite sovereign's are to the social whole, the latter merely aggregating the former – a critique of utility that holds, I would argue, not only if she goes, but *stays*.

Imagine an alternative ending to *Ivanhoe*, one where Rebecca opted to 'stay on': doubtless the Reformers would restrict her sense of the good to the pursuit of her *own* happiness – maximising her *own* pleasure, minimising her *own* pains – because 'sympathy'[66] for *others'* pain or pleasure, *others'* happiness falls outside the utilitarian remit. Even if Rebecca was permitted to practice this other-directed 'sympathy' as a healer, then surely the Reformers, by reason of their utilitarian jurisprudence – at least in its Austinian second generation – would be obliged to *professionalise* that practice, reducing her 'ethics of care' to a protocol of conduct: in short, to a legal *letter* that would kill the ethical *spirit*. For that is precisely where, in spite of all its high-flown flummery about the utility, 'the calculus of felicity', and 'the greatest good for the greatest number', the Benthamic project leads; that is, to the dead letters of John Austin's legal positivism which, in disconnecting the law from (largely faith-based) morality – imaged by Scott in the banishment of Beaumanoir – effectively throws the

---

66 'Among principles adverse to that of utility, that which at this day seems to have most influence in matters of government, is what may be called the principle of sympathy and antipathy' (J. Bentham, J. H. Burns and H. L. A. Hart (eds), *An Introduction to the Principles of Morals and Legislation*, London: Athlone Press, 1970, p. 21 and see also pp. 25 and 58).

normative baby (Rebecca) out with the clerical bathwater (the Templars) by proclaiming law's formal autonomy not only from Ecclesia but *ethics* itself. This move leaves Rebecca caught, as Lacan would phrase it, *entre deux morts*: between a death in the positivist Symbolic (with her desire legislated, her ethics codified) and a death in the pogrom of the Real (with her 'body in pain', consumed by the flames of the English version of the *auto da fé*).

No wonder then that Moorish Spain, clearly no paradise,[67] is so much more attractive to Rebecca – even if this refuge means the renunciation of her sexuality, emblematised in the sparkling diamonds (*I*, p. 400) – the jewel of *eros*? – with which she gifts Rowena during their last meeting. For there Rebecca announces her intention to embrace the life of a saint, albeit a *Jewish* one (a medieval Edith Stein?), who will perform 'good works' amongst 'the sick', 'the hungry' and 'the distressed' (*I*, p. 401). That is, Rebecca will *universalise* – rather than merely collectivise – what has hitherto remained individualised; specifically, her *ethics*, now pluralised across 'the Many' and no longer restricted to, but never ignoring the singularity of 'the One'. In so doing, Rebecca anticipates and becomes the type of Jew whom Marx said in *On the Jewish Question* would go beyond Judaism's particularity, beyond its religio-identic difference, looking forward instead to a new form of humanity: an empathic 'species'-being who is connected rather than separate, caring rather than calculating, ethical rather than utilitarian. All of which portends the possibility a new law, as radicalised as it is socialised, the dissemination of which awaits Rebecca's *return*. This is why I conclude, like the romances of old, with a dream vision: of Rebecca as a crusading jurisprude, returning to England, armed with a new legal ethics and ready to throw down her juridical gauntlet, challenging Bentham and his heirs to a jurisprudential joust. At which final tournament of the law, the clarion call of this Knight of the Fair Countenance would be a novel judgement that proclaims to the hitherto closed kingdom of legal positivism, 'Ethico-legal subjects unite! You have nothing to lose but your utilitarian egotism!'

---

67 Where 'peace and protection' are secured only by the payment of 'ransom' to 'the Moslem' (*I*, p. 399).

CHAPTER 4

# The Monstrous Body of the Law: Wollstonecraft vs. Shelley

## The Alchemy of Romanticism and Rights: The 'New (Legal) Prometheus' of *Frankenstein*

Romanticism reinvents rights. That is the principal claim which this chapter makes, even if – as must be acknowledged at the outset – it is not entirely new. For rights scholarship[1] has long traced its descent from that 'most wanted' of usual Romantic suspects, Rousseau – and behind him, in *francophonie*, Montesquieu, Voltaire and d'Alembert (not to mention, in the anglophone world, Paine, Locke and Hobbes). What, however, distinguishes this chapter, setting *its* central claim off from others, *making it new*, is this: that rights' rich and strange 'alchemy' of reinvention is derived from *an(O)ther* Romanticism, one that is often sidelined if not overlooked altogether; specifically, the *feminist* Romanticism of Mary Wollstonecraft and Mary Shelley. I shall argue that this mother–daughter duo, each exemplary of 'first' and 'second' generation Romanticism, are engaged in an intertextual debate over the nature, content and efficacy of rights discourse, thereby rendering a *novel judgement* that reconceives that discourse's origins and ends. This chapter's second section establishes the terms for this debate by arguing for a legal, specifically *jurisprudential* reading of

---

1 See, for example: G. Robertson, *Crimes Against Humanity: The Search for Global Justice*, London: Penguin Press, 1999, pp. 1–10.

Shelley's *Frankenstein*;[2] that is, a reading in which rights are allegorised in the figure of Frankenstein's monster, and thereby critiqued as the 'monstrous body of the law'. In the third section, I will contextualise this critique of rights, locating *Frankenstein* as a contrary reaction to the previous generation's over-enthusiastic embrace of rights. Sections four and five will situate these two texts – *Frankenstein* and *A Vindication of the Rights of Women*[3] – within a psychoanalytic frame, advancing the thesis that Frankenstein's monster is the 'return of the repressed' body which liberalism, during the French Revolution, first disavowed, then dispatched by regicide and finally supplanted by a disembodied rights discourse.

Hijacked in the next generation by the Industrial Revolution's strong contract and property imperatives, this rights discourse was re-embodied in the early nineteenth-century around the figure of the Capitalist, whose fetish, even 'symptom' rights were (and are). In the sixth section, I will read *Frankenstein* against this immediate backdrop of Capital's hegemonisation of rights discourse, arguing that Frankenstein and his monster, as creator and created, are analogous to that 'New (Legal) Prometheus' – the bourgeois-liberal and his rights. I will argue that *Frankenstein* offers two critiques of this relationship by enacting, through character, setting and plot, two political positions: first, the organic–conservative position, whereby rights (figured in the monster) are seen as destroyer of its creator, the *ancien régime* of the *philosophes* as much as the aristocrats (figured in both Victor Frankenstein and the De Laceys); second, the proto-Marxist position, where rights are seen as not only destroying their creator (Victor) but *themselves*, the created (staged in the last scene of the text where the monster sails off to certain death, accompanying the dead Frankenstein's funeral pyre). Finally, in the seventh section, I will return to a comparative account of Wollstonecraft's and Shelley's texts, situating *A Vindication of the Rights of Women* and *Frankenstein* within the feminist problematic of rights, and arguing that the intertextual debate in which they are engaged may provide, when read holistically, a way out of the philosophical impasses which afflict rights discourse – is it universal or particular? A symptom or a solution? – as much today as it did in their day. So the stakes are high in the novel judgements that Wollstonecraft's and Shelley's respective texts assay because, in their rehabilitation of an explicitly feminist legal and literary

---

2 M. Shelley, *Frankenstein: or The Modern Prometheus*, M. Hindle (ed.), London: Penguin Books, 2003. Hereafter referred to as *F*.

3 M. Wollstonecraft, *A Vindication of the Rights of Woman*, C. H. Poston (ed.), New York: Norton, 1988. Hereafter referred to as *VRW*.

history for rights discourse, they hold out the promise not just of a new critique but of a new *praxis* of rights.

### 'I Shunned My Fellow-Creatures as If Guilty of a Crime' (*F*, P. 55): The Scene of Frankenstein's Crime

One of the most striking features of Mary Shelley's *Frankenstein* is its emphasis on crime, particularly the crime of murder. In fact, the narrative action of the novel consists, largely, in a series of murders: that of Victor Frankenstein's younger brother, William; his best friend, the 'Orientalist', Henry Clerval; and, most dramatically, his fiancée, Elizabeth. All these murders are worthy of any of cinema's serial killers, some examples of which include 'Jigsaw' in *Saw* (2004, dir. James Wan), 'Casanova' in *Kiss the Girls* (1997, dir. Gary Fleder), Daryl Lee in *Copycat* (1995, dir. Jon Amiel), the nameless killer (played by Kevin Spacey) in *Seven* (1995, dir. David Fincher) or, finally, either 'Buffalo Bill' or Dr Hannibal Lecter in *The Silence of the Lambs* (1990, dir. Jonathan Demme). And in their own way, each of these celluloid characters are the imaginative descendants of Frankenstein and, particularly, his monster; for the monster is, with Maturin's Melmouth, one of the first literary serial killers and Shelley's novel is the *ur*-text of the genre, establishing its most familiar conventions. Principal among these is the act of flight and pursuit across a bleak, nightmarish landscape, usually rendered in contemporary films as a dystopic, *noir*-ish, even *Blade Runner*-esque cityscape, an urban variation upon the novel's opening and closing chapters set in the Arctic wastes. Next is the *mise-en-scène* of the 'chamber of horrors', deriving ultimately from Frankenstein's dark, garret laboratory at Ingolstadt ('a solitary chamber or rather cell, at the top of the house, and separated from all the other apartments by a gallery and a staircase, I kept my workshop of filthy creation' *F*, p. 59), but usually transposed to some sort of prosaic subterranean space like a suburban basement where the killer performs his ghoulish labours on the 'body in pain': torturing his victims, preserving their remains, even constructing artefacts out of these remains. Finally, there is the obsession with the images of the dead, conventionally figured in contemporary films by the relentless photographing and photographs of the body of the victim which are displayed so often that they take on the same sort of 'frenzy of the visible' that Linda Williams equates with pornography,[4] and which echo in the novel not only in ghastly

---

4 L. Williams, *Hard Core: Power, Pleasure, and the 'Frenzy of the Visible'*, Berkeley: University of California Press, 1989.

spectacle of the dead Elizabeth on her wedding night ('She was there, lifeless and inanimate, thrown across the bed, her head hanging down, and her pale and distorted features half covered by her hair ... The murderous mark of the fiends' grasp was on her neck, and the breath had ceased to issue from her lips', F, p. 189) but also in the repeated references to the portrait of Frankenstein's own dead mother (F, p. 75, p. 138).

Crime, however, is not *Frankenstein*'s sole focus; detection, forensics and, indeed, punishment figure just as prominently in the text. In fact, the whole legal process is as vividly dramatised by the novel as the law's transgression is in the murderous rampage of the monster. So vivid is this dramatisation, it underwrites the principal claim which this chapter makes; that is, that *Frankenstein* can be read as an *allegory* of the law. Indeed, its treatment of the law is not even as oblique as allegory because much of the novel explicitly represents, as it did with the scene of crime, the physical site of the law's theatre and its discursive dramas: the courtroom. Three such curial examples are provided by the text. First depicted is the trial in Switzerland of Justine, a trusted domestic of the Frankenstein household, wrongfully accused, found guilty and hanged for the death of her young charge, William (F, pp. 79–82). Second, there is the Irish discovery (F, pp. 169–171) and arraignment (F, pp. 175–176) of Victor Frankenstein himself for the murder of Henry Clerval. Significantly, Frankenstein is acquitted here, a verdict which might be read as a vindication of British justice – Ireland then 'enjoying' the benefit of English common law represented by Mr Kirwin – particularly when compared to the gross miscarriage of Justine's Continental, civilian-based and inquisitorial-style trial with its absence of the presumption of innocence: 'I perceived that the popular voice and the countenances of the judges had already condemned my unhappy victim' (F, p. 82). Third and last, there is the interview in the judicial chambers (F, pp. 192–194) – a kind of courtroom scene behind the scenes – with the Genevan magistrate where, treating the magistrate as if he was sort of Calvinist father-confessor, Frankenstein makes a full confession of, and seeks a kind of judicial absolution for the whole diabolical business of his creation and its murderous consequences: 'I trembled with excess of agitation as I said this; there was a frenzy in my manner, and something, I doubt not, of that haughty fierceness which the martyrs of old are said to have possessed' (F, pp. 193–194).

*Frankenstein* is not, however, just a representation of the workings of the legal system. The novel goes much further in that it not only represents but *enacts* the legal system's fundamental discursive processes in the text's overarching narrative act. What is that central narrative act if nothing less than the *production* of a body? This production goes far beyond either the act of rending, eviscerating and torturing 'the body in pain' (in the manner of the 'serial killer' subtext of the novel adverted to in the opening paragraph of this section), or the act of trying, cross-examining and executing the body of punishment (in the manner of the 'legal process' subtext of the novel referred to in the second paragraph); instead, this act takes the form of the actual *construction* of the body. That construction is to be understood literally; namely, of how marrow and bone, flesh and blood and all manner of corporeal bits and pieces are put together so as to be regenerated in the manner of Erasmus Darwin's experiments, 'who preserved a piece of vermicelli in a glass case, till by some extraordinary means it began to move' (F, p. 8), referred to by Mary Shelley in her introduction to the text. Shelley's introduction, however, raises a further question, one which poses a preliminary challenge to my thesis: How is this narrative act of bodily construction at all *legal* when the author's introductory references to Byron and Percy Shelley's discussions of the 'experiments of Dr. Darwin' and 'galvanism' (F, p. 8) (to which she was a 'devout but nearly silent listener', F, p. 8) squarely situates the text's genesis within the frame of science? My claim for a jurisprudential reading, however, is based not so much on what the text actually tells the reader as what it *shows* her.

What the reader is shown in *Frankenstein* is certainly not an experiment recognisable as scientific – as indeed Darwin's were; in fact, the situation is quite the reverse because here both the language and procedures of science are conspicuous by their absence in Frankenstein's laboratory.[5] For example, when hovering on the threshold of his breakthrough, Frankenstein refers to his 'supernatural enthusiasm' (F, p. 50) for this act of bodily construction, a process he analogises to 'magic' (F, p. 51). This language recalls the young Victor's flirtations with alchemy and its practitioners – 'Cornelius Agrippa, Albertus Magnus and Paracelsus, the lords of my imagination' (F, p. 40) – a mode of learning and a line of scholarship at complete odds with, and in sharp contrast to the Enlightenment rationalism of Ingolstadt University, exemplified in his tutors, Krempe and Waldman. This mystification, rhetorical and otherwise, surrounding Frankenstein's act of bodily construction is further heightened and, thereby, obscured by the fact that it is never really dramatised in any technical sense for the reader. The theft of the body parts, their stitching together and their reanimation through the coiled tubing and electrical flashes of the laboratory apparatus are more cinematic rather than novelistic conventions, and

---

5 For a similar point, see: J. Copjec, 'Vampires, Breast-Feeding and Anxiety', in *Read My Desire: Lacan Against the Historicists*, Cambridge, MA: MIT Press, 1994, pp. 124–125.

exist only by way of allusion: 'Who shall conceive the horrors of my secret toil as I dabbled among the unhallowed damps of the grave or tortured the living animal to animate lifeless clay' (F, p. 53). No midnight graveyard forays of resurrection men, let alone scientific protocols are represented here; to the contrary, the monster just comes to life: 'I collected the instruments of life around me, that I might infuse a spark of being into the lifeless thing that lay at my feet. It was already one in the morning... when... I saw the dull yellow eye of the creature open; it breathed hard and a convulsive motion agitated its limbs' (F, p. 56). Even the formula of the discovery remains undisclosed, Frankenstein refusing to reveal it to his auditor, Walton: 'I see by your eagerness and the wonder and hope which your eyes express, my friend, that you expect to be informed of the secret with which I am acquainted; that cannot be: listen patiently until the end of the story, and you will easily perceive why I am reserved upon that subject' (F, p. 51). And this absence of science, either linguistically or technically, suggests, instead, that another kind of construction of the body is taking place: a *social* rather than scientific construction of the body.

### Righting the Revolutionary Body Politic: '*Les Mots, Commes les Choses, Ont Eté des Monstruosities*'[6]

The monster seems to spring *ex nihilo* from Frankenstein's 'fever(ed) imagination' (F, p. 51) an act which recalls, echoes and, indeed, mimics the principal act of bodily construction which this period, broadly conceived of as Romantic, affords. For what Romanticism, and the revolutionary impulses released by it constructs is a new polity, the republic of reason, predicated upon and organised around a new *body*:[7] that of the citizen-subject, the bearer of those liberties, freedoms and equities secured by the social contract and entrenched as the 'rights of man'.[8] But this body, and the polity which it organises, is highly problematic, given that the revolution which inspired its construction was committed to an agenda that, from the first, was profoundly disembodying. This disembodiment takes both literal and figural forms. First, it is literal in the sense that the body in

---

6 J. F. La Harpe, *Du Fanatisme dans la langue révolutionnaire ou de la persécution suscitée par les Barbares du dix-huitième siècle, contre la Religion Chrétienne et ses Ministres*, Paris: Migneret, 1797; cited in L. Hunt, below n. 10, at p. 19.

7 For a more generalised account of the metaphor of the 'body politic', see: E. Kantorowicz, *The King's Two Bodies: A Study in Medieval Political Theology*, Princeton: Princeton University Press, 1957.

8 S. Schama, *Citizens: A Chronicle of the French Revolution*, London: Viking, 1989.

the body politic of the *ancien régime*, condensed in the body of the king, is literally dispatched in the guillotining of King Louis XVI.[9] Second, it is figural[10] in the sense that the revolution inaugurates, in place of the body of the king, the reign of rights, themselves a species of figuration – i.e., language – which are announced in what is, after all, one of the most celebrated of speech acts of the age, the *Declaration of the Rights of Man*.[11] What the illocutionary force of the *Declaration* declares, through the *point de capiton*[12] of rights, is a law of the signifier which, as a signifier, is invested with what Lacan would call the executory force of *coupure*:[13] that is, signification's 'cutting edge'. And what this signifier cuts is nothing less than the body itself – 'the word is the murder of the thing', as Hegel would say[14] – so as to interpellate, in its stead, a subject who is evacuated of drive and drained of need: in short, the rights-bearer.

Given this literal but particularly figural disembodiment of the revolution and, behind it, Romanticism, how can it be said that this historical conjuncture constructs a body, juridical or otherwise? The answer lies in the nature of language, itself double, split between the construction and deconstruction of meaning, a division which one can see at work in the *linguisterie* of rights. For if the language of rights cuts the body in the Real, then that language, as language, reconstructs it in the Symbolic as a figural presence (though literal absence) in much the same way language in Freud's *fort! da!* parable works to restore, by figural substitution (i.e., the exclamation, *fort! da!* accompanying the thrown and recovered spool), the body of his grandson's absent mother.[15] The point being made here is that rights, as a language, *recall* the body to life. This resurrection of the body, however, is

---

9 For an almost Christological reading of the execution, see: C. Lefort, *Democracy and Political Theory*, David Macey (trans.), Minneapolis: University of Minnesota Press, 1988, p. 247.
10 For an explicitly aesthetic – rather than, as here, jurisprudential – reading of the revolution's crisis of representation, see: L. Hunt, *Politics, Culture and Class in the French Revolution*, London: Methuen, 1986.
11 *The French Declaration of the Rights of Man and of the Citizen*, ss.1–17, reproduced in W. Lacquer and B. Rubin (eds), *The Human Rights Reader*, New York: New American Library, 1979, pp. 118–120.
12 Or 'quilting' or 'anchoring point', as Lacan says in 'The Subversion of the Subject and the Dialectic of Desire in the Freudian Unconscious', in J. Lacan, *Ecrits: A Selection*, A. Sheridan (trans.), New York: Norton, 1977, p. 303.
13 Ibid. p. 314.
14 G. W. G. Hegel, *The Phenomenology of Mind*, J. B. Baillie (trans.), London: Allen & Unwin, 1931.
15 S. Freud, 'Beyond the Pleasure Principle', in Peter Gay (ed.), *The Freud Reader*, New York: W. W. Norton, 1995, pp. 599–601.

not real but representational; that is, its revivification is mediated by language itself, namely the tropes of metaphor and metonymy.[16] First, the body is metonymised by rights, cut into bits and pieces of linguistic hands and feet, as well as eyes, ears and mouth. Then, second, these body parts, are metaphorised as, in the latter case (eyes, ears and mouth) in rights of speech, belief and thought; or, in the former case (hands and feet) as rights of movement or association.[17]

This linguistic construction of the body enables the prevailing fantasy of rights discourse; namely, its universalism where rights are deemed to be in every*body* generally but in no*body* in particular. This 'onto-theology' of rights' juridical imaginary – as everywhere and nowhere – links up with, and informs (and is informed by) a specific political project of the Revolution and one strain of Romanticism: that of liberalism. This school of thought promotes a notion of the subject who is, much like that of the *Declaration*'s rights-bearer, an individual whose prevailing feature and overriding value is an autonomy which negates the self (particularly in its reliance upon empty, content-free formulas – such as the Kantian 'categorical imperative') as much as it annuls the social (and its indifference to the 'call of the other'). In locating, however, the *Declaration* within this intellectual context of liberalism, I have rendered problematic the central claim of this chapter. For how is the unmediated, embodied and abjected Real of Frankenstein's monster an allegory of the rights-bearer of the revolution? Particularly when the revolution's liberal–universalist discourse dematerialises the Law's body, substituting in its stead a disembodied, ratiocinative cipher? In short, how are these two figures of Romanticism – the monster and the rights-bearer – connected?

### Romanticism's '*Écriture Féminine*' of the Law: Wollstonecraft as Jurisprude

The connection between the monster and the rights-bearer is supplied, I shall argue, by Mary Shelley's mother, Mary Wollstonecraft. This claim, though, might seem to be a difficult one to sustain given the fact that Shelley never knew her mother, Mary Wollstonecraft having died in childbirth – indeed, at Shelley's birth, or more precisely, a few days after, of puerperal

---

16 R. Jakobson, 'Two Aspects of Language and Two Types of Aphasic Disturbances', in S. Rudy (ed.), *Selected Writings*, vol. 2, The Hague: Mouton, 1971.
17 This semiotic process is more fully developed in: W. MacNeil, 'Law's *Corpus Delicti*: The Fantasmatic Body of Rights Discourse', *Law and Critique* 9(1), 1998, 37–57; and W. MacNeil, 'Taking Rights Symptomatically', *Griffith Law Review* 8(1), 1999, 134–151.

fever on 10 September 1797. Even a cursory acquaintance with Shelley's biography, however, reveals her interest in, indeed her obsession with her mother. Most of this obsession takes the typical, hysterical forms of the nineteenth-century cult of the dead, a pathology which *Frankenstein* dramatises in scenes which highlight the image of Victor's dead mother. For example, upon Victor's return to the family home, subsequent to William's death, he pointedly refers to the presence upon the chimney mantel of 'The picture of my mother', herself depicted 'in an agony of despair, kneeling at the coffin of her dead father' (*F*, p. 75). Interestingly, it is this very image of the mother which provokes William's murder, as the monster confesses to Frankenstein: 'As I fixed my eyes on the child, I saw something glittering on his breast. I took it; it was a portrait of a most lovely woman ... my rage returned: I remembered that I was forever deprived of the delights that such beautiful creatures could bestow' (*F*, p. 138).

These references suggest an almost Marian veneration of the maternal *imago*, and recall another site and style of Marian devotion; namely, that of Mary Wollstonecraft, whose portrait continued to grace the drawing room of the home of her widowed, and then remarried husband, William Godwin (much to the chagrin of his second wife, Jane Vial Clairmont).[18] Indeed, Mary Shelley made something of a shrine of Wollstonecraft's St. Pancras gravesite, to which she would take Shelley as if on pilgrimage.[19] What distinguishes, however, these acts of commemoration from the routine rituals of what Philippe Ariès's calls the 'hour of our death'[20] is Mary Shelley's *reading* of Wollstonecraft's œuvre. As a child and teenager she read her mother's writings over and over again, 'textbooks, stories, her first novel, *Mary*',[21] so that Mary Shelley came to know 'her mother's history in more intimate detail than if Wollstonecraft had lived'.[22] Prominent among this course of reading was Wollstonecraft's *A Vindication of the Rights of Women*. This tract was one of the first (and finest) feminist, but also sociological critiques of rights discourse, a favourite of Mary Shelley's, and, indeed, the very text she was (re)reading, as her journal indicates, while writing *Frankenstein* throughout 1816.[23]

---

18 E. W. Sunstein, *Mary Shelley: Romance and Reality*, Baltimore: Johns Hopkins University Press, 1989, pp. 26–37.
19 Ibid. p. 71.
20 P. Ariès, *The Hour of Our Death*, H. Weaver (trans.), New York: Knopf, 1981.
21 Sunstein, *Mary Shelley*, above n. 18, p. 37.
22 Ibid. p. 53.
23 See the journal entries of Mary Shelley for 7 and 8 December 1816 in M. Shelley, *The Journals of Mary Shelley Vol. I: 1814–1822*, P. Feldman and D. Scott-Kilvert (eds), Oxford: Clarendon Press, 1987, p. 149.

Wollstonecraft's tract inaugurates a long and venerable tradition in the critique of rights. The opening gambit of her proto-critical strategy is to *situate* the autonomous subject of rights, to *particularise* its universalism. In so doing, Wollstonecraft's (and her epigones') critique shows that some-*body* lies behind the discourse of rights 'enjoying' its protection while other bodies lie outside of it, thereby falsifying its claim to be in everybody generally but in nobody in particular. The identity of that somebody is, of course, as Wollstonecraft points out in her prefatory letter to Talleyrand, indicated by the statutory title, *Declaration of the Rights of Man*, thereby excluding 'one half of the human race ... from all participation of government' (*VRW*, p. 5). For the *Declaration*'s liberties, freedoms and equities are, quite literally, the 'rights of man' and, as such, are extended only to men. This androcentricity, however, is not to be confused with the orthodox patriarchy of the *ancien régime*; instead, patriarchy has been reinvented in the 'New Constitution' (*VRW*, p. 5) as the *fraternité* of modernity — what Juliet Flower MacCannell[24] would call the 'regime of the brother'. Wollstonecraft's text argues, implicitly, that the result of this reinvention is, for women, *plus ça change, plus c'est le même chose*, as women are excluded just as much, under the regime of the brother as they are from the 'Law of the Father's Name'.

Here Wollstonecraft's proto-critical legal project becomes more problematic than the contemporary critical legal studies movement of the 1970s and 1980s.[25] While both may make, at least initially, the same critical 'move' — exposing the particular in the universal of rights, the bias in the neutrality of law, the body behind the word of the judgement — ultimately they diverge. Like the earlier Marxist critique of rights, the critical legal studies movement urges an abandonment of this discourse.[26] Wollstonecraft, to the contrary, wants to complete the project of liberalism by redeeming rights through their extension to women (a move aligning her with, in some respects, contemporary critical legal feminism and critical race

---

24 J. F. MacCannell, *The Regime of the Brother: After the Patriarchy*, London: Routledge, 1991.
25 On this movement, see: D. Kairys, *The Politics of Law: A Progressive Critique*, New York: Pantheon Books, 1982. R. Unger, *The Critical Legal Studies Movement*, Cambridge, MA: Harvard University Press, 1986.
26 M. Tushnet, 'An Essay on Rights', *Texas Law Review* 62, 1984, 1386–1404. P. Gabel, 'The Phenomenology of Rights-Consciousness and the Pact of the Withdrawn Selves', *Texas Law Review* 62, 1984, 1563–1600.

theory).[27] Only a certain kind of woman, however, is eligible for this extension; specifically, one who belongs, according to Wollstonecraft, to the most 'natural', least artificial sector of society – that is, the *bourgeoisie*: 'I pay particular attention to those in the middle class, because they appear to be in the most natural state' (*VRW*, p. 9). Wollstonecraft introduces this class qualifier because, at the end of the day, she is a classic *bourgeois*-liberal. This is not just a matter of her class allegiances but philosophical preferences. For Wollstonecraft has no problem with what might be called the *langue* of rights; namely, their systemic imperatives of *bourgeois* autonomous individualism, an organising principle located at the lowest level of their discursive deep structure: 'Independence I have long considered as a grand blessing of life, the basis of every virtue' (*VRW*, p. 3). The only problem for Wollstonecraft concerning rights discourse is that women do not as yet speak it. So the problem for her is as follows: how, then, can women be given a 'voice' (*VRW*, p. 5)? What mechanism will enable them to speak?

This is not only a problem for Wollstonecraft specifically but for liberalism generally; namely, how to allow the particular – not just women, but other forms of 'subalterneity': people of colour, the differently abled, the gay–lesbian alliance, etc. – to speak without changing the universal? Or to alter the metaphor: how to allow the particular to *see* itself in rights' looking glass, hitherto monopolised by the race, class and gender dominant's focalisation? I use this metaphor of the mirror, and its suggestion of an Imaginary hooked onto, and interpenetrating the Symbolic, purposively as it captures in two senses the nub of Wollstonecraft's (and, indeed, the liberal-inspired) critique of the law. This critique preserves, at one and the same time, the law's claims to universalism, and its controlling value of autonomy, all the while acknowledging the particular's exclusion. First, women have been excluded hitherto from the law because its linguistically mediated and constructed body, metonymised and metaphorised by rights, has been 'misrecognised'[28] by those men largely in control of the signifier, 'rights', as their own body, centred around their phallus-as-penis. Second, this particular 'misrecognition' has been able to cloak itself as a universal precisely because this act of focalisation is occurring along a Symbolic–Imaginary

---

27 Especially P. Williams, *The Alchemy of Race and Rights*, Cambridge, MA: Harvard University Press, 1991. Also, R. Delgado, 'Critical Legal Studies and the Realities of Race – Does the Fundamental Contradiction Have a Corollary', *Harvard Civil Rights–Civil Liberties Law Review* 23, 1988, 407.
28 J. Lacan, 'The Mirror Stage as Formative of the Function of the I as revealed in Psychoanalytic Experience', in *Ecrits: A Selection*, above n. 12, p. 6.

axis. So much so that those very men who control the politico-juridical process of rights' discursive formation, interpretation and application can say of the body that this discourse constructs in the Imaginary that this is 'not me' – that is, someone or something different, an Other, an imago of the fantasmatic body – at the very same moment that they can say 'That's me being hailed, that's my image, my reflection in the mirror'.

Wollstonecraft's solution to this monopolisation of the body imago of rights by men (who disavow it as their imago at the very moment that they proclaim it to be theirs) is not to break the mirror, like some rights-sceptical, critical legal or Marxist Lady of Shalott. Rather, Wollstonecraft wants to reposition women in front of it, and away from the mirror in which they now focalise: 'But, till men become attentive to the duty of a father, it is vain to expect women to spend that time in their nursery which they, 'wise in their generation, choose to spend at their glass' (*VRW*, p. 6). The problem with this mirror that women currently focalise into is that it casts a reflection of woman as a figure of seduction soliciting the male gaze, 'that impudent dross of gallantry ... which makes many men stare insultingly at every female they meet' (*VRW*, p. 125). Such a 'lookist' form of 'visual pleasure' confers upon women the dubious power of 'illicit privileges' (*VRW*, p. 6); that is, a status which was enjoyed particularly, according to Wollstonecraft, by the concupiscent Frenchwomen of the old regime and its decadent purlieus, the salon culture.[29] But more than rendering women seductive to others, this mirror seduces women *themselves* with the allures of the image – specifically, their own reflections.

Hence, Wollstonecraft's repeated warnings throughout the text on the dangers of female vanity (*VRW*, pp. 121–131, pp. 186–187) because it is precisely this vanity – this absorption in the mirror-image of themselves and their own beauty – which prevents women from breaking the spell of the Imaginary and entering subjectivity, remaining like 'uncivilized beings who have not yet extended the dominion of the mind' (*VRW*, p. 187).

---

29 Wollstonecraft writes, 'In France there is undoubtedly a more general diffusion of knowledge than in any part of the European world, and I attribute it, in a great measure, to the social intercourse which has long subsisted between the sexes'. However, this advancement of women is actually a retrograde one, because, as she continues, 'in France the very essence of sensuality has been extracted to regale the voluptuary, and a kind of sentimental lust has prevailed, which, together with a system of duplicity that the whole tenor of their political and civil government taught, have given a sinister sort of sagacity to the French character properly termed finesse' (VRW, p. 4). Later she will write, 'In France... men have been the luxurious despots, and women the crafty ministers' (ibid. p. 167).

Wollstonecraft urges such a break from the Imaginary and a concomitant entry into Symbolic by the vouchsafing of rights to women, an act enabling them to take their place alongside men in the realisation of autonomy and, hence, virtue: 'Let woman share the rights and she will emulate the virtues of man' (*VRW*, p. 194). But this 'Machiavellian moment'[30] which the text longs for – the assumption of virtue, the securing of autonomy, the enjoyment of rights – will be brought about, so Wollstonecraft implies, only when women look into another mirror; specifically, that of the law's Symbolic–Imaginary where, like men, they will 'misrecognise' themselves as the body imago reflected back by rights' specularity.

This solution to the problematic of rights – repositioning the excluded particular into the position of the hitherto dominant focaliser – informs not just Wollstonecraft's politics, but, oddly, that strain of contemporary 'identity politics' which would counterpose notions of 'difference' against Wollstonecraft's claims of 'sameness':[31] 'For man and woman, the truth', but also themselves impliedly, 'must be the same' (*VRW*, p. 51). Both the 'sameness' and 'difference' feminism represented, respectively, by Wollstonecraft and 'identity politics', argue for the efficacy of rights, a strategy about which many post-identitarian feminists, like Renata Salecl, are highly ambivalent, claiming it sets the groundwork for the current 'hyperinflation'[32] of rights where all identities, problems and issues are translated into its peculiar discursive terms, and are thereby stymied by the impasse of its call ('I have my rights!') and response ('No, I have my rights!'). But this *excess* of rights which we confront today gets ahead of the historical story being recounted here. For even the most rights-sceptical of the post-identitarians – myself included – would agree with Wollstonecraft that the problem facing her was not too *many* rights but too *few*. 'The *rights* of humanity have been thus confined to the male line from Adam downwards' (*VRW*, p. 87). Indeed, the deleterious effects of this paucity of rights can be seen in women, for whom exclusion from rights, from the Law and from the Symbolic has had the effect of making them '*monstrous*': 'Such a woman is ... a(n) irrational monster' (*VRW*, p. 44), writes Wollstonecraft of upper-class women specifically; though this

---

30 J. G. A. Pocock, *The Machiavellian Moment: Florentine Political Thought and the Atlantic Republican Tradition*, Princeton: Princeton University Press, 1975.
31 Consider, for example, Wollstonecraft's claim that the mind has no gender, against the recent rehabilitation of 'women's ways of knowing'. See M. F. Belenky, *Women's Ways of Knowing: The Development of Self, Voice and Mind*, New York: Basic Books, 1986.
32 R. Salecl, 'Why is Woman a Symptom of Rights?', in *The Spoils of Freedom: Psychoanalysis and Feminism After the Fall of Socialism*, London: Routledge, 1994, p. 155.

observation could be extended, generally, to all women who, through their deprivation of rights, are forced by the 'cunning of exertion' (*VRW*, p. 6) to exercise 'lawless power' (*VRW*, p. 44).

The image of monstrosity deployed by Wollstonecraft here is very interesting in terms of narrative prolepsis, anticipating but also providing a very neat tropological segue into the most famous text of her daughter, Mary Shelley: specifically, *Frankenstein*. This image, in fact, links both texts inextricably, mediating an intertextual relationship of not only literary echoes but also philosophical cross-references and, even, political cross-purposes. For if Wollstonecraft is arguing, through this image, that the *exclusion* of women from rights discourse renders them monstrous, then Mary Shelley's position is the reverse; that is, women's (and, indeed, anyone's) *inclusion* into the language of rights renders them just as much a *monster*, a mutation graphically embodied in Victor Frankenstein's creation. This creation is a literalisation of the body-imago implicit in rights discourse which is deformed, distorted and rendered monstrous – *the monstrous body of the law* – in its hijacking by the socio-economic dominant of the period. Furthermore, this hijacking renders problematic any easy liberal rehabilitation of this discourse, disabling strategies like Wollstonecraft's reformist substitution of one imago for another: for example, the body imago of women for men.

## Frankenstein Was framed! Fair Cops and the Framing of Interpretation

This theme of 'return' – of the abjected body which comes back to disrupt, arrest, even annihilate the very subject which rights 'hail' in its play of imagos – evokes a specific theoretical frame. For an argument organised around, initially, a disavowal of the body (dramatised in the Revolution's installation of a 'lack' in the figural body politic by executing the literal body of the king), then, second, its psychic recurrence (represented in the body's imaginary recall by the new Jacobin socio-symbolic codified in the *Declaration of the Rights of Man*) and, finally, its *actual* return (graphically staged in the maniacal rampage of *Frankenstein*'s monster) mimics the narrative organisation of one of modernity's *grand récits*. I refer, of course, to the meta-narrative of psychoanalysis;[33] specifically, its master story of trauma and repression, psychic disturbance and return, and, lastly, a full-

---

33 As Freud said: '[T]he theory of repression is the pillar upon which the edifice of psychoanalysis rests', S. Freud, 'The History of the Psychoanalytic Movement', in A. A. Brill (trans. and ed.), *The Basic Writings of Sigmund Freud*, New York: Modern Library, 1995, p. 907.

blown 'return of the repressed' in symptomatic form, embodied as a corporeal disruption or deformity – a cough, a tic, a paralysis. It is, however, really with this last scene in the three-part drama of psychoanalysis that this chapter's jurisprudential reading of *Frankenstein* is concerned: namely, that of the bodily inscribed symptom.[34] For it is my central contention that Frankenstein's monster is *that symptom*, that 'return of the repressed' body which deforms and/or disrupts the now supposedly disembodied, but imaginarily re-embodied rights discourse, resituating that discourse, along an axis, as Slavoj Žižek might put it, of the Symbolic–Real (the Order of the Thing, rupturing discourse) rather than the Symbolic–Imaginary (the Order of the Image, interpenetrating discourse).[35]

Of what trauma, though, is Frankenstein's monster, as the 'monstrous body of the law', symptomatic? Franco Moretti[36] has argued, persuasively, that the trauma to which Frankenstein is a response is Capital, and the antagonisms in the socio-Symbolic which it unleashes not just *in* the real but *as* the Real.[37] For, of course, the historical backdrop surrounding *Frankenstein*'s conditions of production were just as conflicted, just as discordant as those of Wollstonecraft's *A Vindication of the Rights of Woman*. The latter, however, was a response to a *political* revolution, the French Revolution of the 1790s, while the former, composed in 1817 and published in that *annus horribilus*, 1819[38] can be read as a response to the

---

34 S. Freud, 'Psychopathology of Everyday Life', in A. A. Brill (trans. and ed.) *The Basic Writings of Sigmund Freud*, New York: Modern Library, 1995, pp. 97–109. See also, S. Žižek, *Enjoy Your Symptom! Jacques Lacan In Hollywood and Out*, London: Routledge, 1992, for a contemporary Lacanian update of this classic Freudian notion. See also: S. Žižek, 'The Ideological *Sinthome*', in *Looking Awry: An Introduction to Jacques Lacan through Popular Culture*, Cambridge, MA: MIT Press, 1991, pp. 130–140. As well: S. Žižek, 'How Did Marx Invent the Symptom?', in *The Sublime Object of Ideology*, New York: Verso, 1989.
35 For the overlap between the Lacanian Symbolic, Imaginary and Real and the role of the symptom in knotting them together, see: S. Žižek, 'Hegelian Language', in *For They Know Not What They Do: Enjoyment As A Political Factor*, London: Verso, 1991, pp. 111–112 and p. 136.
36 F. Moretti, *Signs Taken For Wonders*, London: Verso, 1983.
37 Here I acknowledge an indebtedness to Ernesto Laclau's concept of class antagonism as the rupture which splits society but the Symbolic Order itself, and from which, as Žižek might add, the Real – as *jouissance* but also trauma – emerges in the real. See: E. Laclau, and C. Mouffe, *Hegemony and Socialist Strategy: Towards a Radical Democratic Politics*, London: Verso, 1985, pp. 122–127. But also: S. Žižek, *The Sublime Object of Ideology*, above n. 34, pp. 161–164.
38 Many thanks to Dr Peter Hutchings in driving home for me the political importance and significance of bibliographic criticism, especially in the differences in the 1818 text of

Industrial Revolution[39] and its economic challenges convulsing Europe but, particularly, Britain in the early nineteenth century.[40] Moretti's reading of *Frankenstein* locates the text squarely within this conjuncture, emphasising its allegory of the class struggle with Frankenstein's monster standing in for the proletariat and Frankenstein, himself, as the *bourgeoisie*.

While endorsing and, indeed, taking onboard Moretti's materialist interpretation, I would situate *Frankenstein*'s allegory of Capitalism on the level of ideology rather than praxis. That is, the allegory operates not so much *externally* in the class struggle as *internally* in the psychic conflict which industrialisation (and its fellow travellers, Enlightenment, Romanticism, modernity, etc.) installs in the liberal subject as both the master and slave of the law, the possessor and the possession of rights, now redefined by Capital as the fetish of property and contract rights. It is this *psychomachia* within the liberal subject which is exteriorised and figured in the conflict between Frankenstein and his monster, as they assume, exchange and reverse roles as victor and victim, pursuer and pursued. In so critiquing liberalism and the liberal subject, the text does more than just locate itself politically; in fact, it positions itself intertextually – specifically, as a critique of an(O)ther of liberalism's foundational texts, *A Vindication of the Rights of Women*, and its advocacy of liberalism's favoured offspring, the subject of rights. For in writing *Frankenstein*, Mary Shelley is, in effect, trying to speak to, and debate with the dead; namely, the dead mother, a point to which I will return when I discuss the mother–daughter context of the novel at the end of my article. Before I do so, however, I want to explore my claim in more depth that *Frankenstein* is a critique of liberalism, a critique which begins by representing, as monstrous, the liberal subject of rights.

---

*Frankenstein* and its 1831 revised edition. Indeed, these two editions respectively privilege and valorise the competing critiques of liberalism – either organic conservative (1831) and critical Marxist (1818) – which I map out later in this chapter.

39 Paul O'Flinn makes this point, but links proletarian agitation – Luddism – to earlier Jacobincal activity. See: P. O'Flinn, 'Production and Reproduction: The Case of *Frankenstein*', in P. Humm, P. Stigant and P. Widdowson (eds), *Popular Fictions: Essays in Literature and History*, London: Methuen, 1986, pp. 199–200.

40 Many literary critics have argued, with equal vigour, that *Frankenstein* is an allegory of the French Revolution. See: R. Paulson, *Representations of Revolution (1789–1820)*, New Haven, CT: Yale University Press, 1983; C. Baldick, *In Frankenstein's Shadow*, Oxford: Clarendon Press, 1987; L. Sterrenburg, 'Mary Shelley's Monster: Politics and Psyche in *Frankenstein*', in G. Levine and U. C. Knoepflmacher (eds), *The Endurance of Frankenstein*, Berkeley: University of California Press, 1979; and F. Botting, *Making Monstrous: Frankenstein, Criticism, Theory*, Manchester: Manchester University Press, 1991.

## Mary Shelley as Critic of Liberalism: Aristocratic *frondeuse* or Marxist Revolutionary?

Two different and, indeed, seemingly irreconcilable critiques of liberalism run in tandem throughout Frankenstein, a doubleness which speaks to Mary Shelley's own conflicted politics. On one hand, she is a kind of proto-Marxist, as a political, social and sexual subversive in her youth but also as the wife and, particularly, daughter of radicals, in fact, the leading English Jacobins of the period, Wollstonecraft and William Godwin. Not only an enthusiastic reader of her mother's work, she was just as much taken with her father's *Caleb Williams, Political Justice* and other texts, the values of which she thoroughly internalised.[41] Change, reform, indeed revolution itself would remain for her throughout her youth and young womanhood, the supreme good. Her girlhood idols were those most 'romantic' of revolutionaries, Toussaint L'Overture and Mme. Roland; and her acquaintances through her father numbered most of the political extremists of the time: socialist Robert Owen, Chartist Francis Place, Irish republican Lady Mount Cashell as well as, eventually, atheistic Percy Shelley.[42] On the other hand, Mary Shelley can be characterised as an organic conservative, as befitting the wife, widow and mother of an heir to a baronetcy and stately home. She thoroughly relished this role, and ended her days, like many other ambitious and upwardly mobile women of the period by advancing the career of her son socially (presentation at court, marriage to an aristocrat's widow) and professionally (as a barrister), by taking the cure at Baden-Baden and by railing against the times, especially the revolution of 1848, which she abhorred.[43] Both these political positions – the proto-Marxist and organic conservative critiques of liberalism – have a kind of subtextual thematic presence in *Frankenstein*.

To take the latter example first: the organic conservative critique of liberalism is staged in the monster's encounter with the De Lacey family in chapters III–VIII of the text, an often overlooked episode in the text. The De Laceys are displaced aristocrats ('from a good family', F, p. 119) fleeing imprisonment in France and living abroad, in much reduced circumstances abroad ('it was poverty, and they suffered that evil in a very distressing

---

41 'Mary was incorporating her father's political concepts ... justice ... liberty ... republican in theory, a champion of freedom of expression, press, and religion ... and an egalitarian' (Sunstein, *Mary Shelley*, above n. 18, p. 51).
42 See the chapter, 'To Be Something Great and Good' (ibid. pp. 28–61). Of course, other frequenters of Godwin's home on Skinner Street included more middle-of-the-road or conservative figures such as Hazlitt, Lamb, Coleridge and Wordsworth.
43 Sunstein, *Mary Shelley*, above n. 18, pp. 377–378.

degree', *F*, p. 108), a situation which invites comparison with the clerical and noble *émigrés* fleeing the Revolution a generation before. Frankenstein's monster who tracks, hovers over and insinuates himself into the De Laceys' lives, all the while unbeknownst to them, seems like the very spectre of the Revolution itself, haunting the aristocracy, pursuing them in exile, even burning them out of their places of refuge.[44] This parallelism – the monster as the Revolution, the De Laceys as the old regime – is strengthened by the fact that it is through the De Lacey family that the monster becomes a subject, just as the old regime gave birth to 'the monsters' that destroyed it. Through the De Laceys, the monster satisfies, first, his physical needs, assuaging his hunger and thirst with food stolen from them: 'a loaf of coarse bread' and 'pure water' (*F*, p. 103). Once these basic cravings are satisfied, he moves, in almost Maslovian fashion, from the level of need to that of demand; namely, to a demand for the love he sees enacted around him by his 'adoptive' family: 'It was a lovely sight, even to me, poor wretch! who had never beheld aught beautiful before. The silver hair and benevolent countenance of the aged cottager won my reverence, while the gentle manners of the girl enticed my love' (*F*, p. 104). Finally, he arrives at the level – or rather the *law* – of desire with his entry into language (and perforce, the law of the signifier, the Great Other, the *Law*), through his mimicry of their speech: 'By degrees I made a discovery of still greater moment. I found that these people possessed a method of communicating their experience and feelings to one another by articulate sounds ... This was indeed a godlike science, and I ardently desired to become acquainted with it' (*F*, p. 108).

This virtually Lacanian story of subject formation – from need to demand to desire – resonates not just psychoanalytically but historically, commenting ironically not just upon Enlightenment myth of the 'noble savage' – or the modern Prometheus, rediscovering fire (*F*, p. 101) – but the way in which the *ancien régime*, the society of status, gives rise, through its *philosophes*, academies and salon culture to its very destroyer, the liberal subject of rights, who will replace the status society with the social contract. Frankenstein's monster *is* that destroyer. For like that liberal subject of rights – a position which he comes to occupy when he claims a companion

---

44 There is, of course, another figure wreaking havoc on the De Laceys: Safie's father, the Turkish merchant. It is with this 'Orientalist' figure – Muslim, Eastern, conniving, malevolent – that a postcolonial reading of the text could begin (not for nothing is the monster's first book Volney's *Ruins of Empire*). Perhaps this enraced figure persecuting white gentry is a nod in the direction of that 'Black Jacobin' so beloved of not just Mary Shelley but C. L. R. James – Toussaint L'Overture.

as a 'right' – he is himself steeped in, and a product not only of that culture's canon of republican virtue and romantic overreachers – Plutarch's *Lives*, Goethe's *Sorrows of Young Werther*, Milton's *Paradise Lost* (*F*, pp. 124–125) – but also its law-givers, 'Numa, Solon, and Lygurgus' (*F*, p. 125). This legalism, however, will quickly turn to terror tactics, much as the Revolution's constitutionalism (the Convention of 1789, the 'Oath of the Tennis Court', the *Declaration of the Rights of Man*) turned into the Terror of the Committee of Public Safety with its purges, desacralisation and destruction of property. The acts of public violence are staged here in the monster's burning of the De Lacey cottage (*F*, p. 134), itself echoic of that most vivid of counter-revolutionary images: that of the chateau in flames. Even the exposure of the monster's subfusc presence in the cottage has a historical echo: the De Laceys' horrified reaction – 'The life of my father is in the greatest danger ... My wife and my sister will never recover from their horror' (*F*, p. 134) – recalls and reproduces the aristocratic Burkean horror at the spectre of revolutionary liberalism which they themselves have unleashed and which will dissolve their society's organic ties and tiers of family, clan and caste by juridifying civil society as a site of rights.

This organic conservative critique of liberalism is balanced by the proto-Marxist critique, itself staged in the relationship between Victor Frankenstein and his monstrous creation. This relationship enacts, and thereby critiques liberal politics in the way it, initially, situates control of the creation, the monster, in the creator, Frankenstein, in much the same way that the liberal jurist initially, controls or thinks he controls his *ex nihilo* creation, the rights-bearer – or, indeed, how the capitalist thinks he controls his commodity. In each of these instances, however, these relationships undergo a reversal where it is the capitalist who is commodified by his commodity, the jurist who is juridified by rights discourse because, as *Frankenstein* graphically demonstrates, there comes a moment when the creation *controls* the creator. In the novel, this moment comes during the final showdown between the creator and his creation, following Frankenstein's destruction of his second creation, the intended bride of his monster. The means by which we can discern this reversal is through the voice of the monster, virtually a *voix acousmatique*[45] which shatters what had hitherto been the status quo of submission (the monster had, after all, previously begged Frankenstein to make him a mate who would fulfil and

---

45 M. Chion, 'The Impossible Embodiment', in *Everything You Always Wanted to Know About Lacan ... But Were Afraid to Ask Hitchcock*, London: Verso, 1992, pp. 205–207. See also: Žižek, *Looking Awry*, above n. 34, pp. 125–128.

complete him, 'Oh! my creator, make me happy; let me feel gratitude towards you for one benefit!', *F*, p. 140) and signals the inversion of the relationship of creator and created, by pronouncing like some sort of deranged superego: 'Slave, I before reasoned with you, but you have proved yourself unworthy of my condescension. Remember that I have the power; you believe yourself miserable, but I can make you so wretched that the light of day will be hateful to you. You are my creator, but I am your master – obey!' (*F*, p. 162). The Hegelian language of master and slave used by the monster invites, in its anticipation of Marx, a reading which would see here an allegory of the class struggle, and the revolt of the wage slaves. This is, essentially, Moretti's point: that Frankenstein and the Monster embody the 'ambivalent, dialectical relationship, the same as that which, according to Marx, connects Capital with wage-labour'.[46]

The direct discourse, vocalised in the passage above, suggests, as well, a mental as much as a material struggle; that is, the struggle implicit in liberalism, and especially the way rights discourse can turn philosophically – or more, accurately, *jurisprudentially* – on its creator, the jurist, and the sociolegal dominant for which the jurist stands, namely, the ruling class. For what the monster does here to Frankenstein is exactly what Frankenstein did, earlier, to the monster: each renders the other *alone*.[47] The monster murders Elizabeth on the eve of her nuptials ('I shall be with you on your wedding night', *F*, p. 163) just as Frankenstein destroys his bride ('The wretch saw me destroy the creature on whose future existence he depended for happiness, and, with a howl of devilish despair and revenge, withdrew', *F*, p. 163). Certainly, Frankenstein's act may seem distinguishable, at least initially, from that of the monster, having been motivated, seemingly, by something other than revenge; presumably, he destroys the bride because he does not want to see the proliferation of this kind of monstrosity: 'I had resolved in my own mind, that to create another like the fiend I had first made would be an act of the basest and most atrocious selfishness' (*F*, p. 165). But there is something gratuitous about this act of destruction, a kind of 'wantonness' (*F*, p. 141) to Frankenstein's act: 'I thought with a sensation of madness on my promise of creating another like him, and trembling with passion, tore to pieces the thing upon which I was engaged' (*F*, p. 161). And this passage suggests that Frankenstein is not so much acting ethically – a kind of Kantian renunciation – but following his own

---

46 Moretti, *Signs Taken For Wonders*, above n. 36, p. 85.
47 Many thanks to my former Hong Kong University student, Charles Mo, for his astute observations on this issue.

insane logic, the pathological logic of liberalism which holds loneliness to be a virtue rather than a vice, calling it autonomy.

It is this privileged status of autonomy within liberalism which *Frankenstein* calls into question. After all, it is precisely this virtue that the monster wants to escape from, attributing to it the source of all his vices: 'My vices are the children of a forced solitude that I abhor; and my virtues will necessarily arise when I live in communion with an equal' (*F*, p. 142). His lament is this: 'Shall each man . . . find a wife for his bosom, and each beast have his mate, and I be alone?' (*F*, p. 162). By ensuring, through the murder of Elizabeth, that Frankenstein ends up just as 'alone' as himself, the monster exposes the liberal value of autonomy as a kind of pathologised loneliness which isolates, alienates and anomises the subject to such an extent that it goes insane, like the monster and Frankenstein, both driven by psychotic obsessions of revenge in a mad, mutual pursuit. So Frankenstein and his monster end up as demonic parodies of the liberal subject. Both desire an 'Other' – figured in the symptom of Woman, Elizabeth and the bride – and, through that law of desire (the socio-sexual contract?), a new community. The monster seeks his community in the 'vast wilds of South America' where his 'companion will be the same nature as myself, and will be content with the same fare. We shall make our bed of dried leaves; the sun will shine upon us as on man, and will ripen our food. The picture I present to you is peaceful and human' (*F*, p. 141). Frankenstein seeks his in the small 'circle' of family survivors, 'bound close by the ties of affection and mutual misfortune' and from whom, 'new and dear objects of care will be born to replace those of whom we have been so cruelly deprived' (*F*, p. 184). But both Frankenstein and the monster are bound, by the individualising logic of liberalism and its *point de capiton*, rights, to the respective annihilation of the Other, figured in the double dispatch of Elizabeth and the bride. Furthermore, this annihilation will extend, ultimately, to *themselves*, and *their* mutual deaths, far removed from any social tie (let alone community) in the frozen recesses of the Arctic.

This spectacular self-destruction dramatised at the end of the novel gestures towards a psychoanalysis of liberalism; that is, its subject – the subject of rights – is, above all, the split subject, the divided self conflicted over, and ultimately undone by the binaries of individualism and communitarianism, autonomy and connection, the 'me' and the 'not me' of the specular imago. Moreover, this question of rights' failed subjectivity locates Shelley within a specific political project which goes beyond some generalised (and, ultimately, depoliticised) psychoanalysis of politics, or a politicised psychoanalysis. That politics is neither critical legal (which sees the subject of law, rights and liberalism as a monstrous body) nor conservative (which sees that subject as a threat to the old order which created it). Rather, the point Shelley seems to be making here might properly be called a (Freudo-)Marxist one: that the subject of law, rights and liberalism is a monstrous body which, in destroying the old order, *destroys itself* as well, its own discursive contradictions carrying with it the seeds of its own destruction. Indeed, so anticipatory of (Freudo-) Marxism is this point that one might go so far as to echo Slavoj Žižek[48] in claiming that, long before Freud or, as Žižek opts for, Marx, it was Mary Shelley who invented the symptom.

### I Remember Mama: Mothers, Daughters and the (Non-)Anxiety of Influence

It is at this point, of liberalism's impasse dramatised in *Frankenstein* that I would like to return to Wollstonecraft's *A Vindication of the Rights of Women* so as to draw out, and summarise my conclusions about these two texts. Both of these two texts engage the critique of the law, though they propose, seemingly, two very different conceptions of the law's effect, operation and status. Wollstonecraft says that those *excluded from* the law become monsters; Shelley shows the reverse, how those *included in* the law become monsters. This apparent difference, as irreconcilable as it may seem, is, however, just that – '*apparent*'; because, when read together, these two texts, function as halves which complete a whole, telling two sides of the same story: about the failure of the self both *within* and *outside* the law. This double bind is as startling as it is novel, and could only have emerged from narratives which propose a feminist reading of rights, the law and the socio-Symbolic. For who else but two women, positioned as they are both inside and outside of the socio-Symbolic, could have identified the inherent doubleness of the law and rights, which are – like the Kleinian breast – both the good and bad object, both the instrument of our liberation (Wollstonecraft) and the agent of our destruction (Shelley)?[49]

This doubleness of the law can be intuited, exposed and thought through by Shelley and Wollstonecraft because both traverse, as women – and particularly as 'scribbling women' – the line between the public and the private which rights discourse, and indeed liberalism, at once, erases and

---

48 See Žižek, 'How Did Marx Invent the Symptom?', in *The Sublime Object of Ideology*, above n. 34, pp. 11–55.
49 M. Klein, 'The Importance of Symbol Formation in the Development of the Ego', in R. E. Money-Kyrle, B. Joseph, E. O'Shaughnessy and H. Segal (eds), *Love, Guilt and Reparation and Other Works 1921–1945*, vol. 1 of *The Writings of Melanie Klein*, London: Hogarth Press and the Institute of Psychoanalysis, 1975.

yet redraws throughout the Romantic period. For the political liberalism that arose among and with the first generation of Romanticism, represented in the *Declaration of the Rights of Man*, enabled Wollstonecraft's critique of the 'political as personal' (i.e., if 'Man' in the *Declaration*, then why not 'Woman'?) by rendering the most private and personal of virtues – autonomy – as the most public of political values. While, during the second generation of Romanticism, economic liberalism's hiving off of 'the private' – the workplace, the home, the 'life-world' – as *the* space of individual autonomy free from the public realm authorised Shelley's critique of an unbridled Capitalism manipulating rights to further its own profit-spinning and exploitative ends as a 'monstrous body' of the law. In either case, it is liberalism's public–private divide – simultaneously bounded and unbounded, separate and conjoined – which facilitates the critique of the public by the private (Wollstonecraft) or the private by the public (Shelley); and, furthermore, enables these two women, consigned, historically, by their gender, to the private realm of domesticity to utilise and, indeed, communicate with each other through the hitherto public discourse of the law, now revealed (as well as obscured) by liberalism as doubly personal *and* political.

The acknowledgement, however, by Wollstonecraft and Shelley of the law's doubleness does not reposition their proto-critical legal feminism within the aporias of yesteryear's deconstruction (and through that, postmodernity), 'tracing' both positions – liberal reformist and critical/Marxist – but coming to rest over neither. Instead of miring itself in this impasse of 'undecidability', this (and, perhaps, all) feminist critique engages the law's doubleness because it actually takes critique *somewhere*, opening up rather than occluding an alternative space, a different juridical imaginary. That space, that imaginary is one in which *another Law* can emerge, one based as much on the 'Mother's Body' as that 'Father's Name', enabling the reconstruction of rights on the basis of their universal failure rather than partial success. To elaborate: instead of hailing essentialised, and highly particular identities – e.g., the 'rights of *man*' – a feminist rights discourse would interpellate identities predicated upon their non-identity – the split self, the barred subject – because, as language, the signifier, 'rights', cuts the subject as it constructs it in the Symbolic of the 'Father's Name', as well as shattering the mirror-image at the moment it reflects itself as the maternal *imago* in the Imaginary. It is this certainty of rights' failure – of the Imaginary *méconnaissance* of the body-image, of the Symbolic 'hole' in the subject which language installs instead of a 'whole' subject – which opens up the possibility of rights' reinvention. Paradoxically, this possibility is predicated upon rights' impossibility. For it is precisely the impossibility of

98 • Novel Judgements: Legal Theory as Fiction

ever exhausting rights discourse – of ever saying, rights are now complete, comprehensive, totalised – which renders them inevitable, and ensures their persistence.[50]

In introjecting *A Vindication of the Rights of Women*, Mary Shelley's *Frankenstein* renders a novel judgement that points us in this direction, one which critiques the liberal position from the twin vantages of conservatism and Marxism in order to fulfil rather than supersede the discourse of rights, and its extension to women as advocated by Wollstonecraft. Indeed, in writing *Frankenstein*, Mary Shelley may be attempting to complete Wollstonecraft's 'project of modernity', continuing her work of not only rights' extension but reinvention and, in so doing, thereby fulfilling one of Shelley's driving fantasies: that of the communion with the dead. Throughout her life, Mary Shelley was haunted by the spectre of her mother; her reading of Wollstonecraft's *œuvre*, her visits to her grave and finally the corpus of work which Shelley produced are all, in different ways, attempts to summon up the maternal ghost. That summoning, however, is intended neither to bless nor exorcise, as is often the case in the 'anxiety of influence',[51] mapped by Harold Bloom, running through the relations of literary 'fathers and sons' in this period. In fact, the figure of the dead mother summoned by her daughter here suggests an altogether different model of literary and lineal relations, one that is neither and both Oedipal and anti-Oedipal, and which can, at once, acknowledge and disavow origins, critique but also complete sources: in short, a (non-)anxiety of influence. *Frankenstein* participates in the summoning up of this (non-)anxious spectral influence, being itself a text, as M. H. Abrams would say, of profound 'natural supernaturalism'.[52] Composed for a literary *séance*, *Frankenstein* can be read as a psychic message, relayed beyond the grave where an ectoplasmic receiver on the 'Other Side' might well hear a call which says, in an echo of Freud's celebrated story of the dream of the burning child,[53] 'Mother, can't you see I'm righting?'.

---

50 For further development of this point, see: W. MacNeil, 'Enjoy Your Rights! Three Cases from the Postcolonial Commonwealth', *Public Culture* 9(3), 1997, 377.
51 H. Bloom, *The Anxiety of Influence: A Theory of Poetry*. New York: Oxford University Press, 1973.
52 M. H. Abrams, *Natural Supernaturalism: Tradition and Revolution in Romantic Literature*, New York: Norton, 1973.
53 S. Freud, 'The Interpretation of Dreams', in *The Basic Writings*, above n. 34, pp. 436–437.

CHAPTER 5

# Hawthorne's Haunted House of Law: The Romance of American Legal Realism in *The House of the Seven Gables*

### Predicting a 'Predictive Theory of Law': Hawthorne as '[M]esmerical' Seer of the American Legal Realists, Proto-(Holmes) and Principal (Llewellyn, Frank)

Midpoint in *The House of the Seven Gables*,[1] Hawthorne's 'radical', Holgrave, declares with weary exasperation, 'what slaves we are to bygone times' (*HSG*, p. 157). That 'slavery' turns out to be, as Holgrave elaborates further on the analogy, not only epistemic ('We read in Dead Men's books', *HSG*, p. 158), not only emotive ('We laugh at Dead Men's jokes and cry at Dead Men's pathos', *HSG*, p. 158), but also – and, most interestingly, from a law-and-literature perspective – *jurisprudential*, especially in light of the text's original context of heated curial and legislative debate over the legal status of slaves: 'A Dead Man sits on all our judgement seats; and living judges but search out and repeat his decisions' (*HSG*, p. 158). Is it any wonder that Holgrave's lament is so desperate? For with this Maitland-esque image of the law ruling us, vampire-like, from beyond the grave, he forecloses any sense of escape from history, legal or otherwise. 'Shall we never, never get rid of the Past!' (*HSG*, p. 157), he exclaims, his fervour reaching, in this much quoted passage, full rhetorical (Emersonian?)

---

1 N. Hawthorne, *The House of the Seven Gables*. Intro. M. Oliver. New York: Modern Library, 2001. Hereafter referred to as *HSG*.

pitch. To which the ever sensible Phoebe *might* (deflatingly) respond, puncturing his overblown persiflage with a riposte that says, *All too easily.* 'Might', that is, if she was ever allowed to get a word in edgewise with this yappy 'young man in a hurry', one of a long line of characters in American literature, light on learning, but heavy on opinion, and each with an unshakeable faith in their destiny.

No matter, though, that Phoebe's interjection is imagined – and remains so; because as subsequent events in the narrative quite clearly show, there is no need to flee, like 'the flight of the owlish Clifford and Hepzibah', *history*, and all of its highly overdetermined traumas. Each of which Holgrave enumerates in full, even fulsome detail, the famous Maule 'reserve' (*HSG*, p. 24) absenting itself yet again as he itemises a 'perpetual remorse of conscience, a constantly defeated hope, strife amongst kindred, various misery, a strange form of death, dark suspicion, unspeakable disgrace' (*HSG*, p. 159). For all this litany of past woe however, relief comes *easily* here: in acts and explanations which border on, or *are* sleights of hand. With the release of a clasp behind an ancient portrait, an old safe is revealed and, with it, a much sought after document that (once) promised 'riches beyond the dreams of avarice' comes to light, its Derridean (but also Pyncheonian) 'force of law' (*HSG*, p. 195) now long lapsed, indeed moot. With a flimsy coronial ruling on an uncanny, even supernatural death, anticlimactic after all its fantasmatic build-up (think of Judge Pyncheon *in extremis*, last seen joining the ghostly procession of 'defunct Pyncheons' *HSG*, p. 239), a family curse is exposed as a hereditary malady, and rationalised as 'by no means ... unusual' (*HSG*, p. 266). With the preposterous *deus ex machina* of a 'mesmerical' (*HSG*, p. 267) *séance*, a mysterious 'murder' – that of Uncle Jaffrey Pyncheon, thirty years earlier in the diegesis – is solved as nothing more sinister than a death by natural causes: the same unidentified affliction (apoplexy?), in fact, which kills his nephew – Judge Jaffrey Pyncheon – near the finish of the storyline.

So much for history's supposedly sealed enclosure and Holgrave's 'no exit' from it – last seen I might add, jauntily climbing into the late judge's 'handsome, dark-green barouche' (*HSG*, p. 273) and ready to depart forever that emblem of the 'inescapable past', *so-called* – the House of the Seven Gables – for a brighter (and certainly more prosperous) tomorrow, with those lucky legatees, the recently em-*bourgeoisfied* Hepzibah, Clifford and Phoebe in tow. This ease of departure from 'history', however, is precisely why this chapter wants to break with the historicist and historicising arguments that, hitherto, have dominated, inexorably, the critical literature of *The House of the Seven Gables*, be they either old, and neo-

'marxified' (F. O. Mathiesson)[2] or new, and post-'freudianised' (Neill Matheson).[3] Though, seemingly, at opposite ends of the 'theory' spectrum (the political vs. psychic economy), these two stances are linked, not merely by the homophony of their respective principals' surnames (Mathiesson–Matheson), but by their shared *juridical* inflections: the former, trumpeting, in a now classic explication, the dialectical *law* of historical materialism, with the struggle of 'the classes' being played out in Pyncheon–Maule antithesis (and sublated, however flimsily, in the Phoebe–Holgrave synthesis); the latter, hailing, in a virtuoso interpretation, the psychoanalytic *law* of 'lack' – or the 'lack of a lack' – of which the fabled 'Indian deed' (*HSG*, p. 17) to Waldo County is the principal signifier, its 'encryption' within the recesses of the Pyncheon mansion (behind – where else? – Col. Pyncheon's portrait) but an elaborate architectural metaphor for the introjections of the 'lost object' by the subject of mourning and melancholia.

Each of these positions however – the 'trad' of Mathiesson, the 'rad' of Matheson – *repeat*, rather than respond to, in their alternative readings of the novel and its 'laws', Holgrave's plaintive cry ('Shall we never, never get rid of the Past?', *HSG*, p. 157), endlessly circling history, materialist, melancholic or otherwise. I want to interrupt this critical roundabout (though both materialism and psychoanalysis will remain relevant to my reading) and take *The House of the Seven Gables* elsewhere because, with its ending of escape – a closure, as it were, of history's *dis*closure, with all its secrets revealed, released and set free – the text emboldens its readers to do likewise; that is, to sever the 'connect[ion]' that the novel's preface purports to forge (but its diegesis longs to break) between 'a bygone time with the very present' (*HSG*, p. 4). Not that such a rupture need, by necessity, land the reader in the contemporaneity of Hawthorne's 'very present'. Despite all the up-to-the minute, *à la mode* referencing of the text – to daguerreotypy, to Fourierism, and so forth – that *present*, as the preface all too emphatically states, was 'flitting away' (*HSG*, p. 4) even in Hawthorne's day, let alone our own. So to hitch a reading of *The House of the Seven Gables* to context is to mire that interpretation – like some of the, otherwise admirable, law-and-literature scholarship of the text (e.g., Brook Thomas,[4] but

---

2 F. O. Mathiesson, *American Renaissance: Art and Expression in the Age of Emerson and Whitman*, Oxford: Oxford University Press, 1941.

3 N. Matheson, 'Melancholy History in *The House of the Seven Gables*', *Literature and Psychology* 48(3), 2002, 1–37.

4 B. Thomas, *Cross-Examinations of Law and Literature: Cooper, Hawthorne, Stowe and Melville*, Cambridge: Cambridge University Press, 1990.

also, to a lesser extent, Eric Cheyfitz,[5] Michael T. Gilmore[6] and Walter Benn Michaels)[7] – in an antiquarianism where, however evocative its period detail, daguerreotypy has become just as agedly 'brittle' (*HSG*, p. 68) as Hepzibah's treasure, the Davenport china; and Fourierism, just as 'delicate[ly]' (*HSG*, p. 29) quaint as Clifford's Malbone miniature.

Debates, aired ably and amply by Thomas, Cheyfitz and so forth, over the novel's connection to, and glossing of, for example, the judicial career of Joseph Story or the socio-legal impact of the *Dartmouth College* decision are, from the vantage of the here-and-now, just as much curios in the *étagère* of American legal history as Hepzibah's china and Clifford's miniature, explaining neither how to *read The House of the Seven Gables* nor, more importantly, *why* we should. This is exactly why I want to turn, in this chapter, from 'the present' as much as 'the past' of *The House of the Seven Gables* because it is my principal contention here that, if this text's concerns are at all jurisprudential (as its scholarship insists upon, as much as its storyline – with its nomological tale of a missing deed, a judge and 'murder most foul'), then it's to do with *futurity* and its 'laws'. All of which renders Hawthorne's narrative use (and abuse) of the device of Mesmerism not so fantastically far-fetched as it seemed at first blush – though, by my lights, its deployment now becomes *prospective* rather than retrospective. This is so because, as I shall argue in this chapter, what Hawthorne does in *The House of the Seven Gables* is *predict*; and predict nothing less than what will become in the next generation – or two, even three or four generations hence, its effects being felt still today – *the* principal *American* school of thought, and that nation's one truly original and enduring contribution to global jurisprudence, legal realism. For this is a movement that starts out with, and emanates from 'the predictive theory of law', the moniker of which is the invention of Hawthorne's fellow New Englander, the US Supreme Court's most famous jurist-as-philosopher, the 'Great Dissenter', Mr Justice Oliver Wendell Holmes, Jr.[8]

Though belonging to different generations of the Massachusetts intelligentsia, one pre-, the other post-Civil War (in fact, Hawthorne was a

---

5 E. Cheyfitz, 'The Irresistibleness of Great Literature: Reconstructing Hawthorne's Politics', *American Literary History* 6(3), 1994, 539–558.

6 M. Gilmore, *American Romanticism and the Marketplace*, Chicago: University of Chicago Press, 1985.

7 W. B. Michaels, *Our America: Nativism, Modernism and Pluralism*, Durham, NC: Duke University Press, 1995.

8 O. W. Holmes Jr., in R. A. Posner (ed.), *The Essential Holmes: Selections from the Letters, Speeches, Judicial Opinions, and Other Writings of Oliver Wendell Holmes, Jr.*, Chicago: University of Chicago Press, 1992.

contemporary and friend of Holmes's father, that 'autocrat of the breakfast table', Dr Oliver Wendell Holmes, *Senior*), I contend that Holmes, *Junior* and Hawthorne are involved in an unspoken (ectoplasmic?) dialogue across time, with the latter a kind of 'mesmerical' (*HSG*, p. 267) seer of the former, and with *The House of the Seven Gables* propounding a novel judgement which forecasts American legal realism. Not only of Holmes's predictive theory of law but that of his twentieth-century legal realist epigone, Karl Llewellyn, whose gothicising architectural image of the realists' *bête noire* – legal formalism – as a 'haunted house of law' finds a vivid corollary, as I shall argue in the second section, in Hawthorne's Seven Gables, itself a metaphor for a particular type of law (property) and behind it, political economy (mercantilism), both of which are in the process of being displaced by the very forces of consumerist exchange legal realism will trumpet: contract and Capital. Central to the success of this new logic of consumption is an idea of law that is active rather than static, a function rather than a form. All of which entails a categorical rejection of the hitherto dominant legal formalist conception of the law as a letter, the critique of which I explore in section three by tracking the deleterious effects of the novel's fabled, and now, largely, fantasmatic *lettre volée* – the Indian deed to Waldo County – on Clifford (as obsessional), Hepzibah (as hysteric) and Jaffrey (as psychotic/perverse).

The last of whom stages, in his judicial office as much as personal outlook, all of the legal realists' anxieties – Jerome Frank's as much as Llewellyn's and Holmes's – about judges, the 'Bad Man' and posited rules. Having examined the way in which the text enacts these realist bugbears, this chapter will turn, in its fourth and final section, from critique to 'connubial bliss' – *so rendered*; namely, the puzzling union of Phoebe and Holgrave, whose first words of love are prompted by the presence of death, with Judge Pyncheon's corpse stiffening in the front parlour. This coupling of *eros* and *thanatos*, however, is not the only merger that the Phoebe–Holgrave marriage manages and which resonates with meaning. For, here, I want to push this crucial (and penultimate) point: that in fusing activity and observation, 'law jobs' and 'juristic method' – which Phoebe and Holgrave instantiate so thoroughly – Hawthorne's *The House of the Seven Gables* enacts what I call the 'romance of American legal realism'. A romance which turns out to be, as I shall argue by way of conclusion, quite anti-romantic; to use the language of the preface, one 'rigidly subject' (*HSG*, p. 3) to, and propounding a 'concept of law' drained of any higher meaning or deeper purpose. For Hawthorne, this normative evacuation of the law is disastrous because it demands nothing less than the sacrifice (exorcism?) of the 'quality of mercy' itself, figured in the ghostly Alice Pyncheon, last seen 'float[ing]' free (*HSG*, p. 274) – or is that expelled? –

from the House of the Seven Gables: a departure – of forgiveness and forgetting – from which American jurisprudence has yet to recover.

## '*Seisin*-isation and Its Legal Realist Discontents': The Law of, and as Consumption, in *The House of the Seven Gables*

Diet dominates what lawyers such as Judge Pyncheon might call the *obiter dicta* of *The House of the Seven Gables*. A law-and-literature perspective, however, would recognise a potential *ratio* in such putative asides: that is, a central topos emergent in the narrative margins. For when 'read jurisprudentially' the text's repeated referencing of its characters' respective dietary regimens – and the body types these regimens sustain – is highly purposive, pointing to a much broader thematic running throughout *The House of the Seven Gables*: namely, *consumption*. By which I mean a mode of distribution rather than a method of mastication. For the eating habits on display in the text allegorise, to my way of thinking, nothing less than an economic template; the triangulation of which, however, adheres more to the psychoanalytic (Lacanian) model of Real–Imaginary–Symbolic than, as might be expected, the materialist (Hegelian–Marxist) one of thesis–antithesis–synthesis. Clifford, naturally, embodies consumption in terms of the Real, one of his most prominent features being an un-fillable stomach that comes to define him, characterologically, as little more than a walking 'will-to-eat': 'More, more!', he exclaims Oliver Twist-like over his first breakfast at home, 'This is what I need' (*HSG*, p. 94). Hepzibah, by way of contrast, represents consumption as Imaginary, her daily intake having long consisted of an *imago* of *noblesse oblige* ('I was born a lady, and have always lived one – no matter in what narrowness of means, always a lady!', *HSG*, p. 41) instead of three meals, fair and square: she had fed on 'the shadowy food of aristocratic reminiscence' (*HSG*, p. 34). While Jaffrey Pyncheon is the epitome of Symbolic consumption, his penchant for the fictions of realty – and all the *papier mâché* of possession that goes with 'heap[ing] up', as Uncle Venner says, 'property upon property' (*HSG*, p. 135) – outweighing even the 'large sensual endowments' (*HSG*, p. 236) with which the judge is gifted when it comes to pleasures of the well provisioned table.

Into this triangulated space comes a fourth term, one which will disrupt its triadic organisation because it rings in, much like the 'obstreperous' (*HSG*, p. 69) peal of Hepzibah's cent shop-bell, a new form of consumption, predicated on a different logic *and law* of distribution, even production. That law, and that logic appears, however, in the most unprepossessing of forms: as a minor character who, for all his insignificance to the development of the plot, opens and closes the novel; indeed, he is the one who is singled out, postscripturally, by Herman Melville in his congratulatory letter to Hawthorne, commending him on the publication of *The House of the Seven Gables*.[9] The character I refer to, of course, is that pint-sized pride of Pyncheon-street, Phoebe's infant swain and Hepzibah's first (and last) customer, little Ned Higgins whose prodigious intake of two 'Jim Crow(s)' (*HSG*, p. 45, p. 46), one 'Camel' (*HSG*, p. 60), two 'dromedaries' (*HSG*, p. 72), an 'elephant' (*HSG*, 52), a 'locomotive' (*HSG*, p. 72) and a 'whale' (*HSG*, p. 100) render him a consumer *non pareil*. Not that Ned is without competition here. Many of the other neighbourhood urchins are similarly acquisitive, wanting as Ned does from Hepzibah, the best deal they can cut, even something for nothing; think of the 'shrewd little Yankee' (*HSG*, p. 253) trying to screw more music – all *gratis* – from the 'hurdy-gurdy' (*HSG*, p. 251) of the Italian busker and his tartaned companion, the performing monkey: 'Let him play as long as he likes! If there's nobody to pay him, that's his own lookout' (*HSG*, p. 253). Setting Ned apart, however, from these grubby, coin-cadging hoi polloi is the sheer scale of his custom, the amplification of which transforms him from an ordinary impulse shopper into a tiny tot version of the new economy of capitalist circulation, a microchip of mass consumption; its 'splendid bazaar' (*HSG*, p. 44) now very much in the ascendant and superseding New England's hitherto more modest mercantilist efforts – of which Hepzibah's cent shop is a mere remnant, overshadowed by comparison with '[g]roceries, toy-shops, drygoods stores, with their immense panes of plate-glass, their gorgeous fixtures, their vast and complete assortments of merchandise, in which fortunes had been invested' (*HSG*, p. 44).

Given Hepzibah's imagined 'panorama' (*HSG*, p. 44) of merchandising plenty above, is it any wonder that the last words of dialogue to be spoken of in *The House of the Seven Gables* (as well as some of the first in its contemporary setting) are those of 'Dixey' and his interlocutor, the two 'laboring men' (*HSG*, p. 42) who function as something like the text's chorus, either decrying or applauding the twists and turns of the storyline's 'business' (*HSG*, p. 43, p. 274): be it 'Old Maid Pyncheon's' (*HSG*, p. 274) opening of a cent shop, dismissed, initially, as 'Poor business' (*HSG*, p. 48); or, alternatively, her inheritance of 'a couple of hundred thousand' (*HSG*, p. 274) as 'Pretty good business . . . pretty good business' (*HSG*, p. 274). The effect of this running commentary from a pair of Pyncheon-street's resident fixtures is to pick up upon and reinforce the fundamental insight suggested by Hepzibah's 'vanity fair' vision of commerce's cornucopia above: that the

---

9 H. Melville, 16 April 1851. Letter to Nathaniel Hawthorne. Pittsfield. Reproduced in Hawthorne, *The House of the Seven Gables*, above n. 1, p. 312.

business of America is *business*. More specifically: its economy is now driven by intersubjective *exchange*, a value necessitating a different sort of law, one set apart from the subject–object *possessory* kind that had hitherto dominated this realty-obsessed narrative of home ownership with a juridical thematic that might be called '*seisin*-isation and its discontents'. The new law I refer to is, of course, *contract*. But where in the text is this dynamic form of legality, with all of its fungible imperatives, to be found? Certainly not – at least it would seem at first blush – in that emblem of status (and *stasis*), the House of the Seven Gables, itself a monument, if there ever was one, to property, and its underlying value, exposed here as an (ab)use.

I say so because the right of property here is predicated upon an originary wrong, the criminality of which shifts its valorisation away from Marxian *use* to that of Fourierist, even Proudhonist *ab*use of the 'all property is theft' type; a sentiment uttered repeatedly throughout the text by not only Holgrave and Uncle Venner, but especially Clifford when he proclaims: 'what we call real estate . . . is the broad foundation on which nearly all the guilt of the world rests' (*HSG*, p. 226). With such 'guilt' as its grounding, how can the House of the Seven Gables be anything other than a 'rusty, crazy, creaky, dry-rotted, damp-rotted, dingy, dark, and miserable old dungeon' (*HSG*, p. 224) in which its inmates lie, as Holgrave puts it, like poor Hepzibah, more dead than alive, their 'life-blood chilling in . . . (their) veins' (*HSG*, p. 40)? Coincidentally – or *not*, as I shall argue, Holgrave's carceral analogy here is not too far off the mark from how the legal realists such as Karl Llewellyn depicted the common law in early twentieth-century America: as a space of confinement which threatens to entrap all its nation's citizen-subjects. Of course, Llewellyn *domesticated* this threat by rendering its confining space as – what else? – a benign version of Hawthorne's house, right down to its Yankee provenance, with the latter's seven gables recalled in the former's case-by-case additions, imaged here as the wings of 'one of those old New England farm houses . . . that had another piece stuck on when the first son got married, and another piece stuck on when the second son got married, and a third piece stuck onto the second piece when the first grandchild got married . . . and various other things placed in some kind of queer fashion, none of them having any particular initial plan, none of them having any particular relation to anything'.[10] Indeed, so *ad hoc* is this higgledy-piggledy homestead of law that it prompts Llewellyn to ask: '[w]here was the plan?'.[11]

---

10 K. Llewellyn, Lecture Notes cited in W. Twining, *Karl Llewellyn and the Realist Movement*, London: Weidenfeld & Nicolson, 1973, p. 309.
11 Ibid.

At which point, naturally, a divergence opens up between Llewellyn's house and Hawthorne's because the House of the Seven Gables is most definitely a construct with a 'plan', whether it be a dynastic founding (as in the case of Col. Pyncheon) or a dynastic thwarting (as in the case of Thomas Maule). But Hawthorne's house *is* Llewellyn's to this extent: both are organic, even alive, the latter's accretions endlessly replicating themselves, as if autogenetic (captured in the 'pieces' that, seemingly, spring out of nowhere, and are, iteratively, 'stuck on'); while the former's add-ons are even more explicitly generative, its framework defined in terms of sanguinary flow, secreted from a throbbing and aorta-like centre: its 'very timbers were oozy, as with the moisture of a heart. It was like a great human heart, with a life of its own, and full of rich and sombre reminiscences' (*HSG*, p. 25). What are these 'reminiscences' if not the memory traces of the law? That is, those memes of legal precedent that the structural embellishments of Llewellyn's house metaphorise; a similitude which transforms the Pyncheons' colonial pile, built on a double act of thieving – not only of the Pyncheons 'nicking' its lot from the Maules, but, presumably, the Maules land-grabbing from those decorative figures adorning the Waldo County map, the 'Indians' (*HSG*, p. 31) – into what the legal realists might call a 'haunted house of law' where all who enter seem doomed to remain, etherealised as spirits, ever seeking its sequestered juridical secret, the lost letter of the law.

Such a fate was, according to the legal realists, what awaited their legal formalist opponents. Llewellyn, for example, observed that the legal formalists' slavish devotion to binding authority constricted their movement in the common law's 'old houses' so much so that it threatened real physical damage, precedential tradition betraying rather than bolstering the legal process. For in moving, as was the narrow legal ambit permitted here, 'from one level to the next', an adjudicator was just as likely to find, instead of a solution, himself 'suddenly dropped, bang' by the weight of their legal authorities, 'down an extra step and landed on ... [their] face[s]'. That forensic fall takes on an even more final turn for Hawthorne, going well beyond landing on one's face. Consider Judge Pyncheon – or, for that matter, Uncle Jaffrey, or Gervase, or the Old Colonel; in all their respective housebound tumbles, each of them, literally, are stopped dead in their tracks. Which prompts this question: in light of the death-dealing nature of this 'desolate, decaying, gusty, rusty old house' (*HSG*, p. 26), what is the jurisprude – whom Holmes, after all, compared favourably to an 'architect' The Path of the Law, p. 176[12] – to do here? That is, is s/he to abandon the house

---

12 O. W. Holmes, 'The Path of the Law', in Posner, The Essential Holmes, above n. 8, p. 176. Hereafter referred to as *PL*.

of law, 'trashing' it as s/he goes? Or is s/he to hazard a makeover, tarting the place up for future generations? The almost instant results effected by even Phoebe's modest efforts in Alice's bedroom, its 'practical arrangements' (*HSG*, p. 63) transformed with a 'touch' (*HSG*, p. 64) here and there, militate in favour of the latter and its 'homely witchcraft' (*HSG*, p. 64).

Except, of course, for the fact that this domestic sorcery conjures up the prospect of not only a much more habitable space ('now the Seven Gables will be new-shingled', *HSG*, p. 19), but, as well, the evil spirit driving that renovation: the *samsara* of Col. Pynchon, 'come again' (*HSG*, p. 53) – and, with him, another spin of the ancestral cycle of 'wrong-doing' (*HSG*, p. 4). Given seemingly interminable repetition, the jurisprude-as-architect is left with, in terms of planning options, the former, as outlined above; specifically, fleeing the House of the Seven Gables in the wake of its destruction. No House of Usher-like fate, however, is in store for Hawthorne's house precisely because, unlike Poe's purlieu of incestuous transgression, this abode is haunted by the ghost of *law*; that is, the dead inscription of the deed, its location long forgotten, its efficacy spent, but which, nonetheless, still calls to all the house's inhabitants, hailing them in its interpellative agency. What does this it say? Nothing less than this tantalising prospect: 'boundless wealth! – unimaginable wealth' (*HSG*, p. 271). No wonder so many of the text's characters become as befuddled as they do by the mere thought of what the deed promises, allowing it to cloud their reason, confuse their judgement; for what this document may lack in jurisprudential *effect*, it makes up for in psychological *affect*.

Indeed, by burying law's letter so deep inside what might be called the novel's 'architectural unconscious', Hawthorne accounts for, and signals how the deed's persistent affectivity comes to function in a way that is the precise opposite of, say, Poe's 'purloined letter': the latter's narrative trick was to be forever open to the eye, in plain view of all; while the former's is to be so secreted away from the gapes and gawks of all that it must be mulled over, dwelt upon, imagined. That is to say, law's hidden letter – its *lettre cachée* – solicits *fantasy*. And what a 'plague of fantasies' this buried document triggers, capable, even, of raising the dead; consider the departed 'Pyncheons . . . bound to assemble in the parlour' each midnight (*HSG*, p. 239), all 'try(ing) the picture frame' (*HSG*, p. 240) for the deed. The sheer fantasmatic excess of which prompts this writer to ask: who wrote *The House of the Seven Gables*? Nathaniel Hawthorne or Slavoj Žižek? My question is not (wholly) flippant because this Žižekian plague infects not only the dearly departed but the *living* of the 'here and now', nowhere more so than in that trio of elderly surviving Pyncheons: Clifford, Hepzibah and Jaffrey, all pathologically 'enjoying their symptoms'.

### 'What the Judge had for Breakfast': Law's Letter, the 'Bad Man' and the Subversion (or Perversion?) of the Legal Subject in the Formalist Dialectic of Desire

It would be tempting of course to read into Clifford's case history, the most pathological of the novel's characters: a classic instance of obsessional neurosis, as symptomatised as much by the fetish he makes of his daily routine with Phoebe ('pacing' and 'brooding' without her, *HSG*, p. 119), as all of his strange phobias. For example, note the fuss he makes over the Colonel's portrait, the look of which he cannot 'bear' (*HSG*, p. 97), and which *must* be covered; then, the 'invincible distaste' (*HSG*, p. 117) he has, shamelessly, for the aged visage of Hepzibah; finally, his revulsion at house itself, 'dismal' (*HSG*, p. 97) for one of his 'refined' (*HSG*, p. 95) sensibilities. Not that his sister Hepzibah is so very far off the mark he sets in terms of psychic disturbance; though with her nervous mannerisms – her 'tremors and palpitations' (*HSG*, p. 31) – she approximates more the 'hysteric' (*HSG*, p. 89) than the obsessional. The problem with such a clinical reading, however, is that Hepzibah and Clifford are fully justified in all their anxieties, the two of them having more than enough to either obsess about or hystericise over. Take Hepzibah: though trained for nothing useful – and curiously proud of it – she must now, in her old age, quit her quiet and retiring seclusion in order either to 'earn her own food, or starve!' (*HSG*, p. 34). Or consider Clifford: as paralysing as his persecution complex is, he is absolutely spot on about the very real 'malevolent' influence (*HSG*, p. 270) that his cousin and nemesis, Jaffrey, exercises over and against him as his 'Evil Destiny' (*HSG*, p. 212, p. 226) – proving the truth of the adage, 'Just because you're paranoid, doesn't mean they're not out to get you!' The proximate cause, of course, for the pathology of each is a *traumatic* encounter with the law: in the form of Clifford's arrest, conviction and incarceration. A shock from which neither brother nor sister has recovered, and which has only served to intensify in them the same propensity towards the fantasmatic (the 'delusion of family importance', (*HSG*, p. 18) that the deed-*as*-legality has instilled, aetologically, in *all* the Pyncheons, warping their collective unconscious and its *internal* Law.

Remember how often, in the text, words such as 'fantasy' and 'delusion' are associated with the pair. To give just two examples: Hepzibah has 'longed dreamed' of '*fantasies*' of enrichment (*HSG*, p. 58); '[t]he world' was 'no longer a *delusion*' (*HSG*, p. 122) for Clifford when he is in the company of Phoebe – and so on. Each dreams of escape; though these escapes play out along different lines, speaking to their respective material positions as much as psychological proclivities. For instance: with her *folie de grandeur* about her hitherto exalted but now spent bloodline – 'her antique portraits, pedigrees, coats of arms, records and traditions' (*HSG*, p. 35), an ironic contrast to her abject penury – is it any wonder that Hepzibah's 'dream' takes the form of *rescue* by 'family romance'? For who is it, in the 'strange festal glory' (*HSG*, p. 58) of her mind, that comes to the aid of this forlorn gentlewoman-in-distress other than a bevy of rich *male* relations, surrogate 'Names-of-the-Father', and the respective 'Laws' they personify: an Anglo-Indian nabob (*HSG*, pp. 57–58), a Southern planter (*HSG*, p. 58), an English gentleman (*HSG*, p. 58), each doting and benevolent, and all of them ready to gift Hepzibah with either a remittance '*per annum*' (*HSG*, p. 58), a residence ('Pyncheon Hall', *HSG*, p. 58) or 'unreckonable riches' (*HSG*, p. 58). Clifford, by way of contrast, dreams of *flight* – not so surprising for an *out*law held all too long *in* law; that is, as an actual inmate confined by 'four stone-walls' (*HSG*, p. 96) like some 'yankeefied' Dr Manette. '[T]he South of France', 'Italy', 'Paris' (*HSG*, p. 97); these are *his* places of refuge, glamorous expatriate havens where he will be free, not only from the literal Essex County prison which held him behind its 'iron grates' (*HSG*, p. 96), but also from the figurative one of his own making: his own psychic panopticon and, within it, a *nosological* cell. Instead of these psychological bars, Clifford cries 'I want my happiness!' (*HSG*, p. 136), a protest against his *embodied*, as much as mental incarceration; namely, the detention of *dotage*, especially in the form it takes for him as an infantilised old man, forever confined as an aged 'child' (*HSG*, p. 128) to the charge, however caring, of his 'nurse... guardian... playmate' (*HSG*, p. 125), Phoebe.

In spite, however, of all their manifold psychic (and physical) frailties, neither Hepzibah nor Clifford acts with any kind of sustained follow-through upon their escape fantasies because both, ultimately, remain within the deontological remit of the Law and its socio-Symbolic *sittlichkeit* – albeit on the margins. The latter returns home from prison to a house he hates but a sister he loves (in his way), thereby establishing, against all odds for one so atomised and anomised, a social tie ('What he needed was the love of a very few', *HSG*, p. 269); the former never leaves her home, however down-at-the-heels it has become, keeping up appearances of 'old gentility' (*HSG*, p. 34) even in dire want, and resorting to such shaming means (for her) as *infra dig* 'trade' to maintain herself and her adored brother ('There is nothing but love here Clifford... you are at home', *HSG*, p. 93). Both fulfil, indeed embrace their obligations – to each other as much as 'the other', the law. Even when the Pyncheon siblings fancy themselves guilty somehow of Jaffrey's 'murder' and leave 'the scene of the crime' for their foolhardy railway foray, these 'Two Owls' (*HSG*, p. 217) ultimately return to their Pyncheon-street perch. Neither resiles from the logic of duty, each refusing the call of fantasy, escapist or otherwise; and, by so doing, avoiding the Judge's fate, who descends into what looks to be a murderous and, ultimately, self-destructive psychosis, 'diseased in the mind' (*HSG*, p. 204) because he confuses illusion with actuality, fantasy with fact. For Jaffrey thoroughly embraces Clifford's childhood boast of 'boundless wealth' – 'a thing to laugh at' (*HSG*, p. 202) – as *true*, a misperception that piques his implacable and deranged 'possessive individualism' into action, ever ready – as are all psychotics – to treat his hallucinations as if they were 'real' (*HSG*, p. 272). Despite all his palaver about not being a 'dreaming' man (*HSG*, p. 202), his Honour occupies centre-stage here as the text's principal fantasist, hanging on like grim death (until his own grim death) to a 'delusion' (*HSG*, p. 272) of riches, lost but soon to be found. A finding which, incidentally, the Judge will go to any and all lengths to bring about, transgressing each social norm, committing every kind of crime.

Just recall, for instance, his youthful 'rap sheet' of indictable offences: trespass (committed by breaking into, and searching his uncle's 'private drawers', *HSG*, p. 268), fraud (occasioned by the destruction of a will 'of recent date' in favour of another – Clifford – all the while allowing 'an older one in his own favour ... to remain', *HSG*, p. 268), constructive manslaughter (his uncle's death being the result of his wrongful deed of trespass, itself provoking 'the crisis of a disorder to which the old bachelor had an hereditary liability', *HSG*, p. 268), tampering with evidence (arranging all 'circumstances' at trial to point to the innocent Clifford's guilt, *HSG*, p. 268), and perverting the course of justice (perpetrated in laying 'a scheme that', overall, 'should free himself at the expense of Clifford', *HSG*, p. 268). Not to mention any number of later offences, carried out – ironically – during his supposedly 'exemplary' (*HSG*, p. 267) maturity of 'eminent respectability' (*HSG*, p. 269): abuse of office (confirmed by the 'influence, political ... (and) personal' exercised by him to release Clifford from prison, *HSG*, p. 200), invasion of privacy (verified in his having informants 'constantly and carefully overlook' Clifford's 'deportment and habits', *HSG*, p. 203), intimidation (substantiated in his threat that Clifford will face 'confinement ... for the remainder of his life, in a public asylum' if he does not 'give up his secret', *HSG*, p. 203), even sexual harassment (borne out by 'the sex ... (being) ... too prominent' in the supposedly 'cousinly' kiss he attempts with a very hesitant, indeed resistant Phoebe, *HSG*, p. 103) – to name just a few.

Which prompts me to ask: is there nothing from which Jaffrey Pyncheon will flinch, no wrong he will not do, no law he will not flout? The violation of which, one might add, never attracts even the hint of, at

112 • Novel Judgements: Legal Theory as Fiction

least, *police* detection, let alone state prosecution. In light of this, surely there are few, if any other 'usual suspects' in the line-up of *Novel Judgements*' rogues that are more adept at *evading* legality's sanction by *manipulating* its technicality than Pyncheon, at one and the same time, law-*full* and law-*less*. Unless, of course, it is that other menacing 'man in black', *Bleak House*'s Tulkinghorn, the model for whom – according to Dickens – was none other than Hawthorne's reprobate-turned-'pillar of the community', that 'christian', 'good citizen', 'horticulturalist' and 'gentleman' (*HSG*, p. 23), Judge Jaffrey. Naturally, any reader with even a passing acquaintance of Dickens's biography would well understand why, in his great novel of the law, this former – and, more to the point, *failed* – articled clerk would make a *solicitor* his 'villain of the piece'. But Hawthorne? With little or no experience of legality, why would he make his antagonist not only a lawyer but a *judge* – even if only a bencher of an 'inferior court' (*HSG*, p. 23). Why bestow this 'very desirable and imposing title of judge' on a man such little scruple, even 'inward criminality' (*HSG*, p. 269)? Especially when the model for Pyncheon – Hawthorne's Whig political nemesis (and Holmes's uncle-by-marriage!), Charles Wentworth Upham[13] – was a *clergyman*, not a lawyer. Why then make an officer of the court not only the 'villain of the piece', but such an egregious example of villainy?

Hawthorne's reasons for such a choice may be (and doubtless were) many and varied, including the clerical,[14] the

13 J. R. Mellow identifies not only Upham but Sen. Nathaniel Silsbee as a model for Jaffrey Pyncheon. See: J. R. Mellow, *Nathaniel Hawthorne in His Time*, Boston: Houghton Mifflin Co., 1980. John McWilliams, however, only identifies Upham – as does the Modern Library edition of *The House of the Seven Gables*. See: J. P. McWilliams Jr., *Hawthorne, Melville and the American Character: A Looking Glass Business*, Cambridge: Cambridge University Press, 1984. For a fuller treatment of this colourful politico, minister and expatriate maritimer (born in New Brunswick of United Empire Loyalist heritage – incidentally, the same allegiance of the Revolutionary War Pyncheons), see: G. E. Ellis, *Memoir of Charles Wentworth Upham*, Cambridge: J. Wilson & Son, 1877.
14 Certainly, in this period, anti-clericalism – at least, that aimed at the *contemporary* pulpit – would never have made for good copy, fictional or otherwise, in what was, then, staunchly Protestant New England, Massachusetts in particular. With most of this era's native-born Bay Staters, such as Phoebe and the rest of Pyncheon-street's residents, regular churchgoers, such a stance would be a 'no-go' for even the most radical freethinker (Holgrave included); and this, despite the fact that the unofficial 'Established' faith of the region, Congregationalism, had, of late, come in for some heavy theological drubbing from its sectarian rival, the Unitarianism of the Boston *cognoscenti*. Of course, history, especially in the form of, as Michael Davitt Bell puts it, the 'historical romance of New England' was another matter altogether (M. D. Bell, *Hawthorne and the Historical*

political[15] and the familial.[16] But it is this peculiar yoking of the judicial and the villainous in the figure of Judge Jaffrey Pyncheon which suggests, for me, a jurisprudential analogue; namely, Mr Justice Oliver Wendell Holmes, Jr. – a seemingly bizarre choice in light of the latter's distinguished and nigh-on fifty-year career on the

*Romance of New England*, Princeton: Princeton University Press, 1971); and, there, Hawthorne's work bristles with problematic men of the cloth, *The Scarlet Letter*'s Dimmesdale being the most famous. But a sustained critique, either fictional or factual, of *Ecclesia* in the here-and-now? For Hawthorne and the rest of New England's intellectual 'Brahmin' caste, that would await the arrival of a different sort of clericalism; one found in an 'alien' popery encountered, not only abroad, while touring the Continent (on that topos, see *The Marble Faun*), but, also, at home, having been brought by the steady Irish and, later Italian influx into the region throughout the nineteenth century (the presence of which is registered, textually, in that bizarrest of characters, Pyncheon-street's Italian organ-grinder). Given this historical context – of not so much deference, as a 'hands-off' approach to the present-day clergy – clearly, a change of vocation was in order for Pyncheon-as-Upham.

15 Here, Hawthorne may gesture towards a certain strain of anti-judicialism well and truly in circulation, politically, at the time, American law reformers – such as David Dudley Field – having given vent to Benthamite bromides against judge-made law, promoting in its stead the idea of a code. See: L. Friedmann, *A History of American Law*, New York: Touchstone, 1973. More specifically, see: P. J. King, *Utilitarian Jurisprudence in America: The Influence of Bentham on American Legal Thought in the Nineteenth Century*, New York: Garland Publishers, 1986. That specific reform agenda, though, must be set off against a broader, more generalised juridical background of the courts and their operation, the adjectival and substantive functionality of which – at least, at the highest level – Hawthorne would have thoroughly approved. That is to say, if cross-examined on the matter, Hawthorne would have been clearly on the side of the bench, and its curial orthodoxy, rather than the Benthamites, and their critique of the common law. The bench I refer to, in this instance, is the Taney Supreme Court, notorious, then as much as now, for its 'softness' on slavery and its hostility towards abolition; not for nothing is *Dred Scott* (*Dred Scott* v. *Sandford*, 60 US 19 How. 393 (1857)) its best remembered and most reviled decision. Judicial attitudes with which Hawthorne, ever the good Democrat – Pierce's biographer, after all, and later an office-holder under his administration – would have been in sympathy.

16 Specifically, that of Hawthorne's own troubled family tree, and its blood-stained patriarch, Salem witch-finder general, Judge John Hathorne, the prototype for Col. Pyncheon and, *a fortiori*, his novelistic descendant, Judge Jaffrey Pyncheon, 'the old Pyncheon come again' (*HSG*, p. 19). That said, transgressions such as Jaffrey Pyncheon's, once brought to light, far exceed for sheer heinousness any of the (mis)deeds of the fictional Colonel Pyncheon or the factual Judge Hathorne. For unlike Jaffrey, Colonel Pyncheon did *heed* the law that he was charged to uphold (that is, witchcraft-as-crime), however mixed his motives (admittedly, retributively venal); while Judge Hathorne, according to the historical record, actually *believed* in that dubious law (and remained the only inquisitor never to recant), his motives being *ad idem* with his acts. See: E. H. Miller, *Salem Is My Dwelling Place: A Life of Nathaniel Hawthorne*, Iowa City: University of Iowa, 1991.

bench:[17] a curial tenure of office for which, despite all Holmes's differences of opinion, over the years, with his judicial brethren[18] – or perhaps precisely because of that, he was universally respected, if not idolised. How then can I associate someone as heinous as Judge Pyncheon with someone as – at least in judicial terms – hagiographic as Holmes: the so-called 'Yankee from Olympus'[19]? Wherein lies, as the narrative voice of *The House of Seven Gables* would put it, the 'link' (*HSG*, p. 18) between the two? I want to suggest that this linkage lies specifically in a shared *moral* value, one which Holmes expressly valorises and Hawthorne dramatically enacts: precisely, that of *badness*. Now badness, and its personification – the 'Bad Man' – have come to count, perhaps unduly in the emphasis given each by legal scholars, biographers and the like, as Holmes's core contribution to jurisprudence. But there is good reason for this notoriety *or* notability, however one may wish to characterise it. For it is this flamboyant figure – of law's user and abuser; what might be called in a more current colloquial idiom, the client 'from hell' – who is, according to Holmes, the principal driver on his 'path of law', coursing over its gravel, marking its lanes, pushing its route ever on, all the while paying lip service to, if not outright ignoring its traffic signals and signposts along the way: namely, its rule system.

All of which renders Holmes's 'predictive theory of law' predictable; for the Bad Man's bottom line is that legal process's substantive outcomes – that is, actual rulings, real decisions – provide a far more reliable guide to determining not only what the law *is* but in forecasting what it *will be* than, say, the Sugarman-esque 'law-as-text', with its formal imperatives of discursive systematicity. In short, the Bad Man privileges how courts *act* rather than what they say (or, more to the point, write), as proof positive of the law: 'You will find some text writers telling you that it (law) is something different from what is decided by the courts . . . that it is a system of reason . . . a deduction from principles of ethics or admitted axioms . . . which may or may not coincide with the decisions. But if we take the view of our friend the bad man we shall find he does not care two straws for the axioms or deductions, but that he does want to know what the . . . courts are likely to do in fact. I am much of his mind' (*PL*, p. 163). *Nearly*, but not quite; for the two are coincident, yet not identical: because while Holmes is

---

17 Initially on the Supreme Court of Massachusetts (1883–1903), then latterly on the US Supreme Court, from which he retired in 1932.
18 So much so that he could just as easily have said at the end of his career as he did, encomiastically, at the beginning: 'I venerate the law, and especially our system of law as one of the vastest products of the human mind' (*PL*, p. 173).
19 C. D. Bowen, *Yankee from Olympus*, Boston: Little Brown, 1944.

'much of his mind' (*PL*, p. 163), he is *not* the Bad Man. Nor is the Bad Man, him – or, at least, what he is soon to be: a judge. For in Holmes's predictive theory of law, the Bad Man and the judge are separate and distinct, the latter, being a synecdoche for the legal system in its entirety, a part standing for the *whole*; while the former is that system's *hole*, its point of greatest vulnerability as much as maximum utility, facilitating both the law's avoidance *and* instrumentalisation, as need arises.

That said, the Bad Man is wary of *blatantly* compromising law's integrity, sidestepping any open breach of it; he may shadow the law, testing its ambit, straining its limits – but never to the extent of overtly falling afoul of it, and, thereby, attracting its sanction: '[A] bad man ... who cares nothing for an ethical rule which is believed and practiced by his neighbours is likely nevertheless to care to avoid being made to pay money, and will want to keep out of jail' (*PL*, p. 161). These strategic, indeed sociopathic traits listed above – a lack of principle, an aversion to punishment, but especially a repugnance for *getting caught red-handed*; all could fit, quite easily, into a psychological profile of Jaffrey Pyncheon..., that novelistic instantiation of the Law who stands exposed here as *the* outlaw of the narrative. And, moreover, one who, in his outlawry, manages to shun any sense of shame, as much as he shifts any accusation of blame: contrast Clifford's life-long and soul-destroying mortification ('thoroughly crushed', *HSG*, p. 99) with Jaffrey's 'black and damnable' (*HSG*, p. 269) wrong-doing of which he is in such deep denial that he has 'forgotten' all about it, 'and seldom thought of it again' but as a 'venial matter' (*HSG*, p. 269), easily 'forgiven' (*HSG*, p. 269) and left to 'fade' (*HSG*, p. 269), free from any public scrutiny.

With this erasure of any sense of (legal) responsibility – let alone twinge of conscience, Hawthorne collapses the 'distinction' between 'law' and (*im-*)'morality' (*PL*, p. 161) Holmes worked so hard to maintain,[20] conflating the judge with the Bad Man, and thereby paving the way for what subsequent generations of legal realists and their fellow travellers – Frank, but also Pound, Llewellyn, Cohen and so on – would bemoan as the *baddest* of Bad Men: that odious amalgam, the adjudicator who is wildly discretionary (his decisions turning on the contingencies of politics as much as personality) and, at one and the same time, excessively constrained

---

20  At least, for the purposes of 'learning and understanding the law' (*PL*, p. 161) because, for Holmes, morality – meaning right conduct, virtue, *civitas*, etc. – is inscribed in the very heart of law: 'The law is the witness and external deposit of our moral life. Its history is the history of the moral development of the race. The practice of it, in spite of popular jests, tends to make good citizens and good men' (*PL*, p. 161).

(rendering him the automaton of 'mechanical jurisprudence'), both formlessly free *and* formalistically bound. Before exploring, however, in any further detail the manifold conflicts rending this despised figure, I want to put this question to what I take to be the Bad Man's novelistic prototype – Judge Pyncheon: that is, for all his impressive – yet as far as any police blotter is concerned, still unreported criminal record, in what lies His Honour's badness? The query is a significant one because any answer to it will gesture as much towards Holmes's, as Hawthorne's Bad Man, the two sharing precisely the same nature. The badness of which, as it turns out, inheres in what they are *not*, neither of these figures of law's Imaginary being bad in any truly positive (and legal positivist) sense. That is, both Hawthorne's and Holmes's Bad Men eschew the *obvious* commission of any substantive offence under the 'posited' (or manmade) law. Rather their joint culpability resides in *omission* not commission – in what they do not do, instead of what they do; in other words, their mutual *failure* to act.

Note how Jaffrey gets off scot-free, exonerated of his uncle's death 'by refraining' (*HSG*, p. 268) at Clifford's trial 'to state what he had himself done and witnessed' (*HSG*, p. 268). One could well imagine, if put in a similar position, the Bad Man operating with the same restraint; his minimalist sense of legal duty enabling him to sit back, remain silent and, when spoken to, find it – like Jaffrey did – 'hardly ... necessary to swear to anything false' (*HSG*, p. 268). But for all this, and other similarities between Hawthorne's and Holmes's Bad Men, the latter merely *stalks* the law, whereas the former *becomes* the law, Pyncheon having opted, after his cousin's trial, for a career in the very curial process of which he had made a mockery. A strange choice of profession, to say the least, for such a promisingly delinquent young 'juvie' – which the text tries to explain away on the grounds of the budding *roué* 'reformed' (*HSG*, p. 22). That justification, however, rings false; and, in any event, is almost instantly undercut by the textual admission of the persistence of Jaffrey's overweening will-to-power, still as grasping as before and just as unstoppable until satiated. Indeed, its most recent manifestation is well and truly on display in the good Judge's desire for the highest sort of public 'office' (*HSG*, p. 23), him being content with neither the bench nor Congress, now (over)reaching for nothing less than the state's 'gubernatorial' chair (*HSG*, p. 235) – as the reader learns from the lavish nomination lunch focalised by the text's omniscient narrator with the sponsoring Federalist ward-heelers lamenting the absence of their nominee, the Judge, now, unbeknownst to them, well and truly dead.

No surprises then that Judge Pyncheon is a 'judge without judgments', let alone justice because he is a creature of 'law's politics', driven by his own (considerable) appetites, cannibalising the rules and rule system as he sees fit – fitness, here, being largely a question of whether it satiates his hunger for 'wealth, prosperity and elevated station' (*HSG*, p. 114). This is why the jurisprudentially informed reader need not ask – as Holmes's legal realist descendent, rule-sceptic Jerome Frank did, famously, in the 1930s – as to 'what the judge had for breakfast'[21] because, in this case, it is perfectly clear that Judge Pyncheon, in all his 'fleshly effulgence' (*HSG*, p. 101), has gobbled up the law, leaving behind only curial crumbs at this banquet. Which is more than enough, by the way, to render this engorgement 'not all', a stray juridical morsel thwarting Jaffrey's 'Levianthanic' urge to become, through corporeal introjection, a law unto *himself*. This remainder, of course, is that 'little piece of the Real'; specifically, the deed to Waldo County, the *objet petit a* which so obsesses the Pyncheons 'from generation to generation' (*HSG*, p. 18), and for which Judge Pyncheon has substituted, given that document's disappearance, another set of inscriptions, 'familiar *enough* to capitalists', he condescends to Hepzibah, 'but unnecessary here to be specified' (*HSG*, p. 201). Meaning, Uncle Jaffrey's lost 'paper' wealth – the stock certificates, company shares, bills of exchange, trust accounts, insurance claims, assignments of debts, and so forth; indeed, all the 'big, heavy, solid unrealities' (*HSG*, p. 197) of credit and debit that would have comprised the financial portfolio of a well-heeled, nineteenth-century *rentier* and which went, so inconveniently, astray after said party's untimely decease – or so it is believed.

Which, in turn, his nephew and principal beneficiary pursues so *relentlessly*, thereby displacing onto another 'lost treasure' the same tenacious and implacable drive for ownership that, iteratively, gripped his ancestors in their pursuit of that long vanished, proprietarial 'princedom' (*HSG*, p. 19) of theirs. The secret of which the judge erroneously believes is in the possession of that strangest of *sujets supposés savoir*, Clifford: '[A]t this moment, if he chooses ... (Clifford) can inform me where to find ...

---

21 The well-known maxim – that legal judgement turns on, and is the result of the vagaries of the adjudicator's matutinal meal – is attributed to Jerome Frank or as F. Schauer puts it he was 'saddled with the "what the judge had for breakfast" caricature', see F. Schauer, *Thinking Like a Lawyer: A New Introduction to Legal Reasoning*, Cambridge, MA: Harvard University Press, 2009, p. 130. The pairing of early legal realism with the 'breakfast theory', essentially a glib and cynical reworking of Frank's 'The Basic Myth', from J. Frank, *Law and the Modern Mind*, New Brunswick: Transaction Publishers, 2008, p. 3, has been pervasive in legal jurisprudence texts such as R. Dworkin, *Law's Empire*, London: Fontana Press, 1986, p. 36; M. Davies, *Asking the Law Question*, Sydney: Law Book Co., 2008, p. 164 and M. Leiboff and M. Thomas, *Legal Theories: Context and Practices*, Sydney: Law Book Co., 2009, pp. 375 and 376.

in whatever shape they exist, of the vast amount of Uncle Jaffrey's missing property' (*HSG*, p. 202). While I have adverted earlier to this 'misrecognition' – that is, the mistaken belief in the truth of Clifford's idle taunt of buried treasure – here I want to emphasise the *tangible* shape this sort of secret-as-*idée fixe* takes on, over time and iteratively, for not only the Pyncheons writ large (Clifford, Uncle Jaffrey, Gervase, and so forth), but, in particular, the *judicial* Pyncheons, past (the old Colonel) and present (Judge Jaffrey). That is, in the material form of law's *letter*, be it 'yellow[ed] parchment' (*HSG*, p. 178) or some modern 'schedule' (*HSG*, p. 202), each of which, having gone missing, are now sought, high and low, by them with the same urgency they would (or should) devote to finding and following binding precedent under *stare decisis*.

What both these judicial (mis)judgments revolve around, and disclose is the legal signifier at its purest – at once empty *and* absent; a formal (and formalist) symptom of law at its most literally *script*-ural, and which sits, figuratively, cheek by jowl here (and in Judge Pyncheon's case, what cheeks! what jowls! – the 'lower region of his face' being marked by a 'massive accumulation of animal substance' (*HSG*, p. 101) with the notion of the judge as a-*nomic*; specifically, as a rule-free arbitrator whom even the most 'Solomonic' of 'palm tree justices' would find too much of a swinging bellwether. This conjuncture – of the appetitive (law's insatiable craving) in pursuit of the alphabetic (the legal letter-as-comestible) – is exactly why Hawthorne's novel is such an insightful analepsis of legal realism: because it gives the reader, in the figure of Jaffrey Pyncheon, a startling personification of that movement's principal object of critique and central contradiction – one which complicates my earlier claims of the judge-as-psychotic, expulsive of the Law. Instead of psychotic, Jaffrey Pyncheon turns out to be the perverse judge, who, simultaneously, embraces *and* disavows the rule system, forever transgressing the spirit of the law, paradoxically in his search, *everywhere*, for its letter. Now the question becomes: what – or, more to the point, who – will traverse this legal formalist fantasy, bringing to an end its ever-spiralling and subjectively subversive dialectic of desire driven by and for the agency of law's letter?

Two possibilities, I would like to suggest, present themselves as critical contenders for the role of 'psychic detective' here: the unlikely pair of Hepzibah and Clifford. Those 'horror(s)' (*HSG*, p. 255) – as the reader might query, with the same astonishment as the children of the neighbourhood. With forensic champions such as these – 'lunatics' (*HSG*, p. 150, p. 213), even enfeebled 'imbecile(s)' (*HSG*, p. 123, p. 136, p. 188) – why not opt for that 'cock of the walk', the lordly chanticleer and his 'gallinaceous' (*HSG*, p. 130) brood of 'two wives' (*HSG*, p. 131), 'Speckle' (*HSG*, p. 86) and the rest? Surely they would fit the bill – as the 'Old Bill' of the unconscious – as much as their owners because they turn out to be one and the same, right down to personal features; think of the hens' 'crest(s)' (*HSG*, p. 78) which humorously iterate Hepzibah's much maligned 'horror of a turban' (*HSG*, p. 37). More, though, than just mimic appearances in the way animals often do with their people, this small flock's 'degenerat[ion]' (*HSG*, p. 78) metaphorises another evolutionary law in reverse: the Pyncheons' devoutionary spiral downwards to some cretinous *fin de ligne*. 'The Daguerreotypist once whispered' to Phoebe, and said 'these marks betokened the oddities of the Pyncheon family, and that the chicken itself was a symbol of the life of the old house' (*HSG*, p. 132). All of which *might* suggest a 'eugenics' solution to this case of 'the hereditary' (*HSG*, p. 104) gone awry, something along the lines of Holmes's lawful, yet scandalous decision in *Buck* v. *Bell*,[22] though here, given the long reach of the family tree, the generations would have to be more than doubled, the three of the Bells becoming, 'Seven generations of (Pyncheon) imbeciles are enough' – sterilise! The only problem with this Holmesian injunction, however, is that the text so flatly contradicts its Social Darwinism, *The House of the Seven Gables*' weakest characters outlasting 'the fittest' by not only surviving natural selection's lawful winnowing out but thriving well beyond it into the novel's extradiegetic future.

Think of Clifford: for all the narrative's repeated emphasis on his physical and mental infirmities, it is this very figure of vulnerability who has, quite literally, the *last laugh* on his, seemingly, far more robust cousin, as instanced in the strange euphoria (a 'gusty mirth', emboldening him to 'dance', 'sing' and 'play', *HSG*, p. 215) that overwhelms the ex-con upon discovering his nemesis's body in the Old Colonel's study – if not exactly cold, then at least cooling: 'What an absurd figure', crows Clifford, 'the old fellow cuts now' (*HSG*, p. 216). Elation of this sort, however, should not be read – so I contend – as part and parcel of Clifford's overall pathology; namely, as a form of mania that, with him, functions as the flip side of, and complement to Hepzibah's depressiveness. I would resist, however, such 'wild analysis' because it positions the reader just as uncomfortably as the hapless 'gimlet-eyed' (*HSG*, p. 222) railway passenger was; that is, with him (or her) listening with growing alarm to Clifford's ramblings about 'spiritualize[d]' travel (*HSG*, p. 223) and rotting 'corpse[s]' (*HSG*,

---

22  *Buck* v. *Bell*, 274 US 200 (1927).

p. 226, p. 228), all the while left wondering whether all this is a transcendentalist parody or a psychotic confession? Or, if such *psycho*-analysis is to be indulged, then I would caution the reader, *contra* Matheson, to approach these psychic structures – mania, depression – in the same spirit as the text does; that is, as sources of strength rather than signs of senility: in short, as coping mechanisms, enabling their agent-subjects (Clifford, Hepzibah) to persevere, even triumph over and above Jaffrey's psychotic *hors-loi* by operating within, and between the interstices of the socio-Symbolic Law.

Seen from this light, Clifford's much commented upon evanescence – as a voice 'indistinct' (*HSG*, p. 84) in its intonation; a presence 'faded away' to the point of 'unreality' (*HSG*, p. 84) or 'substantial emptiness' (*HSG*, p. 92) – looks strategic on his part; granted, a form of lunacy, but one very much with its own logic, drawing upon presumably 'an(O)ther Law', *une autre symbolique*: what a certain strand of contemporary gender theory (*à la* Judith Halberstam,[23] Lee Edelman[24] & co.) would hail as a subjectivity of 'unbecoming' which when mobilised, as here, is the only means, in the absence of any sort of civil and political 'right to desire differently', of securing the survival of 'the queer'. For that is precisely what Clifford is: a 'queer', though one tricked out in nineteenth-century drag, his sexual difference being coded as the period's effeminate aestheticisim: 'Beauty would be his life' (*HSG*, p. 94). As a proto-Wildean '[s]ybarite' (*HSG*, p. 95) plonked down amidst Pyncheon-street's neo-Puritans, Clifford's 'delicate taste' (*HSG*, p. 111) may be the only real 'crime' of which he is 'guilty'. A 'love of the beautiful' (*HSG*, p. 111) being, here, 'a love that dare not speak its name' because it is so *contra naturam* Salem's (and New England's) pragmatic ethos that it attracts not only vituperative familial disapproval ('they persecuted his mother in him', *HSG*, p. 54 – meaning his '[f]eminine' side, *HSG*, p. 53) but the strongest sort of community sanction: in fact, the same Reading Gaol-style fate that awaits Wilde, incarceration. No surprises then that Clifford, once released, lives only day to day, taking all in through his 'senses', and gobbling up every meal as if it were his last: 'He ate food with what might almost be termed voracity, and seemed to forget himself ... in the sensual enjoyment which the bountifully spread table afforded' (*HSG*, p. 93). I would like to suggest that he does so because this might very well be his last meal, especially given the hostile normative and juridical

---

23 J. Halberstam, *In a Queer Time and Place: Transgender Bodies, Subcultural Lives*, New York: New York University Press, 2005.
24 L. Edelman, *No Future: Queer Theory and the Death Drive*, Durham, NC: Duke University Press, 2004.

conditions that obtain in this period against Clifford and what might be called, anachronistically, his gender-bending 'LGBTQ' brethren, sodomy being very much on the books in this period, and, previously, pretty much a 'hanging offence'.[25]

Not that this posited socio-legal regime is any better for women, as is amply evidenced by the paucity of options available for Hepzibah as an 'Old Maid' (or, for that matter, Phoebe as a 'Young Maid'). Teaching school, running a cent shop, boarding with or living off more comfortably situated relations; these are the less than attractive avenues that appear open to the (female) talent of this era. In light of these severe limitations, is it any wonder that Hepzibah elects for the autonomy of seclusion, turning inward, feeding off her own being, eating – as it were – her *Dasein*. To interpret, however, Hepzibah's 'withering away' as a symptom of tradition's vulnerability in the face of modernity – as Mathiesson's Marxism might – is as much a characterological *méconnaissance* as reading, heteronormatively, Clifford's aestheticism a weakness. Hepzibah's 'queer and quaint ways' (*HSG*, p. 117) may be *reactive*, but they are most certainly not reactionary – a characterisation more easily attributed to her 'conservative' (*HSG*, p. 139) brother. After all, who is it that first voices something like working-class *ressentiment* against the leisured classes? None other than that *ci-devant* member of the New England gentry, the family-proud Hepzibah, now a fully-fledged 'hucksteress' (*HSG*, p. 35) proletarianised by a day of trading, who, after espying a richly dressed 'lady' (*HSG*, p. 49) from her shop window, has what might be called a 'Madame Defarge moment' of proto-revolutionary status envy: 'Must the whole world toil, that the palms of her hands may be kept white and delicate' (*HSG*, p. 50).

Far then from colluding with, let alone valorising the hegemonic class and gender system which this upper crust *flâneuse* emblematises, Hepzibah as aristo-anorexic registers her protest against that system in the most corporeal of ways; specifically, as an act of resistance which is *somatised*, that is, *written* on her 'shrunken' body (*HSG*, p. 30), as well as inscribed in her 'creaking' joints (*HSG*, p. 28), 'scowling' visage (*HSG*, p. 48) and 'near-sighted' (*HSG*, p. 37) squint. While her attendant speech may attempt to

---

25 All American colonies imposed the death penalty for 'sodomy'. After the Revolution, however, Pennsylvania was the first state to abolish that sentence in 1786, followed in the course of the next generation by most of the other states. Even with these sweeping reforms, though, this sentence remained on the books of North and South Carolina until after the Civil War. See: N. Edsall, *Towards Stonewall: Homosexuality and Society in the Modern Western World*. Charlottesville, VA: University of Virginia, 2003, pp. 127–152.

mitigate this spirit of defiance ('May God forgive me!' is her quickly uttered prayer, following upon her 'sentiment of virulence' above, *HSG*, p. 49), Hepzibah's body, nonetheless, continues to fight on, never surrendering to this system, and the law that supports it. No wonder then it is this odd, seemingly feeble figure of feminine opposition (a 'gaunt, sallow... maiden' of sixty, *HSG*, p. 37), rather than any of the novel's male characters – not Holgrave, not Uncle Venner, certainly not Clifford – who actually confronts that embodiment of the law, Jaffrey Pyncheon. For Hepzibah not only sees – as do many characters, including the *naive* Phoebe – through the Judge's *faux* benignity to his underlying *animus*; alone of all the others, she divulges this *mens rea*, her 'scowl' exposing his 'smile' for the ruse it is: 'In the name of Heaven... give over, I beseech you, this loathsome pretence of affection for your victim! You hate him! Say so, like a man!' (*HSG*, p. 196). So for all her pulmonary murmurs and ticks, the text goes out of its way here and elsewhere to insist upon how 'strong' (*HSG*, p. 85) Hepzibah's heart is, it being but a sign of her latent 'heroism' (*HSG*, p. 115), the 'high, generous and noble' (*HSG*, p. 115) nature of which is concealed behind her brittle vulnerability.

The problem, however, with Hepzibah and Clifford as putative traversers of fantasy is that both, ultimately, are marked by a deficiency –but not in the way in which others in the text would understand that deficiency (either as bubble-blowing infantilism or paralysing shyness, respectively). Though Hepzibah, for example, may have the *power* to carry out this charge of transversal (not surprising for one so thoroughly situated by, and *under* the Law's paternal signifier, 'Pyncheon' – 'born in Pyncheon-street, under the Pyncheon-elm, and in the Pyncheon-house', *HSG*, p. 35), she lacks the knowledge to do so. While Clifford, to take the other example, most definitely has that knowledge – having stumbled across the deed's hidden location in his youth – but lacks any power by which to prosecute it (again, nothing startling here in one who never *really* was a Pyncheon in the first place). One is too much of a Pyncheon, the other too little of one – and neither have the combined *nous* and nerve to venture into the across legal history's layered structures emblematised in Hawthorne Seven Gables, descending its depths to the very foundational 'bottom' (*PL*, p. 175) which, for all his notorious anti-historicism, Holmes argued was a precondition to any sort of legal realism which would want to make good on its promise of nomological rebuilding, free of precedential constraints: 'History ... enables us to make up our minds dispassionately whether the survival which we are enforcing answers any new purpose when it has ceased to answer the old' (*HSG*, p. 191). To that end, one might well ask: who is equipped to make such an exploratory descent, gifted not only with the knowledge of the letter of the law's location, but with the capacity to effect its delivery? As if responding, proleptically, to Holmes, Hawthorne identifies quite clearly, I shall argue, just who will ensure the *arrival* of law's letter; and, in so doing, will bring to an end its psychic hold on all and sundry in his novel by exposing it as the lifeless scribble – moot *and* mute – it so clearly is, thereby arresting its dialectic of desire by traversing, here, its fantasy of legal formalism. Such psychic and physical *pouvoir/savoir* is invested in one, and one figure alone in *The House of the Seven Gables*: none other than Holgrave.

## Getting the (Law-)Job Done: Holgrave as the Legal Realist; Phoebe as the Legal 'Real' (*HSG*, p. 122)

Holgrave? A deliverer of the law? To whom even Phoebe refers to as 'lawless' (*HSG*, p. 75)? Who, himself, rejects freely all laws, let alone courts, including (and especially) the one that ruled against Clifford; for Holgrave impliedly calls this court's authority into question when he suggests that his housemate was 'settled by a competent tribunal, *or one which called itself competent*' (*HSG*, p. 82, italics mine). I italicise the preceding quotation's modifying clause in order to highlight what any jurisprudentially informed reader would recognise instantly in its note of qualification: an utterance of legal *critique*, its 'hermeneutics of (curial) suspicion' being unmistakeable here. Not that the courts are Holgrave's only target. Legal personnel, as much as court processes, attract their fair share of criticism, even when they cross Holgrave's field of vision as aesthetic subjects, caught under the glare of his daguerreotypic gaze. Consider how vividly the 'pictures out of sunshine' (*HSG*, p. 80), which this piercing stare focalises, disclose the 'secret character' (*HSG*, p. 80) of Judge Pyncheon. For, here, Holgrave's much commented upon[26] art of the camera literally brings to light His

---

26 Charles Swan observes Holgrave's 'democratic art' which 'does not allow the operator deferentially to flatter the patron', instead the 'daguerreotype reveals the truth about Judge Pyncheon *and* that the daguerreotype is like the Colonel': C. Swan, '*The House of the Seven Gables*: Hawthorne's Modern Novel of 1848', *Modern Language Review* 86(1), 1991, 9. Similarly, Alfred Hitchcock writes in a much earlier article that, 'Where the shadow falls, a barrier rises which no camera penetrates' where 'the Judge, hiding a black heart beneath sultry smiles' reveals to the reader that 'their composite is Hawthorne himself, a truer portrait than that which looks down on me from my study wall': A. Hitchcock, 'The Relation of the Picture Play to Literature', *English Journal* 4(5), 1915, 293. See also L. B. Levy, 'Picturesque Style in "The House of the Seven Gables" ', *New England Quarterly* 39(2), 1966, 159; R. Thomas, 'Double Exposures: Arresting Images in "Bleak House" and the "The House of the Seven Gables" ', *A Forum on Fiction* 31(1), 1997, 102–103 and 106; A. Trachtenberg, 'Seeing and Believing: Hawthorne's Reflections on the Daguerreotype in "The House of the Seven Gables" ' 9(3), 1997, 466–468, 471 and 476–477.

Honour's putatively hidden nature: one that is 'sly, subtle, hard, imperious and, withal, cold as ice' (*HSG*, p. 80); and, as such, is very much at variance with the 'exceedingly pleasant countenance' (*HSG*, p. 81), the Judge presents to the world at large.

Now such an ideological revelation – of the malign motives underlying the surface sweetness of the law – would be a truly radical gesture, worthy of legality's most vociferous critic; if, that is, the Judge's public–private divide wasn't the worst-kept confidence in Salem, the town's 'diurnal gossip' (*HSG*, p. 106) being so much a-twitter with the 'vast discrepancy' (*HSG*, p. 106) between Jaffrey's exterior ('wherewith he shone like the noonday sun', *HSG*, p. 107) and his interior ('bold, imperious, relentless, crafty', *HSG*, p. 107) that no one, *no one* can fail to conflate his present (as 'The Pyncheon of To-Day', *HSG*, p. 100) with his past (as the spitting image of the Old Pyncheon, whose reincarnation he is). Holgrave's critique of Judge Pyncheon, however, goes further than the 'scandal'-mongering (*HSG*, p. 107) of the local *on dit*. For with his considerable powers of observation, Holgrave divines not only the Judge's fairly obvious animus but the *angoisse* that strains to breaking his relationship with his cousin, Clifford: 'what can Judge Pyncheon have to ... fear from the ... half-torpid Clifford' (*HSG*, p. 188). So the 'impulse' (*HSG*, p. 187) driving Holgrave's critique is not, as he maintains, merely clinical – that is, 'to look on, to analyze, to explain' (*HSG*, p. 187); rather, it is *to solve*, its end-game being the resolution of the above stated 'mystery' (*HSG*, p. 188). As such, Holgrave's critical project in this case is investigatory, in fact forensic and perforce *legal*. All of which confirms Hepzibah's reassuring response to an alarmed Phoebe that, far from being lawless, Holgrave has 'a law of his own' (*HSG*, p. 75).

But what kind of law is Holgrave's? Certainly not a scholastic one – especially in the sense of Roscoe Pound's 'law-in-books', Holgrave having little acquaintance with texts (he 'had read very little', *HSG*, p. 155), even less with education (having had 'the scantiest possible, and obtained by a few winter-months' attendance at a district school', *HSG*, p. 151). This double deficit, however, situates the legalism of Holgrave within a proto-realist, indeed Holmesian vein. For Holmes, famously, argued that the life of the law lies not in bookish, scholastic 'logic', but, rather, in direct, unmediated 'experience'.[27] Which is precisely what Holgrave has in spades – *experience*: be it as a pedlar of cheap scent and 'notions' (*HSG*, p. 152), a self-taught dentist (*HSG*, p. 152), a newspaper editor (*HSG*, p. 152), a shop's sales assistant (*HSG*, p. 152), a packet-ship's official (*HSG*, p. 152),

---

27  O. W. Holmes, 'The Common Law', in Posner, *The Essential Holmes*, above n. 8, p. 237.

up to and including his stint as a Fourierist (*HSG*, p. 152) and his gig as a Mesmerist (*HSG*, p. 152). Not to mention his current career briefs: of course, as a daguerreotypist, but also as an aspiring writer (for such popular periodicals as 'Godey' or 'Graham', *HSG*, p. 183) and a budding politico ('making a speech full of wild and disorganising matter, at a meeting of his banditti-like associates', *HSG*, p. 75). For all this vocational flux though, Holgrave is centred by, and around a personal core that remains *fixed*: 'he had never lost his identity ... (nor) violated the innermost man, but had carried his conscience with him' (*HSG*, p. 152). So Holgrave, like Holmes, most definitely has a set *standpoint*, from which one detects his crime, the other predicts his law – yet each remaining at a remove: the former circling Hepzibah, Clifford and Judge Jaffrey; the latter, shadowing the Bad Man – both 'coolly' (*HSG*, p. 82) attentive, wearing an expression 'not sinister' (*HSG*, p. 135) but 'questionable' (*HSG*, p. 136).

This is precisely the kind of near-autistic detachment that so unnerves Phoebe about Holgrave ('She did not altogether like him', *HSG*, p. 82) and, indeed, frustrates me about Holmes, hitherto one of my favourite legal philosophers. For when will either, as E. M. Forster might put it, *only connect*;[28] that is, leave their owl-like perches, and turn their observations, however 'deep' and 'thoughtful' (*HSG*, p. 135) into participation, their passive spectatorship into active engagement. To wit, when will Holmes-as-Holgrave and Holgrave-as-Holmes actually *do* something; thereby transforming their critique into a construction, their standpoint into a solution, their fixity into a function? In order for that to happen, both await the appearance of what deconstruction would call a 'supplement' – that is, a necessary add-on or X factor, hitherto absent, but the presence of which will temper Holmes's and Holgrave's 'crude, wild, and misty philosophy' (*HSG*, p. 156), putting their psychic predictions and 'inward prophecy' (*HSG*, p. 154) to work. For Holmes, that 'pragmatic sanction' will come in the form of what his principal intellectual heir and successor, mentioned earlier – again, Llewellyn – would call the 'law–job';[29] that is, the functionalisation of the law as an *activity*, the varied nature of which obtains in the list of juridical tasks that follows: 'the disposition of the trouble-case' (*MPL*, p. 1016); 'the preventive channelling of conduct

---

28 E. M. Forster, *Howards End*, Harmondsworth, Middlesex: Penguin Books, 1986, p. 188.
29 K. N. Llewellyn, 'My Philosophy of Law', in M. D. A. Freeman (ed.), *Lloyd's Introduction to Jurisprudence*, 8th edn, London: Thomson Reuters, 2008, pp. 1016–1017. Hereafter referred to as *MPL*.

and expectations' (*MPL*, p. 1016); 'the allocation of authority' (*MPL*, p. 1017); 'the net organization of the society as a whole so as to provide integration, direction, and incentive' (*MPL*, p. 1017); and, lastly, the '[j]uristic method', meaning the 'building up (of) effective traditions of handling, the legal material and tools and people developed for other jobs' (*MPL*, p. 1017).

Hawthorne anticipates this quintessentially Legal Realist contribution to jurisprudence, instantiating these law–jobs – or 'chores' as she, doubtless, would call them – in a character who is 'activity' (*HSG*, p. 73) personified, and, after all, referred to by the text as 'the real' (*HSG*, p. 122): namely, Phoebe. For Phoebe incarnates the Llewellyn-*esque* law–job, enacting in her domestic routine and daily intercourse the various legal pursuits itemised above. Consider the following: how deftly she disposes of a 'trouble-case' by mollifying a 'pettish and nervously restless' (*HSG*, p. 119) Clifford ('Phoebe's presence ... was usually all that he required', *HSG*, p. 119); preventively channels 'too intense' (*HSG*, p. 103) conduct by sidestepping the untoward overtures of Judge Pyncheon ('A young girl – especially if she be a pretty one – can never be too chary of her lips', *HSG*, p. 103*)*; effectively allocates authority, taking change not only of the shop's intake ('what an enormous heap of copper! Positively a copper mountain!', *HSG*, p. 72) but also its provisioning ('We must renew our stock', *HSG*, p. 72); and completely reorganises that microcosm of society in which she finds herself – her ancestral home, integrating its inhabitants: her peculiar cousins, their pets, even their strange lodger – into, and as a whole ('Whatever health, comfort, and natural life exists in the house', says Holgrave, 'is embodied in your person', *HSG*, p. 186), giving them direction, providing them with incentive: again, according to Holgrave, 'They both exist by you' (*HSG*, p. 186).

No wonder Holgrave declares his love to Phoebe with such 'wild enjoyment' (*HSG*, p. 262). His timing may be seriously off (that 'strange moment' (*HSG*, p. 259) in the wake of his discovery of Judge Pyncheon's corpse, mortifying in the Old Colonel's study) and the location insalubrious to say the least (a closed-off, near derelict room in the now deserted Seven Gables, itself a possible crime scene); but surely here is the 'young girl' (*HSG*, p. 154) of which he had earlier fantasised in the narrative, one whose 'intuitive sympathy' (*HSG*, p. 154) would complete him and his investigation into the 'complexity of complexities' (*HSG*, p. 154). For is there nothing Phoebe can't do? Seemingly not, because, as the text states, she so 'spiritual[ises]' (*HSG*, p. 73) activity she may very well figure in her person New England's very real Calvinist credo: the Protestant work ethic, of which she is a *prosopopoeia*. Which prompts me to ask, not why would Holgrave declare himself to her; but, rather, why would the capable Phoebe reciprocate his feelings, accepting suit from someone as unfocused, even erratic as Holgrave – of whose future prospects the text speculates uncertainly, wondering if he may give off, as many potentially promising young men do who fail to live up to their promise, a 'false brilliancy' (*HSG*, p. 156), destined to fade.

I would like to suggest, however, that if Phoebe accepts Holgrave's offer of love – and later, one presumes, marriage – then it is because her juridical 'activity of body, intellect, and heart' (*HSG*, p. 119) is missing one vital element, key to the 'law–jobs' (and her) 'useful purpose' (*HSG*, p. 69): specifically, self-reflexiveness; or what Llewellyn calls the 'juristic method', and its ongoing reformist (re)conceptualisation of the law–jobs, 'doing them better, until they became a source of revelation of new possibility and achievement' (*MPL*, p. 1017). For Phoebe, this sort of meta-activity – the *ur*-law–job – is alien to a nature inclined to 'the Actual' (*HSG*, p. 121); but, for Holgrave, who, after all, fancies himself, first and foremost, 'a thinker' (*HSG*, p. 155), it comes as second nature – or should come, if, that is, he can overcome his allergy to what is, for Holmes, and the other realists, the legal historical starting point for their reformist efforts: namely, 'tradition'. This is, doubtless, why Holgrave does such an about-face towards the end of the narrative, embracing the lasting permanence of 'stone' houses (*HSG*, p. 270), rather than those of 'wood' (*HSG*, p. 270) and the concomitant reorientation in perspective that such a turn to historicity entails. An alteration that would, presumably, exchange the 'new suit' (*HSG*, p. 155) of modernity he had hoped to don for a garment of 'patchwork' (*HSG*, p. 155), stitched out of the past's conventions and precedents.

This highly metaphoric makeover is noteworthy because Holgrave's costume change suggests not only, generally, what he is to become (a 'model-conservative', *HSG*, p. 271), but, specifically, *who* he will be. For 'patches' are already associated with a character in the text – hitherto of some standing, though hardly central, now revealed as essential: that crackerbarrel philosopher of Pyncheon-street, Uncle Venner, whose folk wisdom, as much as attire, is 'patched together too, of different epochs; an epitome of times and fashions' (*HSG*, p. 55). That is the fate of the reformed revolutionary, Holgrave: to mellow (or moulder?) into a kind of fiscal reactionary, forever dropping, like pocket coins, cost-cutting 'sage counsel' (*HSG*, p. 58) of the 'Give no credit!' (*HSG*, p. 58), 'Never take paper money!' (*HSG*, p. 58) and 'Look well to your change!' (*HSG*, p. 58) kind. This sort of parody of capitalist exchange – more *Poor Richard's Almanack* than David Ricardo – is precisely the farce that legal realism pulls off when they take up Holmes's suggestion that law's agent of the future will be the 'man of economics' (*PL*, p. 170). For the economics that legal realism valorises is exactly the kind of dumbed-down banality that Uncle Venner ventriloquises here, and that Holgrave will mime.

This is because these proto-realists (Holgrave, Uncle Venner), like the legal realists proper (Llewellyn, Frank, and so forth), are not interested, for all the former's anarchist agitprop or the latter's New Deal social engineering, in any sustained critique of Capital; indeed, if anything they are firmly in favour of the socio-economic *status quo*, their real object of critique being a formalist legal system, the 'black letters' of which are stifling the market and its operation, preventing it from being truly free. Which is why Hawthorne is so prescient in *The House of the Seven Gables*; though published in 1851 – the last decade of the antebellum era's agrarian and mercantilist order, it forecasts the American political economy's soon-to-be pressing need for a new legal process (as client-focused rather than rule-bound), a new style of adjudication (as substantively oriented rather than formalistically correct) and a new understanding of legality (as 'law-in-action' rather than 'law-in-books') that will aid and abet, in the generation to follow, its post-war industrial take-off. So, here, Hawthorne's novel looks neither to, for all its historical flourishes, the past of Puritan 'punishment' (witch trials, public hangings and so on) nor to, for all of its up-to-the-minute detail, the present of Yankee 'discipline' (the Essex County prison, contemporary curial *causes célèbres*, and so forth), but, instead – to continue the Foucauldian idiom – a future of American 'governmentality' in which the 'romance of American legal realism', by marrying critical form (Holgrave) to constructive function (Phoebe), regulates and releases a new imperium of *laissez-faire*.

There is, however, a jurisprudential price to be paid for the (re)birth of Capital that this (un)holy legal realist union produces; that is, the loss of any sense of a 'higher law', gestured towards in figure of 'sweet Alice Pyncheon' (*HSG*, p. 274), last seen – by Uncle Veneer no less – floating 'heavenward' (*HSG*, p. 274). Whether that celestial ascension be a much longed for exorcism or a dreaded exile remains up for grabs, and I note the way in which the ending's last flourishes confound the strong closure it (seemingly) aspires to by introducing any number of nagging ambiguities: the 'whispered, unintelligible prophecies of the Pyncheon-elm' (*HSG*, p. 274); the 'kaleidoscopic pictures' (*HSG*, p. 274) of Maule's Well. One closural feature, however, remains clear: that 'with one farewell touch of a spirit's joy upon her harpsichord' (*HSG*, p. 274*)*, Alice shuffles off her (im)mortal coil. That Alice, not only departs the House of the Seven Gables, but leaves the earth altogether is troubling, if not tragic. For who – indeed *what* is Alice Pyncheon if not the very 'quality of mercy' itself; recall her touching humility, her tender forgiveness when, under an hypnotic spell, she is summoned, in Holgrave's horror story of her forlorn life – the text's cautionary tale-within-a-tale – to serve, as a final degradation, at the wedding of her psychic master, Thomas Maule: '[W]hen the twain were one, Alice awoke out of her enchanted sleep. Yet no longer proud – humbly, and with a smile all steeped in sadness – she kissed Maule's wife and went her way' (*HSG*, p. 181).

Such Portia-like attributes – forgiveness, humility, mercy – are in short supply in a text in which *no one forgets*, let alone forgives (or shows humility or mercy); everyone, here, clinging to their pride, through thick and thin, even if a range of other affects – love (Hepzibah), sensuality (Clifford), common sense (Phoebe), greed (Jaffrey), curiosity (Holgrave) – would dictate otherwise. That Alice vacates this narrative's obdurate world of '*je me souviens*' drives home the fissure that lies at the heart of legal realism and its flawed 'romance': by reducing the law to a function (Phoebe-as-'law–job') that asks only how it may better perform its functionality (Holgrave's critique, constrained), legal realism empties legality of any *real* value and renders not only un-askable but unanswerable whether this is a good or bad law. In so doing, legal realism set America's jurisprudence on a 'sociological' (instead of legal philosophical) trajectory from which it has never really recovered, even to *this* day. Despite the patent differences between, for example, the 'legal process' school of the 1950s, the 'public policy' wonks of the 1960s, the 'law-and-economics' movement of the 1970s, even the 'critical legal studies' vanguard of the 1980s, all share an identical legacy and *longneur*: as the heirs of legal realism, they suspend any 'rush to judgment' that may smack of 'the merciful', indeed 'the moral', even 'the just'.

Which may account for why American jurisprudence is so bedevilled at present with 'Bad Men' – a present I think both Holmes and Holgrave presage – and all the human rights violations of which they stand indicted, both domestically (for a death penalty which is clearly racialised in its application, and amounts to a kind of juridical lynching) and internationally (for normalising a regime of torture, continuous with and stemming from a legal history of slavery, Indigenous genocide and patriarchal oppression). To argue, as have I, that Hawthorne's dispatch of Alice Pyncheon-as-mercy prefigures such developments may be overstating the case, biting off more – like Ned? – than, interpretively, the novel can chew. That said, I think I can hazard a pretty good guess – strongly evidenced and supported by a text in which the innocent are incarcerated, the judge is the villain and socio-economic 'might' always seems to trump juridical 'right' – on how Hawthorne would react to a legal system which, with its lethal injections and waterboarding, its prisons full to bursting and its outsourced rendition, would make Jaffrey Pyncheon blush with shame. To such a shortfall of justice in the current American legal system, I reckon Hawthorne would respond resoundingly with a comeback his friend and fellow *litterateur*, Herman Melville ascribed, famously, to his work – specifically, *The House of the Seven Gables* – as much as his temperament. Quite simply, Hawthorne would render a novel judgement that says 'NO! in Thunder'.[30]

---

30 H. Melville, 'Letter To Nathaniel Hawthorne, 16 April 1851, Pittsfield' in 'Commentary' in N. Hawthorne, *The House of the Seven Gables*, New York: Random House, 2001, p. 310.

CHAPTER 6

# In Boz We Trust! *Bleak House*'s Reimagination of Trusteeship

### Trust No One!: Dickens, Equity and the Rewriting of the Law of (Dis)Trusts

Trust is on trial in *Bleak House*.[1] Indeed, trust is at the very centre of the text's *cause célèbre*, the never-ending legal dispute of Jarndyce and Jarndyce which, as John Jarndyce himself says, is about 'a will, and the trusts under a will' (*BH*, p. 95). Now a trust, as every schoolchild (or, at least, law student) knows, is Equity's principal contribution to Anglo-American law, being a mechanism whereby goods are held by one (the trustee, the fiduciary) on behalf of, and for the benefit of another (the beneficiary, *cestui que* trust).[2] Or that is the legal *theory*; legal *practice*, however, often tells a different story – to which *Bleak House* amply attests. Nonetheless, it is this law of trusts that structures Dickens's text, driving its involved plot, connecting its many characters, and otherwise holding together a text long and labyrinthine enough to rival even a Chancery suit, like the infamous Jennings case,[3] which ran in the courts for nigh-on seventy years, and upon which Dickens based Jarndyce and Jarndyce. This centrality of trust law – as both narrative

---

1 C. Dickens, *Bleak House*, New York: Modern Library, 2002. Hereafter referred to as *BH*.
2 J. Hackney, *Understanding Equity and Trusts*, London: Sweet & Maxwell, 1996; P. Pettit, *Equity and the Law of Trusts*, London: Butterworths, 2001.
3 Or variously Jennens, or Jennons. See: P. Polden, 'Stranger than Fiction: The Jennens Inheritance in Fact and Fiction', *Common Law World Review* 32, 2003, 211–247 and 338–367.

device and doctrinal innovation – is integral to my analysis of the *Bleak House*. For I want to reclaim in this chapter a certain legalist reading of *Bleak House*, one that, however, has nothing to do with the much commented upon, even overworked topos of curial critique (of Chancery), and all of the strained imputations of reformism (largely legal-process oriented) that go with it. I want to sidestep this debate because, as many of Dickens's contemporaries (and near-contemporaries) were quick to point out[4] – and which he, himself, acknowledged, however grudgingly, in the text's preface[5] – procedural reform had already come to Chancery by the time *Bleak House* was written, rendering such critique by the by, if not otiose.[6]

4  Sir Edward Sugden (later Lord St Leonards) took Dickens to task for his misrepresentation of current Chancery practices in a *Household Words* piece, 'The Martyrs of Chancery', which appeared prior to *Bleak House* – but upon which the novelist based much of his subsequent critique of Equity. See: W. Holdsworth, *Charles Dickens as Legal Historian*, New Haven, CT: Yale University Press, 1929, p. 81. Later, Fitzjames Stephen, Dickens's implacable critic, chastised him in a *Saturday Review* piece published in 1857 for failing to take into account that 'The Court of Chancery was reformed before he published *Bleak House*' (see: J. F. Stephen, 'Mr. Dickens as a Politician', in P. Collins (ed.), *Charles Dickens: The Critical Heritage*, London: Routledge, 1995. Early American law-and-literature scholar, John Marshall Gest repeats much the same criticism at the turn of the century, though in a very vivid metaphoric way: 'Dickens, therefore, did not kill the Chancery snake, but only jumped on it after it was dead'(see: J. M. Gest, 'The Law and Lawyers of Charles Dickens', *American Law Register* 53, 1905, 425).
5  Which opens, of course, with a very telling anecdote: that of Dickens's highly defensive account of the public reprimand he received at the hands of an unnamed Chancery judge – and from which he is clearly stinging (*BH*, xxxiii). While Dickens rejects the accusation of misrepresentation, and affirms the accuracy of his depiction of Chancery, one wonders if the shrillness of tone acknowledges, at least impliedly, the possibility – that on some points – the judge might be right.
6  For example, by the time of the novel's composition, the 'Six Clerks Office' (*BH*, p. 7) of which Dickens writes was long gone, the six clerks – and sworn clerks – having been abolished in 1842. Other reform measures include: the introduction in 1840 of two new vice-chancellors, in 1851 of a new Court of Appeal for Chancery and, in 1852 – in the wake of the report of the Chancery Commission, legislation that abolished the office of the master and introduced a variety of procedural reforms (new rules of evidence permitting oral and cross-examination; regulations empowering Chancery to decide questions of common law, and so forth), as well as the phasing in of an annual salary scheme for court officials and judges, replacing the old corrupt system of case by case payment. See, in addition to Holdsworth, *Charles Dickens as Legal Historian* and Gest, 'The Law and Lawyers of Charles Dickens': J. Oldham, 'A Profusion of Chancery Reform', *Law and History Review* 22(3), 2004, 609–614; M. Lobban, 'Preparing for Fusion: Reforming the Nineteenth Century Court of Chancery, Pt. 1', *Law and History Review* 22(2), 2004, 330; D. Hammer, 'Dickens: The Old Court of Chancery', *Notes and Queries* 17, 1970, 342; T. Fyfe, *Charles Dickens and the Law*, London: Chapman & Hill, 1910.

This is not to suggest, though, that *Bleak House* is thesis-less about the law and/or legality – far from it. Which is why this chapter resists, as well, a mode of interpretation, common enough in a certain Foucault-inspired strand of literary criticism, that displaces the juridical (i.e., Chancery) in favour of the disciplinary (i.e., Inspector Bucket), brilliantly foregrounding the novel's anatomisation of the 'capillaries of power', but, unfortunately, sidelining, if not altogether *ignoring* its very real nomological issues.[7] Instead, I propose a *jurisprudential* reading of *Bleak House* that, contra New Historicism, 'takes law seriously',[8] but, by the same token, is not mired, *a la* Old Historicism,[9] in the essentially antiquarian question of institutional (i.e., court) overhaul. So law as *Begriffsjurisprudenz* – that is, as concept, as idea – is the focus here, my principal argument being this: that what Dickens renders in *Bleak House* is nothing less than a novel judgement reconfiguring the notion, largely

---

7 See D. A. Miller, 'Discipline in Different Voices: Bureaucracy, Police, Family and *Bleak House*', *Representations* 1, 1983, 59–89; see also, D. A. Miller, *The Novel and the Police*, Berkeley: University of California Press, 1988. Ripostes include the Marxist and the Feminist, see: D. La Capra, 'Ideology and Critique in Dickens's *Bleak House*', *Representations* 6, 1984, 116–123; J. Newton, 'Historicisms, New and Old: "Charles Dickens" Meets Marxism, Feminism and West Coast Foucault', *Feminist Studies* 16(3), 1990, 449–470.

8 This is not to suggest that New Historicism always substitutes politics for law in its reading of *Bleak House*. Clearly the following scholars 'take law seriously' but are more concerned with the socio-legal (Dolin), the narrational (Hall), the aesthetic (Thomas) and 'the feminine' (Polloczek) rather than, as here, the jurisprudential. See: K. Dolin, 'Law, Literature and Symbolic Revolution: *Bleak House*', *Australasian Journal of Victorian Studies* 12(1), 2007, 10–18; J. Y. Hall, 'What's Troubling about Esther? Narrating, Policing and Resisting Arrest in *Bleak House*', *Dickens Studies Annual* 22, 1993, 171–194; R. Thomas, 'Making Darkness Visible: Capturing the Criminal and Observing the Law in Victorian Photography and Detective Fiction', in C. Christ and J. Jordan (eds), *Victorian Literature and the Victorian Visual Imagination*, Berkeley: University of California Press, 1995; D. P. Polloczek, 'The Marginal, the Equitable and the Unparalleled: Lady Dedlock's Case in Dickens' *Bleak House*', *New Literary History* 3(2), 1999, 453–478; M. Markey, 'Charles Dickens' *Bleak House*: Mr Tulkinghorn as a Successful Literary Lawyer', *St Thomas LR* 14(4), 2002, 689–758. The following article adopts a jurisprudential approach, but given the range of texts it addresses, is very summary. See: D. H. Lowenstein, 'The Failure of the Act: Conceptions of Law in *The Merchant of Venice, Bleak House, Les Misérables* and Weisberg's *Poethics*', *Cardozo LR* 15(4), 1994, 1139–1234.

9 P. Collins, *Dickens and Crime*, London: MacMillan, 1994. Other historicist studies of Dickens, law and, *inter alia, Bleak House* include: H. House, *The Dickens World*, London: Oxford University Press, 1941; J. Butt, 'Bleak House in the Context of 1851', *Nineteenth Century Fiction* 10, 1955, 1–21; J. Butt, and K. Tillotson, *Dickens at Work*, London: Methuen, 1957; F. R. Leavis and Q. D. Leavis, *Dickens the Novelist*, Harmondsworth: Penguin Books, 1972.

legal,[10] of 'trust' itself, drawing upon but also transforming what has become Equity's law of (*dis*)trusts. To that end, I want to explore in this chapter how the text rewrites this law of (dis)trusts, reinscribing a new notion of lawyerly trusteeship, intensified, amplified and extended well beyond the strict doctrinal confines imposed by Chancery. What might be called, with a nod to pre-eminent sociologist of the professions, Steven Brint, the *lawyer-as-social trustee*.[11] This claim – for a renewed trust in the law, through a revivified law of trusteeship – may strike the reader as odd, if not downright wrong, particularly when, as to law, and its lawyers, one of the not-so-subtle messages of *Bleak House* is 'trust no one!'. But this notion of social trusteeship contrasts markedly, I will argue, with the more traditional trustee functions lawyers perform; that is, the fiduciary relationship, or the duty of highest good faith, but narrowly conceived and obtaining only between lawyer and client. It is the spectacular *failure* of this relationship that *Bleak House* depicts (think of Vholes, Kenge, Guppy, as well as Tulkinghorn), and which this chapter will review, in some detail, in its second section. Section three will shift away, however, from *content* – i.e., the portrayal of lawyering – engaging, instead, the novel's narrative *form*, and the way in which its tale is told. For, there, a distinctly legal undertone emerges, resonates and is *heard* in the text's omniscient third-person narration: what I call the 'barristerial' voice of *Bleak House*. It is in this voice, I shall argue, that the lawyer-as-social trustee speaks, interpellating its readers as judge and jury, summoning them to pass judgement – a novel judgement – on a society that violates its fiduciary duty, as much as transgresses trust.

Nowhere is this breach more in evidence, I assert, then in the narrative of Esther Summerson, that will be read in the fourth section of this chapter, as a kind of affidavit, attesting on an individuated level, to fiduciary's failure, to trust's distrust that the omniscient third-person narrator collectivises.

---

10 The literature on trust is voluminous and I am grateful to my current and former colleagues, Dr Ron Levy (Griffith Law School) and Mr Shaun McVeigh (Faculty of Law, University of Melbourne) for their advice and guidance. See, for example: R. Hardin, *Trust*, Cambridge: Polity Press, 2006; C. Tilly, *Trust and Rule*, New York: Cambridge University Press, 2005; R. Gaita, *Breach of Trust: Truth, Morality and Politics*, Melbourne: Black Inc., 2004; O. O'Neill, *A Question of Trust*, Cambridge: Cambridge University Press, 2002; B. Misztal, *Trust in Modern Societies: The Search for the Bases of Social Order*, Cambridge: Polity Press, 1996; F. Fukuyama, *Trust: The Social Virtues and the Creation of Prosperity*, New York: Free Press, 1995; D. Gambetta, *Trust: Making and Breaking Cooperative Relations*, Oxford: Basil Blackwell, 1988; N. Luhmann, *Trust and Power*, Chichester: John Wiley, 1979.

11 S. Brint, *In An Age of Experts: The Changing Role of Professionals in Politics and Public Life*, Princeton: Princeton University Press, 1994, pp. 5–20, pp. 36–42, p. 114.

When taken together, the effect of these two narratives – at once, individual and collective, private and public – is to solicit a reconceived, indeed reimagined sense of trusteeship, both personal and political, one that neither atomises (as Vholes' marketised or Tulkinghorn's fantasmatic client) nor autonomises (as a domestic ward) the *cestui que* trust. But where is a concrete example of that trusteeship to be found? *Bleak House* eschews such representation and, indeed, rebukes any easy remedies (e.g., Jarndyce's questionable efforts to restore trust among his own family). While the text may *diagnose* the social ills consequent upon the failure of trust – to use a medical rather than legal analogy – it refuses to *prescribe* for them. This refusal accounts for, as I will argue in the fifth and final section of the chapter, the inconclusive conclusion of the novel, but also suggests an ongoing role for the novelist, himself, as a figure of trust.

### The 'Galaxy Gallery' of the British Bar and 'Albion's (Not So) Divine' Attorneys: Barristers vs. Solicitors in *Bleak House*

Look not, however, for this legal figure of social trusteeship amidst the novel's many sketches of lawyers; there, a kind of 'rogues' gallery' of the law emerges, a curial counterpoint to Weevle's high society copper-plated engravings, 'The Galaxy Gallery of British Beauty' and 'Divinities of Albion' (*BH*, p. 283). Only here the 'Law List' this text complies is comprehensive rather than selective, running the gamut from the grand (the Lord Chancellor, Tulkinghorn, Kenge) to the grim (Guppy, Smallweed Jr., Vholes). In so doing, *Bleak House* paints a group portrait of a particular class – the urban, professional *bourgeoisie* (or *petit bourgeoisie*) – who, as a collective, mirror and invert another set of likenesses: the darkened visages of Sir Leicester's aristocratic ancestors ('A staring baronet', a 'shepherdess', etc., *BH*, p. 555), glowering from their frames over Chesney Wold's ominously echoing corridors and walkways. Yet what the reader is *shown* of the law and lawyers in this, admittedly, highly visual novel – think of 'Allegory' emblazoned on Tulkinghorn's office ceiling – is only half the story, a point often overlooked by, and which ultimately undoes the sumptuous televisual adaptations of *Bleak House*.[12] For unlike these instances of law's 'moving image', this text *tells* more than shows; indeed, how the story

---

12 See, especially, the brilliant 1980s dramatisation of *Bleak House*, BBC Television, 1985, starring Denholm Elliott, Diana Rigg and Suzanne Burden. Most recently, the trendier (billed as *Bleak Enders*, screening after popular soap opera, *EastEnders*) but less satisfying *Bleak House*, BBC Television, 2005, starring Dennis Lawson, Gillian Anderson and Anna Maxwell Martin.

is *said* – if I may be permitted this solecism – is the key not only to its aesthetic achievement, but also to its jurisprudential import. Because it is there, in the novel's narration, especially its third-person narrator, that a timbre is caught, a tone is audible, one which yokes *Bleak House*'s socio-legal *content* – the thematic, as I argue, of trusteeship – to a narrative form of lawyerly persuasion: what this chapter designates the text's barristerial voice, and of which more will be said in the following section.

But why is this voice barristerial in the first place? Given, especially, the Bar's fleeting, and largely unprepossessing presence in the novel in the shadowy form of Tangle, Blowers, *et al.* (*BH*, pp. 6–7). This dearth of the Bar, however, should come as no surprise, particularly given Dickens's (over?-) familiarity with the solicitor side of lawyering. After all, as a young man, prior to his early career as a court reporter, and long before his first literary success under the *nom de plume* 'Boz', Dickens had commenced articles as a clerk: first, with a sole practitioner, Charles Malloy, New Square, Lincoln's Inn; second, with a firm, Ellis & Blackmore of Holborn Ct., Gray's Inn.[13] Dickens's career as a trainee in law was undistinguished, and lasted little more than a year (May 1827 to November 1828)[14] from where he departed for Doctor's Commons, and his beat as court reporter there.[15] One wonders, though, if the sting of this early (Rick-like?) 'false start' – or less euphemistically, *failure* – may have lingered, a constant irritant to the success-driven Dickens, only to be salved by donning the mantle of the socially superior branch of the profession, the Bar, and its sneer at its very junior associates, the solicitors? Certainly, Dickens never misses an opportunity to have 'a go' at solicitors; in *Bleak House*, he seems to rehearse every known lawyer joke of the period, many of which – and the stereotypes they reference – are with us today. From the pomposity of Kenge's 'conversation' to the bloodsucking viper that is Vholes, from the vulgar presumption of that proto-geezer, Guppy, to the unholy progeny of 'Law and Equity' (*BH*, p. 272), Smallweed Jr. – whose greatest wish is *be* 'a Guppy' (*BH*, p. 270), Dickens never lets up, either here or elsewhere (think of Uriah Heep in *David Copperfield*), deprecating them, one and all, as 'attorneys' with its 'below the salt' associations of 'pettifoggery'; that is, as venal, but especially *servile* advisers, leeching off their clients.[16]

13 J. Forster, *Forster's Life of Dickens*, George Gissing (ed.), London: Chapman & Hall, 1903, p. 33. See also: A. Wilson, *The World of Charles Dickens*, Harmondsworth: Penguin, 1972, p. 63.
14 Foster, *Forster's Life of Dickens* and Wilson, *The World of Charles Dickens*, ibid.
15 Wilson, *The World of Charles Dickens*, above n. 13, p. 64. E. Johnson, *Charles Dickens: His Tragedy and Triumph*, vol. 1, New York: Simon & Schuster, 1952, pp. 58–59.
16 R. Robson, *The Attorney in Eighteenth Century England*, Cambridge: Cambridge University Press, 1959.

Even so grey and eminence as Mr Tulkinghorn, to whom 'half the Peerage stops to say "How do you do . . .?" ' (*BH*, p. 13), and who is received, as the rank-conscious Sir Leicester rather pointedly puts, '*almost* on a footing of equality with the highest society' (*BH*, p. 560, italics mine), is dismissed as a sort of upper servant, albeit a remarkably privileged one when compared to Rosa, Mercury, even Mrs Rouncewell – *but* still a servant nonetheless: '[the] steward of the legal mysteries, the butler of the legal cellar' (*BH*, p. 13). Of course, this (mis)representation of the lower branch of the profession was out of date even during Dickens's term of articles in the late 1820s – the time-frame within which the diegesis of the novel is set[17] – let alone during the much later period of *Bleak House*'s composition (November 1851– August 1853) and publication (March 1852–September 1853). For the solicitors are *the* professional successes of the nineteenth century. In their steady rise towards respectability, this supposed 'lower' branch of the legal profession, supply a model for other upwardly mobile vocations (e.g., doctors, accountants, surveyors),[18] and even outpace more established callings, such as the barristers – *the* 'status' profession[19] – who are still hamstrung by and dated in their traditions of gentlemanly (i.e., unpaid) practice.[20]

Instead of, and in marked contrast to the obligatory student dinners hosted by the Inn benchers – still the principal qualifying requirement for the Bar, the solicitors are upping, as Steven Brint would have it, their 'occupational'[21] ante by laying down, in addition to articles, far more stringent admissions standards (formal study, examinations).[22] But the innovation that really turns the solicitors from a money-grubbing trade into a learned profession is the promulgation, by new organisations such as the Incorporated Law Society (founded 1824),[23] of ever stricter guidelines

---

17 Legal historian Sir William Holdsworth sets the story as early as 1827, when, of course, Dickens would have been an articled clerk, attending a court presided over by Lord Lyndhurst – and from which experience, presumably, the novelist would have drawn upon for his picture of Equity.
18 See M. S. Larson, *The Rise of Professionalism: A Sociological Analysis*, Berkeley: University of California Press, 1977.
19 Brint, *In an Age of Experts*, above n. 11, pp. 26–27.
20 D. Duman, *The English and Colonial Bars in the Nineteenth Century*, London: Croom Helm, 1983.
21 Brint, *In an Age of Experts*, above n. 11, pp. 31–32.
22 W. R. Cornish and G. Clark, *Law and Society, 1750–1950*. London: Sweet & Maxwell, 1989, pp. 51–53; A. H. Manchester, *Modern Legal History*, London: Butterworths, 1980, pp. 52–54.
23 Cornish and Clark, *Law and Society*, above n. 22, p. 52. See also: M. Birks, *Gentleman of the Law*, London: Stevens & Sons, 1960, pp. 155–157; H. Kirk, *Portrait of a Profession: A History of the Solicitor's Profession, 1100 to the Present Day*, London: Oyez Publisher, 1976, pp. 29–30.

governing lawyer–client relations, borrowed largely from Equity, especially its principal notion of *uberimma fides* – or the 'highest good faith', exercised by the 'fiduciary' in their 'duty of care'. When recast from this equitable vantage, clients resemble nothing less, in these professional precepts, than *cestui que* trusts, or beneficiaries under a trust (to whom good faith is owed), while the solicitor is that figure of fiduciary, the trustee (who is motivated by good faith, acting on behalf of the beneficiary).[24]

Dickens must have been aware of these changes – even if he completely discounted them. For make no mistake about it: Dickens's contempt for attorneys in *Bleak House* is palpable; and he has no hesitation about portraying them in the worst possible light, no matter how successfully they rebrand themselves as 'solicitors', no matter how effectively they cloak themselves in the mantle of trusteeship with all of its correlative fiduciary duties. Think how the text mocks, by association, two of these duties, both so vital to any notion of professional legal conduct that, to this day, they are referred to as 'the standard conception' of lawyering:[25] the duties of partisanship and neutrality.[26] For who is the lawyer in *Bleak House* most closely identified with these duties? None other than the vile Vholes, surely the novel's ethical nadir, but one who is described in what *seems* be one of the narrative's most mordant moments of irony as a 'rock of trust' (*BH*, p. 543). I say ironic because, surely, this 'rock' *crushes* his client to death – but *not* by evading his professional fiduciary duties; rather, by *embracing* them. So the analogy – Vholes as a 'rock of trust' – is anything but ironic. Precisely because Vholes puts into practice, all too well as it turns out, the duties of trust he seems, at least initially, only to mouth as platitudes, pushing them to their (il)logical, nay life-threatening extreme, thereby transforming these fiduciary principles into a law of *distrust*.

Consider his much professed commitment to the duty of partisanship; namely, his obligation to pursue, vigorously, his client's legal interests, at all costs. '[W]hen a client of mine', proclaims Vholes, as if citing a profes-

---

24 Consider what another common law court, the American Supreme Court, said in 1850 of the solicitor/attorney–client relationship: 'There are few of the business relations of life involving a higher trust and confidence than that of attorney and client, or, generally speaking, one more honorably and faithfully discharged; few more anxiously guarded by the law, or governed by sterner principles of morality and justice; and it is the duty of the court to administer them in a corresponding spirit, and to be watchful and industrious, to see that confidence thus reposed shall not be used to the detriment or prejudice of the rights of the party bestowing it' (*Stockton* v. *Ford* 52 US 11 How. 232 (1850)).
25 R. O'Dair, 'The Standard Conception of Legal Ethics', in *Legal Ethics: Cases and Materials*, London: Butterworth, 2001, pp. 134–136.
26 Ibid. p. 135.

sional practice manual, 'laid down a principle which was not of an immoral (that is to say, unlawful) nature, it devolved upon me to carry it out. I have carried it out. I do carry it out' (*BH*, p. 805; see also, p. 524). The problem here with Vholes, however, is not *underperformance*, as one might suspect, at least in the first instance, from his hyperbolic clientism and its ring of protesting too much. Instead, he *over*-invests in the client, doing far *too much* for Rick, and thereby transforming his legal interests into something terrifying; that is, a caged beast, routinely (and cruelly?) put through its paces, but never let off its leash. 'The suit does not sleep', Vholes advises Richard, 'we wake it up, we air it, we walk it about' (*BH*, p. 541). No wonder Rick becomes ever more exhausted as the plot progresses, since he is given no respite from this curial hyperactivity. Not even the complementary duty of lawyering's 'standard conception' – that of neutrality – affords any relief; on the contrary, it exacerbates what Weevle calls Rick's 'smouldering combustion' (*BH*, p. 546), allowing Rick to turn on the spit of Chancery until he too incinerates, without any assistance – or rather *interference* from his lawyer. For assistance *is* interference, at least according to the duty of neutrality which imposes on lawyers a strict policy of non-intervention: a 'hands off' approach, especially when it comes to judging the rightness or wrongness of the client's choices. 'Now sir, upon the chances of Mr. C's game I express to you no opinion, *no* opinion', disclaims Vholes, in a smug statement of not-so-benevolent neglect, 'It might be highly impolitic of Mr. C, after playing so long and so high to leave off; it might be the reverse. I say nothing. No, sir . . . nothing' (*BH*, p. 677). Rock of trust? With a trustee like that, who needs defalcators?

Of course, the reader should expect this of Vholes, the text going out of its way to portray him as *inhuman*, indifferent to the suffering he causes, for all his professions of *faux* sympathy as a father, son, and so forth. Associated, instead, more with the funereal rather than the familial, Vholes seems to have stepped directly out of a crypt; a common enough caricature in the period,[27] gothicising the lawyer as one of the 'living dead', lying in his 'coffin' (*BH*, p. 541), robed in 'black' (BH, p. 524), having, doubtless, 'sired' Richard as a 'Vampire' (*BH*, p. 804).[28] Not that any of the other solicitors – or for that matter, other lawmen – are much better in their effects,

---

27 W. W. Pue and D. Sugarman (ed.), *Law and Vampires: Cultural Histories of Legal Profession*, Oxford: Hart, 2003.
28 It is Esther, who – to her horror – reaches this conclusion, while observing Richard and Vholes together: 'So slow, so eager, so bloodless and gaunt, I felt as if Richard were wasting away beneath the eyes of this adviser, and there were something of the Vampire in him' (*BH*, p. 804, above n. 1).

however well intentioned (or least, less life draining) their motives or methods. Consider the relatively sympathetic figure of 'Conversation' Kenge, whose only real character flaw seems to be that he is in love with 'the sound of his own voice' (*BH*, p. 22) – not necessarily a bad thing for a lawyer. But it is Kenge who sets the stage for Vholes, and his exploitation of young Carstone; Rick, after all, only began to 'pour over' (*BH*, p. 270) the Jarndyce suit during his brief articles in Kenge's office, the first sign of his vulnerability to Chancery (and Vholes). Further, it is Kenge's other clerk, William Guppy, who precipitates what Tulkinghorn only threatens – Lady Dedlock's desertion. For she runs away only when Guppy brings her ladyship word that her secret is betrayed and all is lost (*BH*, pp. 742–743), Sir Leicester having been fully apprised of her disgrace. Finally, it falls to that 'long arm of the law', Inspector Bucket, to complete what Guppy began, and thereby fulfil Tulkinghorn's ultimate goal: her ladyship's destruction. For in giving chase to her flight, ostensibly to rescue her from self-inflicted harm, Bucket achieves the obverse; he literally hounds Lady Dedlock to death.

### 'Dead . . . and Dying Thus around Us Every Day' (*BH*, p. 636): Dickens's Brief and the Barristerial Voice of *Bleak House*

All of which suggests, put not your trust in lawmen of any sort! At least, that is, not in the kind of 'failed fiduciary', the representations of whom, reviewed previously, seem to attract so much attention in *Bleak House*, transfixing the reader's horrified gaze. This is why I have lingered over their eye-catching characterological depictions because they provide such a vivid contrast to what I argue is another, more *powerful* lawyerly presence in the novel, one listened to, rather than looked at; that is, an *ear*ful, instead of an eyeful, and one that reverberates throughout the omniscient third-person narration in a set of asides, questions and declamations which most definitely sound in law. It is here, so I contend, that the barristerial voice is heard, amidst all of the novel's rich heteroglossia. 'Barristerial' because this voice seems to leap off the page, hailing its audience, as counsel would a jury, transforming their scene of reading into a site of judgement – as an imaginary court of conscience; and, in so doing, searching for, appealing to, soliciting . . . what? Namely, trust. But what sort of trust? Certainly not the *private* trust of lawyer–client privilege, as the text makes quite clear in its relentless and ruthless satirising of Vholes & Co., those juridical agents of distrust.

Instead, *Bleak House's* barristerial voice speaks in and on behalf of the *public* trust; that is, the trust of the *many* rather than the *few*. This group trust places law – a reformed and rehabilitated 'Rule of Law', rather than an oppressive law of rules – at the very centre of the liberal polity, and its increasingly democratising and secularising institutions. For this characterisation of the state of the nation describes precisely the England of *Bleak House*; despite the feudal remnants of Chesney Wold and Chancery, it is a society of modernising *change*, however stop–go. Think of that stereotypical example of the 'rising' *bourgeoisie*, Ironmaster Rouncewell, whose parliamentary ambitions so alarm the declining denizens of the old deference culture, the Dedlocks and their country house hangers-on (*BH*, pp. 561–562). In polities (and politics) such as these, a refashioned law, if freed from Equity's medieval maw, would bond 'the social', replacing 'altar and throne', Church and State – Rev. Chadband and Sir Leicester? – as the principal means and modality of trust: the 'glue' holding society together. That social trust would be fostered and sustained through a reliance in, and on law's language (of interdependent rights and duties, connecting each to each), law's fori (of dispute resolution, open to, and binding upon all) and law's actors (judges, lawyers, police) who are trained as, and all too willing to perform a function, as Steven Brint[29] argues, that originates in and comes to predominate as the *beau idéal* of the nineteenth-century professions: that of *social* trustee.

'Social trusteeship' is Brint's inspired coinage for the kind of public-spirited, community-minded figure of authority, legal and otherwise,[30] whom the Victorians came to valorise, and who solicits trust precisely because, for him (and in that period, it always was a *him*) – unlike today's 'experts'[31] – civic responsibility trumps self-interest, professional integrity overrides profits. What disappoints, however, about Brint's notion of trusteeship is an absence of *content* that would define it in terms other than that of generalised fiduciary duty, as well as fidelity, zeal, accountability and so forth.[32] All standards, so susceptible to formalisation (and trivialisation), that *Vholes*, himself, could argue they inform *his* professional practices,

---

29 Brint, *In an Age of Experts*, above n. 11, pp. 36–37. See also the excellent review essay which reads this break-through book, in light of its significance for, and accuracy about the legal profession: K. Anderson, 'A New Class of Lawyers: The Therapeutic as Rights Talk', *Columbia Law Review* 96(4), 1996, 1062–1092.
30 Brint, *In an Age of Experts*, above n. 11, pp. 5–20, pp. 36–42, p. 114. For an excellent discussion of *Bleak House*'s thematic of professionalism, particularly within the context of philanthropic responsibility, see: B. Robbins, 'Telescopic Philanthropy: Professionalism and Responsibility in *Bleak House*', in J. Tambling (ed.), *Bleak House: Charles Dickens*, London: Macmillan Press, 1998, pp. 139–162.
31 Brint, *In an Age of Experts*, above n. 11, pp. 3–20, pp. 37–53, pp. 62–82, p. 132.
32 Ibid. p. 8.

rendering him 'trustworthy', even though he incarnates the 'one great principle of English law' that Brint so decries of the expert 'new class'[33] and their transactional imperatives: 'to make business for itself' (*BH*, p. 537). Which is why Dickens is so crucial here because he out-Brints Brint, so to speak, by dramatising in and through *Bleak House*'s barristerial voice the radical difference between a professionalism grounded in, on one hand, *formal* (and faux) trustworthiness and, on the other, *substantive* (and true) trustworthiness. This difference, I want to argue, turns on a further distinction; namely, the age-old juristic one between law's *letter* and law's *spirit*.

Here is how these oppositions play out. Formal trustworthiness says 'trust me' because I adhere to the letter of the law, and all of its posited professional rules of conduct; while the latter, substantive trustworthiness says nothing expressly of trust, but solicits it nonetheless by engaging law's spirit, that necessary supplement of law's letter, through its direct address of, and to justice – *the* central question of jurisprudence. Formal trustworthiness would limit this question to just *procedures* (e.g., access to counsel and court); conversely, substantive trustworthiness would *contextualise* justice, situating it *socially*. What is right – and just – in a society? Moreover, what is wrong – and unjust – with it? That is the collective 'truth' from which the lawyer-as-social trustee does not flinch and to which the barristerial voice gives expression in *Bleak House*; that is, by revealing the gross *injustice* that lies at this very centre of the society the novel depicts, constituting its principal – and not-so-repressed – trauma. What is that trauma if not the horrific image of cruel 'want' (Tom's All Alone) in the midst of ostentatious 'plenty' (Chesney Wold, the Dedlock town mansion, even Bleak House), figured, especially, in those 'dead' and 'dying thus around us everyday' (*BH*, p. 636) as summoned up in the narrator's special pleading occasioned by Jo's demise and anaphorised as: 'Dead, your Majesty. Dead, my lords and gentlemen. Dead, Right Reverends and Wrong Reverends of every order. Dead, men and women, born with Heavenly compassion in your hearts' (*BH*, p. 636).

Of course, the dead child, and the grief-stricken eulogy it provokes, is a lugubrious speciality of the Dickens *œuvre* – think of Paul Dombey or Little Nell – so much so that the reader might be sorely tempted to agree with a waggish Oscar Wilde that one must have a heart of stone to keep from *laughing*. But what distinguishes the funeral oration for Jo from others is that *Bleak House*'s barristerial voice is not content to leave, as would Buzfuz, Stryver, Jaggers and all the other counsel in Dickens's world, this bit of

---

33 Ibid. pp. 4–6, p. 85, p. 95, pp. 104–105.

bombast as a courtroom flourish. Rather, this voice not only *vocalises* but *focalises*, bringing, through the all-seeing eye of the omniscient third-person narrator, its peoples' court of judging readers to a field of vision that locates Jo's death within a set of material conditions so vividly realised that its novelistic representation prompted public outcries that rivalled Mayhew's sociological study of the London poor.[34] For fiction tops fact here in its portrayal of that sink of iniquity and breeding ground of infection, the slum of 'Tom's All Alone', the 'corrupted blood' of which propagates 'contagion somewhere' (*BH*, p. 614). By 'somewhere' the text's narrative voice really means *everywhere*, the bacillus of Tom's-All-Alone being 'moved on' by the law itself in the form of patient zero, Jo. As a figural *and* literal carrier of diseased disorder, his presence portends all manner of malady, psychic and physical: marital discord amongst the Snagsbys, disfiguring illness at Bleak House, vengeful suspicions confirmed at Tulkinghorn's offices, reaching outward and upwards 'through every order of society, up to the proudest of the proud, and to the highest of the high' (*BH*, p. 616).

This monitoring, by the text, of Jo's condition, tracking its metastasis through the social system as a whole, is significant in terms of socio-legal as well as medical aetiology.[35] For the narrator is not content to isolate, as would a physician (Allan Woodcourt?), the source of *Bleak House*'s pathologies, thereby quarantining any further outbreak (e.g., institutionalising Jo; blockading Tom's All Alone). Rather this voice is more concerned, as a lawyer would be, with *liability*, indeed *responsibility*. Which is why the question posed by the text is the curial one of cause and effect, forging – in that favoured metaphor of tort law – a *chain* of causation. 'What connexion', queries the text's counsel-like voice, as if making an opening statement on the first day of a trial, 'can there be, between the place in Lincolnshire, the house in town, the Mercury in powder, and the whereabout of Jo the outlaw with the broom . . .?' (*BH*, p. 217). Of course, this 'connexion' is made explicit at the novel's end; not, however, by any disembodied barristerial voice. Instead, it is done by the all too physical presence of Bucket, whose ever gesticulating digit – that metonym of discipline, his famous 'fat forefinger' (*BH*, p. 698) – winkles out

---

34 H. Mayhew, *London Labour and the London Poor*, New York: Dover Publications, 1968.
35 *Bleak House* seems to bring out the doctor (rather than lawyer) *manqué* in literary critics with the following engaging the issue of disease, pathology and allied medical issues: G. Benton, ' "And Dying Thus around Us Every Day": Pathology, Ontology and the Discourse of the Diseased Body: A Study of Illness and Contagion in *Bleak House*', *Dickens Quarterly* 11, 1994, 69–80; L. Fasich, 'Dickens and the Diseased Body in *Bleak House*', *Dickens Studies Annual* 24, 1996, 135–151; M. S. Gurney, 'Disease as Device: The Role of Smallpox in *Bleak House*', *Literature and Medicine* 9, 1990, 79–92.

the 'innumerable histories' of this story 'who, from opposite sides of great gulfs, have, nevertheless, been very curiously brought together!' (*BH*, p. 216). Interestingly, though, Bucket's disclosures to Sir Leicester and others at the end of novel, explaining away, Poirot-like, the 'whodunnits' of its plot – like Tulkinghorn's murder – are anything but cliff-hangers, complicating generic claims that *Bleak House* is English literature's first *real* detective novel.

Or if it is, then this novel initiates an exceedingly wan tradition, devoid of any true suspense, let alone satisfactory solutions. For the crime the reader really wants solved in *Bleak House* is not the Christie-style, 'Who killed Tulkinghorn?' – a forerunner of Roger Ackroyd, with all of its closural creakiness: surprise! it was *the French maid* – not the butler – who did it! Rather the solution desired here is to a mystery more social than singular, communal than individual; that is, the crime of Jo's death, itself emblematic of a society in crisis, a nation, as Carlyle would put it, and in terms *Bleak House* affirms, 'dying of inanition'.[36] How did this parlous 'condition of England' come about? Where is blame to be placed? Who *did* this? That is the authentic 'whodunnit' of *Bleak House*, a question the text does not shrink from answering; and does so in the passage that opened this section, implicating *all* – not just the 'usual suspects' of Crown ('your Majesty'), Church ('Right Reverends and Wrong Reverends') and class ('my lords and gentlemen'), but the public itself, 'men and women, born with Heavenly compassion'. In short, all of the novel's readers are called to account here as culpable, co-respondents in the collective crime of those 'dead' and 'dying thus around us everyday', the victims of which include, in addition to Jo, all the others – think of Jenny's baby (*BH*, pp. 109–110) – for whom the text, as social trustee speaks. And not only speaks, but *shows*; for long before Bucket *tells* us how Chesney Wold and Tom's All Alone are connected, the narrator's ken, barristerial or otherwise, *takes* us there: to the sordid back room at Krook's which holds the first of *Bleak House's* many dead bodies, the overdosed corpse of the seriously *déclassé* Capt Hawdon.

It is here, in this literally mortifying scene (*BH*, chs. IX and X), that Dickens provides the fulcrum or axis upon which *Bleak House* turns, the spokes of its many storylines intersecting, not just between 'Jo the outlaw' and the Dedlocks, but Tulkinghorn, Miss Flite, the Snagsbys, Allan Woodcourt, Esther, Ada, Richard, Sjt. George, Guppy, Smallweed and, of course, Krook and Lady Jane, each of whom move through, or pass by here. What's more, the narrator sees not just into all places, but all persons, sensing

---

36 T. Carlyle, *Past and Present*, R. D. Altick (ed.), New York: New York University Press, 1965, p. 7.

their feelings, sussing their motives, like the prosecution proving *mens rea* (i.e., a 'guilty mind'); for the narrator of *Bleak House* knows, as does any good criminal barrister, what good or evil lurks in the hearts of men. Think how the narrator vouchsafes the novel's readers access to the inner workings of so secretive a character as Tulkinghorn, himself a 'reservoir' of client 'confidences' (*BH*, p. 131), yet who is unreadable to everyone else in the novel, 'not knowing whether his whole soul is devoted to the great, or whether he yields them nothing beyond the services he sells' (*BH*, p. 161). But in the course of his first showdown with Lady Dedlock, Tulkinghorn's grudging admiration – the closest he comes to an expression of *affect* – becomes quite clear, the narrator giving the reader a free indirect look-see into the not so 'passionless' (*BH*, p. 502) malignity going on behind the old solicitor's 'mask' (*BH*, p. 160) of a face, his emotions betrayed only by a barely discernible arched eyebrow, a 'hair's-breadth more contracted than usual' (*BH*, p. 566): 'So! Anger, and fear, and shame. All three contending. What power this woman has, to keep these raging passions down! Mr Tulkinghorn's thoughts take such form as he looks at her' (*BH*, p. 566).

This dramatisation of what might be called, with a nod to high positivist jurisprude Hans Kelsen, 'juristic consciousness'[37] – suggests that, instead of Tulkinghorn, it is *the narrator* who is *Bleak House's actual* trustee of secrets, seeing, both inside and outside the book's characters, a virtually Hartian 'internal point of view'[38] of everyone's deepest thoughts, as well as an 'external point of view'[39] of their most shameful acts. If so, does this transference of trusteeship complicate, even challenge the 'socialisation' thesis that I have been arguing for, converting the narrator's voice of social conscience into a ruthless will-to-power? For that, of course, is what Tulkinghorn's trusteeship of secrets does; it *empowers* him at the expense of others: a power which he most certainly *enjoys*[40] – in the darkest Lacanian/Žižekian sense[41] – carrying out. Consider how he badgers Sjt. George (*BH*,

---

37  H. Kelsen, *Pure Theory of Law*, M. Knight (trans.), Berkeley: University of California Press, 1967, p. 116.
38  H. Hart, *The Concept of Law*, Oxford: Oxford University Press, 1961, pp. 89–117, p. 218, p. 222, pp. 240–242, p. 255, p. 270.
39  Ibid. pp. 89–112, p. 138, pp. 240–242, p. 255.
40  See J. F. MacCannell, 'Enjoyment', in E. Wright (ed.), *Feminism and Psychoanalysis: A Critical Dictionary*, Oxford: Blackwell, 1996, pp. 84–88.
41  J. Lacan, 'Kant with Sade', in B. Fink (trans.), *Ecrits: The First Complete Edition in English*, W. W. Norton & Co., London, 2006, p. 645. J. Lacan, 'God and the Jouissance of Woman', in J. Mitchell and J. Rose (eds), *Feminine Sexuality: Jacques Lacan and the Ecole Freudienne*, New York: Pantheon Books, 1982. See also: S. Žižek, *Enjoy Your Symptom! Jacques Lacan In and Out of Hollywood*, London: Routledge, 1992.

pp. 373–374); threatens to put the squeeze on Bagnet – via his deputy, Smallweed (*BH*, pp. 476–477); intimidates the obstreperous Hortense into sullen (if temporary) acquiescence (*BH*, pp. 572–579); and, of course, quietly terrorises Lady Dedlock (*BH*, pp. 566–569, pp. 645–646). And all (un)naturally enough, in the name of *trust*; as he says to Lady Dedlock, during their final and fateful interview, of her scandalous and carefully concealed past, now known fully to him: 'It is my secret, in trust for Sir Leicester and the family' (*BH*, p. 646). Which prompts a further question: Is Tulkinghorn's trusteeship different, in any real sense, from that of the narrator? That is to say, is the only authentic divergence between the indefatigable solicitor of secrets and the barristerial voice of social scruples merely one of degree rather than kind, the latter *aggregating* the individual interests – over which the former exercises his fiduciary duty on a case by case basis – into group version of the *cestui que* trust? In short, are they nothing more than two sides of the same legalistic coin, each breaching their respective remits of trust, the one, the private; the other, the public?

Certainly that would make sense of the third-person narrator's phantasmagorical vision, or less mythopoetically, *psychotic delusion* of London as 'city of dreadful night', wrapped in an omnipresent fog, its 'murk' (*BH*, p. 5) sucking the very light out of the skies, let alone oxygen, with filth accumulating everywhere, infection running rampant, even bodies exploding. For urban decay, nay *disaster* such as this – a forerunner of today's science fiction scenarios of the metropolis *in extremis*? – would appear to be the result of trusting, and disclosing *all* your secrets to 'the outraged majesty of the Law' (*BH*, p. 702), this failing world, of which the narrator-as-social trustee records in intimate and lurid detail, 'outing' all of its hitherto closeted skeletons, being but a massification of the 'dead' and 'dying' clients (*Dead*-lock?) to whom Tulkinghorn, as the personal trustee of their confidences, tends, and for whose dire fates he is, ultimately, responsible. This is because Tulkinghorn is, with all due respect to Alfred Hitchcock, *the trustee who knows too much*.

Knowing too much not only empowers, but, in its information overload, *vertiginises*, leading to a dizzying loss of perspective, one that magnifies the objective at the expense, even the *exclusion* of the subjective. Think of how Tulkinghorn's quasi-masonic *pouvoir/savoir* (*BH*, pp. 559–560) leads him to believe he *knows* his clients' interests better than the clients themselves, and how all too eager he is to forfeit them in order to safeguard that *knowledge*. Consider how easily Lady Dedlock – after all, a client, as much Sir Leicester – is cut loose, left to founder by Tulkinghorn because she is a rival for Sir Leicester's 'trust' (*BH*, p. 569), and the knowledge which that trust brings. No surprises then that he moves her along faster than any bobby does Jo, goading – rather than 'boring' (*BH*, p. 10) – her to death. What *is* surprising however – at least, initially – is just how willing Tulkinghorn is to surrender Sir Leicester's welfare, despite all his blather about his client's 'feelings' and 'honor' (*BH*, p. 571). Clearly, he knows all too well the deleterious consequences that such a blow – Honoria dishonoured – would have for Sir Leicester, so thoroughly is that proud gentleman's considerable *amour propre* implicated in his *amour* for her ladyship.

No such 'consideration' (*BH*, p. 571), however, deters Tulkinghorn; only his death prevents this disclosure. But for Hortense's bullet, Tulkinghorn would have exposed Lady Dedlock to Sir Leicester,[42] reducing him – even earlier in the narrative – to the jabbering paralytic he becomes at its close, with one foot in the grave. Which, of course, retrospectively, parses anew the true import of Tulkinghorn's previously announced attornial cathexis in and of 'Sir Leicester and the baronetcy, Sir Leicester and Chesney Wold, Sir Leicester and his ancestors' (*BH*, p. 569) as turning on anything *but* Sir Leicester because the subject in this passage ('Sir Leicester *and* . . .') is swallowed up by the objects to which it is conjunctively linked: attributes such as a title, a manor, a lineage. For Tulkinghorn's 'sublime object of (legal) ideology' is just that: an object – or rather a set of objects, an 'order of things', as well as an 'imagined community' for which they are a synecdoche. That is, the fantasy of aristocracy, as reified in the passage's checklist of *objet petit a*: 'the baronetcy', 'Chesney Wold', 'the ancestors'. This is precisely why the Dedlocks of *reality* (the flesh and blood Sir Leicester and his lady) *must* be dispatched by Tulkinghorn, their trusty legal advisor; so that the Dedlocks of *the Real* – the noble 'Thing' of England's version of the *ancien régime* – may *live on*, as imaginary legal fictions, in his psychic projections and introjections. Thus, Tulkinghorn enacts, in his role as all-knowing trustee, a psychopathology that a certain strain of psychoanalytically inflected philosophy would call the 'ethics of the Good',[43] animated by a higher cause, for which no sacrifice is too great, even if it means – as here, with Sir Leicester – sacrificing that cause's very *ding-an-sich*.

---

42 At least that is after the second interview with Lady Dedlock, when her dismissal of Rose, in clear contravention of Tulkinghorn's express instruction, shows her to be less biddable – or 'trustworthy' – than originally thought: *BH*, pp. 645–647.
43 See especially, A. Zupancic, *Ethics of the Real: Kant, Lacan*, London: Verso, 2000.

## Equity's Darlings?: Esther's Affidavit and *Bleak House's Cestui Que* Trusts 'at Risk'

No such 'ethics', however, drives the barristerial voice of *Bleak House* and its sense of social trusteeship, because if one attends to the overall shape and pattern of the text, then it is clear that this voice, and the omniscient narration within which it is situated, is, as far as the novel is concerned, 'not-all'.[44] Which is to say, the third-person narrator, barristerial or otherwise, cannot totalise the text – that is, know and understand all of its secrets – because it is but *half* of the narrative. For *Bleak House* (in)famously, is split into two, like the psycho-analytic self; its third-person narrative is off-set by the first person account of little 'Dame Durden' (a.k.a, 'Mother Hubbard', a.k.a. 'Little Woman', a.k.a. 'Cobweb') herself, the notoriously cloying Esther Summerson, and a figure of some controversy in the critical reception of the novel. Long dismissed, even during the heyday of textual treacle – the mid-Victorian period – as 'too sweet to be wholesome', Esther has attracted, of late, a revisionist reading; the doyenne of Dickens studies, Hilary Schor,[45] has argued anew for her centrality to *Bleak House*. Indeed, by Schor's lights, Esther is *the* narrative voice of the novel, suturing its two (discrepant?) halves into a unified whole, not only recounting her own first person storyline, but also ventriloquising that of the third-person narrator's disturbing vision of the 'plague of fantasies', legal and otherwise, besetting Britain. Certainly she's crazy enough[46] to envisage that latter narrative's hallucinatory *longueur* of London as the lowest circle of a Dantesque hell. In fact, Esther may be one of the most psychologically

---

44 This point is also made – albeit in a much more Derridean vein – by Audrey Jaffe. See: A. Jaffe, 'David *Copperfield* and *Bleak House*: On Dividing the Responsibility of Knowing', in J. Tambling (ed.), *New Casebooks Series: Bleak House: Charles Dickens*, New York: St Martin's Press, 1998, p. 164. The extent of the third-person narrator's 'omniscience' is one of the more contested issues in the literary criticism of *Bleak House* with W. J. Harvey and Ellen Serlen weighing in on the side of the all-knowing, while Taylor Stoehr and Catherine Belsey limit and circumscribe that knowledge. See: W. J. Harvey, '*Bleak House*: The Double Narrative', in A. E. Dyson (ed.), *Dickens: Bleak House: A Casebook*, London: Macmillan, 1969, p. 228; E. Serlen, 'The Two Worlds of *Bleak House*', *English Literary History* 43, 1976, 551–566; C. Belsey, *Critical Practice*, London: Methuen, 1980, pp. 80–81; T. Stroehr, '*Bleak House*: The Novel as Dream', in A. E. Dyson (ed.), *Dickens: Bleak House: A Casebook*, London: Macmillan, 1969, p. 236.
45 H. Schor, *Dickens and the Daughter of the House*, Cambridge: Cambridge University Press, 1999, p. 117.
46 A. Zwerdling, 'Esther Summerson rehabilitated', *Publications of the Modern Language Association of America* 88, 1973, 429–439. See also: W. Axton, 'The Trouble with Esther', *Modern Language Quarterly* 26, 1965, 545–546.

damaged characters in the Dickensian *oeuvre*, with something like a 'diary of a mad (Victorian) housewife' emerging in her narrative, and symptomatised in her nervous jangling of her keys, her chronic and ludicrous self-effacement and her bizarre dreams of herself as wholly 'Other', neither human (a 'worm in a garden path', *BH*, p. 480) nor organic (a bead on a 'flaming necklace', *BH*, p. 480).

Is it any wonder that Esther is in such psychic pain? Especially in view of her upbringing: not just 'cold as Christian charity', as one might expect from the stern school of child-rearing adhered to by many in this evangelically minded period; but, more than that, so slamming of self-esteem ('Your mother, Esther, is your disgrace, and you were hers', *BH*, p. 18) and so secluded as to be hermetically sealed, that it calls to mind current scandals of sadistic parents (or guardians), sequestering their children (or charges), such as modern-day Kasper Hausers, in suburban attics or basements and raising them, on the sly, as prisoners. It is *this* fundamental breach of trust and its transgression of boundaries, both psychic and physical, to which Esther Summerson's story attests, transforming her narrative portion of the novel into an affidavit of 'equity's darling'[47] *betrayed*, the *cestui que* trust *violated*. And violated and/or betrayed by the very person charged with her welfare; namely, her godmother/aunt-as-'constructive trustee', the *de facto* rather than *de jure* caretaker of her interests.[48] But Miss Barbary, as this chapter has evidenced amply, is not the only 'failed fiduciary' in *Bleak House*, just as Esther is not the only beneficiary who has been so thoroughly let down. This is why I would argue, *contra* Schor, for the autonomy of the Esther storyline, as separate and distinct on thematic – as much as structural – grounds. Because that narrative *particularises* the breach of social trusteeship the third-person narrator decries *generally*, bristling, as it does, with individual tales of disappointment: not only from the formal *cestui que* trusts of Equity – e.g., the tragic histories of Miss Flite (*BH*, pp. 489–490) and Gridley (*BH*, p. 212) – but, as well, from a range of *quasi-cestui que* trusts,

---

47 The bona fide purchaser for value without notice – a particularly privileged figure, whose claim to ownership will always be upheld in equity even if legal title is questionable, i.e., the property was acquired from someone who had no right to sell, assign, transfer, and so forth. See: D. M. Walker (ed.), *The Oxford Companion to Law*, Oxford: Clarendon Press, 1980, 'Bona fide purchaser', p. 140.
48 A constructive trust is imposed, regardless of any intention, by operation of law in circumstances where it would be unconscionable for the legal owner of the property to assert beneficial ownership. See: Walker, *The Oxford Companion to Law*, 'Constructive Trust', ibid. pp. 280–281.

much like Esther herself, sorely tried by supposedly beneficent friends and families.

For example, think of how Caddy and the rest of the Jellybys – Peepy *et al.* – are left to their own mischievous devices, while their mother pursues 'telescopic philanthropy' (*BH*, p. 35), a send-up of Victorian do-gooder, Caroline Chisholm's much commented upon disregard of domestic order in favour of her considerable overseas mission efforts. Or consider the Pardiggle boys, all outlandishly monikered after obscure saints (Oswald, Egbert, and so forth) and frog-marched by their mother, that parody of the High Church, Mrs Pardiggle, into unwelcoming workers' cottages, their allowances tithed, without any real consent on their part, to the Anglo-Catholic charities – 'Infant Bonds of Joy' for one (*BH*, p. 101) – of their busybody parent's choosing. Or the little 'Coavinses' – the ever ungrammatical Charley and her little brother, Tom – fending for themselves, and ostracised even by their slum neighbours, but one – the kindly landlady, Mrs Blinder – on account of their father's dubious profession as a debt collector. One shudders, of course, to think of the strange upbringing the Skimpole girls (the 'Beauty daughter', the 'Comedy daughter', etc.) must have undergone at hands of Horace – by the way, the only 'child' *not* in danger in *Bleak House*. Of course, the all-time low of neglect is reached in the case of Jo – with that of Jenny's baby a close second – both of whom die in a *context* of pauperised misery, knitting together trusteeship's personal and political, individual and group *failures*.

But it is, however, with 'the wards in Jarndyce and Jarndyce' – Ada and Richard, rather than Miss Flite's latest avian acquisitions – that I am most concerned here because they are victimised not once but twice: first, by Chancery; and second, by their self-appointed guardian, John Jarndyce. While the reader would affirm the former, she might very well query the latter: Jarndyce as a victimiser? Of whose character, no less a critic than Vladimir Nabokov said was one of world literature's 'kind[est]' men?[49] Who acts only for others, never himself, and, thereby, comes to functions as something like the moral centre of the novel? After all, it is Jarndyce who attempts to mediate the central conflict of the story; his cheery invitations to Ada, Rick and Esther to 'meet as old friends, and take the past for granted' (*BH*, p. 62), offering Bleak House as their home and himself as their protector, are intended to 'heal' (*BH*, p. 43) the rift rupturing his kith and kin by establishing a different sort of *trust*. This trust is one released from the baleful influence of the family's Chancery suit, and which will inform a

---

49 V. Nabokov and F. Bowers (eds), *Lectures on Literature*, New York: Harcourt Brace Jovanovich, 1980, p. 106.

*socius*, however small, of 'hopeful change' (*BH*, p. 97), full of love rather than law. That is, a kind of Jarndyce utopia, apart from the world, hunkered down in its Hertfordshire house, but without the bitter isolation that marred Miss Barbary's remote establishment and from which Esther had to be rescued as a child by her guardian's timely intervention. For Bleak House is to be, by Jarndyce's design, a space as free from the *shame* of morality (Miss Barbary, Mrs Rachel), as it is from the *blame* of the law (Jarndyce and Jarndyce). Guilt, either arising from illegitimacy or intestacy, has no place here.

Or so it seems. Because, of course, the problem with this optimistic reading – which takes Jarndyce's benevolence at face value – is that it ignores the very real collapse of trust between the residents of Bleak House: not only in the deep 'estrange[ment]' (*BH*, p. 609) of Rick and Jarndyce, but in the increasing lack of 'frank[ness]' (*BH*, p. 672) between Ada and Esther, as well as the very mixed (and misrecognised) emotions that come to cloud Esther and Jarndyce's relationship. How did this sorry state of affairs come about? Surely the trouble can be traced to no less a source than Jarndyce himself who, for all his rantings against 'Wiglomeration' (*BH*, p. 98) reproduces, in his behaviour, some of the worst excesses of the Chancery bench. For what does Jarndyce do for most of the novel? He *judges.* Not only does he judge, but when he judges, *he judges and finds wanting.* Remember how quick off the mark he is to dismiss the case made by Ada and Richard, discounting their love as youthful infatuation and denying consent to, ironically, the one 'constancy' (*BH*, p. 179) – engagement to his steadfast cousin – that might have saved Rick from the very mindset of which Jarndyce complains; that is, of 'indecision', coupled with a 'habit of putting off', all the while 'trusting to this, that, and the other chance' (*BH*, p. 165). Naturally, avuncular concern for *both* Rick and Ada – as too young, too unsettled, and so on – would be Jarndyce's defence; however, one still wonders if something more untoward is driving Jarndyce, an impropriety captured in the Lord Chancellor's very telling 'pause' (*BH*, p. 31), pregnant with disapproving meaning, when interviewing, in his chambers, the young and beautiful Ada about the suitability of an unmarried man offering her his home and protection. Interestingly, it is this very living arrangement which so nonplussed the Woolsack – assuaged only by the *duenna*-like presence of Esther – that obtains at the end of the narrative, with a now widowed Ada and a still single Jarndyce, together and alone (but for the child, little Richard), snugly, even sexually (?) *in situ*.

This prurient insinuation, however leering it may sound to the reader, has a purpose; for the question I want to pose by it is structural, rather than sensational. That question is this: is John Jarndyce the character type that a certain kind of narratology,[50] at once mythic and psychoanalytic, might call a 'blocking figure', hindering Rick as a potential rival to the psychosexual authority he exercises as the patriarch (primal father?) of his largely feminised household? Further, does Jarndyce's hoarding, as his phallic prerogative, give some credence, at least in highly coded form, to the '[s]elfishness' (*BH*, p. 814) of which he stands accused by Horace Skimpole's, admittedly, mendaciously self-serving – but in this case possibly true? – 'tell all' autobiography, and which is dismissed, so witheringly, by Esther. Speaking of whom, is it not the proposal of marriage to Esther that tips Jarndyce's conduct into the realm of the transgressive, his legal guardianship, hitherto described (repeatedly) as 'fatherly' (*BH*, p. 64, p. 82, p. 235, p. 687) now taking on, in his marital overtures to his ward, a very different paternal function, resting on an entirely *other* law: what might be called, with a nod to leading cultural legal scholar, Peter Goodrich, *Oedipus Lex*?[51]

What sets this 'Law of the Father' apart from the orthodox Freudo-Lacanian conception of prohibition is that the paternal function here carries with it the certainty of its own contravention in the form of incestuous abuse. It is that law (and its criminal double, incest), so I suggest, that one can never evade, no matter how far one retreats into the domestic sphere and, as the Bagnets put it, its 'private ties' (*BH*, p. 663). This is because that law of transgression is sure to follow, like the smallpox infection that invades Bleak House itself. If, that is, this law has not been there, always/already, from the start and spatialised in the architectural form of Bleak House's 'Growlery': that therapeutic 'isolation tank' of a gentleman's study where Jarndyce can vent *his angoisse* about Chancery when the symptomatic 'wind in the East' is blowing. The 'ill wind', as the proverb would have it, 'that blows no good', for it brings with it, in the figure of Jarndyce, a legality even more oppressive than its predecessor, Equity; that is, a law of obscene *jouissance* rather than symbolic prohibition, in which *cestui que* trusts are always 'at risk' because their boundaries are sure to be violated and their trust breached.

### Can't Live with It; Can't Live without It: *Bleak House*'s Trusteeship *à Venir*

So with regard to the representation of the law, *Bleak House* presents its readers, at least on the level of characterological example, with two

---

50 N. Frye, *Anatomy of Criticism: Four Essays*, Princeton: Princeton University Press, 1957, p. 44.
51 P. Goodrich, *Oedipus Lex: Psychoanalysis, History, Law*, Berkeley: University of California Press, 1995.

impossible choices of the 'can't live with it; can't live without it' variety. On the one hand, and in light of the dire depictions of Vholes, Tulkinghorn and the rest, the reader might be inclined to agree with Sjt. George – who says, on the subject of lawyers, 'I don't take kindly to the breed' (*BH*, p. 691) – prompting him or her thereafter to declare their *lebenswelt* a law-free zone. Only the text demonstrates, on the other hand, and in the case of Jarndyce, the futility of an effort like this, such foreclosure, as I have argued, merely conjuring another (and worse) law which will ride roughshod over everything and everyone in its way. All of which suggests that the jurisprudential bottom line of *Bleak House* is anything but expulsive of the law, and may very well be recuperative of it; a thesis that is aired in, and supported by the common sense observation of that most commonsensical of the novel's characters, the 'old girl' herself, Mrs Bagnet. 'It won't do to have truth and justice' on your side, she says to George, you *must* 'have law and lawyers' (*BH*, p. 732). But what sort of law does Mrs Bagnet have in mind? Certainly not equity, emanating as it does from Chancery, that 'most pestilent of hoary sinners' (*BH*, p. 4), as Dickens puts it with his usual flair for understatement. But is the common law any better? Especially given its never-ending round robin with 'Equity' which 'sends questions to Law', while 'Law sends questions back to Equity' (*BH*, p. 96). And what kind of lawyer does she think fitting? To whom can one turn to, and trust?

That question remains unresolved in *Bleak House*, its barristerial voice neither prescribing remedies, judicial or otherwise, nor describing the form which that trust, or the figure which that lawyer, and the law he or she embodies, will take. Which might be why *Bleak House* ends on such an ambiguous, even *bleakly* unsatisfactory note: in mid-sentence with Esther, once again, hemming and hawing about – what else? – *herself*, her humility topos about her 'old looks' (*BH*, p. 861) here looking more like a neurotic form of narcissism, intended to cadge compliments. All the more puzzling, given Esther's remarkable success, against all odds (lacking family, fortune, even a fair face) in securing a stable home (Bleak House north), and a loving family (Allan and their 'two daughters', *BH*, p. 859). Despite this putative note of 'happily ever after', not everything seems settled in *Bleak House's* ending; there is no full and final *closure*, as it were, to its closing – however much the text tries to will it into being (with Charley married, Tom apprenticed, and so forth). This failure to resolve is not only confined to Esther's ongoing personality disorder, but extends to several other characters: Ada, raising her child, but as a single parent, melancholically obsessed with a long gone Richard, forever in widow's weeds; Jarndyce, still unattached, the perpetual bachelor – ever the guardian, never the groom;

even Caddy and Prince (now 'lame', *BH*, p. 859), together and happy, but raising a special needs child – hearing and speech impaired ('deaf and dumb', *BH*, p. 860) – with demands far more labour-intensive than anything Mrs Jellyby and/or old Mr Turveydrop could dictate.

Of course, who better to raise little Esther than the caring Caddy, last seen learning to sign with her child (*BH*, p. 860)? And what a welcome change this novelistic representation of the differently abled is: as a comfort to, rather than a calamity for the mid-Victorian family, free of the maudlin sentimentality that is, for example, Tiny Tim's true 'affliction' (*BH*, p. 860) in *A Christmas Carol*.[52] But, nonetheless, in light of this qualified contentment (is Caddy caring or careworn?) and the more troubling fates outlined above, this question still nags: is this supposed to be a happy ending? If so, then something is amiss, and, indeed, gone missing. What is it? I would like to conclude with this suggestion; namely, that what is missing in *Bleak House* is nothing less than a sense of civil society, a public sphere that will bind the 'private ties' of which the Bagnets speak as central to the socius. For this is *the* core problem in and with *Bleak House*'s world; there is no such thing as society here, a lack which Dickens diagnoses more than 130 years before Mrs Thatcher's notorious pronouncement to that effect. Only for Dickens, unlike the Thatcherites, that rend in the social fabric is catastrophic rather than capitalising: the real 'floodgates' (*BH*, p. 561) so feared by Sir Leicester. Which accounts for why every institutional pillar of society – be it politics, the arts, religion, the ruling class, charity – is so hollowed out in *Bleak House*, and dominated by placemen ('Foodle', 'Doodle', *et al.*, *BH*, p. 384), frauds (Skimpole, Turveydrop), hypocrites (Rev. and Mrs Chadband), twittery (the 'debilitated cousin', *BH*, p. 560; Volumnia) or the misguided (Mrs Jellyby, Mrs Pardiggle). None of these actors are any better – and some are worse – than the lawyers ('Chizzle', 'Mizzle', *BH*, p. 7) manning the courts. Only medicine gets off reasonably lightly; though, bear in mind, that all Dr Woodcourt – *pharmakon*-ic as the doctor who kills as his cure – has to do is show up, and, without fail, someone in the text will die, be it Nemo/Hawdon, Jo, Lady Dedlock or Richard.

What will call a halt to *Bleak House*'s mounting body count, and the *anomie* of which it is but a sign? Is there a *praxis* of reciprocal obligations or a language of responsibility that will restore trust in and to these

---

52 For the most recent and, to my mind, most sophisticated theorisation of disability and its Other, 'ableism', see: F. K. Campbell, *Contours of Ableism: The Production of Disability and Abledness*, London: Palgrave Macmillan, 2009.

institutions, linking the small, precarious islands of 'private ties' in the text – Bleak House, north and south – into a greater, connected public whole? Law, of course, as a practical *and* discursive system of rights and duties is the obvious answer: as a social adhesive potentially binding each to each. If, that is, it wasn't so hampered by such a limited sense of trust: as client-based rather than collective oriented; as a creature of Equity, narrowly conceived, rather than a more broadly based construction of the equitable interest, writ large. In short, law remains locked into a version of itself as one of (dis)trust – of any and all. Which is why Dickens is so crucial a figure here because his text-as-novel judgement gestures towards an(O)ther jurisprudence, one going *beyond* this law in its representational *content*, but only by *returning* to it in its narrational *form*. That is, by alerting the reader to the limits of legalistic notions of (dis)trust through *Bleak House*'s characters (Vholes, Tulkinghorn, Jarndyce), plot (Jarndyce and Jaryndyce) and language (where 'trust' becomes the text's 'floating signifier'),[53] all the while sounding a voice *of*, and *in* law that not only speaks, as social trustee, on behalf of the communal – of those 'dead' and 'dying' – but listens to, indeed takes the testimony of its individual *cestuis que* trust: of Esther and those like her. In so doing, *Bleak House* sketches, in its narrative dialogism – one that gives utterance both to the 'Symbolic Law' (the barristerial voice) *and* its qualifying 'Other' (Esther's affidavit) – the possibility of a renewed socius predicated upon an alternative legality: a law of trust, and a trust in the law. That law, and the reimagined trusteeship it calls forth, is still, as Derrida might say, *a venir* – or 'to come', its final arrival, postponed by what Steve Brint calls the 'age of the expert'. But until that day, surely

---

53 To give just a few (but varied) instances of where this 'sign of the times' crops up in the text: when presented with the household keys to Bleak House, Esther Summerson is 'quite lost in the magnitude of (her) trust' (*BH*, p. 69); Jarndyce, in turn, characterises Esther's face as 'trusting, trusty' (*BH*, p. 95); Mrs Pardiggle, 'trust(s)' that her charitable interventions are 'improving to others' (*BH*, p. 103); Weevle (a.k.a. Jobling) divulges to Guppy that he (groundlessly) 'trusted to things coming round' (*BH*, p. 276); Ada, ever constant, assures a thwarted Richard that 'You may trust in me' (*BH*, p. 336); Phil Squod's comical dispatch of Smallweed, Sr. from Sjt. George's shooting gallery is described as assistance of 'shorter trust' (*BH*, p. 371); little Charley Neckett is the worthy repository of her mistress' 'trust' (*BH*, p. 433); Woodcourt accepts his charge from Esther to look in upon, and after Richard as a 'trust and . . . a sacred one' (*BH*, p. 613); Sir Leicester must 'trust' (*BH*, p. 747), in Inspector Bucket's efforts to find Lady Dedlock; and the Dedlock family attorney, Tulkinghorn, is referred to – in what must be the text's blackest moment of black comedy – as one of the 'trustiest representatives' of the law (*BH*, p. 302).

the reader can count on Dickens's legal *fictions* – such as *Bleak House* – to anticipate, summon up and hold forth on this legal *faction*, at least imaginatively; so much so that, pending the law and lawyers' real assumption of social trusteeship, we can say, echoing another polity's slogan of group reliance, it is 'In Boz We Trust'.

CHAPTER 7

# Two on a Guillotine? Courts and 'Crits' in *A Tale of Two Cities*

### A Tale of Two Trials: *Bourgeois*–Liberal Legality and Revolutionary Justice in *A Tale of Two Cities*

In *A Tale of Two Cities*,[1] everything comes in twos: not just the title's two cities (London, Paris), but two heroes (Carton, Darnay), two villains (the Bros. St. Evremonde), two informants (Cly, Barsad), two *tricoteuses* (Mme. Defarge, The Vengeance) and, especially, *two trials*. After all, the book pretty much opens and closes with a trial; in each case, of Charles Darnay, the identity of whom as double defendant connects the novel's parallel yet hitherto distinct narratives, their storylines intersecting as he takes the stand twice. So *A Tale of Two Cities* could be described as, essentially, a 'courtroom drama', its trial scenes anchoring the text; if only, that is, its competing scenes of the French Revolution (the storming of the Bastille, the Reign of Terror, and so forth) did not, retroactively, overwhelm, even obliterate practically everything else about the novel *including* the law, here drowned in the blood of its insurrectionary politics. Though it must be said that this politics – as lawless as it seems, with heads rolling and bodies mounting – is predicated upon a kind of legality and vice-versa; that is, in *A Tale of Two Cities*, legality *is* political and the political, legal, no less in

---

1 C. Dickens, *A Tale of Two Cities*, London: Penguin Books, 1970. Hereafter referred to as *ATTC*.

England than in France. For Charles Darnay only *just* escapes the hangman's noose at Tyburn, as surely as he misses, *barely*, his appointment with the operator of the Place de la Revolution's guillotine, for what are, in both cases, *political* offences: as a poor refugee in London accused of treason; as a returned *émigré* in Paris condemned for counter-revolutionary activities.

This is why *A Tale of Two Cities* invites, indeed *commands* – like some 'sovereign' as theorised by legal positivism, be it royalist king or republican 'General Will' – a *jurisprudential* reading. For the text renders a novel judgement on the law–politics nexus that complicates, even confounds Dickens's reputation as a critic of legalism – let alone as a radical reformer – and disrupts, in the process, its own balanced binaries ('the best of times', 'the worst of times', *ATTC*, p. 35), not the least of which are curial. After reviewing, in the chapter's second section, the trials of Charles Darnay, I will argue that *A Tale of Two Cities* comes down squarely on the side of what might be called, *à la* cod-Marx, '*bourgeois*–liberal legality', exemplified in its criminal proceeding at London's Old Bailey, all while rejecting its alternative inversion, the 'revolutionary justice' meted out in the Conciergerie by its infamous tribunal. This vote of confidence, however, on the text's part for *bourgeois*–liberal legality – or more simply, the Rule of Law, as codified by A.V. Dicey[2] – is not based upon with what this type of law purports to *do*; specifically, hear both sides, remain impartial, render fair judgement. Rather it is what this law does *not* do – that is, its *failure* to establish a case, then convict and perforce execute – which is, ironically, the very grounds, I contend, for its success; whereas, by way of contrast, the tribunal's success, and its revolutionary 'rough justice' which *does* very much grasp its cases' nub, is precisely what constitutes its failure.

Nowhere is this failure more spectacularly dramatised, as I will demonstrate in this chapter's third section, than in *A Tale of Two Cities'* depiction of Paris under the Terror as a society in the grip of the regime of *truth*: a truth vouchsafed by a law that understands far too much and from which nothing is hidden – where there are no secrets, legal or otherwise. This accounts for *A Tale of Two Cities'* valorisation, as I will maintain in this chapter's fourth section, of a law that *forgets* rather than remembers; an act of repression that is associated, by my lights, with Jarvis Lorry and the values of Capital which he, as Tellson's emissary, emblematises. All of which seals, as I contend in the fifth (and final) section, the fate of barrister, Sydney Carton, who is positioned by the text as law's *sujet supposé*

---

2 A. V. Dicey, *Introduction to the Study of the Law of the Constitution*, E. C. S. Wade (intro.), London: Macmillan, 1959.

*savoir*;[3] that is, the agent of legal critique deemed to know its political machinations, but, equally, its manufacture of truth. This is, of course, 'too much information', and explains why Sydney Carton *must die*. For it *his* critical legal knowledge that threatens the delicate equilibrium of the Rule of Law and its imaginary lures that save (rather than slice) us. This is why, in answer to my chapter's quizzical title – and *contra* its 1960s horror film reference[4] – there can be only *one* on a guillotine in *A Tale of Two Cities*; and that one is 'the crit', the figure of law's politics, who is sacrificed to save 'the courts' and the Rule of Law itself. A tragic loss, as it turns out, for the law; and one which, I shall argue by way of conclusion, jurisprudence – and Dickens? – *still* mourn, thereby opening up the possibility for legal critique's resurrection and *return*.

### The Trials of Charles Darnay: Stryver of the Bailey vs. the Tribunal's *J'accuse*

What irked lawyer-*cum*-reviewer, Fitzjames Stephen, the most about *A Tale of Two Cities* – and he loathed almost everything about the book – is its (mis-)representation of Charles Darnay's treason trial in London, itself based on a 1780 Old Bailey case, *R. v. Lamotte*. That case was, as in the novel, a proceeding against a young French nobleman, resident in London at the time of the American Revolution, though here found guilty of spying on behalf of his government, then of course allied with the colonists against the British. And is it any wonder this curial portrayal is *so* provoking? Because what Dickens, the former court reporter, renders here is not so much a trial as a *travesty*, replete with the following irregularities: suborned witnesses (Barsad and Cly are double agents, at once in the pocket of the Marquis St. Evremonde, as well as 'regular government pay . . . to lay traps', *ATTC*, p. 98); a 'hung jury' atmosphere ('the accused . . . was . . . being mentally hanged, beheaded, and quartered, by everybody there', *ATTC*, p. 93); the most scurrilous *ad hominem* form of prosecution (Charles is excoriated by the Attorney General as a figure of 'real wickedness' and 'infamy', *ATTC*, p. 95, p. 96); and a presiding judge who, in his capricious biases, seems enlisted from, indeed a charter member of that common law coterie anathematised by Jeremy Bentham and his followers as 'Judge & Co.' (consider his mental indictment of Darnay for 'that . . . heresy about

---

3   J. Lacan, 'The Four Fundamental Concepts of Psycho-Analysis', in A. Sheridan (trans.) *The Seminar of Jacques Lacan: Book XI*, London: Hogarth Press, 1977.
4   *Two on a Guillotine*, Directed by W. Conrad, Warner Bros: USA, 1965.

George Washington', *ATTC*, p. 102). No surprises then that Stephen went running for proof to the *State Trials* where he found, much to his satisfaction, quite the reverse: 'it would be perfectly impossible', he writes in a well-known riposte, 'to imagine a fairer trial than De La Motte's, or stronger evidence than that on which he was convicted'.[5] Stephen continues: 'The counsel for the Crown said not one word about the character of the approver, and so far was the judge from pressing hard upon the prisoner ... he excluded evidence offered against him which in almost any other country would have been all but conclusive'.[6]

One senses, however, that for all of the above, what really drives Stephen spare is the humour with which the trial is treated – a rare comic instance in a book which is seriously short of laughs. For Dickens does have some fun here, parodying the language of the law, sending up its empty rhetorical flourishes in phrases such as 'wickedly, falsely, traitorously' (*ATTC*, p. 93), all 'adverbiously' (*ATTC*, p. 93) repetitious in his rather delicious turn of phrase. The effect of this hyperbole is to *ironise* the Attorney General's opening address to bench and jury, undercutting its encomium to that shadiest of characters, the spy Barsad, by its very overstatement, calling into question his characterisation as a 'shining citizen' (*ATTC*, p. 96), whom 'Providence' (*ATTC*, p. 96) itself had guided 'to ferret out the nature of the prisoner's schemes' (*ATTC*, p. 95) and to whom a statue should be erected if 'Britain, as in ancient Greece and Rome' did such things to honour 'patriotism' (*ATTC*, p. 96). Is that 'patriotism' as in the last refuge of scoundrels? Certainly that is the Johnsonian dictum, indeed *obiter dictum* that the reader would take from this forensic flight of fancy. A fancy that becomes farcical with Stryver's grilling of this 'immaculate and unimpeachable' (*ATTC*, p. 96) witness in a scattershot of scathing interrogatives, of which the following is typical: 'Of what profession? Gentleman. Ever been kicked? Might have been. Frequently? No. Ever kicked downstairs? Decidedly not; once received a kick on the top of a staircase and fell down-stairs of his own accord. Kicked on the occasion for cheating at dice?' (*ATTC*, p. 96)[7] – and so on.

---

5 Sir J. F. Stephen, '*A Tale of Two Cities*', *Saturday Review* 17, 1961, 741–743. G. Hood and L. Lane (eds), *The Dickens Critics*, Ithaca: Cornell University Press, 1859, pp. 38–46, at p. 46.
6 Ibid.
7 Well and truly worthy of Stryver's courtroom model, that *succès de scandale* of the nineteenth-century Bar, Edwin James, QC – whose pomposity ('out-rumpoling' Rumpole) as much as propensity for peculation would surely have sent a shudder down Stephen's ramrod Victorian spine, or for that matter, any other respectable lawyerly reader acquainted with the text's real-life analogue.

But what must have been the last legal straw for Stephen, breaking his bencher's back, is the fact that in *R. v. Darnay*, the defendant goes free, fully acquitted and released under his own recognisance when, clearly, he is guilty of *something*. Not, of course, treason, the evidence of which is tainted and its attesters compromised. But what of a related, albeit lesser offence? Namely, *sedition* which sets a far lower bar for its *actus reus* (or 'guilty act') than treason, requiring only an *utterance* against civil authority, rather than active aid in support of the enemy. Surely Charles has done just that, satisfying this standard when he said to no less a credible 'witness for the prosecution' than Lucie Manette that the American Revolution was the result of England's 'wrong and foolish' mismanagement and that one day 'George Washington might gain almost as great a name as George the Third' (*ATTC*, p. 102). Naturally, the text intends this comment to be taken by its readers, gifted with the benefit of hindsight, as a statement of the obvious, history's judgement being all too clear here. But as an historical novel, *A Tale of Two Cities* invites its readers not only to judge the past but enter into it, identifying with the period's concerns, even anxieties – like the alarm bells Charles's remarks must have set off for the auditors of 1780, no matter how much Lucie tries to trivialise them as a joke intended 'to beguile the time' (*ATTC*, p. 102). For England, in the period in which the novel was set, was waging a war much like the contemporary War on Terror, it being a conflict both *within* (the colonists overseas, as well as their domestic sympathisers, back 'home') and *without* (involving age-old enemies like France and Spain, each weighing in, decisively, on the American side) the British Empire.

Mention of France above brings me to the novel's 'salt in the wound'; at least for readers such as Stephen, already injured by Dickens's gross misrepresentation of the common law. For what really must add insult to their injury here is that it is *French* revolutionary justice that gets its law *right*, as much as the English courts get it *wrong*. I will identify, in due course, exactly what the Parisian tribunal is spot on about, as I have, previously, spelled out where the London court went awry; but, I want to ask here, as a preliminary question, how can I make this argument in the first place? Particularly when the text goes out of its way to caricature the Revolution's exceedingly limited form of legality in terms of such crudity that it outstrips, easily, the Rumpolesque brio of the Old Bailey, reaching a frenzied, even psychotic pitch that anticipates, and far surpasses juridico-political polemics such as Zola's *J'accuse*. Indeed, accusation rather than arraignment, denunciation rather than deposition is, as the text would have it, the order of the day at this 'dread Tribunal' (*ATTC*, p. 309), rendering its hearings more of a pantomime than a legal proceeding. What with its 'little or no order'

(*ATTC*, p. 344), and its course continually disrupted either by the shrieks of its 'turbulent audience' (*ATTC*, p. 311) – e.g., 'Take off his head!' (*ATTC*, p. 31) – or by the obsessive ringing by that fetish object, the president's bell, the tribunal evinces little, or no consistency of procedure. Even worse is the case of the tribunal's substantive legal reasoning; there, its verdicts are an incoherent and dizzying array of about-faces, swinging wildly from acquittal to conviction, reneging today in its judgment of yesterday, itself a violation of *res judicata* and the prohibition against being tried twice for the same offence. For instance, Charles is exonerated, initially, and carried in triumph from the court in a 'wild, dreamlike procession' (*ATTC*, p. 315); then, subsequently, on the next day, he is excoriated as 'a notorious oppressor of the People' (*ATTC*, p. 362) and condemned to 'Death within four and twenty hours' (*ATTC*, p. 362).

Now my query is this: why the curial overkill in this, the showiest of show trials? Of course, Dickens is cribbing from Carlyle here, the latter's *French Revolution*[8] justifying this sort of portrayal – the tribunal as a chamber of judicial horrors – as being rooted in historical fact; namely, public prosecutor Fouquier-Tinville's notorious kangaroo courts that sent thousands to the guillotine, including, lastly and fittingly, himself. Additionally, though, I would like to suggest another source, one grounded more in psychological *affect* than historical authority and turning on attitudes that are as much anti-Continental as they are crypto-Carlylean; that is, the largely hostile feelings on the part of the Great British public – as much as their lawyers – towards, *inter alia*, European legal practices, of which France is typical. For what Dickens gives vent to in *A Tale of Two Cities* is a view, then (still?) rife in the United Kingdom, as much in the 1850s as in the 1790s, that, when compared to the common law's adversarialism (lawyer as 'hired gun', judge as umpire, trial as a fight between two parties), the French inquisitorial system (judge led, counsel subordinate, and a trial in single-minded pursuit of the facts) has been more capricious, often heavy-handed, even dictatorial, whether it was, as here, radical–revolutionary or, previously, reactionary–royalist, each being two sides of the same despotic coin. After all, 'law and order' under the *ancien régime* comes across not much better (and, possibly, *worse*) than the Terror. Think, for example, of Gaspard – that lesser version of Damiens, the favourite regicide of Foucault[9] as much as Dickens (*ATTC*, p. 200) – whose

---

8 T. Carlyle, *The French Revolution: A History*, London: Dent, 1906.
9 M. Foucault, *Discipline and Punish: The Birth of the Prison*, A. Sheridan (trans.), New York: Pantheon, 1977.

corpse is left hanging after his execution over the village well, poisoning its waters and punishing the community in a kind of collective reprisal for the murder of their landlord, the old Marquis (*ATTC*, p. 201).

A detail such as this one, of the pre-1789 juridical order, when coupled with those of the post-1789 order, resonate with and reinforce on the part of the reader a Pross-like chauvinism – national, ethnic, religious but especially *legal* – airing an *animus* against 'foreign' principles of law at odds with the rights of free-born Englishmen (like *their* presumption of guilt rather than *ours* of innocence, that Lucie-like 'golden thread' of the common law *ATTC*, p. 239). Dickens, however, complicates this sort of tub-thumping for British justice by reminding the reader repeatedly that, for England, this was the age of 'the hangman' (*ATTC*, p. 37) as well as the Bloody Code: 'today, taking the life of an atrocious murderer, and tomorrow of a wretched pilferer who had robbed a farmer's boy of sixpence' (*ATTC*, p. 37). But there *is* a difference between England and France, despite the similarity implied by the novel's celebrated contrastive opening; a divergence which goes to the text's contemporary 'scene of writing' (1859), rather than the shifting time frame of its past storyline (1775, 1780, 1793, 1757, 1767 and so on). For the point that Dickens seems to make here is that England's worst abuses of what Foucault might call law-as-punishment are truly *historical,* having been reformed (by Bentham, Brougham, and so on) or about to be (like Chancery); whereas, in France, its disciplinary – but also punitive – politics of revolutionary justice are locked into a *cycle* of repetition of which 1848 (and the fall of *another* French monarchy, that of the 'citizen-king', Louis-Philippe) is the most recent instance (with the 'July Revolution' of 1830, a not so distant memory; and the Paris Commune of 1870, not too far in the future).

So the tribunal's representation in *A Tale of Two Cities* comes freighted with an enormous amount of baggage: historical, ideological but, particularly, *jurisprudential.* All the more startling then that it, *quite correctly*, convicts Charles Darnay. For under the terms the 'law of the Suspected' (*ATTC*, p. 302), be they broadly or strictly construed, Charles *is* guilty and stands condemned to death, a judgement that Darnay's very *presence* in Paris confirms rather than contests. This is because Darnay is not accused here, as he was in England, of having *done* something; that is, of committing an act with intent, like treason, which would raise all sorts of highly justiciable issues, such as intention and its proof. Rather, in France, he is charged with *who he is*, not what he has done, because *identity* – specifically *class identity* – is the key issue for revolutionary justice: think of the Kulaks under Stalin, or the landlords under Mao. It is precisely this accusation of identity, encoded as the status offence of being a returned aristocratic 'emigrant' (*ATTC*, p. 278) and, perforce an 'Enemy of the Republic', that is established beyond all (un)reasonable doubt at Darnay's hearings before the tribunal. Not that Charles does all he can to argue the contrary, portraying himself (rather piously) as a *déclassé* who, having renounced his high 'station' (*ATTC*, p. 312), has reinvented himself as a solid *petit bourgeois* Londoner living by his 'own industry' (*ATTC*, p. 312), instead of on 'the overladen people of France' (*ATTC*, p. 312). The problem, however, with Charles's self-presentation – as *the* embodiment of the Weberian Protestant work ethic – is that it the text so flatly contradicts it.[10] For it is Charles's feelings of compassion for an 'old servant' (*ATTC*, p. 271), Gabelle, who petitioned his aid not only on the grounds of 'justice' and 'generosity' (*ATTC*, p. 270), but, also, 'because of the honour of . . . (his) noble name' (*ATTC*, p. 270), addressing him in his letter by his former title, 'Monsieur Heretofore The Marquis' (*ATTC*, p. 270). In short, by appealing to his innate *noblesse oblige* as a feudal overlord, a strategy which succeeds and prompts Charles's return, thereby *affirming* the very aristocratic, emigrant identity with which he is charged.

Of course, Dr Manette's timely courtroom character reference 'save[s]' (*ATTC*, p. 316) Charles. Subsequently, however, that strategy is turned against both of them at the second tribunal by those real masters tribunal trickery, the Defarges, who cite not only themselves as accusers of Darnay, but Manette, whose Gramsci-like prison notebooks will attest, they contend, that his future son-in-law is, indeed, 'one of a family of tyrants, one of a race proscribed' (*ATTC*, p. 345). The term 'race' is, as literary critic Maia von Sneideren[11] has noted, a striking one, and will be picked up later on in the text, echoed in the soon-to-be read out dying declaration of Thérèse Defarge's nameless brother, whose last words were witnessed (in 1757), then afterwards recorded (in 1767) by Manette, the attending physician. *In extremis*, and within earshot of Manette, young Defarge gasps: 'Marquis . . . in the days when all these things are to be answered for, I summon you and yours, to the last of your bad race, to answer for them' (*ATTC*, p. 356). What the phraseology of this death-bed denunciation suggests ('the last of your bad *race*'), when taken with the wording of the previously cited deposition of the Defarges ('one of a *race* proscribed'), is that the French Revolution is more than a conflict of ideologies (Liberty, Equality, Fraternity *vs.* the Divine Right of Kings), more than a clash of

---

10 The same point is made by M. L. von Sneideren, 'An Amazingly Good Jackal: Race and Labour in Dickens' *A Tale of Two Cities*', *South Atlantic Review* 66(2), 2001, 64–90.
11 Ibid.

classes (the aristocracy *vs.* the common people), but something far more fundamental, genetic as much as genealogical – what is bred in the bone, wired in the blood.

And blood *will* tell – a truism of which the old, family-proud (s)nobs of eighteenth-century Versailles would have approved heartily; and to which Darwin (1859 is also the year of publication for *The Origin of Species*) and similarly inspired scientists (e.g., Mendel, Spencer) of Dickens's day are giving fresh currency, remaking nineteenth-century notions of humanity in light of their new template, race – understood now in *biological*, as much as familial terms.[12] Manette, himself a type of Enlightenment scientist, anticipates this template, nowhere more so than in his own testimonial, cited below, and which cries out for what international law would now term 'racial genocide' directed at, ironically, his own descendants. For it is Lucie and her daughter, Little Lucie, both St. Evremondes – one by marriage, the other by descent – who are the unwitting targets of the curse Manette calls down upon the family of his former nemeses, damning them in terms ('to the last of their race') that not only look back to the Old Testament's ukases 'unto the seventh generation', but forward, uncannily, to the Nazis and their eugenic Nuremberg laws. He writes in a kind of ecstasy of 'unbearable agony' (*ATTC*, p. 302), the *jouissance* of racism: 'And them and their descendants, to the last of their race, I, Alexandre Manette, unhappy prisoner, do ... denounce to the times when all these things shall be answered for. I denounce them to Heaven and Earth' (*ATTC*, p. 361). No wonder then that after this evidence is tendered the normally contained Thérèse Defarge gloats – Vengeance like – 'Save him now, my doctor, save him' (*ATTC*, p. 362). For how is Manette to save Charles from *himself*? Despite all his secrets and lies, disguises and deceptions – as Darnay, d'Aulnais, St. Evremonde – *A Tale of Two Cities*' putative protagonist stands here absolutely exposed in all his biological and familial *truth*, the hereditary foe of the *Volk* and vermin fit only for 'extermination' (*ATTC*, p. 369).

**Through the Looking Glass of the Law: *A Tale of Two Cities*' Curial Dialectic of Recognition and *Méconnaissance***

The startling suggestion that Dickens makes here is that the tribunal of revolutionary justice, far from being the stage-managed sham *bourgeois*–

---

12 For an excellent and in-depth analysis of the concept of blood and its connections to, and differences from race in *A Tale of Two Cities*, see von Sneideren, above n. 10.

liberal legality wants it to be, in fact, actualises *the truth*. 'Patriots, I speak the truth!' (*ATTC*, p. 346), shouts The Vengeance, endorsing the veracity of the tribunal's proceedings as much as the Defarges' evidence. But the question arises here: what enables the tribunal to realise the truth? Is there a mechanism – or lack thereof – the presence or absence of which functionalises this grand truth-telling claim? Certainly there is an *absence* of legal representation, lawyers having gone on walkabout in the novel's depiction of revolutionary France, even more so than the *ci-devant* 'laughing ladies and fine lords' (*ATTC*, p. 203). So one reason that the tribunal may winkle out the truth is because there is no lawyerly *presence* here to gum up the works by, for example, testing evidence, objecting to irregularities and otherwise arresting the all-too-efficient wheels of justice from spinning out of control. No wonder that one of the most vociferous critics of the Revolution turns out to be the advocate, Stryver; his diatribes against it ('the most pestilent and blasphemous code devilry that was ever known', *ATTC*, p. 269) are a tacit recognition that its tribunals anticipate the rise of what David Saunders would call 'anti-lawyers',[13] well and truly represented in its results-driven, process-averse and highly politicised prosecutors.

But the notion that really seems to have gone missing from *A Tale of Two Cities*' tribunal scenes is any sense of what might be called 'the juridical imaginary'; namely, that psychic space of *nomos* informing the physical space of the tribunal, one that would provide it with a set of presumptions and principles, duties and rights – such as the right to counsel. Which raises one of the most striking paradoxes about revolutionary justice; despite its jurisprudential grounding in a theory of rights – the 'rights of man' – it has no qualms, nonetheless, in *waiving* those very grounds, as when, for example, the tribunal blithely pronounces, 'Emigrants have no rights' (*ATTC*, p. 280). This erasure of rights is possible – that is, both as sayable and doable – in the land of the *Declaration of the Rights of Man* precisely because revolutionary justice no longer operates, as Jacques Lacan would put it, on the level of the Imaginary (juridical or otherwise), but, instead, on the level of the Real. In fact, the revolutionary Real – of rupture, of trauma, of 'the Thing' – has fractured forever the previously extant Imaginary, figured in the *ancien régime*'s 'Fancy Ball' (*ATTC*, p. 138). Parading itself on several occasions throughout *A Tale of Two Cities* (*ATTC*, pp. 134–138; pp. 203–204), this gathering comprises a *grotesquerie* of two social orders, with the 'usual suspects' (Monseigneur in Town, the Farmer-

---

13  D. Saunders, *Anti-Lawyers: Religion and the Critics of Law and State*, London: Routledge, 1997.

General, etc.), taking the lead, followed by charlatans and fakirs of all stripes: not only clergy without faith, doctors without cure, intellectuals without ideas (*ATTC*, p. 136), but, even more bizarre, sects such as 'Convulsionists' (*ATTC*, p. 137)

Ultimately, though, there is no difference between the above two orders of the Old Regime – either its 'Centre' of power (*ATTC*, p. 137), or its 'Circumference' of fantasy (*ATTC*, p. 137). Both are being eaten away, in Dickens's vivid phrase, by the 'leprosy of unreality' (*ATTC*, p. 137), with each soon to be de-corporealised by revolutionary justice as spectres: 'Ghosts all! The ghost of beauty, the ghost of stateliness, the ghost of elegance' (*ATTC*, p. 285). What a vivid contrast is provided by England and its juridical imaginary. Not that Dickens is oblivious to own country's history of revolt against duly constituted legal authority, 'British orthodoxy' (*ATTC*, p. 267) having seen fit to throw off its own Bourbon equivalent, the 'merry Stuarts' (*ATTC*, p. 135), quite content to sell England by the pound. The irony, of course, is heavy here, with the implication that there was nothing very 'merry' to begin with about the Stuarts; even less so at their end, with the overthrow of James II, as Dickens suggests elsewhere,[14] powered more by a desire to *restore* rather than revolt against the law. For what the Glorious Revolution of 1689 did was entrench, constitutionally, what was already there in the first place – however threatened by Stuart absolutism; namely, rights (in the form of the Bill of Rights) and representative government (ensured by the Act of Settlement), two measures which guarantee that linchpin of *bourgeois*–liberal legalism and its juridical imaginary, the Rule of Law.

Central to this imaginary, and the kind of legalism it sustains, is the Rule of Law formulation as propounded, later, by A.V. Dicey in his celebrated *Introduction to the Study of the Law of the Constitution*: first, that everyone is deserving of equal treatment under the law ('every man, whatever be his rank or condition, is subject to the ordinary law of the realm and amenable to the jurisdiction of the ordinary tribunals');[15] and, second, that no one is 'above' it.[16] Certainly, at first blush, nobody is above, at least the *common law* in A Tale of Two Cities – but some*thing* well and truly is; specifically, the hard, reflective surface of a 'mirror', suspended from the courtroom ceiling which hangs, Damocles like, 'over the prisoner's' – meaning Charles's – 'head' (*ATTC*, 94). By placing, literally, this very distinctive, decorative

---

14 C. Dickens, *A Child's History of England*, London: Chapman & Hall, 1905.
15 Dicey, *Introduction to the Study of the Law of the Constitution*, above n. 2, p. 193.
16 Ibid.

feature within the Old Bailey, Dickens's scene figuratively summons up, as above the law, the very realm of nomological ideology itself; that is, the juridical imaginary which physically encompasses the court's docket here in what Lacan taught was that Imaginary order's source and seminal metaphor – the mirror of the celebrated 'mirror phase':

> Over the prisoner's head there was a mirror, to throw the light down upon him. Crowds of the wicked and the wretched had been reflected in it, and had passed from its surface and this earth's together. Haunted in a most ghastly manner that abominable place would have been, if the glass could ever have rendered back its reflections, as the ocean is one day to give up its dead. Some passing thought of the infamy and disgrace for which it had been reserved, may have struck the prisoner's mind. Be that as it may, a change in his position making him conscious of a bar of light across his face, he looked up; and when he saw the glass his face flushed.
>
> (Dickens, *A Tale of Two Cities*, p. 94)

This remarkable passage suggests a reading that is not only Lacanian but, at least initially, an *Althusserian* one – if Lacan inspired. How? In its imaging of England's juridical imaginary as a mirror that is not only a witness to past offenders, long gone ('crowds of the wicked and the wretched' who had passed before its 'surface', prior to leaving the earth altogether) but is capable, in its specularity, of 'hailing' the prisoner, Darnay (throwing 'light down upon him'), this passage invokes the Althusserian notion of ideological interpellation. To wit, the mirror 'interpellates' – as Louis Althusser would put it[17] – Charles as the ideological subject of law; that is, as the perpetrator of crime (he *did* say all those naughty things about George III), the commission of which, however unintended and/or minor, is confirmed not only by Charles' facial flush (owing to a 'passing thought of . . . infamy and disgrace') but in the 'bar of light across his face' – a brightness that says, in a positive act of identic recognition, 'Guilty!'.

This Althusserian reading, however, is complicated, even subverted by the passage itself when it interjects: 'Haunted in a most ghastly manner that abominable place would have been, if the glass could ever have rendered back its reflections, as the ocean is one day to give up its dead'. Here the text shifts,

---

17 L. Althusser, 'Ideology and Ideological State Apparatuses (Notes towards an Investigation)', in L. Althusser, *Essays on Ideology*, New York: Verso, 1984, pp. 1–60.

in its eerie maritime simile of the court as a corpse-strewn Atlantic ('the ocean ... to give up its dead'), from an Althusserian view of the juridical imaginary (where the guilty, are forever before the law, 'haunting' it, spectrally) to one that is more properly Lacanian, especially when it qualifies this ectoplasmic encounter as contingent upon a condition: 'if the glass could ever have rendered back its reflections'. For according to Lacan,[18] the Imaginary's specularity is distinguished, as here in the looking-glass of the law, by its *failure* to reflect; that is, its *méconnaissance* or, more simply, 'misrecognition', the subject being obscured, distorted, seen through a glass, darkly. This is precisely why Charles goes free; he is misrecognised by a juridical imaginary that not only fails to reflect, but in fact *refracts* who he is: is he Carton or Darnay? And this failure of England's juridical imaginary to disclose the identic truth of its (putative) criminal subject is, paradoxically for Dickens, the basis of its success in that, at the very least, it does not destroy its accused – or, for that matter, anyone else. Which is a perfect chiastic reversal of France's *lack* of imaginary where revolutionary justice *fails* (its death sentences destroying, eventually, everyone: litigants, witnesses, prosecutors) in succeeding all too well (in determining guilt and securing conviction).

This chiasmus obtains because the French system of revolutionary justice, as unmediated by an Imaginary, creates a short-circuit between the Symbolic to the Real, running directly from the former's letter that literally kills – i.e., Mme Defarge's knitted list of denunciations – to the latter's 'body in pain', imaged in that most 'thing'-like of monstrous Things; specifically, the severed head – the most gruesome textual example of which is that of the Bastille's erstwhile governor, his own 'hewed off' by Mme Defarge herself (*ATTC*, p. 249). England's phlegmatic law – the common law, or *bourgeois*–liberal legality – by way of contrast, may lack, as Miss Pross would say, 'imagination' (*ATTC*, p. 127), and all the blood-soaked drama that goes with it; but *it has an Imaginary*, symbolised in the courtroom mirror, the reflection of which produces an ongoing process of doubling, like Carton for Darnay, and vice-versa. This imaginary doubling introduces a radical indeterminacy into the law's Symbolic and its system of differences, forever disseminating aliases and alibis, mitigations and exceptions, *obiters* and dissents. All of which not only renders undecidable if Charles is Sydney – or Sydney, Charles – but thwarts, indeed disables any resolute claims to speak, jurisprudentially or otherwise, the *whole truth and nothing but the truth*.

---

18 J. Lacan, 'The Mirror Stage as Formative of the Function of the I', in A. Sheridan (trans.), *Ecrits: A Selection*, New York: Norton, 1977.

And a good thing too – for if *A Tale of Two Cities* conveys anything approximating a moral, it is the importance of *not* telling the whole truth; in fact, of holding back, of keeping a secret. 'A wonderful fact to reflect upon', says the text in a tantalising aside, is 'that every human creature is constituted to be that profound secret and mystery to every other' (*ATTC*, p. 44). Not that *all* secrets are kept in *A Tale of Two Cities* – or should be. After all, Carton unburdens himself of *his* secret in the love his 'bleeding' (*ATTC*, p. 238) heart has for Lucie. '[Y]ou have been the last dream of my soul' (*ATTC*, p. 181), he confides, a declaration gesturing, possibly, towards Dickens's own secret love for Ellen Ternan.[19] But that secret, like the Dickens–Ternan affair, is almost instantly secreted away (a confidence 'reposed in your pure and innocent breast ... alone, and will be shared by no one', *ATTC*, p. 183), to be held in reserve, until its promise of 'sacrifice for you and those dear to you' (*ATTC*, p. 183) can be redeemed in an eleventh-hour rescue of Charles – himself held, tellingly, 'in secret' (*ATTC*, p. 280, p. 284, pp. 285–286) at La Force. So some secrets, clearly, are to be divulged. But every secret? What would the effect be if, for example, all London's 'darkly clustered houses' – its 'room[s]', its 'beating heart[s]' – imparted their 'secret[s]' (*ATTC*, p. 44)? Are there some secrets better left hidden, unsaid and undisturbed? This certainly seems to be the case in the novel's depiction of another city, Paris under The Terror, where no one (like Charles), and nothing (like Manette's prison testimonial) remains secret for long. For the City of Light, unlike Dickens's London, is awash in the blinding revelation of *truth*, its revolutionary justice bringing all the wrongs of the past, hitherto shrouded in secrecy, out into the glare of the open.

This is because revolutionary justice is not content to remain on the level of surface, merely *identifying* the criminal subject(s). Instead, this form of legality goes further, plumbing the deep structure of crime, in all of its secrecy. Nowhere more so than by bringing before the tribunal's unflinching gaze the novel's hitherto undisclosed 'primal scene' – or, at least, that is, its after-effects, as registered in Manette's hitherto secreted carceral affidavit; namely, the brutal rape of Thérèse Defarge's beautiful older sister, left to die of shock, bound to her bed in silk scarves, bemoaning the untimely fates of her father, husband and brother (*ATTC*, p. 351). Each of whom die at the hand or by the act of the brothers St. Evremonde: the first, killed by grief (*ATTC*, p. 355); the next, literally worked to death (*ATTC*, p. 355); the last, slain at sword point (*ATTC*, pp. 355–356). In bringing this scene of

---

19 Certainly Dickens's biographer Fred Kaplan suggests that Lucie Manette was modelled on Dickens's mistress of his declining years, actress Ellen Ternan. See: F. Kaplan, *Dickens: A Biography*, London: Hodder & Stoughton, 1988, pp. 415–416.

*sexual*, as well as *social* oppression into the juridical field of vision, revolutionary justice realises not only a 'politics of the law', but its *psychoanalysis*, recovering in the deeply denied memories of Manette what might be called a counter-'family romance'. Or, better yet, and in a more philosophical vein, an anti-*Oedipe*, figured in the St. Evremonde twins, whose fraternity here conflates to function as a paternity more anal than phallic: that is, as a doubled 'primal father', their monopolisation of *eros* placing them on the side of Real 'enjoyment' rather than Symbolic repression.

Which is odd, given that it is the old Marquis who says to Charles, 'Repression is the only lasting philosophy' (*ATTC*, p. 153), But then, of course, this is not so odd, given that 'Father Enjoyment', as Slavoj Žižek would call Monseigneur in the Country,[20] literally represses everyone and everything – *except repression itself*, destroying the victims of his 'philosophy of the bedroom' (like Thérèse Defarge's family) and dispatching all witnesses (like Manette) to the 'political unconscious' of the *ancien régime*, the Bastille, thereby foreclosing the Law and the responsibility for one's actions it imposes. The problem, however, with this foreclosure is that what is expelled from the Symbolic (Manette and his attestation to heinous yet unpunished crime) *returns in the Real* (much as Charles' anxious mother feared: 'I have a presentiment that if no other innocent atonement is made for this, it will one day be required of him', *ATTC*, p. 360). That is, as an 'enjoyment' even more destructive than that of the 'primal father', now regendered as the 'symptom of Woman' in what is, arguably, one of the most psychotic characters in Dickens's *œuvre*, Thérèse Defarge. For she is a figure of id-like drive, going well beyond the 'pleasure principle' of the St Evremondes and their ilk – think of 'Monseigneur in Town', whose morning chocolate is a metaphor for France being drained to the dregs by the aristocracy (*ATTC*, p. 134). Instead, she embodies the terrifying force of *thanatos* itself; that is, the 'death drive', more unstoppable than Nature itself. 'Tell the Wind and the Fire', she exclaims to the more moderate Ernest, 'where to stop; not me!' (*ATTC*, p. 371).

Only the death of those 'doomed to destruction and extermination' (*ATTC*, p. 37) will satisfy Mme. Defarge, whose corporealisation of *thanatos* is yoked, here, to a higher law – *retribution*, 'The Vengeance' being not only her sidekick but her very reason for being, and the principle of which (unjust deserts?) is textualised in the warp and woof of her knitted list of infamy. Herein, for Dickens, likes the real danger of revolutionary justice,

---

20 S. Žižek, *Enjoy Your Symptom! Jacques Lacan In Hollywood and Out*, London: Routledge, 1992.

and which tips the scales – as if there was any doubt – clearly in favour of *bourgeois*–liberal legality, and its juridical imaginary. This is because in actualising the truth (Defarge's and Manette's denunciatory texts, each attesting to socio-sexual oppression), revolutionary justice releases *trauma* itself from the Bastille of the unconscious, encouraging it to run amok, coursing through Paris, 'stain[ing]' and 'smear[ing]' (*ATTC*, p. 291) its inhabitants with the blood of its victims, all the while challenging and undoing any and all kinds of phallic authority – whether it be Real ('Father Enjoyment') or Symbolic ('Father Repression') – because it is none other than feminine *jouissance* itself. Nowhere is this dark force – the feminine as *outlaw*, as well as *outside* the law – more graphically imaged than in the revolutionary crowd scenes for which *A Tale of Two Cities* is cinematically celebrated, and where a gendered analysis of the text would begin.

Such an analysis would examine how, here, Dickens taps into and spectacularises a fear (and loathing) of 'the feminine' – indeed, of all sexual difference – encoded as the *canaille*. Think of that strange, cross-dressed mob assembled by the Grindstone, 'false eyebrows and false moustaches' (*ATTC*, p. 291) offset by their torn finery: the 'spoils of women's lace and silk and ribbon' (*ATTC*, p. 291). Or that carnivalesque, even 'queer' conga line of a dance – the 'Carmagnole' (*ATTC*, p. 308) – making its way through the Parisian boulevards, The Vengeance leading its strange formation steps, where 'women danced together, men danced together' (*ATTC*, p. 307). Finally and most (in)famously, in the *tricoteuses* of Paris, clustered around, and iteratively, 'knitting, knitting' (*ATTC*, p. 216) beneath that monument to castration, the *vagina dentata of* Mme La Guillotine, their gaze arrested by the rolling heads of the clerical and aristocratic *corps morcelé*. Ultimately, though, the textual effect solicited by this revolutionary 'frenzy of the visible' – its scenes of dismemberment, a kind of politicised pornography of snuff – is not the arrest, but the *aversion* of the readerly gaze. This is the case because I will argue in this chapter's next section that what Dickens enjoins here is the *non*-enjoyment of the symptom of trauma, one that says categorically rejects the truth of revolutionary justice and its politics of the law, opting instead for a 'politics of forgetting', supported and sustained by *bourgeois*–liberal legality and its juridical imaginary of *méconnaissance*.

### Jarvis Lorry, Tellson's Bank and the Politics of Forgetting: Capitalising Law, Legalising Capital

If there is a character in *A Tale of Two Cities* who embodies what I have called its 'politics of forgetting', then it is Jarvis Lorry, Tellson's tireless clerk. Nowhere is the politics which Lorry figures more vividly dramatised than in the scenes depicting Dr Manette's seemingly inexplicable psychotic relapse on the very day of Charles and Lucie's wedding, subsequent to his prenuptial *in camera* interview with his prospective son-in-law from which he emerges 'deadly pale' as if 'the old air of avoidance and dread had lately passed over him' (*ATTC,* p. 223). The text elides the content of the interview; presumably, the revelation of Charles' real identity, a narrative omission that points the reader away from the relapse's aetiology (which, in any event, will come to light at the tribunal), and towards its symptomatic after-effects and treatment. For Charles and Lucie's departure for their honeymoon signals in Dr Manette a full-blown 'return of the repressed', symptomatised in his delusional reversion to the old prison identity of the shoemaker of 'One Hundred and Five, North Tower' (*ATTC,* p. 73), and which Lorry discovers: 'Mr. Lorry . . . went himself into the Doctor's room. The bench was turned towards the light, as it had been when he had seen the shoemaker at his work before, and his head was bent down, and he was very busy' (*ATTC,* p. 224).

What follows is a course of treatment – walks, casual conversation, the appearance of normalcy while keeping close watch – all prescribed by Lorry, and culminating in, when the worst of Manette's psychosis has passed, a kind of 'talking cure' with Manette as analysand and Lorry as analyst who, speaking *en passant* with the doctor, gives this diagnosis, under the guise of discussing a case study: 'My dear Manette . . . It is a case of a shock from which he has recovered, so completely, as to be a highly intelligent man, capable of close application of mind . . . But, unfortunately, there has been . . . a slight relapse' (*ATTC,* p. 229). By distancing the situation at hand as one pertaining to some third party, Lorry elicits, by way of counter-transference ('Now, my dear Manette . . . I want guiding . . . Tell me, how does this relapse come about?', *ATTC,* p. 230), a *self*-diagnosis on Manette's part in his capacity as medical consultant ('I believe . . . that there had been a strong and extraordinary revival of the train of thought and remembrance that was the first cause of the malady', *ATTC,* p. 231) and a prescription for cure, the key step of which is the 'letting go', by the doctor, of his fetish object: the 'old companion' of the cobbler's bench, 'hacked . . . to pieces' by Mr Lorry, 'while Miss Pross held the candle as if she was assisting at a murder' (*ATTC,* p. 235).

The analogy drawn here between the destruction of the bench and 'murder' is striking, not the least because this criminological simile seems to situate Lorry as a psychoanalyst of Lacan's *école freudienne*. For Lorry urges Manette to substitute Law of the signifier (that is, the discourse of analysis) for the obsessional object, a Lacanian counselling strategy that

174 • Novel Judgements: Legal Theory as Fiction

Lorry not only entreats but enacts, his own self-description being that of a 'speaking machine' (*ATTC,* p. 54) without the affect of 'feelings' (*ATTC,* p. 55): in short, as an instantiation of the mechanical Symbolic, and its dead letters. So Lorry's intervention here – smashing the bench – makes perfect psychoanalytic sense in that it 'acts out' the central dictum of Lacan that the 'word is the murder of the thing'.[21] Instead of the 'thing' – the symptom *not* to be enjoyed here – Lorry urges Manette to embrace his signifying 'lack',[22] as an effect of language which is, at once, professional (the voice of science), and paternal (the metaphor of fatherhood). Indeed, Lorry speaks for, and on behalf of the *Nom du Père*, though, interestingly, he is the least 'phallic' character in the novel, described by Miss Pross as an old 'bachelor' even in his 'cradle' (*ATTC,* p. 222). Nevertheless, it is Lorry who reinstates *A Tale of Two Cities'* most significant intersubjective tie – the bond between father and child – as the mediator reuniting Manette with Lucie, acting *in loco parentis* (though at a distance) for Lucie by managing, as a 'man of business' (*ATTC,* p. 54), Manette's property during the long years of the doctor's incarceration.

This association between property and paternity renders Lorry a figure, first and foremost, of Symbolic exchange, upholding a contract which is, as much, *social* (restoring not only parent and child, but husband and wife; namely, Charles to Lucie, by aiding and abetting their escape from Paris in his carriage) as *financial* (bequeathing an estate which, as Carton foretells, will 'enrich', Charles, Lucie and their children as his heirs *ATTC,* p. 404), thereby establishing his true 'business' as what Robertson Davies would call 'fifth business';[23] that is, as the character who is neither hero nor villain, but who, nevertheless donates an agency, an instrument, a means which is crucial to the narrative – here, a new *Law.* What is the Law for which Lorry stands and speaks? Surely, it is the Law of finance Capital, the very apotheosis of the Symbolic's exchange values, institutionally concretised in the text in Tellson's Bank, that forerunner of globalisation which, with offices both in London and Paris, traverses the novel's central binary, its two cities. Moreover, Tellson's is the repository of all the characters' private affairs: of Manette's property (as well as his personhood, Lorry escorting him to safety in England); of Lucie's

---

21 '*Le mot est le meutre de la chose*' quoted in J.-A. Miller, 'Language: Much Ado About What?', in E. Ragland-Sullivan and M. Bracher (eds), *Lacan and the Subject of Language,* London: Routledge, 1990, p. 30.
22 J. Lacan, 'Function and Field of Speech and Language in Psychoanalysis', in Sheridan, *Ecrits: A Selection,* above n. 18.
23 R. Davies, *Fifth Business,* New York: Viking, 1970.

wardship (Lorry, also, having brought her to England as a child); of Charles's identity (Tellson's is the address to which Gabelle sends his letter to Charles); even, of Monseigneur's funds (at least, for those who made 'provident remittances', *ATTC*, p. 264).

As such, Tellson's anticipates Niklas Luhmann's characterisation of financial services as the 'memory bank' of modernity.[24] But Tellson's is as much a space of *forgetting* as it is of memory, and what it denies, suppresses, even *represses* is the fundamental antagonism upon which Capital is built; specifically, the class war imaged in the figure of 'Death' hovering over it, and meted out to 'the forger . . .; the utterer of a bad note . . .; the purloiner of forty shillings and six pence . . .; the coiner of a bad shilling . . .; the sounders of three-fourths of the notes in the whole gamut of Crime' (*ATTC*, p. 84). Not for nothing then is Tellson's situated next to Temple Bar, historically the forbidding site for the display of treasonous heads. This contiguity suggests a function for the English bank similar to that of the Bastille in France; that is, as the 'unconscious' of society – though reconfigured here as a commercial rather than carceral institution, as befits England as a 'nation of shopkeepers'. All of which implies, in its parallelism, the possibility that Tellson's may meet the same historical fate visited upon the Bastille. For if the Bastille could be stormed and its secrets released, not only in the shape of its seven prisoners (*ATTC*, p. 249), but in the form of Manette's affidavit, then why not Tellson's? Why wouldn't it be stormed, if not by a *jacquerie*, then by their English equivalents? By either the English Jacobins of the novel's time frame or by the Chartists of Dickens's own day?

Tellson's and Capital are insulated from this assault by the common law's aporias of *méconnaissance*, precisely because neither can arrest, let alone control *bourgeois*–liberal legality's endless *différance*. So Capital (as well as Tellson's) can make good here on its central ideological claim that it is a creature rather than a creator of law, thereby endorsing the prevailing jurisprudential assertion of the day, made by legal positivism, that the law enjoys a systemic autonomy with no 'necessary connection' to, principally, morality, and the ecclesiastical obscurantism which, then, was its prop. With this declaration of (jurisprudential) independence, *bourgeois*–liberal legalism's reformist project was free to embark, throughout the mid-century, on a systemic rationalisation of the common law. This reordering takes the form of practical, institutional changes: in the 1850s, in the

---

24 N. Luhmann, *Observations on Modernity*, W. Whobery (trans.), Stanford: Stanford University Press, 1998.

176 • Novel Judgements: Legal Theory as Fiction

simplification of court procedures, the regularisation of remedial relief and the establishment of the Court of Appeal;[25] in the 1870s, in the fusing the systems of equity and common law under the Judicature Acts. But these rationalising reforms, and the autonomic space which enables them, are 'always/already' compromised; that is, they are only *relative* because, 'in the last instance', the Imaginary specularity of the common law is focalised by the *same* predominant gaze of blindness and insight prevalent in the pre-positivist legal regime. Though now this gaze is restricted by, and to the exchange values of 'His Majesty the Economy' rather than the 'queen of the sciences', theology. Whose gaze is this? Surely it belongs to none other than the common law judge, hitherto the *bête noire* of Bentham and the Benthamites, now rehabilitated by Austin's version of legal positivism, the formalist imperatives of which were best served by the *con*formist 'expository jurisprudence' rife on the bench, rather than the *re*formist 'censorial jurisprudence' driven by the legislator's utility calculus.

Dickens gestures towards this rehabilitation of the judge by 'second wave' (Austinian) legal positivism with a character who only makes an appearance in *A Tale of Two Cities* by way of postscript: in Carton's concluding 'vision of judgement'. There, on the scaffold, Carton famously foresees evil punished and virtue rewarded with Barsad, Cly, Defarge, The Vengeance, the Juryman, all perishing, ironically, by their very 'retributive instrument' (*ATTC*, p. 404), the guillotine; while Charles, Lucie, Dr Manette and Mr Lorry live out their lives in England that are 'peaceful, useful, prosperous and happy' (*ATTC*, p. 404). The prophecy does not stop there, Carton foreseeing another child born to Charles and Lucie: a boy, 'who bears my name' (*ATTC*, p. 404), presumably, Sydney Carton Darnay (C. D. for Charles Dickens?). This character, in fact, may grow up to be the novel's nameless narrator because it is *he* who is envisaged telling *his* son – also Sydney Carton Darnay – Carton's tale: 'I hear him tell the child my story, with a tender and faltering voice' (*ATTC*, p. 404). But Darnay does more, however, than just memorialise Carton by naming and narration. For he achieves, as Carton presages, the *professional* success that eluded his namesake: 'I see that ... man winning his way up the path of life which once was mine. I see him winning it so well, that my name is made illustrious there by the light of his ... I see him foremost of just *judges*' (*ATTC*, p. 404, italics mine). So Sydney Darnay will redeem Carton's wasted

---

25 Common Law Procedure Act 1852, 15 & 16 Vict., c. 76. For a fuller, historical treatment of this and other, related acts, see: W. R. Cornish and G. de N. Clarke, *Law and Society in England, 1750–1950*, London: Sweet & Maxwell, 1989, pp. 41–43.

promise by becoming one of the great Victorian judges – Lord Darnay, Justice of Appeal in Ordinary? – worthy to sit alongside Blackburn, Lyndhurst, Selborne and St. Leonards.

It is this character whose elevation to the bench coincides with, and, indeed, allegorises the mid-Victorian triumph of the Austinian *imago*, so celebrated subsequently – and nostalgically – by Dicey;[26] that is, of the formalist, expository judge, seated, one can well imagine, on an elevated bench very much like the one the judge occupies in the Old Bailey, in a court just as bedizened with mirror and all. Which is why Dicey's Rule of Law folderol about no one being 'above the law' is outed so categorically in *A Tale of Two Cities* as, ultimately, the cheat it is – nowhere more so than in this vivid imagery of curial mirroring. For it precisely the Old Bailey's mirror – a metaphor for the common law's mirrored Imaginary, if ever there was one – that will attract and reflect back this judicial focaliser's gaze, and with it, his own class affinities; which, in turn, will inform, indeed compel his application of such class-based, *bourgeois*–liberal doctrines such as freedom of contract, sanctity of property, and so forth. All of which is to say: if the common law's juridical imaginary resists a complete 'totalisation' of the French revolutionary sort, then it certainly solicits a more elastic (though no less effective) 'hegemonisation' of the Gramscian/Laclau-*esque*[27] kind through such courtroom collusions with Capital's contractual and proprietarial imperatives in which *someone* is very much 'above the law'. But who, for all his manifest control of legal process, is a someone still able to disclaim any judicial bias skewing (as Stanley Fish would put it)[28] the law's 'formal existence' because his gaze of judgement is only a *reflection*, merely an *image* – and therefore something 'Other' to the judge himself.

This judicial sleight of hand – now you see the judge, now you don't – is carried off largely unnoticed here; unnoticed, that is, by all, *except one*. That 'one' is none other than Stryver's 'jackal' (*ATTC*, p. 117) and junior counsel, Sydney Carton, whose studied indifference and dissolute languor conceals

---

26 Of whom Dicey remarks, with regret, that 'a certain distrust both of the law and of the judges' has grown up, leading to 'a marked decline' in '[t]he ancient veneration for the rule of law has in England suffered during the last thirty years' (A.V. Dicey, *Introduction to the Study of the Law of the Constitution*, above n. 2, p. 1886).
27 For this much more layered, complex and contingent understanding of 'hegemony', see: E. Laclau and C. Mouffe, *Hegemony and Socialist Strategy: Towards a Radical Democratic Politics*, London: Verso, 1985.
28 See S. Fish, 'The Law Wishes to Have a Formal Existence', in H. A. Veeser (ed.), *The Stanley Fish Reader*, Oxford: Blackwell Publishers, 1999, pp. 165–206.

*his* penetrating gaze. For it is Carton, the ever alert barrister, who *sees through* the juridical imaginary's reflections and refractions, here literalised in that very *mirror* hanging over the court at the trial of Charles Darnay. There, the text draws attention to Carton's seemingly distracted – though anything but unfocused – *longueur*, 'looking at the ceiling of the court' (*ATTC*, p. 103). The suggestion here is that only Carton senses how fragile this curial *salon des glaces* actually is, and how effortlessly its Imaginary identic lures of interpellation can be exploited; in this case, by freeing Charles on the grounds that he is Carton's mirror-image ('they were sufficiently like each other to surprise, not only the witness, but everybody present', *ATTC*, p. 104), a *trompe l'œil* of subjectivity.

### 'The Mirror Cracked from Side to Side': Sydney Carton *Must* Be Sacrificed! (And Resurrected?)

If that kind of manipulation comes so easily to Carton, so the text seems to warn, then what of the temptation to *trash* – that is, to smash – law's mirror? After all, Carton is more than an adept at legal systems without such a mirrored Imaginary. Think how well, for example, he plays the *political* game in France, sidestepping the specularity of law altogether by threatening Barsad (*ATTC*, pp. 330–334), securing access to the Conciergerie (*ATTC*, p. 334, p. 379), and pulling off the final 'switch and bait' that will save Darnay (*ATTC*, pp. 379–383). So Carton might be described, with a nod to Carl Schmitt,[29] as a figure of 'exceptionality', capable of standing both outside the juridical imaginary (manipulating its politics), as well as within it (massaging its processes). It is this *doubleness* – a 'Double of coarse deportment' (*ATTC*, p. 114), as the text refers to him – that renders Carton an adversarial prototype of nomological (post-)modernity; namely, that of the critical legal lawyer, positioned as this figure is, similarly, along the fault lines, indeed, at the very crux of law–politics. Which raises this final question: if Carton is the proto-'crit', the potential trasher of the bourgeois– liberal legality, then what is to prevent him from exposing its central contradiction, hitherto cloaked by its juridical imaginary; specifically, that the common law is at once, *independent* of, yet *instrumental* to the economy? The answer is, according to jittery common lawyers, nothing at all. This is why, by their legalistic lights, 'Carton *must* be sacrificed!' because

---

29 C. Schmitt, *Political Theology*, G. Schwab (trans.), Cambridge, MA: MIT Press, 1985. See also: G. Agamben, *State of Exception*, K. Attell (trans.), Chicago: University of Chicago Press, 2005.

he is, as Lacan might put it, the *sujet supposé savoir*; that is, he is the subject presumed to know – and know too much at that. For that knowledge *empowers* the Carton the critical legal lawyer, rendering him capable of cracking, like some Marxist Lady of Shalott, the looking-glass of juridical imaginary, thereby releasing the 'politics of the law' of revolutionary enjoyment.

Or so *bourgeois*–liberal legalism would have it, *conflating* the consequences of revolutionary 'mirror-cracking' and legal critique, as much as *inflating* Carton's cynicism about the law into a dangerous (deconstructive?) nihilism. By these (paranoid) lights, Carton's death will allow the law to *live*. No surprises then when Carton is left to his fate in Paris by that very *embodiment* of the new Law of Capital, Jarvis Lorry – the only character in the text to suspect, and indeed approve of his plan of self-sacrifice. Thus, Carton's demise stems from not so much the Parisian tribunal's revolutionary justice as that of *bourgeois*–liberal legality itself, figured by Lorry. It is *he* who sends legal critique by tacit agreement to the scaffold. Why? Of course, in the terms of the plot and its immediate demands: to escape the Terror, Lorry spiriting, once again, his friends, out of France and to safety in England. But in broader, thematic terms, I would suggest that Lorry *the banker* – that is, the finance capitalist – does so to ensure the persistence of a common law culture. For that legal culture is predicated upon a strict doctrinal formalism which, paradoxically, works *in tandem* with an economic instrumentalism that will ensure the nineteenth century triumph of the global free market: a triumph which has its *naissance* in the eighteenth century. That birth, however, could have been stillborn, strangled in its nativity, so Lorry and his City brethren would fantasise, by a 'politics of the law' originating either in revolutionary enjoyment or critical nihilism, yet each inimical to Capital. Carton's decease, however, sets up an alternative legal historical trajectory, pointing to, indeed disclosing *A Tale of Two Cities*' fundamental jurisprudential insight: that the iron grip of *bourgeois*–liberal legalism on the juridical imaginary is contingent upon, as much as is revolutionary justice, an act of *violence*. This jurispathology – not only of Coverian 'pain and suffering', but Cartonian *blood and guts* – will immunise the Rule of Law, and its judiciary (i.e., Lord Justice Darnay), against any challenge, securing its ongoing hegemony, as well as shutting down other ways of *re*imagining legality and, with it, the possibility of reform.

This is a tragedy for the law because, of course, reform *is* needed – however problematic, as I have argued, Dickens's views might be on the issue. Even critique 'on a rampage' – i.e., revolutionary justice – can be justified because, as the little seamstress suggests, it might very well deliver on its promises of a better life for its citizen-subjects:[30] 'If the Republic really does good to the poor, they ... (may) come to be less hungry, and in all ways to suffer less' (*ATTC*, p. 403). So legal critique's dispatch – and with it, the possibility of social reform – turns out to be a terrible loss to the law, and the *socius* it regulates. This is a passing that all progressive jurisprudes should mourn, much as Lucie does for Carton until her dying day: 'I see her, an old woman, weeping for me on the anniversary of this day' (*ATTC*, p. 404). Which prompts this 'crit' to ask: Is there no possibility of legal critique's comeback, its *resurrection*? Carton, of course, holds out this promise when he goes to the guillotine repeating the Anglican burial service: 'I am the Resurrection and the Life ... he that believeth in me, though he were dead, yet shall he live' (*ATTC*, p. 403). This prayer for resurrection, amidst *A Tale of Two Cities*' famous last words ('It is a far, far better thing that I do', and so on, *ATTC*, p. 404), takes the novel back to its opening, and to a character, hitherto minor, now revealed as core; namely, Jerry Cruncher, Tellson's indefatigable courier and grave robber *extraordinaire*, who for all his hostility to his wife's 'flopping' (*ATTC*, p. 86) turns out to be the real agent of, and, indeed, true believer in *resurrection*. Surely it is from Jerry, the 'Resurrection-Man' (*ATTC*, p. 194), that legal critique awaits the delivery of a message of hope, liberating it from this state of spectral abandonment – outside the law, yet haunting it – with a novel judgement that says '*recalled to life*' (*ATTC*, p. 41).

---

30 This point is made as well by Hilary Schor in her excellent reading of, *inter alia*, *A Tale of Two Cities*, in ch. 3 of her superb study: H. Schor, *Dickens and the Daughter of the House*, Cambridge: Cambridge University Press, 2005.

CHAPTER **8**

# Beyond Governmentality: The Question of Justice in *Great Expectations*

## An Anti-Foucauldian Dickens? Governmentality and Its Discontents

In one of the most suggestive asides in *Great Expectations*,[1] Joe Gargery, the novel's moral centre – and, as it turns out, most perspicacious critic – says of his formidable wife, Mrs Joe: 'Your sister is given to government' (*GE*, p. 44). This remark, as Joe himself might exclaim, is 'astonishing' (*GE*, p. 95), precisely because it anticipates and even underwrites a certain critical legal reading of *Great Expectations*, one indebted to that great theorist of 'governmentality',[2] Michel Foucault. There is, however, nothing novel in a Foucauldian reading of *Great Expectations*. Jeremy Tambling's excellent 'Prison-Bound: Dickens and Foucault',[3] for instance, makes a compelling case for a 'Foucauldian Dickens',[4] meticulously cataloguing the disciplinary devices (the Prison, the panoptical gaze, the carceral society) and punishment

---

1 C. Dickens, *Great Expectations*, New York: Bantam Books, 1982. Hereafter, referred to as *GE*.
2 M. Foucault, 'Governmentality', P. Pasquino (trans.), *Ideology and Consciousness* 6, 1979/1983, 5–21.
3 J. Tambling, 'Prison-Bound: Dickens and Foucault', in R. Sell (ed.), *New Casebooks: Great Expectations*, New York: St Martin's Press, 1994, pp. 123–142.
4 This remark is found in an earlier version of Tambling's article, ibid. p. 2 delivered to the Postmodern Legal Theory Workshop at the Faculty of Law, University of Hong Kong, Hong Kong, autumn, 1996.

motifs (fantasies of guilt and shame) which saturate, indeed oversaturate *Great Expectations*. In stressing, however, Foucault's earlier project of discipline and punish, Tambling ends up inadvertently reproducing, albeit within a much more sophisticated theoretical frame, the historicist insights and observations of an earlier generation of scholarship on Dickens and the law; for example, Philip Collins on the Prison,[5] Humphrey House on Bentham[6] and the Leavises on guilt and shame.[7] In this chapter, I want to break this cycle of critical repetition (which mimics the repetitions, doublings and foldings-in of the narrative), and shift the debate away from standard socio-legal discussions of Dickens – be they old historicist or early Foucauldian – and towards what I take to be the key historical, political and, especially, *jurisprudential* issue of *Great Expectations*; specifically, the emergence of 'governmentality' in Victorian society, political economy and law.

I will argue in the second section that Magwitch's return to Britain from Australia dramatises the advent of governmentality in *Great Expectations*, representing its concerns with 'security, territory, population'[8] in the surveillance apparatuses of the Customs House. This portrayal of governmentality's appearance accounts for why, in *Great Expectations*, Dickens oscillates in his depiction of the law as everywhere and nowhere, an absent presence and a present absence. For governmentality, at once, displaces the law as the organising principle of 'the social' (i.e., the Rule of Law), all the while successfully (re)functionalising it as a 'tactic' of social control. This governmental retooling of the law, I contend in the third section, hooks up with, and is reinforced by English jurisprudence of the mid-nineteenth century, then embarked on redefining the law either as largely retributive (as did Fitzjames Stephen) or principally distributive (as did John Stuart Mill). I assert in the fourth section – that, in so redefining the law, Victorian legal theory, virtually, has rendered un-askable, let alone unanswerable any question of *justice*, trivialising the law as a mere tactic of power, figured in the character of Jaggers, and dooming it to repeat rather than resolve the injustices – themselves retributive and distributive – of the period. I continue in the fifth section that this deadlock of retributive and distributive repetition is enacted in the doubled ending of *Great Expectations*. All of which takes me to the crux of this chapter's argument; that is, by representing, so vividly, in *Great Expectations*, how a society without a theory of justice is destined to duplicate

---

5 P. Collins, *Dickens and Crime*, London: Macmillan, 1994.
6 H. House, *The Dickens World*, Oxford: Oxford University Press, 1941.
7 F. R. and Q. D. Leavis, *Dickens the Novelist*, Harmondsworth: Penguin Books, 1972.
8 Foucault, 'Governmentality', above n. 2, p. 20.

its injustices, Dickens passes a novel judgement on modernity's governmentalisation of the law – and, indeed, politics, economy and society – as described by Foucault. In fact, Dickens may very well be the first anti-Foucauldian, anticipating Baudrillard's call to 'forget Foucault',[9] in order to take us, in *Great Expectations*, 'beyond governmentality' and towards an (O)ther juridical imaginary with a revivified (deconstructive?) theory of justice.

## Magwitch's Return: The Emergence of Governmentality in *Great Expectations*

Chapter 39 is the key 'recognition' scene[10] in *Great Expectations*; here Pip's illusions, or rather self-delusions – that Miss Havisham is his benefactress, that she intends Estella for him – are shattered ('all a mere dream', *GE*, p. 301) as the real source of his 'great expectations' (*GE*, p. 129) are revealed: in the largesse of the returned felon, and now successful outback 'sheepfarmer' (*GE*, p. 296), Abel Magwitch. I would like to suggest, however, that this chapter's significance lies not only in its plot twist ('All the truth of my position came flashing on me', *GE*, p. 297), but in the thematic turn it introduces in the narrative's abiding concern with the law. For what emerges here is not only the 'truth' (*GE*, p. 297) of the text, but a new regime of what Foucault might call *pouvoir/savoir* – 'power/knowledge' – which supersedes, even displaces, the law's role, as hitherto depicted in the novel. Up until this point in *Great Expectations*, Dickens had represented the law as thematically central; a centrality rendered, however, in terms of an earlier Foucauldian project – namely, that of discipline and punish. The regime of discipline is, of course, omnipresent in *Great Expectations*. From the 'black' (*GE*, p. 36), Benthamite hulks brooding over the Marshes ('moored by massive rusty chains ... [it] seemed to be ironed like the prisoners', *GE*, p. 36) to Jaggers' 'dismal' (*GE*, p. 151), sepulchral chambers (decorated with death masks and a chair, upholstered in 'deadly, black horsehair' with 'nails like a coffin', *GE*, p. 152) within the gloom of the 'grim stone' (*GE*, p. 152) of a panoptic Newgate, discipline casts its 'shadow', to use Stewart Macauley's rich metaphor,[11] over the setting, style and

---

9 J. Baudrillard and S. Lotringer, *Forget Foucault*, N. Dufresne (trans.), New York: Semiotext(e), 1987.
10 Peter Brooks also makes the same point in: P. Brooks, 'Repetition, Repression, and Return: *Great Expectations* and the Study of the Plot', in Sell, *New Casebooks: Great Expectations*, 1994, above n. 3, p. 102.
11 S. Macauley, 'Non-Contractual Relations in Business: A Preliminary Study', *American Sociological Review* 28(1), 1963, 55.

structure of the novel. This penumbral ubiquity of discipline, however, should not obscure punishment's lingering presence, the tokens of which the text constantly refers: the 'gibbet ... which once held a pirate' by the Marshes (*GE*, p. 5), as well as the 'gallows', 'whip'-stand and 'debtors' door' of Newgate (*GE*, p. 152). Chapter 39, however, marks, with Magwitch's return – the return of the criminal and colonial repressed? – the emergence of a new regime which supersedes (though it incorporates)[12] discipline and punish: what Foucault would call 'governmentality'.

'Governmentality' is defined by Foucault as a form of governance, arising in the eighteenth century and coincident with the emergence of the nation-state, which raises and renders problematic the following questions: 'How to govern oneself, how to be governed, how to govern others, how to accept him who governs us, how to become the best possible governor'.[13] Historically, these core questions of governance have been answered by reference to some sort of normative standard like 'the common good'. Governmentality, however, abandons this discourse of normativity – and its controlling sign, legal sovereignty – in favour of a new discursive logic, one which takes as its focus the economy of objects. 'One governs things'[14] – or so proclaims governmentality. But these things include not only 'wealth, resources, means of subsistence' but 'men',[15] for governmentality's mode of governance anticipates the Marxist notion of reification by 'thingifying' the inhabitants of the polity as 'population'. Indeed, population makes governmentality possible, its massification calling forth techniques of social engineering and statistical survey. So governmentality amounts, according to Foucault, to the monitoring of the flows and ebbs of population both within and across state boundaries, the territorial integrity of which are secured as much by the disciplinary apparatuses of surveillance ('schools, manufactories, armies')[16] as traditional notions of national sovereignty. Hence, Foucault's handy slogan reducing governmentality to three principal policy concerns: 'security, territory, population'.[17]

---

12 On this point, Foucault writes: 'We must consequently see things not in terms of the substitution for a society of sovereignty of a disciplinary society and the subsequent replacement of a disciplinary society by a governmental one; in reality we have a triangle: sovereignty–discipline–government' ('Governmentality', above n. 2, p. 19).
13 Ibid. p. 5.
14 Ibid. p. 11.
15 Ibid.
16 Ibid. p. 19.
17 Ibid. p. 20.

Magwitch's return in Chapter 39 transgresses this triple agenda, thereby mobilising and operationalising governmentality. First, Magwitch's return runs against, even subverts the control of population flows that governmentality had made, since its inception, its 'primary target'.[18] After all, transportation is just one attempt on the part of government to dispose of a surplus population on the move (Magwitch was a 'tramping' man before he met up with Compeyson, *GE*, p. 322), rendered rootless – and, ultimately, criminalised – by industrialisation: a strategy of displacement for dealing with the displaced. Second, Magwitch's return violates 'territory', literally the national borders of Britain from which he is barred, under penalty of death, by the Law of Return: 'It's death to come back', Magwitch says, 'I should of certainty be hanged if took' (*GE*, p. 301). A figurative frontier, however, is also crossed by Magwitch's return, one as internal and psychic as the other was external and physical. For Magwitch's return is motivated by what Freud would call a *Wunsch*, a wish; that is, he wishes to experience directly, rather than merely imagine the 'gentleman' he has 'made' (*GE*, p. 298), thereby confusing the boundaries between fantasy and reality and, as Foucault notes, the strict separation of public and private which governmentality 'polices'.[19]

I set off 'police' above because the actual police of the era – these were the 'days', as the text tells us, of 'Bow Street' (*GE*, p. 114) – are conspicuous by their absence in Chapter 39, and thereafter in the novel. This absence is odd, given that this part of the narrative from here on in is concerned primarily with detection, arrest and arraignment; logically, police matters of law enforcement. Instead, however, of the police, governmental bureaucrats of what Oliver MacDonagh would call 'the Victorian administrative state'[20] take charge here: for it is the Customs House's 'galley' (*GE*, p. 411), rather than Bow Street's finest which gives 'hot pursuit' to Magwitch in his dramatic attempted escape, engineered by Pip, along the Thames. Of course, the presence here of the Customs House's agents, rather than the police, makes perfect sense in that Magwitch is trying to flee the country after making an illegal entry, thereby violating the integrity of the borders which it is the Customs House's brief to *secure*. I stress 'secure' because 'security' is the third and final aspect of governmentality, a function with

---

18 Ibid. p. 19.
19 Foucault writes: 'it is the tactics of government which make possible the continual definition and redefinition of what is within the competence of the State and what is not, the public versus the private' (ibid. p. 21).
20 O. MacDonagh, 'The Nineteenth-Century Revolution in Government: A Reappraisal', *Historical Journal* 1, 1958, 52–67.

which the Customs House is clearly invested here, discharging it, effectively and efficiently: not only in its capture of Magwitch, but in its extensive surveillance system, dependent on paid informants, which Magwitch's return activates. For from the moment Magwitch appears in Chapter 39, he is being watched; and, by no less a person than his old partner-in-crime turned nemesis, Compeyson, now at liberty and in the pay, presumably, of the Customs House. No wonder Pip, having settled Magwitch for the night – after, tellingly, closing 'the shutters, so that no light might be seen from without' (*GE*, p. 301) – hears or thinks he hears 'pursuers' (*GE*, p. 302) outside his flat ('Twice I could have sworn there was a knocking and whispering at the outer door', *GE*, p. 302), an anxiety uncannily proleptic of the narrative's climactic chase scene in Chapter 54. For it will be Compeyson, as one of the pursuers on the Customs House galley, who identifies Magwitch for the officers – ironically, his last act before his erstwhile sidekick plunges him to a watery grave.

Magwitch is not, however, the only prey being stalked here. Pip's movements, as well, are being monitored, as, indeed, chapter 40 soon discloses. For someone *is* casing Pip's flat. That someone turns out to be the 'something' (*GE*, p. 303), as Pip phrases it, of Orlick, the novel's most psychopathic character, no mean feat in a narrative which includes Miss Havisham (her 'sick fancies' being a classic case of psychosis, *GE*, p. 54), Jaggers (an obsessive-compulsive; think of his constant hand-washing, *GE*, p. 76) and, even Pip, himself (delusional, e.g., hallucinating Miss Havisham hanging from a rafter at Satis House on two occasions, *GE*, p. 59, p. 373). Like Bradley Headstone in *Our Mutual Friend*, Orlick is the Dickensian precursor of that pervasive figure of contemporary popular culture, the 'serial killer'; or, rather, nascent serial killer, sheer luck – in the unlikely form of 'Trabb's boy' (*GE*, p. 399) – thwarting his attempted murder of Pip in the old sluicehouse. Where is governmentality's 'security' service here? Of course, no borders are transgressed in Orlick's case, thereby explaining the blind eye which, in this instance, Customs House's usually penetrating panopticism turns here. But does this blindness on the part of the Customs House mean, necessarily, that the entire field of vision of governmentality is obscured? Where, for example, are those other agents of governmentality, the police?[21] Naturally, Pip and Herbert would be loath to report this offence, as any 'such course' would prove 'fatal to Provis' (*GE*, p. 401), as well as, possibly,

---

21 Foucault explicitly connects the police and governmentality when he writes: 'the same principles as the good government of the State, is just at this time beginning to be called "police" ' ('Governmentality', above n. 2, p. 10).

to themselves, both acting as accessories, as the criminal law would have it, 'after the fact' in aiding and abetting a returned convict. But even if the police were notified, one suspects that they would fudge the investigation, getting it wrong just like they did with Orlick's first attempt at murder, his grievous bodily assault on Mrs Joe where, in a forensic style bordering on the Clouseau-esque, '[t]hey took up several obviously wrong people, and they ran their heads very hard against wrong ideas, and persisted in trying to fit the circumstances to the ideas, instead of trying to extract ideas from the circumstances' (*GE*, p. 114). All of which points to the highly uncertain, even indeterminate role of the police – and, indeed, the law – in *Great Expectations*. For if there is any truism about the law in the novel, it is this: the law is always there when you need it *least*, but nowhere to be found when you need it *most*.

### The Map of Misjudgement: Retributive and Distributive Justice in Victorian Jurisprudence

This is one of the great puzzles in a novel full of puzzles; that is, how the law can be everywhere in the narrative, but nowhere – too much, in some cases, and too little, by far, in others? For the law in *Great Expectations* is, at once, an overwhelming presence, terrifyingly effective on occasion (think of Magwitch's sentence of fourteen years for 'putting stolen notes into circulation', *GE*, p. 326), but more often than not a spectacularly dysfunctional absence, so much so that the narrative's litany of failed prosecutions (e.g., Molly, Estella's birth mother, goes free of the murder of another 'tramping woman', despite her obvious guilt, *GE*, p. 365), 'technical' convictions (e.g., Orlick is jailed for burgling Uncle Pumblechook rather than his far more serious assaults on Pip and Mrs Joe, *GE*, 434) and wildly discrepant sentences (e.g., think of Compeyson's seven years, compared to Magwitch's fourteen for the same offence) constitute what might be called, with a nod to Harold Bloom, a 'map of misjudgement',[22] lacking either rhyme or reason. A critical legal reading, however, would take exception here, arguing that there is a method to the madness, an order amidst the chaos of the map of misjudgement – though it only becomes apparent only when reformulated as the question: is this an issue of interest to the officials of the law? If not, then little legal consistency will be evinced in, say, whether one member of the *Lumpenproletariat* is acquitted or convicted of another's murder (as in the case of Molly and her victim) or whether an assault between members

---

22  H. Bloom, *The Map of Misreading*, New York: Oxford University Press, 1975.

188 • Novel Judgements: Legal Theory as Fiction

of the artisanal working-class is fully investigated or not (like the example of Mrs Joe). If, however, some issue close to official interests is at stake, like the sanctity of property (in the instance of Orlick), then legal redress is swift and sure. Also to be counted upon for consistent results is class affinity or aversion, class allies being assured of leniency – consider Compeyson's treatment – with class enemies being certain of harshness, as Abel Magwitch learns to his bitter regret at his felony trial with Compeyson, prior to his transportation. For Magwitch is convicted before he is tried, and, largely, as he tells Pip, on the basis of his class background, a prejudgement evidenced by the prosecution,[23] the defence,[24] the cross-examination of witnesses[25] and the judicial summation.[26] The story Magwitch tells here is a familiar one, as much in his own day as today, carrying with it the critical legal insight, anticipated in the nineteenth century by both Karl Marx[27] and

---

23 Magwitch says: 'I noticed first of all what a gentleman Compeyson looked . . . and what a common sort of wretch I looked. When the prosecution opened, I noticed how heavy it all bore on me, and how light on him' (*GE*, p. 325).

24 Magwitch ventriloquises the Crown prosecutor, addressing the court with the following: 'My lord . . . here you has afore you . . . two persons . . .; one, the younger, well brought up . . .; one, the elder, ill brought up . . .; one, the younger, seldom if ever seen in these transactions, and only suspected; t'other, the elder, always seen in 'em and always wi' guilt brought home' (ibid.).

25 Of the defence counsel's slanted argument, Magwitch says this: 'warn't it him as had been know'd by witnesses in such clubs and societies, and nowt to his disadvantage? And warn't it me that had been tried before' (ibid.).

26 Of which, Magwitch says: 'ain't it him as the judge is sorry for, because he mighta have so well, and ain't it me as the judge perceives to be the old offender of violent passion, likely to come to worse' (ibid.).

27 As I have noted before in the second volume of *Capital*, Marx writes of the contract for free labour as that:

> innate Eden of the rights of man. There alone rule Freedom, Equality, Property and Bentham. Freedom, because both buyer and seller of a commodity, say of free agents, and the agreement they come to, is but the form in which they give legal expression to their common will. Equality because each enters into relation with the other, as with a simple owner of commodities and they exchange equivalent for equivalent. Property, because each disposes only of what is his own. And Bentham, because each looks only to himself . . . On leaving this sphere of simple . . . commodities . . . we think we can perceive a change in the physiogamy of our *dramatis personae*. He, who before was the money-owner, now strides in front as capitalist; the possessor of labour-power follows as his labourer. The one with an air of importance, smirking, intent on business; the other, timid and holding back, like one who is bringing his own hide to market and has nothing to expect but – a hiding.
>
> (K. Marx, *Capital: A Critique of Political Economy, Volume I, The Process of Production Capital*, S. Moore and E. Aveling (trans.), F. Engels (ed.), Moscow: Progress Publishers, 1954, p. 416).

Anatole France,[28] that the 'law is politics', and especially, *class* politics, its autonomy having been hijacked by *bourgeois* social biases and economic interests.

While endorsing and, indeed, taking onboard Magwitch's critical legal, even Marxist reading of his trial, I would, nonetheless, 'foucauldianise' it to this extent: specifically, that the law, if it has been hi-jacked in this era, has hi-jacked *itself* from within, not outside of its discursive regime. That is, the 'politics of the law' is an effect, not so much, as critical legal studies or Marxism would have it, of legal discourse's manipulation by external forces (i.e., the *bourgeoisie*) for their own instrumental ends (i.e., *bourgeois*–liberal political economy), as it is, as Foucault would counter,[29] of legal discourse's own *auto*-manipulation, a kind of discursive self-instrumentalisation. Or to put it another way, if the law has been hi-jacked here, then it is because legal discourse has 'morphed' itself into another Foucauldian regime of power/knowledge, precisely the very form of power/knowledge that the state is taking in this period.

That is to say, *the law is self-governmentalising*, becoming what Foucault would call a 'tactic' of control.[30] This 'tacticalisation' of law through its self-governmentalisation, however, differs from the correlative governmentalisation of the state to the extent that it is characterised, negatively, more by what it does not do than by any positive programme (e.g., 'security, population, territory') that it does do. For what the law ceases to do in this period – both practically in the judgements of the courts and, theoretically, in the writings of jurisprudes – is to ask those very questions which, historically, have dominated jurisprudence: What is 'the right'? What is 'the good'? And what, especially, is 'the just'? These questions become as much un-askable as they were always unanswerable here. This is because mid-Victorian legal theory has internalised, as much its judicial practice, the lessons of the previous generation's Austinian

---

28 France writes in 1894 of the 'majestic egalitarianism of the law, which forbids rich and poor alike to sleep under bridges, to beg in the streets, and to steal bread', quoted in: S. Bottomley and S. Parker, *Law in Context*, Annandale, VA: Federation Press, 1994.

29 See, e.g., Foucault in 'Politics and the Study of Discourse' where he writes that change – or rather 'discontinuity' – in the 'history of the mind is to be located, first and foremost, [w]ithin a given discursive formation, detecting the changes which affect its objects, operations, concepts, theoretical options', in M. Foucault, 'Politics and the Study of Discourse', in G. Burchell, C. Gordon and P. Miller (eds), *The Foucault Effect: Studies in Governmentality*, Chicago: University of Chicago Press, 1991, p. 56.

30 Foucault writes, 'in the case of government it's not a matter of imposing laws on men, but rather of disposing things, that is to say to employ tactics rather than laws, and if need be to use the laws themselves as tactics' ('Governmentality', above n. 2, p. 13).

positivism[31] and evacuated itself of any real theory of justice, aside from the crude formulation of either retribution or distribution. Who are we to punish? Where are we to deliver the goods?; these are the only two jurisprudential questions to survive the nuclear blast of positivism (exploding the connection between law and morality) and its formalist fallout.

Mid-Victorian legal theory (and practice) still lies heavy under formalism's nuclear winter, but two largely, non-formalist theoretical schools – engaging, however minimally, with at least some issues of law's spirit rather than, exclusively, its letter – may be discerned, emerging out of the rubble. But, ultimately, both collude with formalism because they confine their ambit to either one or the other of the questions above: one school, broadly moral-authoritarian addresses the question of retribution; the other school, largely utilitarian–liberal, engages the question of distribution. Representing the former, moral position is Fitzjames Stephen,[32] the celebrated codifier of the criminal law in a variety of colonial territories (e.g., India, Canada, Queensland), whose understanding of the law – naturally enough for a criminal lawyer – is retributive. He writes in his riposte to liberalism, *Liberty, Equality, Fraternity*: '[Criminal] acts have in fact been forbidden and subjected to punishment not only because they are dangerous to society, but also for gratifying the feeling of hatred – call it revenge, resentment, or what you will'.[33] So Stephen conceives of the law largely, as a stick to beat people with, enforcing good behaviour through coerced obedience, thereby maintaining the social order – and its hierarchies of status – through that shibboleth authoritarians hold most dear, 'law and order'.

Exemplifying the latter, utilitarian strand is John Stuart Mill, the leading philosopher of his day, whose sense of the law is, principally, distributive, though the 'greatest happiness principle' upon which his sense of law rests is 'progressive'; that is, a return to the best *Benthamite* reformism, and a repudiation of its reactionary Austinian revision. He writes in *Utilitarianism* that the 'highest abstract standard of social and distributive justice . . . rests upon a still deeper foundation, being an emanation from the first princi-

---

31 For the impact of Austin on the legal profession, see: R. Cotterrell, *The Politics of Jurisprudence: A Critical Introduction to Legal Philosophy*, London: Butterworths, 1989, pp. 79–82.

32 For the most interesting jurisprudential discussion of Fitzjames Stephen, see: S. McVeigh and P. Rush, 'Cutting Our Losses: Criminal Legal Doctrine', in P. Rush, S. McVeigh and A. Young, *Criminal Legal Doctrine*, Aldershot: Dartmouth Press, 1997.

33 J. F. Stephen, *Liberty, Equality, Fraternity*, R. J. White (ed.), London: University of Cambridge Press, 1967, p. 152.

ples of morals ... the very meaning of Utility',[34] a sentiment which is further qualified in *On Liberty* where he continues: 'I regard utility as the ultimate appeal on all ethical questions; but it must be utility in the largest sense, grounded on the permanent interests of man as a progressive being'.[35] So for Mill the law is viewed as a carrot to induce but not compel obedience, advancing the 'greatest good for the greatest number', all the while enabling, as long as no 'harm' (*TE*, p. 201) to another is involved, the free exercise of that value most cherished by liberals, individual autonomy. Despite, however, their differences, Stephen and Mill share, implicitly, a similar belief, and, more to the point inspire a theory and practice that the law, far from being some privileged, *a priori* 'transcendental signifier' (best expressed in a Rule of Law doctrine which precedes and, indeed, creates, variously, the king, the social contract or parliamentary supremacy, rather than vice-versa), is nothing more than an instrument, a technique, a *tactic* serving, logistically, some other goal or purpose, be it the punitive or facilitative, retributive or distributive.

### The Tactics of Power and the Power of Tactics: Governmentalised Law

The question remains though: why this tacticalisation, and perforce, *trivialisation* of the law, as a technique or instrument, subordinate to, and merely executing some extra-legal public policy, be it retribution or distribution? And, moreover, why would the law trivialise *itself* as a governmental tactic in its own legal theory and juridical practice? From a Foucauldian perspective, the answer is simple: power. Governmental tacticalisation (or tactical governmentalisation) *empowers* as much as trivialises the law. Indeed, empowerment is an *effect* of trivialisation, because in devolving from the anchoring fixity (*point de capiton*?) of punishment's Rule of Law into a mere tactic of governmentality – whether retributive or distributive – governmentalised law is rendered *manoeuvrable*; that is, flexible and supple enough to traverse what one governmentalist, Pasquale Pasquino calls the 'polymorphous universe ... of power'[36] which governmentality

---

34 J. S. Mill, 'Utilitarianism', in M. Warnock (ed.), *Utilitarianism and On Liberty*, London: William Collins, 1962.
35 J. S. Mill, 'On Liberty', in J. S. Mill, *Three Essays: On Liberty, Representative Government and the Subjection of Women*, Oxford: University Press, 1975, p. 16. Hereafter, referred to as *TE*.
36 P. Pasquino, 'Theatrum Politicum: The Genealogy of Capital – Police and the State of Prosperity', in Burchell *et al.*, *The Foucault Effect: Studies in Governmentality*, above n. 29, p. 107.

has reconfigured in this epoch. For the cartography of power is dramatically uneven in, and under nineteenth-century governmentality. At certain points, it is overaccreted with governmental control, notably at its policed and patrolled frontiers, those national boundaries through which labour, immigration and goods flow. However, at others points – namely those domestic spaces of civil society, the market and the 'lifeworld' – that governmental control is much more diffuse, if not dispersed altogether. This dispersion of power occurs because governmentality's emergence is coextensive with the formation of Capital, its *laissez-faire* notions pitting, as another governmentalist, Graham Burchell notes, 'the heterogeneity and incompatibility of the principles regulating non-totalisable multiplicity of economic subjects of interest' against the 'totalising unity of legal-political sovereignty'.[37] All of which is to say that under the governmentality–Capital conjuncture, Capital commands the civil realm of the market – of the *distribution*, as Žižek might put it, of 'enjoyment' and its 'theft' – while governmentality regulates the state sphere of security, through its mechanisms of retribution (informants, police, lawyers, courts, jailers and executioners).

Of course, there is nothing particularly Foucauldian in this unpacking of the civil society–state authority divide (or alternatively, the private–public distinction) under the governmentality–Capital conjuncture; indeed, critical legal studies echoes it as one of its principal themes, and Marxism anticipates it by well over one hundred years. But what is unique about the Foucauldian position, however, is the radical contingency which it discerns in the boundaries between governmentality and Capital, which, as always shifting, moving or being redrawn, open up what Burchell (1991) calls a 'hybrid space . . . in which public law is coupled with forms of 'private' power and authority'. And it is precisely within this indeterminate, interstitial space that in *Great Expectations* Dickens squarely situates the law, hybridised as both private power (Capital) and public authority (governmentality) in the novel's most menacing figure, of whom everyone is 'afraid' (*GE*, p. 224). A fear which must be read as heavily ironic; for in a narrative that depicts such a dread-inspiring 'rogues' gallery' of killers, thieves and fraudsters, this figure turns out to be (who else?) *the lawyer*, Mr Jaggers.

---

37 G. Burchell, 'Peculiar Interests: Civil Society and Governing The System of Natural Liberty', in Burchell *et al.*, ibid. p. 137.

### The 'Clean Hands' of Equity: Jaggers as the Governmental Lawyer

Jaggers is the *prosopopoeic* figure of the self-governmentalised (and Capitalised) law, shuttling, as he does, back and forth between his public role as a criminal defender (securing, for example, Molly's acquittal, as well as defending most of the London demimondaine) and his private, civil capacity (as Magwitch's 'agent', *GE*, p. 128; as Pip's 'guardian', *GE*, p. 131; and Miss Havisham's 'man of business', *GE*, p. 164). This movement is literalised in Jaggers' constant *peripateia* between Little Britain and Satis House, between the Marsh country and London. But no matter where Jaggers pops up (and he pops up everywhere),[38] he is forever the 'hired gun', acting on and under strict 'instructions' (*GE*, p. 269): the perfect instrument of his clients' interests. And it is exactly this instrumentality which empowers Jaggers, investing him with all the tactical force that the law commands under governmentality's – at least, theoretical – 'trivialisation' of it: both its retributive coercion and its distributive facility. As to the former, think how effectively, and chillingly he disciplines and punishes his housekeeper and former client, Molly, the 'wild beast tamed', *GE*, p. 187; while, as to the latter, consider how all the 'portable property' (*GE*, p. 187) in the narrative – Miss Havisham's, Pip's, Magwitch's – passes through his (over-washed) hands as trustee, literally the 'clean hands' of equity. In fact, Jaggers' tactical force is enhanced its very instrumentality; that is, by the very fact that it is so client driven, so private, so secret. Indeed, he is credited with knowing all the 'secrets' of Newgate (*GE*, p. 251), so much so that his governance is the very form of which E.P. Thompson might call the 'secret state',[39] a kind of governmentality within governmentality.

It is, however, not just Newgate's secrets that Jaggers is privy to, but, as Estella comments 'the secrets of every place' (*GE*, p. 251), and especially every*one* in *Great Expectations*; for example, the secret of Estella's parentage, as well as the source of Pip's 'great expectations'. As the repository of these secrets, Jaggers can be compared to Tulkinghorn in *Bleak House*, another figure of legal menace; as I have argued in Chapter 6, it is *his* ferreting out of the secret of Esther Summerson's parentage which drives Lady Dedlock, ultimately, to her death. Jaggers, however, goes further than Tulkinghorn in his knowledge of secrets, for the *savoir* which is truly the source of his *pouvoir* is not only of the origins of people but the ends to which they tend:

---

38 Even in Joe's local, 'The Three Jolly Bargemen' where he cross-examines Wopsle and, first, divulges Pip's 'great expectations' (*GE*, p. 129).
39 E. P. Thompson, *Writing by Candlelight*, London: Merlin, 1980.

the secrets of their desire. For Jaggers knows what people *want*. And what they want in *Great Expectations* is nothing less than *revenge*. In fact, the entire plot of the novel turns on revenge schemes which Jaggers facilitates through his retributive and distributive power. Take the example of Miss Havisham's 'revenge', as Herbert puts it, 'on all the male sex' (*GE*, p. 164), consequent upon her jilting by the scoundrel, Compeyson on their putative wedding day.[40] Her reprisal against men (and, indeed, the system of patriarchy *in toto*) is expedited by Jaggers' timely supply of an instrument of retribution, the infant, Estella: 'I had been shut up in these rooms a long time', confesses Miss Havisham to Pip, 'when I told ... [Jaggers] that I wanted a little girl to rear and love, and save from my fate ... He told me that he would look about him for such an orphan child. One night he brought her here asleep, and I called her Estella' (*GE*, p. 372).

Or take the instance of Magwitch's revenge against a class society as quick to penalise him as to be merciful to the *faux* genteel Compeyson. Ironically, these class biases are reproduced, even upon transportation, in the carceral society of Australia: 'The blood horses of them colonists' as Magwitch confides to Pip, 'fling up the dust over me as I was walking [and] one of 'em says to another "He was a convict, a few years ago, and is a ignorant common fellow now, for all he's lucky"' (*GE*, p. 300). What keeps Magwitch 'a-going' (*GE*, p. 300), however, is not the reality of his New World success as it is his fantasy of Old World redress: 'you owns stock and land; which on you owns a brought-up London gentleman' (*GE*, p. 300). And it is this revenge fantasy that is realised by, and through Jaggers' distributive mediation: 'it was the money left me and the gains of the first few year, wot I sent home to Mr. Jaggers – all for you – when he first come arter you, agreeable to my letter' (*GE*, p. 300). So, in both cases – that of Magwitch as much as Miss Havisham – Jaggers is the man who can make dreams (or worst nightmares) come true, an odd job for the law, however 'tacticalised', given that its historic, symbolic mandate is to *pro*scribe (not propagate) the imaginary, traversing what Žižek would call its 'plague of fantasies'[41] and subjecting its aggressivity to the governmentality's 'theme of reason'.[42]

---

40 At precisely 'twenty minutes to nine' (*GE*, p. 168), the time at which all clocks were stopped at Satis House.
41 S. Žižek, *The Plague of Fantasies*, London: Verso, 1997.
42 Foucault writes, 'the art of government ... organises itself around the theme of the reason of the State' ('Governmentality', above n. 2, p. 14).

## *Great Expectations* as 'Revenge Tragedy': Governmentality as Injustice

All of which raises the question: Why is the law, in the form of Jaggers, colluding with, rather than conspiring against revenge? Why, moreover, is *Great Expectations*, largely, a story of revenge, so much so that it might be fairly described as a Victorian version of the seventeenth-century 'revenge tragedy'? Surely this genre, and the atavistic impulse that it dramatises, works against the 'modernity' which the text of *Great Expectations* insists upon, locating it within a regime that predates 'discipline and punish', let alone governmentality. And, if *Great Expectations is*, as I have been arguing, a record of governmentality's emergence, then how can this regime with its claims to 'reason'[43] coexist with the bloodlust of revenge? In short, why (and how) this short-circuit between the modern and the primitive? I want to suggest that this short-circuit occurs *precisely* because of governmentalisation; that is, it is *through* governmentality's 'sleep of reason' that revenge, as 'the return of the repressed', emerges from the 'political unconscious', symptomatised as the dominant social, economic *and juristic* theme not only in Dickens's text but in the context – the mid-century body politic – which it figures. For the highly overdetermined conjuncture that *Great Expectations* captures, and freeze-frames is the installation of a rupture – concealed and revealed by the plague of revenge fantasies – at the very centre of Victorian society, and provoked by governmentalisation's emptying of not only the law, but the social itself of any theory of justice, at the very moment Capital,[44] and its modalities of exchange (not for nothing is Uncle Pumblechook's cry 'More Capital', *GE*, p. 145), reification (think of Magwitch who surveys Pip 'with an air of admiring proprietorship', *GE*, p. 309) and commodity fetishism (consider Miss Havisham and her jewels, with which Estella is equated if not identified: 'Miss Havisham . . . had put some of the most beautiful jewels . . . into Estella's hair, and about her bosom and arm', *GE*, p. 226), are crisscrossing the social with all sorts of antagonisms, and the injustices to which these antagonisms give rise. As Joe says, 'one man's a blacksmith, and one's a whitesmith and one's a goldsmith, and one's a coppersmith. Diwisions among such must come' (*GE*, p. 209).

---

43 As Foucault writes, 'the State is governed according to rational principles which are intrinsic to it and which cannot be derived solely from natural or divine laws or the principles of wisdom and prudence; the State, like Nature, has its own proper rationality' (ibid.).

44 Like Capital, governmentality is also concerned with the management of 'men and things', the implication being, Foucault hints at, that men *are* things, as the Marxist doctrine of reification (thingification) would have it (ibid. p. 10).

So what Dickens portrays in *Great Expectations* is a society fraught with injustices, arising from various antagonisms – some gendered (as in Miss Havisham's case), some class-specific (as with Magwitch), some even enraced (suggested by the reference to Magwitch as Compeyson's 'black slave', *GE*, p. 324) – at the very instance that society is deprived of the theoretical or practical means of rectifying them. For, without a theory of justice, there is no way to strategise a solution to these social injustices – aside from the techniques of retribution and distribution. And these techniques, particularly in their deployment by Jaggers, reveal themselves, towards the end of the novel, to be collusive with, rather than dispositive of injustice, precisely because they *repeat* rather than resolve the original wrongs, themselves either retributive or distributive. Nowhere is this more in evidence than in the spectacular backfiring of the revenge schemes exploiting these retributive and distributive techniques. For example, Miss Havisham's fantasy of revenge ultimately turns on her, repeating the trauma of her own 'broken' (*GE*, p. 53) heart, as she witnesses, aghast, what, after all she had desired in the first place: Pip's utter, emotional desolation at the hands of hands of her affect-less, retributive weapon, Estella. 'You can break his heart' (*GE*, p. 54), says Miss Havisham, encouragingly, to her young protégée, upon the occasion of Pip's first visit to Satis House. But consider Miss Havisham's reaction when that heart *is* broken many years later by Estella's engagement to the brutish but well-connected Bentley Drummle. In her final and fatal interview with Pip, the day after he had declared, in an 'ecstasy of unhappiness' (*GE*, p. 338), his love for Estella to be as undying as it is doomed (so he believes) to be unrequited, Miss Havisham cries remorsefully: 'Until you spoke to her the other day, and until I saw in you a looking-glass that showed me what I once felt myself, I did not know what I had done. What have I done! What have I done!' (*GE*, p. 371).

Magwitch makes out somewhat better than Miss Havisham; his *protégé* Pip actually undergoes a change of heart at the very end of the narrative, softening towards the old 'warmint' (*GE*, p. 297), and providing him the solace and support he needs: 'what's best of all', Magwitch confides to Pip while incarcerated in Newgate awaiting his sentence, 'you've been more comfortable alonger me since I was under a dark cloud than when the sun shone' (*GE*, p. 428). But, prior to this eleventh-hour alteration of affections, Magwitch had suffered the same volte-face as Miss Havisham, returning eagerly to England to experience, vicariously, his distributive stake in the class society – 'the gentleman what I made', Pip (*GE*, p. 307) – only to be met with, in his *protégé*'s initial reaction, the same ruling-class contempt he has experienced all of his life: 'The abhorrence', Pip thinks to himself, 'in which I held the man, the dread I had of him, the repugnance with which I shrank from him could not have been exceeded if he had been some terrible beast' (*GE*, p. 298). For Magwitch, this encounter with the Real of his desire ends in tears: 'I saw with amazement', notes Pip after his haughty 'welcome' to Magwitch, 'that his eyes were full of tears' (*GE*, p. 296). These tears parallel those of his feminine counterpart, Miss Havisham, whose last interview with Estella ends 'with her head in her hands' (*GE*, p. 285), and her lachrymose wail, 'But to be proud and hard to me . . . Estella, Estella, Estella, to be proud and hard to me!' (*GE*, p. 285).

More than disappoint though – thereby proving the truth of the old saw that it is often a curse to get what you wished for – Miss Havisham's and Magwitch's fantasies of revenge destroy *them*, disturbing neither of their critical targets, the gender hierarchy or the class system. Magwitch may die comforted by Pip, *but he dies in prison*, awaiting a death sentence. An even crueller fate, however, awaits Miss Havisham; she is literally consumed by the Real of her desire; namely, by the 'great flaming light' (*GE*, p. 373) from her lit wedding dress, ablaze from a stray ember. This gruesome self-immolation recalls Freud's famous story of the burning child, only here the cry becomes: Pip, can't you see I'm burning? Neither of these deaths, moreover, achieves anything like strong narrative closure such as would shut down the cycle of vengeful repetition (and its techniques of retribution and distribution) in *Great Expectations*. Indeed, quite the reverse, as the deaths of Miss Havisham and Magwitch merely set the stage for another spin of the wheel of (mis) fortune, a cyclic repetition enacted in the doubled ending of the novel.

**The Sense of (Un)Ending: Repetition as Politics in *Great Expectations***

That *Great Expectations* has not one, but *two* endings – Dickens substituting, at Bulwer-Lytton's suggestion,[45] a 'happy ending' of Pip and Estella together for his original, cynical ending of Pip and Estella apart – is one of the great scandals of Victorian literary studies, to be deplored (as catering to, according to John Irving,[46] the nineteenth-century reading public's taste for cheap sentiment and strong closure), apologised for (as consistent with,

---

45 E. Johnson, *Charles Dickens: His Tragedy and Triumph*, Harmondsworth: Penguin, 1979, p. 491.
46 Irving writes in his Introduction to the Bantam edition of *Great Expectations*: 'This is mechanical matchmaking; it is not realistic; it is overly tidy; it is overly tidy . . . Dickens hopefulness strikes us as mere wishful thinking. Dickens' original ending to *Great Expectations* . . . is thought by most modern critics to be the proper (and certainly the modern) conclusion – from which Dickens shied away; away from such a change of heart and mind, he is accused of selling out' (*GE*, pp. xviii–xix).

argues Edgar Johnson, the author's 'desperate hope'[47] for, and belief in the novel's theme of 'great expectations'), or simply ignored (any additional ending having been rendered otiose, so argues Peter Brooks,[48] with Magwitch's return and the solutions he brings to the novel's mysteries). I would like to suggest, however, that each of these critical positions misses the mark by ignoring or sidelining the *form* of the ending – the real issue being: why, on Dickens's part, the compulsion to repeat? – at the expense of its content and questions like: were Pip and Estella really meant for one another? My emphasis on form, however, would read *Great Expectations* not so much, like Peter Brooks does, as a novel in search of a plot, as a narrative in pursuit of a *politics*: a politics articulated through, and as repetition. For it is in the very doubling of the endings, and its creation of a narrative split, that, as Slavoj Žižek would say, the 'ideological project'[49] of *Great Expectations* becomes clear, albeit in all of its inconsistencies; namely, its political message of *governmental critique* is conveyed *through* its formal medium of narrative splitting between a 'happy' and cynical ending, each of which exposes, and thereby undoes the law's retributive and distributive limits under governmentality in the fantasmatic repetitions of revenge.

Take the first, cynical ending of *Great Expectations*: there, Pip and Estella meet many years later, by happenstance, on a crowded London street, where a 'greatly changed' (*GE*, p. 453) Estella, chastened by 'suffering' (*GE*, p. 453), indicates to Pip, by 'her hand and in her voice, and in her touch' (*GE*, p. 453) that, despite 'Miss Havisham's teaching' (*GE*, p. 454), she has grown 'a heart to understand what ... [his] heart used to be' (*GE*, p. 454). Their irrevocable parting at the end of this chance interview, however, would seem to *confirm* rather than contradict Miss Havisham's teaching, because the failure of Pip's love for Estella to produce any kind of lasting union *fulfils* instead of frustrates Miss Havisham's retributive schemes against phallocracy which, if translated into Lacanese, would say, 'there is no sexual relationship'.[50] Instead of the (im)possibility of sex, there is only

---

47 Johnson, *Charles Dickens*, above n. 45, p. 491.
48 Brooks writes: 'The real ending may take place with Pip's recognition and acceptance of Magwitch after his recapture – this is certainly the ethical *denouement* – and his acceptance of a continuing existence without a plot, as celibate clerk for Clarrikers'. The pages that follow might simply be *obiter dicta*: Brooks, 'Repetition, Repression, and Return', above n. 10, p. 106).
49 Žižek writes 'the failed ending is the usual place at which the inconsistency of the work's ideological project becomes visible' (*The Plague of Fantasies*, above n. 41, p. 145).
50 J. Lacan, 'On Feminine Sexuality, the Limits of Love and Knowledge, 1972–1973', *Encore: The Seminar of Jacques Lacan, Book XX*, J.-A. Miller (ed.), B. Fink (trans.), New York: W. W. Norton & Co., 1998, p. 6.

the fantasy of love, the symptom of which is Estella, whose 'heartless' unreality suggests '*La Femme n'existe pas*' (Lacan 1998: 7) as much as *La Belle Dame Sans Merci*. Indeed, she is the symptom to be 'enjoyed', in the darkest Lacanian–Žižekian sense of that word, both by Miss Havisham ('Did I never give her a burning love', exclaims Miss Havisham, 'inseparable from jealousy at all times, and from sharp pain', *GE*, p. 284) and Pip ('I never had one hour's happiness in her society', thinks Pip, 'and yet my mind all round the four-and-twenty hours was harping on the happiness of having her with me unto death', *GE*, p. 281), each to their extreme prejudice, her fantasmatic hold undoing the two of them in the end.

In fact, everyone in *Great Expectations* is 'undone' by love, defined by Miss Havisham in the most chilling of retributive terms: 'I'll tell you . . . what real love is. It is blind devotion, unquestioning self-humiliation, utter submission, trust and belief against yourself and against the whole world, giving up your whole heart and soul to the smiter' (*GE*, p. 224). This grim view of human relations is borne out by the text; in fact, all the novel's characters are smote when smitten, either a 'beater' or a 'cringer' (*GE*, p. 322), as Jaggers puts it. This dichotomy of 'beating and cringing' (*GE*, p. 322) is played out in most of the relationships of the narrative, the retributive dysfunctionality of which spans not just the disastrous Compeyson–Havisham coupling, but Joe and Mrs Joe (who is as much a 'mo-gul' on a 'ram-page' to Joe as she is to Pip, *GE*, p. 44), Joe's parents (whose father 'hammered away at my mother most onmerciful', *GE*, p. 42) and, of course, Bentley Drummle and Estella (whose flight from her battering husband in the first ending has a distinctly Ann Brontë-ish quality to it, recalling that other great Victorian novel of spousal abuse, *The Tenant of Wildfell Hall*).

These depressing depictions of love Victorian style resonate as much politically as psychoanalytically. This is because they affirm Lacan's theory of gender difference, all the while pointing to the limits of retribution's role as a jurisprudential strategy under governmentality. For if retribution's end result is *more* retribution, so much so that 'there is no sexual relationship', only an ever-widening spiral of domestic violence (think of Estella, the *object* as much as the subject of retribution), then this pattern of punitive escalation calls into question, even judges and finds wanting not just the technologies of retributive jurisprudence, but its very vision of society; namely, Fitzjames Stephen's sentimentalisation of the status society and its 'restraints' of class and caste, kith and kin, and, especially man and wife. Stephen naturalised the inequities of these relationships with an aqueous analogy, comparing '[t]he life of the great mass of men' to 'a watercourse guided this way or that by a system of dams, sluices, weirs, and embankments'.[51] Dickens de-naturalises the ersatz organicism of this trope in *Great Expectations* by representing, and thereby exposing Victorian civil society – especially the domestic sphere of love and marriage – as a site of sanction at its most physically coercive, enforced, variously, by the fist of Joe's father, by Mrs Joe's rolling pin 'Tickler', and by Bentley Drummle's 'compound of pride, brutality and meanness' (*GE*, p. 453). This *exposé* of marriage *à la mode* reveals the whole structure of 'Victorian values', trumpeted by Stephen and the moral-authoritarian agenda of retribution, to be a smokescreen for governmental repression not just of women by men but of the lower orders by their 'betters', because for Stephen the social norm is one of class war: 'I believe', says Stephen, 'that between all classes of men there are and always will be real occasions of enmity and strife'.[52]

If governmentality's retributive jurisprudence is reprised but also rebuked in the first, cynical ending of *Great Expectations*, then the second, happy ending does the same for distributive jurisprudence. This claim, however, would seem to run against the scholarly grain; most Dickens' specialists see, not without justification, sentimental cop-out rather than trenchant political critique in this rewrite. But in bringing Pip and Estella together for a meeting from which Pip can see 'no shadow of another parting' (*GE*, p. 451), so rich is it in the moving confessions of past fault ('There was a long hard time', admits Estella, 'when I kept from remembrance... what I had thrown away... But since... I have given it a place in my heart', *GE*, p. 451) and tender admissions of present affection ('You have always held a place in *my* heart', assures Pip, *GE*, p. 451), the second ending, oddly, speaks to, and indeed realises Magwitch's fantasy of distribution. How is this so? How can the lush romanticism of the second ending – a moonrise, a ruined garden, a solitary figure espied in the mists – evoke distribution's utility calculus? Largely, because the liberal version of utilitarianism which Magwitch embodies places its faith, as does this ending, in the individual, and their autonomous ability to *choose*, despite social obstacles. After all, how does Magwitch avenge himself against the blockages and barriers he experienced from a class society? Certainly not by any sort of *social* solution, such as agitating for, and organising working-class dissent – clearly an option here, this being the era of *Das Capital*, as much as Wemmick's 'Ca-pi-tal' (*GE*, p. 185). Instead, however, of class solidarity, Magwitch opts for the 'false consciousness' of liberal individualism, seeking redress in endowing another working-class lad, Pip, with the autonomy of

---

51 J. F. Stephen, *Liberty, Equality, Fraternity*, above n. 33, note at p. 64.
52 Ibid. p. 226.

'great expectations' – and all the choices that implies – which Magwitch, in turn, chooses to watch over, and witness by returning to England.

It is precisely this autonomous freedom to choose that Pip and Estella exercise here, sloughing off a past of thwarted desire and distorted values; instead, they choose to come together here, presenting a united front of personal happiness against the social, political and economic inequities of the social. So what the second, happy ending of *Great Expectations* represents is the liberal valorisation of the personal over the political, the individual over the collective because, for liberalism (to mimic Lacanese) 'there is no social relationship'; meaning, that is, no social relationship beyond the individuated ties of civil society. A note of uncertainty, however, is introduced in this ending by Estella's insistence that they 'will continue friends apart' (*GE*, p. 451). Why does Estella close this ending with the shadow of a doubt? Surely, because she more than anyone else has been 'bent and broken' (*GE*, p. 451) by civil society, especially the realm of domesticity, supposedly, according to Mill and other liberals, the most private and protected of spaces, but which turns out to be a site of the most mercenary values, emblematised in the worst kind of *mariage de convenance*, Estella's 'brass' for Drummle's 'class': 'The ground belongs to me', says Estella to Pip, referring to the lot upon which Satis House once stood, and which now she is forced to sell, 'It was the only possession I have not relinquished. Everything else has gone from me, little by little, but I have kept this. It was the subject of the only determined resistance I made in all those wretched years . . . I came here to take leave of it before it changed' (*GE*, p. 450). What Estella's pending homelessness drives home here, just as what her uncertainty about her future with Pip may point to, is that there is no escape in a class society from (mis)distribution's calculus of (in)felicity; that is, the private world of 'home and hearth' is just as tainted by, and, indeed, thoroughly implicated in the market arena of 'getting and spending', and all of its sharp practices, misappropriations and inequities.

Any attempt to draw a line between these two overlapping and interpenetrating spheres of market and marriage, political and personal is doomed in *Great Expectations*. Nowhere is this failure more forcefully rendered than in Pip's unwitting exposure of Wemmick to Jaggers, as a man, who, in his chambers in Little Britain, publicly proclaims from his 'letter box mouth' (*GE*, p. 195) the stern platitudes of distribution ('Every man's business is portable property', *GE*, p. 381), while privately parodying Victorian domesticity in Walworth at his 'pleasant home' (*GE*, p. 383) shared with his old father, the 'Aged P.' (*GE*, p. 277). Pip's inadvertent revelation of Wemmick's 'cheerful playful ways' (*GE*, p. 383) brings his double life – indeed, a kind of Jekyll and Hyde of liberalism's private–public divide – into the cold, hard glare of Jaggers' field of vision. The suggestion being that this schizophrenic existence may no longer be sustained, at least in its present employ: 'a misgiving crossed me', says Pip, 'that Wemmick would be instantly dismissed' (*GE*, p. 383). So the implication both here and in the second ending is that the sphere of the personal is no fortress against politico-economic forces. Indeed, these forces may well invade the personal – as Bentley Drummle does to Estella, and as Jaggers may do to Wemmick's faux 'castle' (*GE*, p. 194). This is because the jurisprudence of distribution has so thoroughly confused the two, blurring the distinction between the market and morals, knowing as it does – even in the work of Mill (with his talk of the 'marketplace of ideas'), let alone Austin or Bentham (Bounderby and Gradgrind?) – this: the price of everything, *but* the value of nothing.

### Forget Foucault? Beyond Governmentality: Justice as Deconstruction

So the doubled ending of *Great Expectations* works to dramatise but also expose the twin fantasies of the period – distribution and retribution – and, by extension, the governmentality of the law, state and society of which these fantasies are the main ideological prop. Hence, *Great Expectations* is not so much a novel of governmentality's emergence, as it is one of governmentality's *limits*, inviting, urging and demanding that jurisprudence (as well as juridical practice) go 'beyond governmentality'. But where is jurisprudence to go? Quite obviously: to a new theory of justice. Dickens, himself, makes this move explicit in his article, 'Five New Points of Criminal Law' where he privileges the 'spirit' of the law over its 'perplexed letter', claiming its rightful jurisprudential parentage as the 'child of Justice', rather than the 'Artful Dodger' of empty rhetoric and nitpicking forensics.[53] But the question arises: Does this return to law's origins mean, necessarily, for Dickens, the recuperation of the past of natural law, the quality of mercy, and by implication, the retributive threat of the executioner? Or does it mean for Dickens going back to the future of Rawlsian justice with its distributive fantasies of fairness secured by the 'veil of ignorance'?[54] I would argue that *Great Expectations* situates Dickens in neither time-frame, but would locate itself (and himself) in the 'future anterior'[55] of postmod-

---

53 C. Dickens, 'Five Points of Criminal Law', in P. Collins, *Dickens and Crime*, London: Macmillan, 1994, p. 191.
54 J. Rawls, *A Theory of Justice*, Oxford: Oxford University Press, 1971.
55 J.-F. Lyotard, *The Postmodern Condition: A Report on Knowledge*, G. Bennington and B. Massumi (trans.), Minneapolis: University of Minnesota Press, 1989, p. 81.

ernism, plumping for a definition of justice which is neither modernist (with its fantasies of distribution and retribution) nor Foucauldian (with its triad of discipline–punish–governmentality), but rather between and beyond both. For this postmodern version of justice would 'forget Foucault' as much as modernity, thereby exposing governmentality's not so 'mystical foundations of authority'[56] through a critique of its retributive and distributive tactics. It is precisely towards this postmodern conception of justice which Dickens in *Great Expectations* may point in urging jurisprudence to go beyond governmentality, beyond its retributive and distributive versions of justice. All of which might lead one to suppose that Jacques Derrida rather than Charles Dickens is the real author of *Great Expectations* because what this novel seems to advocate is a vision of justice *as deconstruction* through the deconstruction of justice.

This deconstruction of justice by justice as deconstruction, however, would not take jurisprudence, as institutionalists such as David Saunders fear,[57] *beyond* the law as *within* it, restoring a sense of incalculability to distribution's utility, of uncertainty to retribution's 'just measure of pain': in short, rendering the moment of decision-making *undecidable*. This is not to defer decision-making indefinitely. On the contrary, a decision *must* be made. But as Derrida instructs, its very decisiveness is predicated upon indecision, upon the play of precedents and the aporias of procedures. This dissemination of legal meaning ensures the endless *différance* of judgement, at once 'jurispathic' and 'jurisgenerative',[58] deconstructive and reconstructive, enabling, as Sandra Berns might say,[59] new legal stories to be told, new juridical voices to be heard. I would like to conclude by arguing that if one of these 'different voices' of the law is heard in *Great Expectations*, then it is precisely the one with which opened this chapter, and which suggested its theme of governmentality; namely, the voice of Joe Gargery. As I stated at the outset, Joe is *Great Expectations*' most perspicacious critic, not just because he discerns its theme, but because he anticipates its critique, propounding a novel judgement that, implicitly, urges jurisprudence to go 'beyond governmentality', and envisages an alternative juridical imaginary. That imaginary would tell, as Joe does, a new legal story organised around

---

56 J. Derrida, 'Force of Law: The "Mystical Foundations of Authority"', M. Quaintance (trans.), *Cardozo Law Review* 11, 1989–90, 921–1045.
57 D. Saunders, 'Law, Politics and Religion: Some Early Modern Lessons for Today's Humanities', Professorial Lecture: Griffith University, Nathan Campus, Brisbane, Qld, Australia, 19 May 1999.
58 R. Cover, 'Violence and the Word', *Yale Law Journal* 95(7), 1986, 1601–1629.
59 S. Berns, *To Speak as a Judge: Difference, Voice and Power*, Aldershot: Ashgate, 1999.

morality ('There's one thing you may be sure of Pip . . . namely, that lies is lies', *GE*, p. 64), forgiveness ('Oh, dear old Pip, old chap . . . God knows I forgive you, if I have anythink to forgive', *GE*, p. 446) and an ethic of care ('For the tenderness of Joe was so beautifully proportioned to my need that I was like a child in his hands', *GE*, p. 434). But it is, especially, Joe's focus on law's Other – justice – in which a new legal voice is heard, in which a new legal story emerges, because he redefines justice in virtually Levinasian terms as a justice *of the Other*: an Other to whom justice solicits, comforts and assures, with one of the most poignant and touching of novel judgements in the affirming interrogative, 'Ever the best of friends, ain't us Pip?' (*GE*, p. 436).

# A Jurisprudential Postscript: Century's Close and the End of the Meta-Narrative of Law?

*Novel Judgements* closes with a reading of *Great Expectations*, published in 1861, while it opened with one of *Pride and Prejudice*, published in 1813. As to the literary texts in between: all are spaced at intervals, to a greater or lesser extent, in that half-century's progress: *Frankenstein*, 1818; *Ivanhoe*, 1819; *The House of the Seven Gables*, 1851; *Bleak House*, 1852; and *A Tale of Two Cities*, 1859. If, however, one factors in the legal texts under consideration here, then the historical sweep of this book widens considerably. For it stretches as far back as the late eighteenth century – beginning in 1787, the publication of Bentham's pamphlet, *Defence of Usury* – then extends well into the early twentieth century, concluding, roughly, with the appearance of the first legal realist tracts of Llewellyn (*The Bramble Bush: On Our Law and Its Study*) and Frank (*Law and the Modern Mind*) in 1930. Wedged in between these dates – what a certain kind of historiography might call 'the (very) *long* nineteenth century' – is an array of juridico-political treatises such as Wollstonecraft's *A Vindication of the Rights of Woman* (1792), Bentham's *Introduction to the Principles and Morals of Legislation* (1823), Austin's *The Province of Jurisprudence Determined* (1832), Mill's *On Utilitarianism* (1861), Stephen's *Liberty, Equality, Fraternity* (1874), Dicey's *Introduction to the Study of the Law of the Constitution* (1886) and Holmes's 'The Path of Law' (1897). For all my chronological ordering here however, I want to stress that I am not making, necessarily, a historical argument in this book. At least, not one, principally, about such well-worked *wissenschaftlich* themes and/or devices in a certain 'positivised' account of legal theory's development, all overlapping and intersecting 'schools' and 'movements' (e.g., how Bentham influenced Austin influenced Mill, and so on).

Nor am I concerned, for that matter, with a certain kind of historicist literary criticism (Old or New) clustering around 'the rise of the novel' be it, for example, the growth of realism, the development of free indirect discourse or the triumph of 'character as fate'. This is not to dismiss the significance of that kind of 'critico-historical' inquiry; but my purpose in *Novel Judgements* is otherwise, and seeks to align 'the literary' with 'the legal' in order to ask how the one reads the other *differently* – and vice-versa. For my interest in these hitherto discrete discourses is how they link up with, hook onto, and illuminate *an(O)ther* intertextual history, one that goes, I hasten to add, well beyond 'law-and-literature' as it has been traditionally understood; for example, parsing the literary trope in the jurisprudential essay, or explicating the novelistic representation of court processes. Rather, the historical intertext this book engages is organised around, and by a 'concept of law' in its broadest philosophical sense, one that takes onboard and knits together nomological topoi as diverse as desire, transgression, sovereignty, rights, utility, trusteeship, retribution, distribution, governmentality, and so forth. I refer, of course, to that most anchoring – but also elastic and elusive – of legal notions, the Rule of Law. This explains why this study is, largely, a nineteenth-century one – whether defined as long, short or somewhere in between. For that period was the chrysalis of modern (and postmodern) jurisprudence, giving forth, and form to the Rule of Law as the *degree zero* of legal philosophy, past and present. It is this nomological 'quilting point' that will become, throughout the century, the juridical imaginary's equivalent of that era's most touted and questionable meta-narrative: namely, that of 'progress' be it liberal or socialist, heralding the era of markets or Marx. As a result of this hegemony, a range of ancillary jurisprudential theories proliferated during that century, theorising – and legitimating – the Rule of Law: legal positivism, utilitarianism, rights theory, formalism, legal liberalism and so forth. Each in their own way are a support of the status quo, ensuring not only the persistence of the Rule of Law, but trumpeting its *inevitability*.

With the dawn of the twentieth century, however, an ideological shift occurs, one that bears witness to the emergence of new, more sceptical forms of legal theory *challenging* not only the Rule of Law's claims to access to justice, impartiality of hearing and consistency of judgment, but its *raison d'être*. These movements of legal *critique* – sociological jurisprudence, legal realism, public policy analysis, the 'legal process' school, law in context, critical legal studies, critical legal feminism, critical race theory, cultural legal studies, postmodern jurisprudence – will occur and recur throughout the century. This ebb and flow of legal critique, however, is prefigured in, and overdetermined by the Rule of Law itself. For what might be called the Rule of Law's *thesis* – of full and fair procedures available to all – gives rise to its *antithesis* – critique – in much the same way, during this period, Capital organises its dialectical opposite, Labour. So there is an undercurrent, critical of the Rule of Law, running throughout the nineteenth century's various discourses of power/knowledge, replete with jurisprudential possibilities, charged with curial alternatives. This undercurrent, I have argued, finds its most vivid expression, neither in the period's established 'trad' jurisprudence (and legal history), nor its emerging 'rad' socio-legal disciplines (criminology, penology, etc.), but, rather, in a hugely popular (and still somewhat dubious) aesthetic medium, the novel – *the* prototype of what I have called elsewhere, *lex populi*.[1] Indeed, the wager of this book has been to release these novels' respective subtexts of legal critique, often heavily coded in terms of the domestic, the interior, the private, through a new interpretive method: that is, 'reading jurisprudentially'.

When 'read jurisprudentially', the private sphere these texts depict – country houses, family dynamics, friendship, unrequited love, courtship, marriage – are *publicised*, so to speak, as profoundly *legal* in their concerns. And not only legal; but *critical* of that legality. For these texts disclose how, under the nineteenth-century's new industrial mode of production, *all* relationships – personal and political, private and public – are mediated by not just law's heavy-handed coerciveness, and its prescriptive and/or proscriptive content ('Thou shalt not . . .'), but its near invisible *forms*: the language of the bargain, the discourse of ownership, the idiom of *Recht*, each a superstructural prop of the infrastructure of Capital. In rendering visible what has become so naturalised as to be unseen, these texts put the Rule of Law on trial and render a novel judgement, passing a sentence of critique. Some of these sentences turn on plot devices (an entail bypassing – and disinheriting – the female line; a missing will, and the trusts it sets up gone seriously awry; a deed to vast holdings, long hidden) or settings (revolutionary tribunals, Chancery, a colonial witch trial) that are recognisably legal. But, more often than not, legal critique comes in the form of characters seemingly remote from the law: characters such as Elizabeth Bennet, Rebecca of York, Frankenstein's monster, Holgrave, Esther Summerson

---

1 W. P. MacNeil, *Lex Populi: The Jurisprudence of Popular Culture*. Stanford: Stanford University Press, 2007.

and Joe Gargery (as well as the more legalistic, Carton and Bucket) – each of whom rebuke the Rule of Law in its various permutations, be it defined as the 'command of the sovereign', the 'nonsense upon stilts' of natural rights, utility's felicific calculus, the 'clean hands' of equity, the call of a higher justice, the sanctity of property, or the letter of the law.

As neutralised and nullified as they so often are here – married or killed off, exiled or executed – these figures of legal critique point the reader to another space, another scene of *nomos*; that is, a legality re-envisaged by their narratives' very images and metaphors, their plot twists and textual tropes. What sort of law might that be? What would it look like? What shape would it take? These texts, and the novel judgements they propound, provide something like a jurisprudential cornucopia, their responses instantiated variously as follows: sometimes, a dwelling (Pemberley, Bleak House); sometimes, a message, spoken (Jo to Pip) or unspoken (Mary Shelley to Mary Wollstonecraft); sometimes a positive act, be it a departure (Rebecca), a disclosure (Holgrave) or a sacrifice (Sydney Carton). When read together and taken as a whole, what these spaces and signs, movements and modes gesture towards is a place of law open to all and free of possessive imperatives, in which the legal letter is married to the spirit, in which rights disseminate equally, in which a duty of care extends to, and embraces all, in which no one is the chattel of another and each a legal subject of their own world. That is, they point to a site of *justice*, the novelistic rendering of which might be called, following British jurisprude Herbert Hart, law's 'noble dream'. It is this reverie of the law that our era – often in the wake of anti-legalist 'nightmares',[2] be they totalitarian, authoritarian, even liberal–democratic – seeks to realise, especially in the rethinking of rights (of the *group* as much as the individual), of equality (of *outcomes* as much as opportunities), of the Rule of Law (of equitable *results* in addition to just procedures). Within this context of a reconceived 'juridical (un)conscious', the 'imagination of critique' plays a valuable role, and sets the stage for law's re-visioning, nowhere more so than in the novels under consideration in this book, and their highly *imaginative* judgements. For these novel judgements, when read jurisprudentially, do more than just judge the law and find it wanting; they construct *something* at the very moment they combust it, positing, impliedly, a judgement of the law that is truly *novel*: that is, by making it *new* again. A *new* law re-theorised, fictively, for a *new* era.

2 H. L. A. Hart, 'American Jurisprudence through English eyes: The Nightmare and the Noble Dream', *Georgia Law Review* 11(5), 1977, 969–989.

# Bibliography

Abrams, M. H., *Natural Supernaturalism: Tradition and Revolution in Romantic Literature*, New York: Norton, 1973.

Agamben, G., *State of Exception*, K. Attell (trans.), Chicago: University of Chicago Press, 2005.

Althusser, L., 'Ideology and Ideological State Apparatuses (Notes towards an Investigation)', in L. Althusser, *Essays on Ideology*, New York: Verso, 1984.

Anderson, K., 'A New Class of Lawyers: The Therapeutic as Rights Talk', *Columbia Law Review* 96(4), 1996.

Ariès, P., *The Hour of Our Death*, Weaver, H. (trans), New York: Knopf, 1981.

Aristodemou, M., *Law and Literature: Journeys from Her to Eternity*, Oxford: Oxford University Press, 2000.

Austen, J., *Pride and Prejudice*, Gray, D. (ed.), New York: Norton, 1993.

—— 'Letter to J. Edward Austen, 16 December 1816', in D. Gray (ed.), *Pride and Prejudice*, New York: Norton, 1993.

Austin, J., *The Province of Jurisprudence Determined* and *The Uses of the Study of Jurisprudence*, London: Weidenfeld & Nicolson, 1954.

Axton, W., 'The Trouble with Esther', *Modern Language Quarterly* 26, 1965.

Baldick, C., *In Frankenstein's Shadow*, Oxford: Clarendon Press, 1987.

Battaglia, F. J., '*The House of the Seven Gables*: New Light on Old Problems', *PMLA* 82(7), 1967.

Baudrillard, J. and Lotringer, S., *Forget Foucault*, N. Dufresne (trans.), New York: Semiotext(e), 1987.

Behrendt, L. and Fraser, E., 'A Colonial and Legal Narrative', in I., McCalum and A., McGrath (eds), *Proof and Truth: The Humanist as Expert*, Canberra: Australian Academy of the Sciences, 2003.

Beiderwell, B., *Power and Punishment in Scott's Novels*, Athens, GA: University of Georgia Press, 1992.
Belenky, M. F., *Women's Ways of Knowing: The Development of Self, Voice and Mind*, New York: Basic Books, 1986.
Bell, M. D., *Hawthorne and the Historical Romance of New England*, Princeton: Princeton University Press, 1971.
Belsey, C., *Critical Practice*, London: Methuen, 1980.
Bentham, J., *Defence of Usury*, London: Routledge, 1787.
—— *Strictures on the Exclusionary System as Pursued in the National Society's Schools*, London: E. Wilson, 1816.
—— *Church of Englandism and Its Catechism Examined*, London: E. Wilson, 1818.
—— *Reasons Against the Repeal of the Usury Laws*, London: J. Murray, 1825.
—— *The Rationale for Punishment*, London: R. Heward, 1830.
—— 'Preface to the First Edition' of *A Fragment on Government, or a Comment on the Commentaries* in J. Bowring (ed.), *The Works of Jeremy Bentham*, vol. 1, Edinburgh: William Tait, 1843.
—— 'Scotch Reform' (1843), in J. Bowring (ed.), *The Works of Jeremy Bentham*, vol. 5, Edinburgh: William Tait. Available at: http://oll.libertyfund.org/title/1996 (accessed 2 January 2009).
—— in H. L. A. Hart (ed.), *Limits of Jurisprudence Defined*, London: Athlone Press, 1970.
—— in J. H. Burns and H. L. A Hart (eds), *An Introduction to the Principles of Morals and Legislation*, Oxford: Clarendon Press, 1970.
—— in J. H. Burns and H. L. A. Hart (eds), *A Comment on the Commentaries and A Fragment on Government*, London: University of London Athlone Press, 1977.
—— in F. Rosen and J. H. Burns (eds), *Constitutional Code: Vol. 1*, Oxford: Clarendon Press, 1983.
—— 'Anarchical Fallacies', in J. Waldron (ed.), *'Nonsense upon Stilts: Bentham, Burke and Marx on the Rights of Man'*, New York: Methuen, 1987.
—— 'Truth versus Ashhurst; or Law As It Is Contrasted With What It Is Said To Be', in J. Bowing (ed.), *The Works of Jeremy Bentham*, vol. 5, Bristol: Thoemmes Press, 1995.
—— in J. H. Burns and H. L. A. Hart (eds), *An Introduction to the Principles of Morals and Legislation*, Oxford: Clarendon Press, 1996.
—— 'Legislator of the World', in P. Schofield and J. Harris (eds), *Writings on Codification, Law and Education*, New York: Oxford University Press, 1998.
Benton, G., ' "And Dying Thus Around Us Every Day": Pathology, Ontology and the Discourse of the Diseased Body: A Study of Illness and Contagion in *Bleak House*', *Dickens Quarterly* 11, 1994.
Berns, S., *To Speak as a Judge: Difference, Voice and Power*, Aldershot: Ashgate, 1999.
Best, S., *The Fugitive's Properties: Law and the Poetics of Possession*, Chicago: University of Chicago Press, 2004.
Birks, M., *Gentleman of the Law*, London: Stevens & Sons, 1960.
Black, C. F., *The Land is the Source of the Law: A Dialogic Encounter with Indigenous Jurisprudence*, London: Routledge, 2010.
Blackstone, W., *Commentaries on the Laws of England*, Chicago: University of Chicago Press, 1979.

Bloom, H., *The Anxiety of Influence: A Theory of Poetry*. New York: Oxford University Press, 1973.
—— *The Map of Misreading*, New York: Oxford University Press, 1975.
Botting, F., *Making Monstrous: Frankenstein, Criticism, Theory*, Manchester: Manchester University Press, 1991.
Bottomley, S. and Parker, S., *Law in Context*, Annandale: The Federation Press, 1994.
Bowen, C. D., *Yankee from Olympus*, Boston: Little Brown, 1944.
Brint, S., In An Age of Experts: The Changing Role of Professionals in Politics and Public Life, Princeton: Princeton University Press, 1994.
Brooks, P., 'Repetition, Repression, and Return: *Great Expectations* and the Study of the Plot', in R. Sell (ed.), *New Casebooks: Great Expectations*, New York: St. Martin's Press, 1994.
—— *Troubling Confessions: Speaking Guilt in Law and Literature*, Chicago: University of Chicago Press, 2000.
Brontë, E., *Wuthering Heights*, in C. Brontë, E. Brontë and A. Brontë, *The Brontës: Three Great Novels*, Oxford: Oxford University Press, 1994.
Burchell, G., 'Peculiar Interests: Civil Society and Governing The System of Natural Liberty', in G. Burchell, C. Gordon and P. Miller (eds), *The Foucault Effect: Studies in Governmentality*, Hemel Hempstead, England: Harvester Wheatsheaf, 1991.
Butler, M., *Jane Austen and the War of Ideas*, Oxford: Clarendon Press, 1975.
Butt, J., '*Bleak House* in the Context of 1851', *Nineteenth Century Fiction* 10, 1955.
—— and Tillotson, K., *Dickens at Work*, London: Methuen, 1957.
Cagidemetrio, A., 'A Plea for Fictional Histories and Old-Time "Jewesses" ', in W. Stollers (ed.), *The Invention of Ethnicity*, New York: Oxford University Press, 1989.
Cameron, S., *The Corporeal Self: Allegories of the Body in Hawthorne and Melville*, Baltimore: Johns Hopkins University Press, 1981.
Campbell, F. K., *Contours of Ableism: The Production of Disability and Abledness*, London: Palgrave Macmillan, 2009.
Cardozo, B. N., *Law and Literature and Other Essays and Addresses*, New York: Harcourt, Brace & Co, 1931.
Carlyle, T., *The French Revolution: A History*, London: Dent, 1906.
—— *Past and Present*, R. D. Altick (ed.), New York: New York University Press, 1965.
Chandler, J., *England in 1819: The Politics of Literary Culture and the Case of Romantic Historicism*, Chicago: University of Chicago Press, 1998.
Chaplin, S., 'Fictions of Origin: Law, Abjection, Difference', *Law and Critique* 16(2), 2005.
—— *The Gothic and the Rule of Law, 1764–1820*, New York: Palgrave Macmillan, 2007.
Cheyfitz, E., 'The Irresistibleness of Great Literature: Reconstructing Hawthorne's Politics', *American Literary History* 6(3), 1994.
Chion, M., 'The Impossible Embodiment', in *Everything You Always Wanted to Know About Lacan. . .But Were Afraid to Ask Hitchcock*, London: Verso, 1992.
Clapham, J. H., *An Economic History of Modern Britain: The Early Railway Age, 1820–1850*, Cambridge: Cambridge University Press, 1926.
Cohen, F., 'Transcendental Nonsense and the Functional Approach', *Columbia LR* 35, 1935.
Collins, P., *Dickens and Crime*, London: Macmillan, 1994.

Copjec, J., 'Vampires, Breast-Feeding and Anxiety', in *Read My Desire: Lacan Against the Historicists*, Cambridge, MA: MIT Press, 1994.

Cornell, D., *Beyond Accommodation: Ethical Feminism, Deconstruction and the Law*, London: Routledge, 1991.

—— 'The Maternal and the Feminine: Social Reality, Fantasy and Ethical Relation', in *Beyond Accommodation: Ethical Feminism, Deconstruction and the Law*, London: Routledge, 1991.

Cornish, W. R. and Clark, G. de N., *Law and Society in England, 1750–1950*, London: Sweet & Maxwell, 1989.

Cotterrell, R., *The Politics of Jurisprudence: A Critical Introduction to Legal Philosophy*, London: Butterworths, 1989.

Cover, R., 'Violence and the Word', *Yale Law Journal* 95(7), 1986.

Crane, G., *Race, Citizenship and Law in American Literature*, Cambridge: Cambridge University Press, 2002.

Creed, B., *The Monstrous-Feminine: Film, Feminism, Psychoanalysis*, London: Routledge, 1993.

Cutmore, J. (ed.), *Quarterly Review Archive*, John Murray: London. Available at: www.rc.umd.edu/reference/qr (accessed 10 October 2010).

Daiches, D., *Sir Walter Scott and His World*, London: Thames & Hudson, 1971.

Davies, M., *Asking the Law Question*, Sydney: Law Book Co., 2008.

Davies, R., *Fifth Business*, New York: Viking, 1970.

Delgado, R., 'Critical Legal Studies and the Realities of Race – Does the Fundamental Contradiction Have a Corollary?', *Harvard Civil Rights–Civil Liberties Law Review* 23, 1988.

Derrida, J., 'Force of Law: The "Mystical Foundations of Authority"', M. Quaintance (trans.), *Cardozo Law Review* 11, 1989–90.

Dickens, C., *A Child's History of England*, London: Chapman & Hall, 1905.

—— *A Tale of Two Cities*, London: Penguin Books, 1970.

—— *Great Expectations*, New York: Bantam Books, 1982.

—— 'Five Points of Criminal Law', in P. Collins, *Dickens and Crime*, London: Macmillan, 1994.

—— *Bleak House*, New York: Modern Library, 2002.

Dicey, A. V., *Introduction to the Study of the Law of the Constitution*, E. C. S. Wade (intro.), London: Macmillan, 1959.

Dillingham, W. B., 'Structure and Theme in "The House of the Seven Gables"', *Nineteenth Century Fiction* 14(1), 1959.

Dimock, W. C., *Residues of Justice: Literature, Law, Philosophy*, Berkeley: University of California Press, 1996.

Dinwiddy, J. R. R., *Radicalism and Reform in Britain, 1780–1850*, London: Continuum, 1992.

Dolin, K., *Fiction and the Law: Legal Discourse in Victorian and Modernist Literature*, Cambridge: Cambridge University Press, 1999

—— *A Critical Introduction to Law and Literature*, Cambridge: Cambridge University Press, 2007

—— 'Law, Literature and Symbolic Revolution: *Bleak House*', *Australasian Journal of Victorian Studies* 12(1), 2007.

Douzinas, C., *Justice Miscarried: Ethics and Aesthetics in Law*, London: Harvester Wheatsheaf, 1994.
Duckworth, A. M., *The Improvement of the Estate: A Study of Jane Austen's Novels*, Baltimore: Johns Hopkins University Press, 1971.
Duman, D., *The English and Colonial Bars in the Nineteenth Century*, London: Croom Helm, 1983.
Dworkin, R., *Law's Empire*, Fontana Press: London, 1986.
Dyer, G., 'Ivanhoe, Chivalry, and the Murder of Mary Ashford', *Criticism* 39(3), 1997.
Edelman, L., *No Future: Queer Theory and the Death Drive*, Durham, NC: Duke University Press, 2004.
*Edinburgh Review*, 27 December 1816.
Edsall, N., *Towards Stonewall: Homosexuality and Society in the Modern Western World*, Charlottesville, VA: University of Virginia Press, 2003.
Eliot, G., *Middlemarch*, Oxford: Oxford University Press, 2008.
Ellis, G. E., *Memoir of Charles Wentworth Upham*, Cambridge: J. Wilson & Son, 1877.
Erlanger, H., 'Is It Time for a New Legal Realism?', *Wisconsin LR* 2, 2005.
Fasich, L., 'Dickens and the Diseased Body in *Bleak House*', *Dickens Studies Annual* 24, 1996.
Ferguson, R. A., *Law and Letters in American Culture*, Cambridge, MA: Harvard University Press, 1984.
—— *The American Enlightenment 1750–1820*, Cambridge, MA: Harvard University Press, 1997.
—— *Reading the Early Republic*, Cambridge, MA: Harvard University Press, 2004.
—— *The Trial in American Life*, Chicago: University of Chicago Press, 2007.
Fish, S., 'The Law Wishes to Have a Formal Existence', in H. A. Veeser (ed.), *The Stanley Fish Reader*, Oxford: Blackwell Publishers, 1999.
Forster, E. M., *Howards End*, London: Arnold, 1947.
Forster, J., *Forster's Life of Dickens*, George Gissing (ed.), London: Chapman & Hall, 1903.
Foucault, M., *Discipline and Punish: The Birth of the Prison*, A. Sheridan (trans.), New York: Pantheon, 1977.
—— 'Governmentality', P. Pasquino (trans.), *Ideology and Consciousness* 6, 1979/1983.
—— 'Politics and the Study of Discourse', in G. Burchell, C. Gordon and P. Miller (eds), *The Foucault Effect: Studies in Governmentality*, Chicago: University of Chicago Press, 1991.
Frank, J., *Law and the Modern Mind*, New Brunswick, NJ: Transaction Publishers, 2008.
Freeman, M. D. A., *Lloyd's Introduction to Jurisprudence*, London: Sweet & Maxwell, 1994.
Freud, S., 'Beyond the Pleasure Principle', in *The Freud Reader*, Peter Gay (ed.), New York: W. W. Norton, 1995.
—— 'Psychopathology of Everyday Life', in A. A. Brill (trans. and ed.), *The Basic Writings of Sigmund Freud*, New York: Modern Library, 1995.
—— 'The History of the Psychoanalytic Movement', in A. A. Brill (trans. and ed.), *The Basic Writings of Sigmund Freud*, New York: Modern Library, 1995.
—— 'The Interpretation of Dreams', in A. A. Brill (trans. and ed.), *The Basic Writings of Sigmund Freud*, New York: Modern Library, 1995.

Friedmann, L., *A History of American Law*, New York: Touchstone, 1973.
Frug, M. J., *Postmodern Legal Feminism*, New York: Routledge, 1992.
—— 'Progressive Feminist Legal Scholarship: Can We Claim a "Different Voice?"', in *Postmodern Legal Feminism*, New York: Routledge, 1992.
Frye, N., *The Anatomy of Criticism: Four Essays*, Princeton: Princeton University Press, 1957.
Fukuyama, F., *Trust: The Social Virtues and the Creation of Prosperity*, New York: Free Press, 1995.
Fyfe, T., *Charles Dickens and the Law*, London: Chapman & Hill, 1910.
Gabel, P., 'The Phenomenology of Rights-Consciousness and the Pact of the Withdrawn Selves', *Texas Law Review* 62, 1984.
Gaita, R., *Breach of Trust: Truth, Morality and Politics*, Melbourne: Black Inc., 2004.
Galsworthy, J., *The Forsyte Saga*, London: Headline Review, 2007.
Gambetta, D., *Trust: Making and Breaking Cooperative Relations*, Oxford: Basil Blackwell, 1988.
Geary, A., *Law and Aesthetics*, Oxford: Hart Publishing, 2001.
Gest, J. M., 'The Law and Lawyers of Charles Dickens', *American Law Register* 53, 1905.
Gilligan, C., *In a Different Voice: Psychological Theory and Women's Development*, Cambridge, MA: Harvard University Press, 1982.
Gilmore, M., *American Romanticism and the Marketplace*, Chicago: University of Chicago Press, 1985.
Glen, P., 'The Deconstruction and Reification of Law in Franz Kafka's *Before the Law* and *The Trial*', *Southern California Interdisciplinary Law Journal* 17, 2007.
Goodman, N., *Shifting the Blame: Literature, Law and the Theory of Accidents in Nineteenth Century America*, Princeton: Princeton University Press, 1998.
Goodrich, P., *Oedipus Lex: Psychoanalysis, History, Law*, Berkeley: University of California Press, 1995.
Goodwin, M., 'The Black Woman in the Attic: Law, Metaphor and Madness in *Jane Eyre*', *Rutgers Law Journal* 30, 1999.
Grahame, J., *Defence of the Usury Laws Against the Arguments of Mr Bentham*, Edinburgh: Printed for A. Constable, 1817.
Gramsci, A., in D. Forgacs (ed.), *An Antonio Gramsci Reader: Selected Writings 1916–1935*, New York: Schocken Books, 1988.
Green, M. S., 'Legal Realism as a Theory of Law', *William and Mary LR* 46, 2005.
Grey, T. C., *The Wallace Stevens Case: Law and the Practice of Poetry*, Cambridge, MA: Harvard University Press, 1991.
Grierson, J. C., *Sir Walter Scott*, New York: Clarendon Press, 1979.
Grossman, J., *The Art of the Alibi: English Law Courts and the Novel*, Baltimore: Johns Hopkins University Press, 2002.
Guest, J. M., *The Lawyer in Literature*, Boston: Boston Book Company, 1913.
Gurney, M. S., 'Disease as Device: The Role of Smallpox in *Bleak House*', *Literature and Medicine* 9, 1990.
Hackney, J., *Understanding Equity and Trusts*, London: Street and Maxwell, 1996.
Halberstam, J., *In a Queer Time and Place: Transgender Bodies, Subcultural Lives*, New York: New York University Press, 2005.
Hall, J. Y., 'What's Troubling About Esther? Narrating, Policing and Resisting Arrest in *Bleak House*', *Dickens Studies Annual* 22, 1993.

Hammer, D., 'Dickens: The Old Court of Chancery', *Notes and Queries* 17, 1970.
Hardin, R., *Trust*, Cambridge: Polity Press, 2006.
Harding, D. W., 'Regulated Hatred: An Aspect in the Work of Jane Austen', *Scrutiny* 8, 1940.
Harmon, A. G., *Eternal Bonds and True Contracts: Law and Nature in Shakespeare's Problem Plays*, Albany: State University of New York Press, 2004.
Hart, H. L. A., *The Concept of Law*, Oxford: Oxford University Press, 1961.
—— 'American Jurisprudence through English eyes: The nightmare and the noble dream', *Georgia Law Review* 11(5), 1977.
Harvey, W. J., '*Bleak House:* The Double Narrative', in A. E. Dyson (ed.), *Dickens: Bleak House: A Casebook*, London: Macmillan, 1969.
Hawthorne, N., *The House of the Seven Gables*, New York: Modern Library, 2001.
Hegel, G. W. G., *The Phenomenology of Mind*, J. B. Baillie (trans.), London: Allen & Unwin, 1931.
Heinzelman, S. S. and Wiseman, Z., *Representing Women: Law, Literature and Feminism*, Durham, NC: Duke University Press, 1994.
Hitchcock, A., 'The Relation of the Picture Play to Literature', *English Journal* 4(5), 1915.
Hobbes, T., in M. Missner (ed.), *Leviathan*, New York: Pearson Longman, 2008.
Holdsworth, Sir. W., *Charles Dickens as a Legal Historian*, New Haven, CT: Yale University Press 1929.
Holmes, O. W., 'Law in Science and Science in Law', in R. A. Posner (ed.), *The Essential Holmes: Selections from the Letters, Speeches, Judicial Opinions and Other Writings of Oliver Wendell Holmes Jr.*, Chicago: University of Chicago Press, 1992.
—— 'The Path of the Law', in R. A. Posner (ed.), *The Essential Holmes: Selections from the Letters, Speeches, Judicial Opinions and Other Writings of Oliver Wendell Holmes Jr.*, Chicago: University of Chicago Press, 1992.
—— 'The Common Law', in R. A. Posner (ed.), *The Essential Holmes: Selections from the Letters, Speeches, Judicial Opinions and Other Writings of Oliver Wendell Holmes Jr.*, Chicago: University of Chicago Press, 1992.
Homer, S., *A History of Interest Rates*, New Brunswick, NJ: Rutgers University Press, 1963.
Hood G. and Lane, L. (eds), *The Dickens Critics*, Ithaca, NY: Cornell University Press, 1859.
House H., *The Dickens World*, London: Oxford University Press, 1941.
Hunt, L., *Politics, Culture and Class in the French Revolution*, London: Methuen, 1986.
Hutchings, P., *The Criminal Spectre in Law, Literature and Aesthetics: Incriminating Subjects*, London: Routledge, 2001.
—— 'Modern Forensics: Photography and Other Suspects', *Cardozo Studies in Law and Literature* 9(2), 1997.
Hutton, R. H., *Sir Walter Scott*, London: Macmillan, 1929.
Jaffe, A., '*David Copperfield* and *Bleak House*: On Dividing the Responsibility of Knowing', in J. Tambling (ed.), *New Casebooks Series: Bleak House: Charles Dickens*, New York: St. Martin's Press, 1998.
Jakobson, R., 'Two Aspects of Language and Two Types of Aphasic Disturbances', in S. Rudy (ed.), *Selected Writings*, vol. 2, The Hague: Mouton, 1971.
Johnson, E., *Charles Dickens: His Tragedy and Triumph*, vol. 1, New York: Simon & Schuster, 1952.

—— *Charles Dickens: His Tragedy and Triumph*, Harmondsworth: Penguin, 1979.
Johnson, P., *A History of Christianity*, London: Weidenfeld & Nicolson, 1976.
Kairys, D., *The Politics of Law: A Progressive Critique*, New York: Pantheon Books, 1982.
Kalman, L., *Legal Realism at Yale, 1927–1960*, Chapel Hill, NC: University of North Carolina Press, 1986.
Kaplan, F., *Dickens: A Biography*, London: Hodder & Stoughton, 1988.
Kantorowicz, E., *The King's Two Bodies: A Study in Medieval Political Theology*, Princeton: Princeton University Press, 1957.
Kelsen, H., *Pure Theory of Law*, M. Knight (trans.), Berkeley: University of California Press, 1967.
King, P. J., *Utilitarian Jurisprudence in America: The Influence of Bentham on American Legal Thought in the Nineteenth Century*, New York: Garland Publishers, 1986.
Kirk, H., *Portrait of a Profession: A History of the Solicitor's Profession, 1100 to the Present Day*, London: Oyez Publisher, 1976.
Klein, M., 'The Importance of Symbol Formation in the Development of the Ego', in R. E. Money-Kyrle, B. Joseph, E. O'Shaughnessy and H. Segal (eds), *Love, Guilt and Reparation and Other Works 1921–1945*, vol. 1 of *The Writings of Melanie Klein*, London: Hogarth Press and the Institute of Psychoanalysis, 1975.
Korobkin, L. H., *Criminal Conversations: Sentimentality and Nineteenth-Century Legal Sources of Adultery*, New York: Columbia University Press, 1998.
La Harpe, J. F., *Du Fanatisme dans la langue révolutionnaire ou de la persécution suscitée par les Barbares du dix-huitième Siècle, contre la Religion Chrétienne et ses Ministres*, Paris: Migneret, 1797.
Lacan, J., *Ecrits: A Selection*, A. Sheridan (ed. and trans.), New York: Norton, 1977.
—— 'Function and Field of Speech and Language in Psychoanalysis', in A. Sheridan (ed. and trans.) *Ecrits: A Selection*, New York: Norton, 1977.
—— 'The Four Fundamental Concepts of Psycho-Analysis', in A. Sheridan (trans.) *The Seminar of Jacques Lacan: Book XI*, London: Hogarth Press, 1977.
—— 'The Mirror Stage as Formative of the Function of the I as revealed in Psychoanalytic Experience', in A. Sheridan (trans.), *Ecrits: A Selection*, New York: Norton, 1977.
—— 'The Subversion of the Subject and the Dialectic of Desire in the Freudian Unconscious', in A. Sheridan (trans.), *Ecrits: A Selection*, New York: Norton, 1977.
—— 'God and the Jouissance of Woman', in J. Mitchell and J. Rose (eds), *Feminine Sexuality: Jacques Lacan and the Ecole Freudienne*, New York: Pantheon Books, 1982.
—— 'The Paradoxes of Ethics or Have You Acted in Conformity with Your Desire?', in J.-A. Miller (ed.) and D. Porter (trans.), *The Seminar of Jacques Lacan: Book VII The Ethics of Psychoanalysis 1959–1960*, New York: W. W. Norton, 1992.
—— *The Seminar of Jacques Lacan, Book VII: The Ethics of Psychoanalysis, 1959–1960*, New York: W. W. Norton, 1992.
—— 'The Mirror Stage as Formative of the Function of the I as Revealed in Psychoanalytic Experience', in A. Sheridan (trans.), *Ecrits: A Selection*, New York: Norton, 1997.
—— 'On Feminine Sexuality, the Limits of Love and Knowledge, 1972–1973', in *Encore: The Seminar of Jacques Lacan, Book XX*, J.-A. Miller (ed.), B. Fink (trans.), New York: W. W. Norton & Co., 1998.
—— 'Kant with Sade', in B. Fink (trans.), *Ecrits: The First Complete Edition in English*, London: W. W. Norton & Co., 2006.

Lacey, N., *Women, Crime, and Character: From Moll Flanders to Tess of the D'Urbervilles*, Oxford: Oxford University Press, 2008.
Laclau, E. and Mouffe, C., *Hegemony and Socialist Strategy: Towards a Radical Democratic Politics*, London: Verso, 1985.
La Capra, D., 'Ideology and Critique in Dicken's *Bleak House*', *Representations* 6, 1984.
—— 'Declaration of the Rights of Man and the Citizen', in W. Lacquer and B. Rubin (eds), *The Human Rights Reader*, New York: New American Library, 1979.
Larson, M. S., *The Rise of Professionalism: A Sociological Analysis*, Berkeley: University of California Press, 1977.
Leavis, F. R. and Q. D., *Dickens the Novelist*, Harmondsworth: Penguin Books, 1972.
Lefort, C., *Democracy and Political Theory*, D. Macey (trans.), Minneapolis: University of Minnesota Press, 1988.
Leiboff, M. and Thomas, M., *Legal Theories: Contexts and Practices*, Sydney: Law Book Co., 2009.
Levy, L. B., 'Picturesque Style in *The House of the Seven Gables*', *New England Quarterly* 39(2), 1966.
Lewin, J., 'Jewish Heritage and Secular Inheritance in Walter Scott's *Ivanhoe*', *ANQ* 19(1), 2006.
Llewellyn, K. N., in W. Twining, *Karl Llewellyn and the Realist Movement*, London: Weidenfeld & Nicolson, 1973.
—— 'My Philosophy of Law', in M. D. A. Freeman (ed.), *Lloyd's Introduction to Jurisprudence Eighth Edition*, London: Thomson Reuters, 2008.
Lobban, M., 'Preparing for Fusion: Reforming the Nineteenth Century Court of Chancery, Pt 1', *Law and History Review* 22(2), 2004.
Lockhart, J. G., *Memoirs of the Life of Sir Walter Scott*, Boston: Mifflin and Co., 1901.
Lowenstein, D. H., 'The Failure of the Act: Conceptions of Law in *The Merchant of Venice, Bleak House, Les Misérables* and Weisberg's *Poethics*', *Cardozo LR* 15(4) 1994.
Luhmann, N., *Trust and Power*, Chichester: John Wiley, 1979.
—— *Observations on Modernity*, W. Whobery (trans.), Stanford: Stanford University Press, 1998.
Lyotard, J.-F., *The Postmodern Condition: A Report on Knowledge*, G. Bennington and B. Massumi (trans.), Minneapolis: University of Minnesota Press, 1989.
Macauley, S., 'Non-Contractual Relations in Business: A Preliminary Study', *American Sociological Review* 28(1), 1963.
MacCannell, J. F., *The Regime of the Brother: After the Patriarchy*, London: Routledge, 1991.
—— 'Enjoyment', in *Feminism and Psychoanalysis: A Critical Dictionary*, E. Wright (ed.), Oxford: Blackwell, 1996.
MacDonagh, O., 'The Nineteenth-Century Revolution in Government: A Reappraisal', *History Journal* 1, 1958.
McGill, M., *American Literature and the Culture of Reprinting 1834–1853*, Philadelphia: University of Pennsylvania Press, 2003.
MacKinnon, C., *Feminism Unmodified: Discourse on Law and Life*, Cambridge, MA: Harvard University Press, 1987.
MacNeil, W. P., 'Enjoy Your Rights! Three Cases from the Postcolonial Commonwealth', *Public Culture* 9(3), 1997.

—— 'John Austin or Jane Austen? The Province of Jurisprudence Determined in *Pride and Prejudice*', *Law, Text, Culture* 4(2), 1998.

—— 'Law's *Corpus Delicti*: The Fantasmatic Body of Rights Discourse', *Law and Critique* 9(1), 1998.

—— 'Beyond Governmentality: Retributive, Distributive and Deconstructive Justice in Great Expectations', *Australian Feminist Law Journal* 13, 1999.

—— 'Taking Rights Symptomatically', *Griffith Law Review* 8(1), 1999.

—— 'The Monstrous Body of the Law: Wollstonecraft vs. Shelley', *Australian Feminist Law Journal* 12, 1999.

—— 'A Tale of Two Trials: Revolutionary Enjoyment, Liberal Legalism and the Sacrifice of Critique in Dickens's A Tale of Two Cities', in A. Sarat and P. Ewick (eds), *Studies in Law, Politics and Society*, Oxford: Elsevier Science Ltd., 2000.

—— *Lex Populi: The Jurisprudence of Popular Culture*, Stanford, CA: Stanford University Press, 2007.

MacPherson, S., 'Rent to Own; or What's Entailed in *Pride and Prejudice*', *Representations* 82(1), 2003.

McVeigh S. and Rush, P., 'Cutting Our Losses: Criminal Legal Doctrine', in P. Rush, S. McVeigh and A. Young (eds), *Criminal Legal Doctrine*, Aldershot: Dartmouth Press, 1997.

McWilliams, J. P. Jr., *Hawthorne, Melville and the American Character: A Looking Glass Business*, Cambridge: Cambridge University Press, 1984.

Maine, H. S., *Ancient Law*, Sir F. Pollock (ed.), Boston: Beacon Press, 1963.

Manchester, A. H., *Modern Legal History*, London: Butterworths, 1980.

Markey, M., 'Charles Dickens' *Bleak House:* Mr Tulkinghorn as a Successful Literary Lawyer', *St Thomas LR* 14(4), 2002.

Marx, K., 'On the Jewish Question', in *Works of Karl Marx 1844*, A. Blunden and M. Grant (eds), 1844.

—— *Capital: A Critique of Political Economy, Volume I, The Process of Production Capital*, S. Moore and E. Aveling (trans.), F. Engels (ed.), Moscow: Progress Publishers, 1954.

—— *Capital: A Critique of Political Economy*, S. Moore and E. Aveling (trans.), F. Engels (ed.), New York: International Publishers, 1967.

Matheson, N., 'Melancholy History in The House of the Seven Gables', *Literature and Psychology* 48(3), 2002.

Mathiesson, F. O., *American Renaissance: Art and Expression in the Age of Emerson and Whitman*, Oxford: Oxford University Press, 1941.

Matthias, P., *The First Industrial Nation: An Economic History of Britain, 1700–1914*, London: Hartwell, 1969.

Mayhew, H., *London Labour and the London Poor*, New York: Dover Publications, 1968.

Mellow, J. R., *Nathaniel Hawthorne in His Time*, Boston: Houghton Mifflin Co. John McWilliams, 1980.

Melville, H., 'Letter to Nathaniel Hawthorne: 16 April 1851, Pittsfield', reproduced in N. Hawthorne, *The House of the Seven Gables*, M. Oliver (ed.), New York: Modern Library, 2001.

Mergenthal, S., 'The Shadow of Shylock: Scott's *Ivanhoe* and Edgewoth's *Harrington*', in H. Alexander and D. Hewitt (eds), *Scott in Carnival: Selected Papers of the Fourth*

*International Scott Conference, Edinburgh 1991*, 1993, Aberdeen: Association for Scottish Literary Studies.
Michaels, W. B., *Our America: Nativism, Modernism and Pluralism*, Durham, NC: Duke University Press, 1995.
Mill, J. S., 'Utilitarianism', in M. Warnock (ed.), *Utilitarianism and On Liberty*, London: William Collins, 1962.
—— 'On Liberty', in J. S. Mill, *Three Essays: On Liberty, Representative Government and the Subjection of Women*, Oxford: University Press, 1975.
Miller, D. A., 'Discipline in Different Voices: Bureaucracy, Police, Family and *Bleak House*', *Representations* 1, 1983.
—— *The Novel and the Police*, Berkeley: University of California Press, 1988.
Miller, E. H., *Salem is My Dwelling Place: A Life of Nathaniel Hawthorne*, Iowa: University of Iowa, 1991.
Miller, J-A. 'Language: Much Ado About What?', in E. Ragland-Sullivan and M. Bracher (eds), *Lacan and the Subject of Language*, London: Routledge, 1990.
Millgate, J., 'Making It New: Scott, Constable, Ballantyne and the Publication of *Ivanhoe*', *Studies in English Literature, 1500–1900* 34(4), 1994.
Misztal, B., *Trust in Modern Societies: The Search for the Bases of Social Order*, Cambridge: Polity Press, 1996.
Moretti, F., *Signs Taken For Wonders*, London: Verso, 1983.
Morgan, E., *The Aesthetics of International Law*, Buffalo: University of Toronto Press, 2007.
Morison, W. L., *John Austin*, London: Edward Arnold, 1982.
Mudrick, M., *Jane Austen: Irony as Defense and Discovery*, Princeton: Princeton University Press, 1952.
Murav, H., *Russia's Legal Fictions*, Ann Arbor: University of Michigan Press, 1998.
Nabokov, V. and Bowers, F. (eds), *Lectures on Literature*, New York: Harcourt Brace Jovanovich, 1980.
Naman, A. A., *The Jew in the Victorian Novel*, New York: AMS Press, 1980.
Neale, F., *Essay on Money-Lending: containing a defence of legal restrictions on the rate of interest, and an answer to the objections of Mr. Bentham*, London: W. Pickering, T. White (printer), 1826.
Newton, J., 'Historicisms, New and Old: "Charles Dickens" Meets Marxism, Feminism and West Coat Foucault', *Feminist Studies* 16(3), 1990.
O'Connell, L., 'Proper ceremony: the political origins of the marriage plot', unpublished manuscript, forthcoming.
O'Dair, R., 'The Standard Conception of Legal Ethics', in *Legal Ethics: Cases and Materials*. London: Butterworth, 2001.
Ogden, C. K., *Bentham's Theory of Fictions*, Edinburgh: Edinburgh Press, 1932.
O'Flinn, P., 'Production and Reproduction: The Case of *Frankenstein*', in P. Humm, P. Stigant and P. Widdowson (eds), *Popular Fictions: Essays in Literature and History*, London: Methuen, 1986.
Oldham, J., 'A Profusion of Chancery Reform', *Law and History Review* 22(3), 2004.
O'Neill, O., *A Question of Trust*, Cambridge: Cambridge University Press, 2002.
Orman, C., *The Wizard of the North: The Life of Sir Walter Scott*, London: Hodder & Stoughton, 1973.

Pasquino, P., 'Theatrum Politicum: The Genealogy of Capital – Police and the State of Prosperity', in G. Burchell, C. Gordon and P. Miller (eds), *The Foucault Effect: Studies in Governmentality*, Chicago: University of Chicago Press, 1991.
Paulson, R., *Representations of Revolution (1789–1820)*, New Haven, CT: Yale University Press, 1983.
Pettit, P., *Equity and the Law of Trusts*, Croydon: Butterworths, 2001.
Pether, P., 'Fiduciary Duties', Congreve's *The Way of the World*', Australian Journal of Law and Society 7, 1991.
—— 'Sex, Lies and Defamation: The Bush Lawyer of Wessex', *Cardozo Studies in Law and Literature* 6, 1994.
—— 'Measured Judgements? Histories, Pedagogies and the Possibility of Equity', *Law and Literature* 14(3), 2002.
—— 'Is There Anything Outside the Class? Law, Literature, and Pedagogy', *Cardozo LR* 26, 2005.
—— 'Regarding the Miller Girls: Daisy, Judith and the Seeming Paradox of *In Re: Grand Jury Subpoena, Judith Miller*', *Law and Literature* 19(2), 2007.
Pocock, J. G. A., *The Machiavellian Moment: Florentine Political Thought and the Atlantic Republican Tradition*, Princeton: Princeton University Press, 1975.
Poe, E. A., 'The Fall of the House of Usher', in D. Galloway (ed.), *Selected Writings of Edgar Allan Poe: Poems, Tales, Essays and Reviews*, Harmondsworth: Penguin, 1967.
—— 'The Purloined Letter', in D. Galloway (ed.), *Selected Writings of Edgar Allan Poe: Poems, Tales, Essays and Reviews*, Harmondsworth: Penguin, 1967.
Polden, P., 'Stranger than Fiction: The Jennens Inheritance in Fact and Fiction', *Common Law World Review* 32, 2003.
Polloczek, D. P., 'The Marginal, the Equitable and the Unparalleled: Lady Dedlock's Case in Dickens' *Bleak House*', *New Literary History* 3(2), 1999.
Posner, R. A. (ed.), *The Essential Holmes: Selections from the Letters, Speeches, Judicial Opinions and Other Writings of Oliver Wendell Holmes Jr.*, Chicago: University of Chicago Press, 1992.
Pound, R., 'Law in Books and Law in Action', *American Law Review* 44(12), 1910.
Pue, W. W. and D. Sugarman (ed.), *Law and Vampires: Cultural Histories of Legal Profession*, Oxford: Hart, 2003.
*Quarterly Review*, 33 December 1825.
Raffield, P., *Images and Cultures of Law in Early Modern England: Justice and Political Power, 1558–1660*, Cambridge: Cambridge University Press, 2004.
—— *Shakespeare's Imaginary Constitution: Late Elizabethan Politics and the Theatre of the Law*, Oxford: Hart Publishing, 2011.
Ragaz, S., 'Walter Scott and the *Quarterly Review*', in J. Cutmore (ed.), *Conservatism and the Quarterly Review*, London: Pickering & Chatto, 2007.
Ragussis, M., 'Writing Nationalist History: England, the Conversion of the Jews, and Ivanhoe', *ELH* 60(1), 1993.
Rawls, J., *A Theory of Justice*, Oxford: University Press, 1971.
Reichman, R., 'Mourning, Owning, Owing', *American Imago* 64(3), 2007.
—— *The Affective Life of Law: Legal Modernism and the Literary Imagination*, Stanford: Stanford University Press, 2009.
Riffaterre, M., *Fictional Truth*, Baltimore: Johns Hopkins University Press, 1990.

Robbins, B., 'Telescopic Philanthropy: Professionalism and Responsibility in *Bleak House*', in J. Tambling (ed.), *Bleak House: Charles Dickens*, London: Macmillan Press, 1998.

Robertson, G., *Crimes Against Humanity: The Search for Global Justice*, London: Penguin Press, 1999.

Robson, R., *The Attorney in Eighteenth Century England*, Cambridge: Cambridge University Press, 1959.

Rodensky, L., *The Crime in Mind: Criminal Responsibility and the Victorian Novel*, New York: Oxford University Press, 2003.

Rosenberg, E., *From Shylock to Svengali: Jewish Stereotypes in English Fiction*, Stanford: Stanford University Press, 1960.

Russett, M., 'Meter, Identity, Voice: Untranslating "Christabel" ', *Studies in English Literature, 1500–1900* 43(4), 2003.

Sade, D.A.F. de, *Justine, Philosophy in the Bedroom and Other Writings*, New York: Grove Press, 1990.

Saïd, E., *Culture and Imperialism*, London: Vintage Press, 1994.

Salecl, R., 'Why is Woman a Symptom of Rights?', in *The Spoils of Freedom: Psychoanalysis and Feminism After the Fall of Socialism*, London: Routledge, 1994.

Saunders, D., *Anti-Lawyers: Religion and the Critics of Law and State*, London: Routledge, 1997.

—— 'Law, politics and religion: some early modern lessons for today's humanities', Professorial Lecture: Griffith University, Nathan Campus, Brisbane, Qld, Australia, 19 May 1999.

Schama, S., *Citizens: A Chronicle of the French Revolution*, London: Viking, 1989.

Schauer, F., *Thinking Like a Lawyer: A New Introduction to Legal Reasoning*, Cambridge, MA: Harvard University Press, 2009.

Schmitt, C., *Political Theology: Four Chapters on the Concept of Sovereignty*, G. Schwab (trans.), Cambridge, MA: MIT Press, 1985.

Schor H. and Stolzenberg, N., 'Bastard Daughters and Illegitimate Mothers: Burning Down the Courthouse in *Bastard Out of Carolina* and *Bleak House*', *Yearbook of Research in English and American Literature: REAL* 18, 2002.

—— *Dickens and the Daughter of the House*, Cambridge: Cambridge University Press, 1999.

—— *Dickens and the Daughter of the House*, Cambridge: Cambridge University Press, 2005.

Schroeder, J. L., *The Triumph of Venus: The Erotics of the Market*. Berkeley: University of California Press, 2004.

Scott, Sir W., *Waverley*, Andrew Hook (ed.), London: Penguin, 1972.

—— *Ivanhoe*, G. Tulloch (ed.), London: Penguin, 2000.

Serlen, E., 'The Two Worlds of *Bleak House*', *English Literary History* 43, 1976.

Shatto, S., *The Companion to 'Bleak House'*, London: Unwin Hyman, 1988.

Shelley, M., *The Journals of Mary Shelley Vol. I: 1814–1822*, P. Feldman and D. Scott-Kilvert (eds), Oxford: Clarendon Press, 1987.

—— *Frankenstein: or The Modern Prometheus*, M. Hindle (ed.), London: Penguin Books, 2003.

Slaughter, J., *Human Rights, Inc.: The World Novel, Narrative Form and International Law*, New York: Fordham University Press, 2007.

Smith, J. M., 'I am a Gentleman's Daughter: A Marxist–Feminist Reading of *Pride and Prejudice*', in M. M. Folsom (ed.), *Approaches to Teaching Austen's 'Pride and Prejudice'*, New York: MLA, 1993.
Stephen, J. F.,'A Tale of Two Cities', *Saturday Review* 17, 1961.
—— *Liberty, Equality, Fraternity*, R. J. White (ed.), London: University of Cambridge Press, 1967.
—— 'The Licence of Modern Novelists', in S. Wall (ed.), *Charles Dickens: A Critical Anthology*, Harmondsworth: Penguin, 1970.
—— 'Mr Dickens as a Politician', in P. Collins (ed.), *Charles Dickens: The Critical Heritage*, London: Routledge, 1995.
Stephen, L., *Hours in a Library*, vol. 1, London: J. Murray, 1917.
Sterrenburg, L., 'Mary Shelley's Monster: Politics and Psyche in *Frankenstein*', in G. Levine and U. C. Knoepflmacher (eds), *The Endurance of Frankenstein*, Berkeley: University of California Press, 1979.
Stewart, S., *Crimes of Writing: Problems in the Containment of Representation*, New York: Oxford University Press, 1994.
Stroehr, T., '*Bleak House*: The Novel as Dream', in A. E. Dyson (ed.), *Dickens: Bleak House: A Casebook*, London: Macmillan, 1969.
Sunstein, E. W., *Mary Shelley: Romance and Reality*, Baltimore: The Johns Hopkins University Press, 1989.
Swan, C., 'The House of the Seven Gables: Hawthorne's Modern Novel of 1848', *Modern Language Review* 86(1), 1991.
Tambling, J., 'Prison-Bound: Dickens and Foucault', in R. Sell (ed.), *New Casebooks: Great Expectations*, New York: St. Martin's Press, 1994.
—— 'Prison-bound: Dickens, Foucault and *Great Expectations*', paper presented at Postmodern Legal Theory Workshop at the Faulty of Law, University of Hong Kong, Hong Kong, autumn, 1996.
'The French Declaration of the Rights of Man and of the Citizen', reproduced in W. Lacquer and B. Rubin (eds), *The Human Rights Reader*, New York: New American Library, 1979.
Thomas, B., ' "The House of the Seven Gables": Reading the Romance of America', *PMLA* 97(2), 1982.
—— *Cross-Examinations of Law and Literature: Cooper, Hawthorne, Stowe and Melville*, New York: Cambridge University Press, 1987.
—— *Cross-Examinations of Law and Literature: Cooper, Hawthorne, Stowe and Melville*, Cambridge: Cambridge University Press, 1990.
—— *American Literary Realism and the Failed Promise of Contract*, Berkeley: University of California Press, 1997.
—— *Civic Myths: A Law and Literature Approach to Citizenship*, Chapel Hill, NC: University of North Carolina, 2007.
Thomas, R., 'Double Exposures: Arresting Images in *Bleak House* and *The House of the Seven Gables*', *A Forum on Fiction* 31(1), 1997.
—— 'Making Darkness Visible: Capturing the Criminal and Observing the Law in Victorian Photography and Detective Fiction', in C. Christ and J. Jordan (eds), *Victorian Literature and the Victorian Visual Imagination*, Berkeley: University of California Press, 1995.

Thompson, E. P., *Writing by Candlelight*, London: Merlin, 1980.
Tolkien, J. R. R., *The Lord of the Rings*, Boston: Houghton Mifflin, 1965.
Threadgold, T., 'Deconstruction and the Possibility of Justice: Critical and Cultural Difference', *Law, Text, Culture* 1, 1994.
Tilly, C., *Trust and Rule*, New York: Cambridge University Press, 2005.
Trachtenberg, A., 'Seeing and Believing: Hawthorne's Reflections on the Daguerreotype in *The House of the Seven Gables*', *American Literary History* 9(3), 1997.
Treitel, G. H., 'Jane Austen and the Law', *Law Quarterly Review* 100, 1984.
Tucker, G. H., *A Goodly Heritage*, Manchester: Carcanet, 1983.
Tushnet, M., 'An Essay on Rights', *Texas Law Review* 62, 1984.
Twining, W., *Karl Llewellyn and the Realist Movement*, London: Weidenfeld & Nicolson, 1973.
Unger, R., *The Critical Legal Studies Movement*, Cambridge, MA: Harvard University Press, 1986.
von Sneideren, M. L., 'An Amazingly Good Jackal: Race and Labour in Dickens' *A Tale of Two Cities*', *South Atlantic Review* 66(2), 2001.
Walker, D. M, *The Oxford Companion to Law*, Oxford: Clarendon Press, 1980.
Ward, I., *Shakespeare and the Legal Imagination*, London: Butterworths, 1999.
—— 'A Love of Justice: The Legal and Political Thought of William Godwin', *Journal of Legal History* 25(1), 2004.
Waugh, E., *Brideshead Revisited*, Harlow: Longmans, 1968.
Weisberg, R., 'Wigmore's Legal Novels: New Resources for the Expansive Lawyer', *Northwestern Law Review* 71, 1976.
—— *The Failure of the Word: The Protagonist as Lawyer in Modern Fiction*, New Haven, CT: Yale University Press; Weisberg, 1984.
—— *When Lawyers Write*, New York: Little Brown, 1987.
—— *Poethics and Other Strategies of Law and Literature*. London: Butterworths, 1992.
Welsh, A., *From Copyright to Copperfield: The Identity of Dickens*, Cambridge, MA: Harvard University Press, 1987.
—— *Strong Representations: Narrative and Circumstantial Evidence in England*, Baltimore: Johns Hopkins University Press, 1992.
Wheatley, K., 'Plotting the Success of the *Quarterly Review*', in J. Cutmore (ed.), *Conservatism and the Quarterly Review*, London: Pickering & Chatto, 2007.
White, J. B., *When Words Lose Their Meaning: Constitutions and Reconstitutions of Language, Character and Community*, Chicago: University of Chicago Press, 1984.
—— *Heracles' Bow: Essays on the Rhetoric and Poetics of Law*, Madison, Wisconsin: University of Wisconsin Press, 1985.
—— *Justice as Translation: An Essay in Cultural and Legal Criticism*, Chicago: University of Chicago Press, 1990.
—— *Acts of Hope: Creating Authority in Literature, Law and Politics*, Chicago: University of Chicago Press, 1994.
White, T. H., *The Once and Future King*, New York: Putnam, 1958.
Wigmore, J. H., 'A List of Legal Novels', *Illinois Law Review* 2, 1907–1908.
—— 'A List of 100 Legal Novels', *Illinois Law Review* 17, 1922–1923.
Williams, L., *Hard Core: Power, Pleasure, and the 'Frenzy of the Visible'*, Berkeley: University of California Press, 1989.

Williams, M., *Empty Justice: One Hundred Years of Law, Literature and Philosophy: Existential, Feminist and Normative Perspectives in Literary Jurisprudence*, London: Routledge-Cavendish, 2002.
—— *Secrets and Laws: Collected Essays in Law, Lives and Literature*, London: Routledge-Cavendish, 2005.
Williams, P., *The Alchemy of Race and Rights*, Cambridge, MA: Harvard University Press, 1991.
Wilson A., *The World of Charles Dickens*, Harmondsworth: Penguin, 1972.
Wollstonecraft, M., *A Vindication of the Rights of Woman*, C. H. Poston (ed.), New York: Norton, 1988.
Wright, N. E., Ferguson, M. W., Buck, A. R. (eds), *Women, Property and the Letters of the Law in Early Modern England*, Toronto: University of Toronto Press, 2004.
Young, A., 'The Waste Land of the Law: The Wordless Song of the Rape Victim', *Melbourne University Law Review* 22, 1998.
Zatlin, L. G., *The Nineteenth Century Anglo-Jewish Novel*, Boston: Twayne Publishers, 1981.
Žižek, S., *The Sublime Object of Ideology*, London: Verso, 1989.
—— 'How Did Marx Invent the Symptom?', in *The Sublime Object of Ideology*, London: Verso, 1989.
—— *For They Know Not What They Do: Enjoyment as a Political Factor*, London: Verso, 1991.
—— 'The Ideological Sinthome', in *Looking Awry: An Introduction to Jacques Lacan through Popular Culture*, Cambridge, MA: MIT Press, 1991.
—— *Looking Awry: An Introduction to Jacques Lacan through Popular Culture*, Cambridge, MA: MIT Press, 1991.
—— 'Hegelian Language', in *For They Know Not What They Do: Enjoyment As A Political Factor*, London: Verso, 1991.
—— *Enjoy Your Symptom! Jacques Lacan In Hollywood and Out*, London: Routledge, 1992.
—— *The Plague of Fantasies*, London: Verso, 1997.
Zupancic, A., *Ethics of the Real: Kant, Lacan*. London: Verso, 2000.
Zwerdling, A., 'Esther Summerson Rehabilitated', *Publications of the Modern Language Association of America* 88, 1973.

## Primary Legal Sources

### Cases

*Ashford* v. *Thornton* (1818) 1 B & Ald 405
*Buck* v. *Bell*, 274 US 200 (1927)
*Dred Scott* v. *Sandford*, 60 US 19 How. 393 (1857)
*Prigg* v. *Pennsylvania*, 41 US 539 (1842)
*Stockton* v. *Ford*, 52 US 11 How. 232 (1850)
*United States* v. *Libellants and Claimants of the Schooner Amistad*, 40 US 15 Pet. 518 (1841)

## Legislation
Common Law Procedure Act 1852
Criminal Law Amendment Act 1885
Parl. Deb. XXXII, 1 Feb.–6 March 1816
Parl. Deb. XXXIV, 26 Apr.–2 July 1816
Parl. Deb. Vol. 5, 3 Apr.–11 July, 1821
Statute of 12 Anne
Statute of 12 Carl. II
Statute of 5 Edw. VI
Statute of 6 Edw. VI
Statute of 13 Eliz.
Statute of 37 Hen. VIII
Statute of 21 Jac. I
Statute of 1 Vict.
Statute of 13 Vict.
Statute of 14 Vict.
Statute of 3 Will. IV
Statute of 4 Will. IV

## Discography
'What's Love Got to Do with It?', Performed by Tina Turner, from *Private Dancer*, Capitol Records, 1984

## Filmography
*Ivanhoe*, Directed by D. Canfield, UK/USA: Columbia Pictures, 1952
*The Adventures of Robin Hood*, Directed by M. Curtiz and W. Keighley, USA: Warner Bros., 1938
*Two on A Guillotine*, Directed by W. Conrad, USA: Warner Bros., 1965

## TV Series
*Bleak House*, Directed by J. Chadwick and S. White, UK: BBC Television, 2005
*Bleak House*, Directed by R. Devenish, UK: BBC Television, 1985
*Ivanhoe*, Directed by D. Coupland, UK/USA: Columbia Pictures, 1982
*Ivanhoe*, Directed by D. Maloney, UK: BBC, 1970
*Ivanhoe*, Directed by S. Orme, UK/USA: A&E Television Networks, 1997
*Ivanhoe*, Directed by P. Rogers, B. Coote and H. Smith, UK: Screen Gems Television, 1958

# Index

Abrams, M.H. 98
Agamben, G. 65, 178
age of consent 24
Alembert, Jean le Rond d' 75
Althusser, L. 168
American legal realism 205; *The House of the Seven Gables* see separate entry
Anderson, K. 141
anti-clericalism 112; *see also* religion
anti-judicialism 113; *see also* judges
anti-Semitism 48–9, 50–1, 54–5, 71
Aries, P. 83
Aristodemou, M. 7, 11
*Ashford* v. *Thornton* (1818) 61
Austen, Jane 2, 3, 44; *Emma* 45; *Mansfield Park* 21–2; *Persuasion* 45; *Pride and Prejudice* see separate entry
Austin, John 4, 73–4, 176, 189–90, 205; *Pride and Prejudice* 15–16, 22, 23, 36–43, 45–6
autonomy 26, 95, 97
Axton, W. 148

'Bad Men' 115–16, 129
Baldick, C. 90

barristers *see Bleak House*
Barthes, R. 14
Baudrillard, J. 183
Behrendt, L. 5
Beiderwell, B.J. 4, 49
Belenky, M.F. 87
Bell, M.D. 112
Belsey, C. 148
Bentham, Jeremy 4, 38, 159, 163, 176, 205; Blackstone 59; *Defence of Usury* 49, 50, 51–5, 205; French Revolution 59; *Ivanhoe* see separate entry; 'Judge & Co' or Judge and Code 49, 55–63; Marx 26; natural rights 59; pannomion 62; *Pride and Prejudice* 27–9, 36, 39, 42; *Scotch Reform* 56
Benton, G. 143
Berns, S. 203
Best, S. 2, 5
Birks, M. 137
Black, C.F. 8
Blackstone, W. 59
*Bleak House* 4, 6, 10, 12, 18, 36, 131–5, 193, 205; barristerial voice 136, 140–7, 155; barristers vs solicitors 135–40;

'equity's darling' at risk 148–52; trusteeship *à venir* 152–6
Bloom, H. 98, 187
Botting, F. 90
Bottomley, S. 189
bourgeois–liberal 85; legality see *A Tale of Two Cities*
Bowen, C.D. 114
*Brideshead Revisited* 35
Brint, S. 134, 137, 141–2, 156
Brontë, Emily 35
Brooks, P. 6, 183, 198
*Buck* v. *Bell* (1927) 119
Burchell, G. 192
Butler, M. 42, 45
Butt, J. 133

Cagidemetrio, A. 50
Campbell, F.K. 154
capital 10, 207; *Frankenstein* 89–90, 93, 97; *Great Expectations* 192, 195; *The House of the Seven Gables* 103, 105, 128; *Pride and Prejudice* 26, 28–9, 45; rights discourse 76; *A Tale of Two Cities* 158, 172–9; usury 54
capital punishment 4, 128
Cardozo, B.N. 3
Carlyle, T. 144, 162
categorical imperative 71, 82
Chancery Court 132
Chandler, J. 72
Chaplin, S. 5
Cheyfitz, E. 102
*A Child's History of England* 167
Chion, M. 93
chivalry 49, 63–4
*A Christmas Carol* 154
civil society–state authority divide 192
Clairmont, Jane Vial 83
Clapham, J.H. 52
class 12, 46, 154; *Bleak House* 135, 137, 141, 144, 147, 154; bourgeois–liberal see separate entry; *Frankenstein* 90, 94; *Great Expectations* 188–9, 194, 196–7, 199–200, 201; *The House of the Seven Gables* 101, 119, 123; *Pride and Prejudice* 12, 23, 27, 29–33, 38, 44–5; *A Vindication of the Rights of Woman* 85, 87

clericalism 113; see also religion
Cohen, F.S. 115
Collins, P. 3, 133, 182, 202
colonisers 17, 21–2, 46, 107, 161, 194
command theory of law see Austin, John
commodity fetishism 195
consent 43, 44; age of 24
contract law 2, 5, 76; *Frankenstein* 90; freedom of contract 26; *The House of the Seven Gables* 103, 106; *Pride and Prejudice* 10, 23, 25–6, 28–9, 34, 45
Copjec, J. 79
*Copycat* (1995) 77
copyright 2, 3, 5
Cornell, D. 31
Cornish, W.R. 137, 176
Cotterrell, R. 190
Court of Appeal 176
Cover, R. 61, 203
Crane, G. 7
Creed, B. 29
critical legal studies (CLS) 69, 84, 129, 188–9, 192, 207; *Pride and Prejudice* 46
Cutmore, J. 53

Daiches, D. 70
Darwin, Charles 165
*David Copperfield* 136
Davies, M. 11, 117
Davies, R. 174
death penalty 4, 129
Delgado, R. 85
Derrida, J. 15, 203
Dicey, A.V. 4, 158, 167, 177, 205
Dickens, Charles 3; *Bleak House* see separate entry; *A Child's History of England* 167; *A Christmas Carol* 154; *David Copperfield* 136; *Great Expectations* see separate entry; *Our Mutual Friend* 186; trainee in law 136
Diderot, D. 44
Dimock, W.C. 7
Dinwiddy, J.R.R. 48

disability 154
distributive justice *see Great Expectations*
divine law 12, 38, 48, 58–60
Dolin, K. 6, 11, 133
Douzinas, C. 6
Duckworth, A.M. 3, 42, 45
Duman, D. 137
Dworkin, R. 22, 117
Dyer, G. 61

Edelman, L. 120
Edsall, N. 121
Eliot, G.: *Middlemarch* 28, 35
Ellis, G.E. 116
*Emma* 45
entail 4, 24–5, 31
equality 208
equity: *Great Expectations*: 'clean hands' of 193–4; trusteeship *see Bleak House*
eternal law of God 12, 38, 48, 58–60
ethics: care, ethic of 204; of the Good: *Bleak House* 147; *Ivanhoe* 48, 49–50, 58, 71–4; *see also* morality

Fasich, L. 143
feminism 5, 7, 31–2, 46; critical legal 31, 84, 207; post-identitarian 87; *see also* gender; rights discourse
Ferguson, R. 3
fetishism, commodity 195
feudalism 39, 49
fiduciary relationship 134, 138, 141, 146
financial services 175
Fish, S. 177
Flynn, Erroll 66
formalism, legal 103, 107, 123, 206
Forster, E.M. 35, 125
Forster, J. 136
*The Forsyte Saga* 35
Foucault, M. 162, 181, 182, 183, 184, 185, 186, 189, 194, 195
France 76, 80–1, 86, 93; revolutionary justice *see A Tale of Two Cities*
France, Anatole 189
Frank, J. 103, 115, 117, 120, 128, 205

*Frankenstein* 10, 16–17, 75–7, 96–8, 205; construction of the body 79–80; crime of murder 77–8; critique of liberalism 90–6; framing of interpretation 88–90; legal system 78; righting the revolutionary body politic 80–2; Wollstonecraft 82–8, 90, 96–8
Frazer, J.G. 32
freedom of contract 26
Freeman, M.D.A. 40
Freud, S. 32, 81, 88, 89, 98
Friedmann, L. 113
Frug, M.J. 31
Frye, N. 67, 152
Fukuyama, F. 134
Fyfe, T. 132

Gabel, P. 84
Gaita, R. 134
Galsworthy, J. 35
Gambetta, D. 134
Geary, A. 8
gender 12, 38; entail 24–5, 31; *Great Expectations* 196, 197, 198–200; *The House of the Seven Gables* 119, 123, 128; *A Tale of Two Cities* 172; *see also* feminism
Gest, J.M. 132
Gilligan, C. 43
Gilmore, M.T. 102
Glen, P. 5
Glorious Revolution (1689) 167
Godwin, William 83, 91
Goethe, J.W. von 93
good faith 134, 138
Goodman, N. 2, 5
Goodrich, P. 11, 152
Goodwin, M. 5
governmentality 60; *Great Expectations* see separate entry
Grahame, J. 53
Gramsci, A. 43
*Great Expectations* 10, 12, 181–3, 205; beyond governmentality: justice as deconstruction 202–4; 'clean hands' of equity: Jaggers as governmental lawyer

193–4; Magwitch's return: emergence of governmentality 183–7; 'revenge tragedy': governmentality as injustice 195–7; sense of (un)ending: repetition as politics 197–202; tactics of power and power of tactics: governmentalised law 191–2
Grey, T.C. 2–3
Grierson, H.J.C. 70
Grossman, J. 2, 5
Guest, J.M. 4
Gurney, M.S. 143

Hackney, J. 131
Halberstam, J. 120
Hall, J.Y. 133
Hammer, D. 132
Hardin, R. 134
Harding, D.W. 45
Harmon, A.G. 2, 5
Hart, H.L.A. 145, 208
Harvey, W.J. 148
Hathorne, Judge John 113
Hawthorne, Nathaniel 6; *The House of the Seven Gables* see separate entry
Hegel, G.W.G. 81
Heinzelman, S.S. 7
Hitchcock, A. 123
Hobbes, T. 65, 75
Holdsworth, W. 3, 132, 137
Holmes, O.W., Jr 4, 102–3, 107, 113, 114–15, 122, 123, 124, 125, 127, 129, 205
Holmes, O.W., Sr 103
Homer, S. 52
homosexuality 85, 121
Hood, G. 160
House, H. 133, 182
*The House of the Seven Gables* 10, 17–18, 36, 205; fantasmatic agency of law's letter: subversion of legal subject in formalist dialectic of desire 109–23; getting the (law-)job done: Holgrave as legal realist and Phoebe as legal 'real' 123–30; predicting American legal realism 99–104; '*seisin*-isation and its legal realist discontents': the law of, and as consumption 104–8
*Howards End* 35
human rights 129
Hunt, L. 81
Hutchings, P. 6, 11, 89
Hutton, R.H. 70

identity politics 87
Industrial Revolution 76, 90
inheritance law 2, 35–6; entail 4, 24–5, 31
interest 51, 52
international law 2
Irving, J. 197
*Ivanhoe* 10, 15–16, 47–50, 205; *avant la loi*: Rebecca, Ivanhoe and the return of the King-as-Benthamite 63–71; exile of ethics and morality 71–4; 'Judge & Co' or Judge and Code: Lucas de Beaumanoir 49, 55–63; moneylending: Bentham and Scott 48–9, 50–5

Jaffe, A. 148
Jakobson, R. 82
James, Edwin 160
James II 167
Jews: *Ivanhoe* 48–9, 50–1, 54–5, 71, 74
Johnson, E. 136, 197, 198
Johnson, P. 32
judges: anti-judicialism 113; *Ivanhoe*: 'Judge & Co' or Judge and Code 49, 55–63
jurisprudentially, reading 12–15, 207–8
justice 4, 9, 11; as deconstruction *see Great Expectations*; revolutionary *see A Tale of Two Cities*

Kairys, D. 84
Kant, I. 30, 82
Kantorowicz, E. 80
Kaplan, F. 170
Kelsen, H. 145
King, P.J. 113
Kirk, H. 137
*Kiss the Girls* (1997) 77

Klein, M. 96
Korobkin, L.H. 2

La Capra, D. 133
La Harpe, J.F. 80
Lacan, J. 9, 30, 33, 72, 81, 85, 145, 159, 168, 169, 174, 198, 199
Lacey, N. 9
Laclau, E. 89, 177
Lacquer, W. 59, 81
Larson, M.S. 137
law-and-economics movement 28
lawyer-as-social trustee *see Bleak House*
Leavis, F.R. 133, 182
Lefort, C. 81
legal formalism 103, 107, 123, 206
legal positivism 11, 189–90, 206; *Bleak House* 145; *Ivanhoe* 48, 49–50, 52, 55, 58, 67, 73–4; *Pride and Prejudice* 22, 36–43, 45–6; *A Tale of Two Cities* 175–6
legal realism 205; *The House of the Seven Gables* see separate entry
Leiboff, M. 117
Levinasian 'face of the Other' 48, 72
Levy, L.B. 123
Lewin, J. 50
liberalism 85, 190–1, 201, 206; *Frankenstein* 76, 82, 90–7; *A Vindication of the Rights of Woman* 84, 85, 96–7
libertinism 60
Llewellyn, K.N. 103, 106–7, 115, 125, 127, 128, 205
Lobban, M. 132
Locke, J. 75
Lockhart, J.G. 70
Louis XVI 81
Lowenstein, D.H. 133
Luhmann, N. 134, 175
Lyotard, J.-F. 202

Macauley, S. 183
MacCannell, J.F. 84, 145
MacDonagh, O. 72, 185
McGill, M. 2, 5

MacKinnon, C. 13
MacNeil, W.P. 13, 82, 98
MacPherson, S. 2, 4
McVeigh, S. 190
McWilliams, J.P., Jr 112
Maine, H.S. 26
Manchester, A.H. 137
*Mansfield Park* 21–2
Markey, M. 133
Marx, K. 26, 48, 54, 69, 74, 94, 188–9
Matheson, N. 101
Mathiesson, F.O. 101
matriarchy 32
Matthias, P. 52
Mayhew, H. 143
Mellow, J.R. 112
Melville, H. 105, 130
Mendel, G. 165
mercantilism 103, 105, 128
Mergenthal, S. 50
meta-narrative of psychoanalysis 88–9
method: reading jurisprudentially 12–15, 207–8
Michaels, W.B. 102
*Middlemarch* 28, 35
Mill, J.S. 4, 182, 190–1, 201, 202, 205
Miller, D.A. 6, 133
Miller, E.H. 113
Miller, J.-A. 174
Millgate, J. 47
Milton, John 93
Misztal, B. 134
Mo, Charles 94
moneylending: Bentham and Scott 48–9, 50–5
Montesquieu 75
moral-authoritarianism 190, 200
morality 4, 9, 45; *Bleak House* 151; *The House of the Seven Gables* 119, 128; *Ivanhoe* 48, 50, 52, 55, 58, 73–4; *see also* ethics
Moretti, F. 89–90, 94
Morgan, E. 2, 5
Morison, W.L. 40, 42, 45
Mudrick, M. 45
Murav, H. 2, 5

Nabokov, V. 150
Naman, A.A. 50
natural law 11, 12, 33–4, 37–8, 45, 52, 59–60
Neale, F. 53
Newton, J. 133

O'Connell, L. 10
O'Dair, R. 138
O'Flinn, P. 90
Ogden, C.K. 62
Oldham, J. 132
O'Neill, O. 134
Orman, C. 70
*Our Mutual Friend* 186

Paine, T. 75
pannomion 62
Pasquino, P. 191
patriarchy 31, 32, 46, 152, 194
Paulson, R. 90
*Persuasion* 45
Pether, P. 8, 11
Pettit, P. 131
Plutarch 93
Pocock, J.G.A. 87
Poe, Edgar Allan 6, 108
Polden, P. 131
police 6; *Great Expectations* 185–7, 192; *The House of the Seven Gables* 112
politics–law nexus: *Great Expectations* 188–9; *Pride and Prejudice* 44–6; *A Tale of Two Cities* see separate entry
Polloczek, D.P. 133
pornography 6, 77
positivism, legal 11, 189–90, 206; *Bleak House* 145; *Ivanhoe* 48, 49–50, 52, 55, 58, 67, 73–4; *Pride and Prejudice* 22, 36–43, 45–6; *A Tale of Two Cities* 175–6
Pound, R. 115
predictive theory of law 102–3, 115
*Pride and Prejudice* 12, 15–16, 21–3, 205; Austinian sovereign: command of Mr Darcy and censure of Elizabeth-as-censor 38–43; calculus of felicity 27–9; contract 10, 23, 25–6, 28–9, 34, 45; critical legal insight 46; entail 4, 24–5, 31; Lady Catherine as figure of totem and taboo 29–33; politics of law in Austin and Austen 44–6; positivist house of law 33–8; siting/sighting the law in 23–6; status to contract 26
prisons 128
private–public distinction 96–7, 207; *Great Expectations* 192, 201–2; *The House of the Seven Gables* 123
property law 2, 76, 90, 103, 106
Protestant work ethic 126, 164
psychoanalysis, meta-narrative of 88–9
public–private distinction 96–7, 207; *Great Expectations* 192, 201–2; *The House of the Seven Gables* 123
Pue, W.W. 139

race 2, 5, 12, 46, 84–5, 207; death penalty 129; *Great Expectations* 196; *A Tale of Two Cities* 164–5
Raffield, P. 6–7
Ragaz, S. 53
Ragussis, M. 50
rape 5, 24
Rawls, J. 202
reading jurisprudentially 12–15, 207–8
Reform Bill (1832) 44
reform of Chancery 132
Reichman, R. 6
reification/thingification 10, 184, 195
religion 33, 45, 51–2, 57–8; *Bleak House* 144, 154; *The House of the Seven Gables* 112; Jews: *Ivanhoe* 48–9, 50–1, 54–5, 71, 74
rendition 130
retribution: *Great Expectations* see separate entry; *A Tale of Two Cities* 171–2
'revenge tragedy', *Great Expectations* as 195–7
revolutionary justice see *A Tale of Two Cities*
Riffaterre, M. 34–5
rights discourse 7, 208; alchemy of Romanticism and rights 75–7;

Index • 233

'hyperinflation' of rights 87; liberalism 76, 82, 90–7; righting the revolutionary body politic 80–2; Wollstonecraft 83–8
Robbins, B. 141
Robertson, G. 75
Robson, R. 136
Rodensky, L. 2, 5
Roman law 56, 62
Romanticism *see* rights discourse
Rosenberg, E. 50
Rousseau, Jean Jacques 75
rule of law 4, 9, 11, 206–8; *A Tale of Two Cities* 158, 159, 167, 177, 179; *Bleak House* 141; *Great Expectations* 182, 191; *Pride and Prejudice* 38
Russett, M. 2, 5

Sade, M. 60, 71
Saïd, E. 21–2
Salecl, R. 87
Saunders, D. 166, 203
*Saw* (2004) 77
Schama, S. 80
Schauer, F. 117
Schmitt, C. 67, 178
Schor, H. 5, 148, 180
Schroeder, J.L. 69
science 79–80, 165
Scotland 56, 62
Scott, Sir Walter 4; *Ivanhoe see* separate entry; money 70; *Waverley* 66
Serlen, E. 148
*Seven* (1995) 77
sexual difference 120–21, 172; *see also* gender
Shakespeare 2, 50, 51
Shelley, Mary 82–3, 91, 98; *Frankenstein see* separate entry
silence 43
*The Silence of the Lambs* (1990) 77
Silsbee, Nathaniel 112
Slaughter, J. 7
Smith, J.M. 31
social contract 26, 80, 92
social trusteeship *see Bleak House*
socio-sexual oppression 170–2

sodomy 121
solicitors *see Bleak House*
sovereignty: Austen's Austinian sovereign 38–43, 46; *Ivanhoe*: Rebecca, Ivanhoe and the return of the King-as-Benthamite 63–71
Spencer, H. 165
state authority–civil society divide 192
status society 26, 199–200; *Frankenstein* 92; *Pride and Prejudice* 25–6, 29, 33–4
Stephen, J.F. 3, 4, 132, 159, 160, 190, 191, 199–200, 205
Stephen, L. 57
Sterrenburg, L. 90
Stevens, W. 3
Stewart, S. 6
*Stockton* v. *Ford* (1850) 138
Stroehr, T. 148
Stuart monarchy 167
succession 35–6; entail 4, 24–5, 31
Sugden, Edward 132
Sunstein, E.W. 83, 91
Swan, C. 123

*A Tale of Two Cities* 10, 12, 18–19, 157–9, 178–80, 205; adversarial system 162–3; dialectic of recognition and méconnaissance 165–72; inquisitorial system 162–3; politics of forgetting: capitalising law, legalising capital 172–8; race 164–5; trials of Charles Darnay 159–65
Tambling, J. 181–2
*The Tenant of Wildfell Hall* 199
Ternan, Ellen 170
thingification/reification 10, 184, 195
Thomas, B. 3, 101–2
Thomas, R. 123, 133
Thompson, E.P. 193
Threadgold, T. 5–6
Tilly, C. 134
Tolkien, J.R.R. 66
torture 129
Trachtenberg, A. 123
Treitel, G.H. 4

trial by combat 60–1
trusteeship *see Bleak House*
Tucker, G.H. 44
Tushnet, M. 84

*uberimma fides* 138
Unger, R. 84
universalism 74, 82, 84, 85
Upham, Charles Wentworth 112
usury: Bentham and Scott 48–9, 50–5
utilitarianism 206; *Great Expectations* 190–1, 200; *Ivanhoe* 49–50, 58, 62, 69–74; *Pride and Prejudice* 22–3, 27–9, 38–9, 40

*A Vindication of the Rights of Woman* 16–17, 31, 75–7, 89, 90, 96–8, 205; class 85, 87; critique of rights discourse 83–8; extension of rights to women 84–8; female vanity 86
Voltaire 75
von Sneidern, M.L. 164, 165

Walker, D.M. 149
Ward, I. 2
waterboarding 130
Waugh, E. 35

*Waverley* 66
Weisberg, R. 8
Welsh, A. 3
Wheatley, K. 53
White, J.B. 8
White, T.H. 66
Wigmore, J.H. 3
Wilde, Oscar 142
Williams, L. 77
Williams, M. 7, 11
Williams, P. 85
Wilson, A. 136
witchcraft 56, 108, 113, 128
Wollstonecraft, Mary 4, 82–3, 91; *A Vindication of the Rights of Woman* see separate entry
Wright, N.E. 5
*Wuthering Heights* 35

Young, A. 5

Zatlin, L.G. 50
Žižek, S. 30, 61, 71, 89, 93, 96, 108, 145, 171, 194, 198
Zola, E. 161
Zupancic, A. 147
Zwerdling, A. 148

CPSIA information can be obtained
at www.ICGtesting.com
Printed in the USA
BVHW07s0946030618
518053BV00002B/6/P